PEARSON CUSTOM
BUSINESS RESOURCES

Compiled by

Accounting Information Systems
Pearson Custom edition of Romney 12/ed
Second Printing
University of Baltimore

Pearson Learning Solutions

New York   Boston   San Francisco
London   Toronto   Sydney   Tokyo   Singapore   Madrid
Mexico City   Munich   Paris   Cape Town   Hong Kong   Montreal

Senior Vice President, Editorial and Marketing: Patrick F. Boles
Editor: Ana Díaz-Caneja
Development Editor: Abbey Lee Briggs
Operations Manager: Eric M. Kenney
Production Manager: Jennifer Berry
Art Director: Renée Sartell
Cover Designer: Renée Sartell

Cover Art: Courtesy of EyeWire/Getty Images and PhotoDisc/Getty Images. Photodisc, "Globe surrounded by business people on computer monitors," courtesy of Photodisc/Getty Images. Dave Cutler (Artist), "Man Dropping Coins Into Glass Jar," courtesy of David Cutler/Images.com. Dave Cutler (Artist), "Three Coins in Glass Jar," courtesy of David Cutler/Images.com. Dean Turner, "Stock Vector: Global Finance" Courtesy of Dean Turner/iStockphoto. Hal Bergman, "Refinery Silhouette" Courtesy of Hal Bergman/iStockphoto. Dan Barnes, "Cargo Container Ship Aerial View" Courtesy of Dan Barnes/iStockphoto. Franc Podgorsek, "Stock Numbers" Courtesy of Franc Podgorsek/iStockphoto. "Customer in Line at Grocery Store" Courtesy of Digital Vision Photography/Veer Inc. Owaki-Kulla, "Pumping Gas" Courtesy of Flirt Photography/Veer Inc. Lynn Johnson, "Yunnan Province, People's Republic of China" Courtesy of Lynn Johnson/Getty Images, Inc. Thomas Bendy, "Student Typing" Courtesy of Thomas Bendy/iStockphoto.

This special edition published in cooperation with Pearson Learning Solutions.

Printed in the United States of America.

Please visit our web site at *www.pearsoncustom.com*.

Attention bookstores: For permission to return any unsold stock, contact us at *pe-uscustomreturns@pearson.com*.

Pearson Learning Solutions, 501 Boylston Street, Suite 900, Boston, MA 02116
A Pearson Education Company
www.pearsoned.com

ISBN 10: 1-256-17327-4
ISBN 13: 978-1-256-17327-4

Editorial Advisory Board

Contents

Chapter 1

Accounting Information Systems: An Overview

From Chapter 1 of *Accounting Information Systems*, 12/e. Marshall B. Romney. Paul John Steinbart. Copyright © 2012 by Pearson Education. Published by Prentice Hall. All rights reserved.

Accounting Information Systems: An Overview

Learning Objectives

After studying this chapter, you should be able to:

1. Distinguish data from information, discuss the characteristics of useful information, and explain how to determine the value of information.

2. Explain the decisions an organization makes and the information needed to make them.

3. Identify the information that passes between internal and external parties and an AIS.

4. Describe the major business processes present in most companies.

5. Explain what an accounting information system (AIS) is and describe its basic functions.

6. Discuss how an AIS can add value to an organization.

7. Explain how an AIS and corporate strategy affect each other.

8. Explain the role an AIS plays in a company's value chain.

INTEGRATIVE CASE S&S

After working for years as a regional manager for a retail organization, Scott Parry opened his own business with Susan Gonzalez, one of his district managers, as his partner. They formed S&S to sell appliances and consumer electronics. Scott and Susan pursued a "clicks and bricks" strategy by renting a building in a busy part of town and adding an electronic storefront.

Scott and Susan invested enough money to see them through the first six months. They will hire 15 employees within the next two weeks—three to stock the shelves, four sales representatives, six checkout clerks, and two to develop and maintain the electronic storefront.

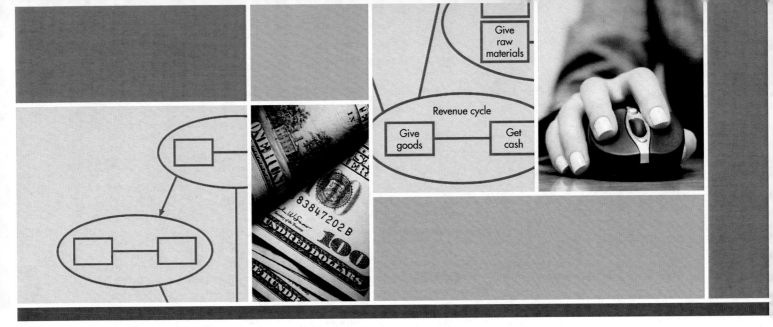

Scott and Susan will host S&S's grand opening in five weeks. To meet that deadline, they have to address the following important issues:

1. What decisions do they need to make to be successful and profitable? For example:
   a. How should they price products to be competitive yet earn a profit?
   b. Should they extend credit, and, if so, on what terms? How can they accurately track what customers owe and pay?
   c. How should they hire, train, and supervise employees? What compensation and benefits package should they offer? How should they process payroll?
   d. How can they track cash inflows and outflows to avoid a cash squeeze?
   e. What is the appropriate product mix? What inventory quantities should they carry, given their limited showroom space?
2. What information do Scott and Susan need to make those decisions?
   a. What information do the external entities they interact with need?
   b. What information do management and other employees need?
   c. How can they gather, store, and disseminate that information?
3. What business processes are needed, and how should they be carried out?
4. What functionality should be provided on the Web site?

Although Scott and Susan could use an educated guess or "gut feeling" to make these decisions, they know they can make better decisions if they obtain additional information. A well-designed *accounting information system (AIS)* can solve these issues and provide the information they need to make any remaining decisions.

Introduction

We begin this chapter by explaining important terms and discussing the kinds of information that organizations need and the business processes used to produce that information. We continue with an exploration of what an accounting information system (AIS) is, how an AIS adds value to an organization, how an AIS and corporate strategy affect each other, and the role of the AIS in the value chain.

A *system* is a set of two or more interrelated components that interact to achieve a goal. Most systems are composed of smaller subsystems that support the larger system. For example, a college of business is a system composed of various departments, each of which is a subsystem. Moreover, the college itself is a subsystem of the university.

Each subsystem is designed to achieve one or more organizational goals. Changes in subsystems cannot be made without considering the effect on other subsystems and on the system as a whole. *Goal conflict* occurs when a subsystem is inconsistent with the goals of another subsystem or with the system as a whole. *Goal congruence* occurs when a subsystem achieves its goals while contributing to the organization's overall goal. The larger the organization and the more complicated the system, the more difficult it is to achieve goal congruence.

Data are facts that are collected, recorded, stored, and processed by an information system. Businesses need to collect several kinds of data, such as the activities that take place, the resources affected by the activities, and the people who participate in the activity. For example, the business needs to collect data about a sale (date, total amount), the resource sold (good or service, quantity sold, unit price), and the people who participated (customer, salesperson).

Information is data that have been organized and processed to provide meaning and improve the decision-making process. As a rule, users make better decisions as the quantity and quality of information increase.

However, there are limits to the amount of information the human mind can absorb and process. *Information overload* occurs when those limits are passed, resulting in a decline in decision-making quality and an increase in the cost of providing that information. Information system designers use *information technology (IT)* to help decision makers more effectively filter and condense information. For example, Walmart has over 500 terabytes (trillions of bytes) of data in its data warehouse. That is equivalent to 2,000 miles of bookshelves, or about 100 million digital photos. Walmart has invested heavily in IT so it can effectively collect, store, analyze, and manage data to provide useful information.

The *value of information* is the benefit produced by the information minus the cost of producing it. Benefits of information are reduced uncertainty, improved decisions, and improved ability to plan and schedule activities. The costs are the time and resources spent to produce and distribute the information. Information costs and benefits can be difficult to quantify, and it is difficult to determine the value of information before it has been produced and utilized. Nevertheless, the expected value of information should be calculated as effectively as possible so that the costs of producing the information do not exceed its benefits.

To illustrate the value of information, consider the case of 7-Eleven. In 1973, a Japanese company licensed the very successful 7-Eleven name from Southland Corporation. As it opened its stores, 7-Eleven Japan invested heavily in IT, but the U.S. stores did not. Each 7-Eleven store in Japan was given a computer that:

- Keeps track of the 3,000 items sold in each store and determines what products are moving, at what time of day, and under what weather conditions.
- Keeps track of what and when customers buy to make sure it has in stock the products most frequently purchased.
- Orders sandwiches and rice dishes from suppliers automatically. Orders are placed and filled three times a day so that stores always have fresh food. In addition, 7-Eleven allows its suppliers to access sales data in their computers so that they can forecast demand.
- Coordinates deliveries with suppliers. This reduces deliveries from 34 to 12 a day, resulting in less clerical receiving time.
- Prepares a color graphic display that indicates which store areas contribute the most to sales and profits.

Average daily sales of 7-Eleven Japan were 30% higher and its operating margins almost double those of its closest competitor. What happened to Southland and its 7-Eleven stores in the United States? Profits declined, and Southland eventually had to file for bankruptcy. Who came to the company's rescue? Along with its parent company, 7-Eleven Japan purchased 64% of Southland.

Table 1 presents seven characteristics that make information useful and meaningful.

TABLE 1 Characteristics of Useful Information

Relevant	Reduces uncertainty, improves decision making, or confirms or corrects prior expectations.
Reliable	Free from error or bias; accurately represents organization events or activities.
Complete	Does not omit important aspects of the events or activities it measures.
Timely	Provided in time for decision makers to make decisions.
Understandable	Presented in a useful and intelligible format.
Verifiable	Two independent, knowledgeable people produce the same information.
Accessible	Available to users when they need it and in a format they can use.

Information Needs and Business Processes

All organizations need information in order to make effective decisions. In addition, all organizations have certain business processes that they are continuously engaged in. A *business process* is a set of related, coordinated, and structured activities and tasks that are performed by a person or by a computer or a machine, and that help accomplish a specific organizational goal.

To make effective decisions, organizations must decide what decisions they need to make, what information they need to make the decisions, and how to gather and process the data needed to produce the information. This data gathering and processing is often tied to the basic business processes in an organization. To illustrate the process of identifying information needs and business processes, let's return to our case study of S&S.

Information Needs

Scott and Susan decide they must understand how S&S functions before they can identify the information they need to manage S&S effectively. Then they can determine the types of data and procedures they will need to collect and produce that information. They created Table 2 to summarize part of their analysis. It lists S&S's basic business processes, some key decisions that need to be made for each process, and information they need to make the decisions.

Scott and Susan realize that the list is not exhaustive, but they are satisfied that it provides a good overview of S&S. They also recognize that not all the information needs listed in the right-hand column will be produced internally by S&S. Information about payment terms for merchandise purchases, for example, will be provided by vendors. Thus, S&S must effectively integrate external data with internally generated data so that Scott and Susan can use both types of information to run S&S.

S&S will interact with many external parties, such as customers, vendors, and governmental agencies, as well as with internal parties such as management and employees. To get a better handle on the more important interactions with these parties, they prepared Figure 1.

Business Processes

Scott decides to reorganize the business processes listed in Table 2 into groups of related transactions. A *transaction* is an agreement between two entities to exchange goods or services or any other event that can be measured in economic terms by an organization. Examples include selling goods to customers, buying inventory from suppliers, and paying employees. The process that begins with capturing transaction data and ends with informational output, such as the financial statements, is called *transaction processing*.

Many business activities are pairs of events involved in a *give-get exchange*. Most organizations engage in a small number of give-get exchanges, but each type of exchange happens many times. For example, S&S will have thousands of sales to customers every year in exchange for cash. Likewise, S&S will continuously buy inventory from suppliers in exchange for cash.

TABLE 2 Overview of S&S's Business Processes, Key Decisions, and Information Needs

Business Processes	Key Decisions	Information Needs
Acquire capital	How much Find investors or borrow funds If borrowing, obtaining best terms	Cash flow projections Pro forma financial statements Loan amortization schedule
Acquire building and equipment	Size of building Amount of equipment Rent or buy Location How to depreciate	Capacity needs Building and equipment prices Market study Tax tables and depreciation regulations
Hire and train employees	Experience requirements How to assess integrity and competence of applicants How to train employees	Job descriptions Applicant job history and skills
Acquire inventory	What models to carry How much to purchase How to manage inventory (store, control, etc.) Which vendors	Market analyses Inventory status reports Vendor performance
Advertising and marketing	Which media Content	Cost analyses Market coverage
Sell merchandise	Markup percentage Offer in-house credit Which credit cards to accept	Pro forma income statement Credit card costs Customer credit status
Collect payments from customers	If offering credit, what terms How to handle cash receipts	Customer account status Accounts receivable aging report Accounts receivable records
Pay employees	Amount to pay Deductions and withholdings Process payroll in-house or use outside service	Sales (for commissions) Time worked (hourly employees) W-4 forms Costs of external payroll service
Pay taxes	Payroll tax requirements Sales tax requirements	Government regulations Total wage expense Total sales
Pay vendors	Whom to pay When to pay How much to pay	Vendor invoices Accounts payable records Payment terms

FIGURE 1

Interactions Between S&S and External and Internal Parties

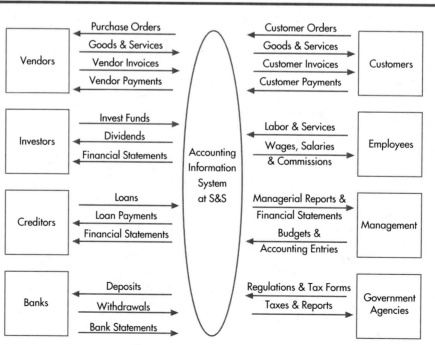

These exchanges can be grouped into five major *business processes or transaction cycles*:

- The *revenue cycle*, where goods and services are sold for cash or a future promise to receive cash.
- The *expenditure cycle*, where companies purchase inventory for resale or raw materials to use in producing products in exchange for cash or a future promise to pay cash.
- The *production* or *conversion cycle*, where raw materials are transformed into finished goods.
- The *human resources/payroll cycle*, where employees are hired, trained, compensated, evaluated, promoted, and terminated.
- The *financing cycle*, where companies sell shares in the company to investors and borrow money and where investors are paid dividends and interest is paid on loans.

These cycles process a few related transactions repeatedly. For example, most revenue cycle transactions are either selling goods or services to customers or collecting cash for those sales. Figure 2 shows the main transaction cycles and the give-get exchange inherent in each cycle.

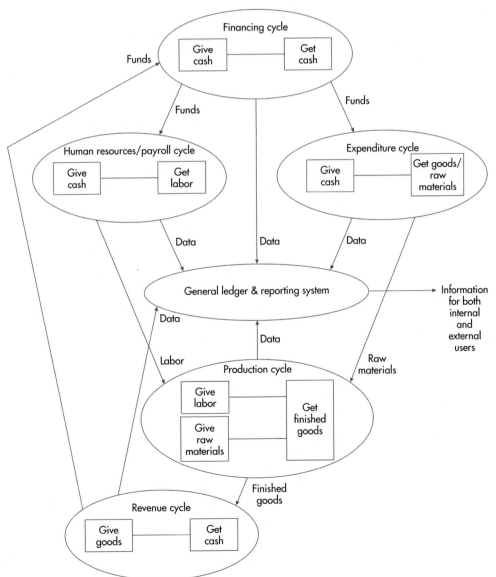

FIGURE 2

The AIS and Its Subsystems

These basic give-get exchanges are supported by a number of other business activities. For example, S&S may need to answer a number of customer inquiries and check inventory levels before it can make a sale. Likewise, it may have to check customer credit before a credit sale is made. Accounts receivable will have to be increased each time a credit sale is made and decreased each time a customer payment is received. Table 3 lists the major activities in each transaction cycle.

TABLE 3 Common Cycle Activities

Transaction Cycle	Major Activities in the Cycle
Revenue	Receive and answer customer inquiries
	Take customer orders and enter them into the AIS
	Approve credit sales
	Check inventory availability
	Initiate back orders for goods out of stock
	Pick and pack customer orders
	Ship goods to customers or perform services
	Bill customers for goods shipped or services performed
	Update (increase) sales and accounts receivable
	Receive customer payments and deposit them in the bank
	Update (reduce) accounts receivable
	Handle sales returns, discounts, allowances, and bad debts
	Prepare management reports
	Send appropriate information to the other cycles
Expenditure	Request that goods and services be purchased
	Prepare, approve, and send purchase orders to vendors
	Receive goods and services and complete a receiving report
	Store goods
	Receive vendor invoices
	Update (increase) accounts payable
	Approve vendor invoices for payment
	Pay vendors for goods and services
	Update (reduce) accounts payable
	Handle purchase returns, discounts, and allowances
	Prepare management reports
	Send appropriate information to the other cycles
Human Resources/Payroll	Recruit, hire, and train new employees
	Evaluate employee performance and promote employees
	Discharge employees
	Update payroll records
	Collect and validate time, attendance, and commission data
	Prepare and disburse payroll
	Calculate and disburse taxes and benefit payments
	Prepare employee and management reports
	Send appropriate information to the other cycles
Production	Design products
	Forecast, plan, and schedule production
	Request raw materials for production
	Manufacture products
	Store finished products
	Accumulate costs for products manufactured
	Prepare management reports
	Send appropriate information to the other cycles
Financing	Forecast cash needs
	Sell stock/securities to investors
	Borrow money from lenders
	Pay dividends to investors and interest to lenders
	Retire debt
	Prepare management reports
	Send appropriate information to the other cycles

Notice that the last activity listed in Table 3 for each transaction cycle is "Send appropriate information to the other cycles." Figure 2 shows how these various transaction cycles relate to one another and interface with the **general ledger and reporting system**, which is used to generate information for both management and external parties.

In many accounting software packages, the various transaction cycles are implemented as separate modules. Not every organization needs to implement every module. Retail stores like S&S, for example, do not have a production cycle and would not implement that module. Moreover, some types of organizations have unique requirements. Financial institutions, for example, have demand deposit and installment-loan cycles that relate to transactions involving customer accounts and loans, respectively. In addition, the nature of a given transaction cycle differs across different types of organizations. For example, the expenditure cycle of a service company, such as a public accounting or a law firm, does not involve processing transactions related to the purchase, receipt, and payment for merchandise that will be resold to customers.

Each transaction cycle can include many different business processes or activities. Each business process can be relatively simple or quite complex. Focus 1 shows how Toyota's attention to continuously improving its business processes has helped it become the largest and most profitable automobile manufacturer in the world.

FOCUS 1 — Improving Business Processes Helps Drive Toyota's Success

Toyota's Georgetown, Kentucky, manufacturing plant, its largest in North America, is the size of 156 football fields, employs 7,000 people, and produces a new car every 55 seconds. Because Toyota produces a high-quality car at a lower cost than its competitors do, it is now the largest automobile manufacturer in the world, a title General Motors had for almost a hundred years.

A major factor in its success is the Toyota Production System (TPS), which is a set of philosophies, principles, and business processes supported by IT. Its goal is to improve continually so Toyota has the most effective and most efficient manufacturing and business processes possible. Toyota willingly shares TPS and its manufacturing and business processes with its suppliers to help them improve their quality and efficiency. It also shares TPS with its competitors, knowing that by the time they duplicate it Toyota will have greatly improved TPS.

The following are some of the principles and business processes on which TPS is built and which Toyota's information systems must support and enable:

- Performance-monitoring software warns assembly line workers of equipment problems. Workers stop production whenever necessary to prevent or correct defects.
- Their just-in-time (JIT) inventory system is one of the most sophisticated in the world. Driverless carts take parts to assembly stations when they are needed so that inventory does not pile up. Suppliers must meet rigid delivery standards. Four hours before they are needed, Toyota software electronically notifies Johnson Controls of exactly what kind of car seats are needed for each car and the exact order in which they must be shipped.

- Continuous improvement is a critical and ongoing process. No process or detail is too small or insignificant to improve. Technology is especially important in the continuous improvement process. This emphasis on continuous improvement creates a culture that values continuous learning and embraces change.
- Electronic displays connected to the manufacturing equipment help workers monitor the assembly line. Information is communicated by light colors (green means the process is operating correctly, yellow means a problem is being investigated, and red means the assembly line has stopped) and by printed messages (which machine malfunctioned, its speed and temperature when it broke down, and who was operating the machine).
- Electronic quality control devices, such as an electronic sensor on a tool or a beam of light, monitor a process. These devices let a computer know when a tool is not used or a required part is not picked up and used at the appropriate time.
- More than half of Toyota's information systems employees work in operations at its plants so they can accompany executives, team leaders, and factory workers when they go to solve assembly line problems.

In summary, Toyota has a very clear and in-depth understanding of the business processes that make it successful, continuously improves those process, and understands the role information systems play in managing, supporting, and facilitating those processes.

Source: Mel Duvall, "What's Driving Toyota?" *Baseline Magazine,* September 5, 2006.

After preparing Tables 2 and 3 and Figures 1 and 2, Scott and Susan believe that they understand S&S well enough to begin shopping for an information system. Susan recalled a previous employer that had several separate information systems, because their software was not designed to accommodate the information needs of all managers. She also vividly recalled attending one meeting where she witnessed the negative effects of having multiple systems. The head of marketing had one report on year-to-date sales by product, the production manager had a different report that contained different sales figures, and the controller's report, which was produced by the general ledger system, had yet a third version of year-to-date sales. Over an hour was wasted trying to reconcile those different reports! Susan vowed that she would make sure that S&S did not ever find itself in such a mess. She would make sure that any system selected would have the capability to integrate both financial and nonfinancial data about S&S's various business processes so that everyone could pull information from the same system.

Accounting Information Systems

It has often been said that accounting is the language of business. If that is the case, then an *accounting information system (AIS)* is the intelligence—the information-providing vehicle—of that language.

Accounting is a data identification, collection, and storage process as well as an information development, measurement, and communication process. By definition, accounting is an information system, since an AIS collects, records, stores, and processes accounting and other data to produce information for decision makers. This is illustrated in Figure 3.

An AIS can be a paper-and-pencil manual system, a complex system using the latest in IT, or something in between. Regardless of the approach taken, the process is the same. The AIS must collect, enter, process, store, and report data and information. The paper and pencil or the computer hardware and software are merely the tools used to produce the information.

This text does not distinguish an AIS from other information systems. Instead, our viewpoint is that the AIS can and should be the organization's primary information system and that it provides users with the information they need to perform their jobs.

There are six components of an AIS:

1. The *people* who use the system
2. The *procedures and instructions* used to collect, process, and store data
3. The *data* about the organization and its business activities
4. The *software* used to process the data
5. The *information technology infrastructure*, including the computers, peripheral devices, and network communications devices used in the AIS
6. The *internal controls and security measures* that safeguard AIS data

These six components enable an AIS to fulfill three important business functions:

1. Collect and store data about organizational activities, resources, and personnel. Organizations have a number of business processes, such as making a sale or purchasing raw materials, which are repeated frequently.
2. Transform data into information so management can plan, execute, control, and evaluate activities, resources, and personnel. Decision making is discussed in detail later in this chapter.
3. Provide adequate controls to safeguard the organization's assets and data.

Since accounting data comes from an AIS, AIS knowledge and skills are critical to an accountant's career success. Interacting with an AIS is one of the most important activities that accountants perform. Other important AIS-related activities include designing internal control

FIGURE 3

An AIS Processes Data to Produce Information for Decision Makers

systems and business process improvements. Focus 2 explains a specialty to designate that certain CPAs have an in-depth knowledge of AIS topics.

How an AIS Can Add Value to an Organization

A well-designed AIS can add value to an organization by:

1. *Improving the quality and reducing the costs of products or services.* For example, an AIS can monitor machinery so operators are notified immediately when performance falls outside acceptable quality limits. This helps maintain product quality, reduces waste, and lowers costs.
2. *Improving efficiency.* For example, timely information makes a just-in-time manufacturing approach possible, as it requires constant, accurate, up-to-date information about raw materials inventories and their locations.
3. *Sharing knowledge.* Sharing knowledge and expertise can improve operations and provide a competitive advantage. For example, CPA firms use their information systems to share best practices and to support communication between offices. Employees can search the corporate database to identify experts to provide assistance for a particular client; thus, a CPA firm's international expertise can be made available to any local client.
4. *Improving the efficiency and effectiveness of its supply chain.* For example, allowing customers to directly access inventory and sales order entry systems can reduce sales and marketing costs, thereby increasing customer retention rates.
5. *Improving the internal control structure.* An AIS with the proper internal control structure can protect systems from fraud, errors, system failures, and disasters.
6. *Improving decision making.* Improved decision making is vitally important and is discussed below in more detail.

 F O CUS 2 CITP—An IT Specialty Designation for CPAs

The American Institute of Certified Public Accountants (AICPA) offers several specialty designations for CPAs. The CITP (Certified Information Technology Professional) designation reflects the AICPA's recognition of the importance of information technology and its interrelationship with accounting. A CITP possesses a broad range of technological knowledge and understands how organizations use IT to achieve their business objectives.

There are many reasons to earn the CITP certification:

● Because only CPAs can be CITPs, this certification further differentiates you from others in the marketplace.
● It affirms your value as an IT specialist and increases your value to your employer or clients.
● It is a great "calling card" for IT people who want to be leaders in industry, public practice, government, or academia.
● It opens the doors to new technology-related roles and opportunities.
● Automatic membership in the IT Section, which allows you to meet, share best practices, network, and communicate with other CITPs. You can also receive monthly CITP newsletters and other communications, attend monthly CITP Webinars, and access exclusive CITP resources and content on the IT Center Web site.

To qualify for the CITP designation, you must be a CPA and a member of the AICPA. You must earn 100 points in the areas of business experience, lifelong learning, and an optional exam. Candidates must earn a minimum of 15 points, up to a maximum of 75 points, in the area of business experience. The number of points awarded depends on the number of hours spent working in the following areas in the three-year period preceding application for the CITP designation:

● IT Strategic Planning
● Information Systems Management
● Systems Architecture
● Business Applications and E-Business
● Security, Privacy, and Contingency Planning
● Systems Development, Acquisition, and Project Management
● Systems Auditing and Internal Control
● Databases and Database Management

You must also earn a minimum of 30 points, up to a maximum of 70 points, in lifelong learning, which includes continuing education, additional degrees, and obtaining or maintaining other technology-related certifications.

Candidates who have earned at least 60 points in business experience and lifelong learning can earn 40 points by passing an exam that covers the eight previously mentioned topical areas.

Decision making is a complex, multistep activity: identify the problem, collect and interpret information, evaluate ways to solve the problem, select a solution methodology, and implement the solution. An AIS can provide assistance in all phases of decision making. Reports can help to identify potential problems. Decision models and analytical tools can be provided to users. Query languages can gather relevant data to help make the decision. Various tools, such as graphical interfaces, can help the decision maker interpret decision model results, evaluate them, and choose among alternative courses of action. In addition, the AIS can provide feedback on the results of actions.

An AIS can help improve decision making in several ways:

- It can identify situations requiring management action. For example, a cost report with a large variance might stimulate management to investigate and, if necessary, take corrective action.
- It can reduce uncertainty and thereby provide a basis for choosing among alternative actions.
- It can store information about the results of previous decisions, which provides valuable feedback that can be used to improve future decisions. For example, if a company tries a particular marketing strategy and the information gathered indicates that it did not succeed, the company can use that information to select a different marketing strategy.
- It can provide accurate information in a timely manner. For example, Walmart has an enormous database that contains detailed information about sales transactions at each of its stores. It uses this information to optimize the amount of each product carried at each store.
- It analyzes sales data to discover items that are purchased together, and it uses such information to improve the layout of merchandise to encourage additional sales of related items. In a similar vein, Amazon.com uses its database of sales activity to suggest additional books for customers to purchase.

Focus 3 discusses how information technology adds value to UPS.

FOCUS 3   The Use of Technology by UPS

UPS used to invest heavily in training its employees to perform tasks in less time but spent little money on IT. Today, because of the value added to its business, UPS spends well over $1 billion a year on IT. That is much more than it spends on trucks and about as much as it spends on airplanes. UPS has 4,700 employees devoted to developing and maintaining proprietary software and a Web site that 20 million people visit each day. Its 15 mainframe computers and 9,000 servers allow UPS customers to control each shipment (16 million a day) from the time a delivery order is initiated to the time it arrives at its destination. Here is how the system works:

- Customers use UPS software or the UPS Web site to initiate a delivery. They create, print, and attach labels to their shipment containing detailed sender information and the time the shipment should arrive.
- They schedule a pickup time electronically.
- The UPS system routes the label information to the distribution center closest to the shipment's destination.
- At the distribution center, proprietary software uses the destination, desired arrival time, traffic and weather conditions, and street information (one-way streets, etc.) to create the most efficient delivery route. Drivers have handheld computers with a global positioning system (GPS) that guide their routes.

- The system creates a label that specifies where to put the shipment on the delivery truck so the earliest shipments are nearest the driver. Drivers average 100 pickups and deliveries a day, and boxes loaded out of order can delay the driver up to 30 minutes.
- Customers can use the UPS Web site to reroute or track their shipment. The GPS allows UPS to predict accurately the shipment's approximate arrival time.
- The handheld computer is programmed to beep at the driver if a shipment is delivered to the wrong address or forgotten.

UPS's commitment to IT has produced dramatic results. Recent system improvements allowed drivers to make seven to nine more stops each day, reduced the number of miles UPS drives each year by 1.9 million, and saved over $600 million per year in operating costs.

However, UPS is not congratulating itself on how well it has used IT to improve its business. The UPS system is a work in progress. UPS continues to innovate and find ways to use IT to become even more efficient and better serve the customer.

Source: Corey Dade, "How UPS Went from Low-Tech to an IT Power—and Where It's Headed Next," _The Wall Street Journal,_ July 24, 2006, R4.

The AIS and Corporate Strategy

Since most organizations have limited resources, it is important to identify the AIS improvements likely to yield the greatest return. Making a wise decision requires an understanding of the organization's overall business strategy. To illustrate, consider the results of a *CIO* magazine survey of five hundred Chief Information Officers. Asked to identify the three most important skill sets for a CIO, over 75% put strategic thinking and planning on their list.

Figure 4 shows three factors that influence the design of an AIS: developments in IT, business strategy, and organizational culture. It is also important to recognize that the design of the AIS can also influence the organization's culture by controlling the flow of information within the organization. For example, an AIS that makes information easily accessible and widely available is likely to increase pressures for more decentralization and autonomy.

IT developments can affect business strategy. For example, the Internet has profoundly affected the way many activities are performed, significantly affecting both strategy and strategic positioning. The Internet dramatically cuts costs, thereby helping companies to implement a low-cost strategy. If every company used the Internet to adopt a low-cost strategy, then the effects might be problematic. Indeed, one possible outcome may be intense price competition among firms, with the likely result that most of the cost savings provided by the Internet get passed on to the industry's customers, rather than being retained in the form of higher profits. Moreover, because every company can use the Internet to streamline its activities, a company is unlikely to gain a sustainable long-term competitive advantage.

Many other technological advances affect company strategy and provide an opportunity to gain a competitive advantage. An example is **predictive analysis**, which uses data warehouses and complex algorithms to forecast future events, based on historical trends and calculated probabilities. Predictive analysis provides an educated guess of what one may expect to see in the near future, allowing companies to make better business decisions and improve their processes. FedEx uses predictive analysis to predict, with 65% to 90% accuracy, how customers respond to price changes and new services. Blue Cross Blue Shield of Tennessee uses a neural-based predictive model to predict the health care that specific patients will need, the severity of illnesses, and organ failures. Stock market analysts are using predictive analysis to predict short-term trends in the stock market.

An organization's AIS plays an important role in helping it adopt and maintain a strategic position. Achieving a close fit among activities requires that data be collected about each activity. It is also important that the information system collect and integrate both financial and nonfinancial data about the organization's activities.

The Role of the AIS in the Value Chain

To provide value to their customers, most organizations perform a number of different activities. Figure 5 shows that those activities can be conceptualized as forming a **value chain** consisting of five **primary activities** that directly provide value to customers:

1. *Inbound logistics*   consists of receiving, storing, and distributing the materials an organization uses to create the services and products it sells. For example, an automobile manufacturer receives, handles, and stores steel, glass, and rubber.
2. *Operations*   activities transform inputs into final products or services. For example, assembly line activities convert raw materials into a finished car.

FIGURE 4

Factors Influencing Design of the AIS

FIGURE 5

The Value Chain

3. *Outbound logistics* activities distribute finished products or services to customers. An example is shipping automobiles to car dealers.
4. *Marketing and sales* activities help customers buy the organization's products or services. Advertising is an example of a marketing and sales activity.
5. *Service* activities provide post-sale support to customers. Examples include repair and maintenance services.

Support activities allow the five primary activities to be performed efficiently and effectively. They are grouped into four categories:

1. *Firm infrastructure* is the accounting, finance, legal, and general administration activities that allow an organization to function. The AIS is part of the firm infrastructure.
2. *Human resources* activities include recruiting, hiring, training, and compensating employees.
3. *Technology* activities improve a product or service. Examples include research and development, investments in IT, and product design.
4. *Purchasing* activities procure raw materials, supplies, machinery, and the buildings used to carry out the primary activities.

Using IT to redesign supply chain systems yields tremendous benefits and cost savings. For example, Tennessee Valley Authority, a power generator, reengineered its supply chain and created an enterprisewide system that provides up-to-the-minute information, rather than the "current once a day" system that it replaced. The new system replaced 20 smaller and incompatible systems, reduced head count by 89 people, and saved $270 million in its first five years.

An organization's value chain is a part of a larger system called a *supply chain*. As shown in Figure 6, a manufacturing organization interacts with its suppliers and distributors. By paying attention to its supply chain, a company can improve its performance by helping the others in the supply chain to improve their performance. For example, S&S can improve its purchasing and inbound logistics activities by implementing a more efficient just-in-time inventory management system that reduces its costs and minimizes the capital tied up in inventory. S&S can reap additional benefits if it links its new systems with its suppliers so they can perform their primary value chain activities more efficiently. For example, by providing more detailed and timely information about its inventory needs, S&S suppliers can more efficiently plan their production schedules. Part of the resultant cost reduction can be passed on to S&S in the form of lower product costs.

The problems created by an ineffective supply chain are illustrated by Limited Brands. Limited experienced explosive growth, including acquisitions of other retail companies such as Victoria's Secret and Abercrombie & Fitch. These acquisitions left Limited with a tangled web of over 60 incompatible information systems. The problems came to a head one night when 400 trailers converged on a distribution center parking lot that could fit only 150 trailers. The trailers blocked traffic along all the highways around the distribution center and caused countless traffic and community

FIGURE 6

The Supply Chain

problems. No one in Limited knew where all the trailers came from, what the merchandise was, or where it was to be sent. Chaos reigned for some time, until the merchandise could be routed to stores and other distribution centers. Limited solved many of its problems by installing a new, integrated system that greatly improved its supply chain processes and technologies. Developing the new system was not easy. Limited has over a thousand suppliers and sells its merchandise using various platforms, including retail stores, the Internet, catalogs, and third-party retailers.

Summary and Case Conclusion

Susan and Scott reflected on what they had done to try and understand what decisions S&S would need to make and the information needed to make them. They had begun by obtaining an understanding of S&S's basic business processes and of the key decisions that must be made to operate the business effectively. They followed that with an analysis of the internal and external parties that the AIS would have to interact with and the information the AIS would have to provide them.

Since S&S is a retail merchandising company, its business processes could be described in terms of four basic transaction cycles:

1. The *revenue cycle* encompasses all transactions involving sales to customers and the collection of cash receipts for those sales.
2. The *expenditure cycle* encompasses all transactions involving the purchase of and payment for the merchandise sold by S&S, as well as other services it consumes, such as rent and utilities.
3. The *human resources/payroll cycle* encompasses all the transactions involving the hiring, training, and payment of employees.
4. The *financing cycle* encompasses all transactions involving the investment of capital in the company, borrowing money, payment of interest, and loan repayments.

These four cycles interface with the *general ledger and reporting system*, which consists of all activities related to the preparation of financial statements and other managerial reports.

Scott and Susan will need a well-designed AIS to provide the information they need to effectively plan, manage, and control their business. Their AIS must be able to process data about sales and cash receipts, purchasing and paying for merchandise and services, payroll and tax-related transactions, and acquiring and paying for fixed assets. The company's AIS must also provide the information needed to prepare financial statements.

Fortunately, there are many computer-based accounting packages available for the retail industry. As they begin looking at various software packages, however, Scott and Susan quickly learn that considerable accounting knowledge is required to choose the one that will best fit their business. Because neither has an accounting background, Scott and Susan decide that their next task will be to hire an accountant.

Key Terms

system
goal conflict
goal congruence
data
information
information overload
information technology (IT)
value of information
business process
transaction

transaction processing
give-get exchange
business processes or transaction cycles
revenue cycle
expenditure cycle
production (conversion) cycle
human resources/payroll cycle
financing cycle

general ledger and reporting system
accounting information system (AIS)
predictive analysis
value chain
primary activities
support activities
supply chain

15

AIS IN ACTION

Chapter Quiz

1. Data differ from information in which way?
   a. Data are output, and information is input.
   b. Information is output, and data are input.
   c. Data are meaningful bits of information.
   d. There is no difference.

2. Which of the following is NOT a characteristic that makes information useful?
   a. It is reliable.   b. It is timely.   c. It is inexpensive.   d. It is relevant.

3. Which of the following is a primary activity in the value chain?
   a. purchasing   c. post-sales service
   b. accounting   d. human resource management

4. Which transaction cycle includes interactions between an organization and its suppliers?
   a. revenue cycle   c. human resources/payroll cycle
   b. expenditure cycle   d. general ledger and reporting system

5. Which of the following is NOT a means by which information improves decision making?
   a. increases information overload
   b. reduces uncertainty
   c. provides feedback about the effectiveness of prior decisions
   d. identifies situations requiring management action

6. In the value chain concept, upgrading IT is considered what kind of activity?
   a. primary activity   c. service activity
   b. support activity   d. structured activity

7. In which cycle does a company ship goods to customers?
   a. production cycle   c. revenue cycle
   b. financing cycle   d. expenditure cycle

8. Which of the following is a function of an AIS?
   a. reducing the need to identify a strategy and strategic position
   b. transforming data into useful information
   c. allocating organizational resources
   d. automating all decision making

9. A firm, its suppliers, and its customers collectively form which of the following?
   a. supply chain   b. value chain   c. ERP system   d. AIS

10. A report telling how well all approved vendors have performed in the prior 12 months is
    information that is MOST needed in which business process?
    a. paying vendors   c. selling merchandise
    b. acquiring inventory   d. paying employees

Discussion Questions

1. The value of information is the difference between the benefits realized from using that
   information and the costs of producing it. Would you, or any organization, ever produce
   information if its expected costs exceeded its benefits? If so, provide some examples. If
   not, why not?

2. Can the characteristics of useful information listed in Table 1 be met simultaneously?
   Or does achieving one mean sacrificing another?

3. You and a few of your classmates decided to become entrepreneurs. You came up with a great idea for a new mobile phone application that you think will make lots of money. Your business plan won second place in a local competition, and you are using the $10,000 prize to support yourselves as you start your company.
   a. Identify the key decisions you need to make to be successful entrepreneurs, the information you need to make them, and the business processes you will need to engage in.
   b. Your company will need to exchange information with various external parties. Identify the external parties, and specify the information received from and sent to each of them.

4. How do an organization's business processes and lines of business affect the design of its AIS? Give several examples of how differences among organizations are reflected in their AIS.

5. Figure 4 shows that organizational culture and the design of an AIS influence one another. What does this imply about the degree to which an innovative system developed by one company can be transferred to another company?

6. Figure 4 shows that developments in IT affect both an organization's strategy and the design of its AIS. How can a company determine whether it is spending too much, too little, or just enough on IT?

7. Apply the value chain concept to S&S. Explain how it would perform the various primary and support activities.

8. Information technology enables organizations to easily collect large amounts of information about employees. Discuss the following issues:
   a. To what extent should management monitor employees' e-mail?
   b. To what extent should management monitor which Web sites employees visit?
   c. To what extent should management monitor employee performance by, for example, using software to track keystrokes per hour or some other unit of time? If such information is collected, how should it be used?
   d. Should companies use software to electronically "shred" all traces of e-mail?
   e. Under what circumstances and to whom is it appropriate for a company to distribute information it collects about the people who visit its Web site?

Problems

1. Information technology is continually changing the nature of accounting and the role of accountants. Write a two-page report describing what you think the nature of the accounting function and the accounting information system in a large company will be like in the year 2020.

2. The annual report is considered by some to be the single most important printed document that companies produce. In recent years, annual reports have become large documents. They now include such sections as letters to the stockholders, descriptions of the business, operating highlights, financial review, management discussion and analysis, a discussion of company internal controls, segment reporting, inflation data, and the basic financial statements. The expansion has been due in part to a general increase in the degree of sophistication and complexity in accounting standards and disclosure requirements for financial reporting.

   The expansion also is reflective of the change in the composition and level of sophistication of users. Current users include not only stockholders but also financial and securities analysts, potential investors, lending institutions, stockbrokers, customers, employees, and—whether the reporting company likes it or not—competitors. Thus, a report that was originally designed as a device for communicating basic financial information now attempts to meet the diverse needs of an ever-expanding audience.

   Users hold conflicting views on the value of annual reports. Some argue that they fail to provide enough information, whereas others believe that disclosures in annual reports have expanded to the point where they create information overload. Others argue that the future of most companies depends on acceptance by the investing public and by its customers; therefore, companies should take this opportunity to communicate well-defined corporate strategies.

Required

a. Identify and discuss the basic factors of communication that must be considered in the presentation of the annual report.

b. Discuss the communication problems a corporation faces in preparing the annual report that result from the diversity of the users being addressed.

c. Select two types of information found in an annual report, other than the financial statements and accompanying footnotes, and describe how they are helpful to the users of annual reports.

d. Discuss at least two advantages and two disadvantages of stating well-defined corporate strategies in the annual report.

e. Evaluate the effectiveness of annual reports in fulfilling the information needs of the following current and potential users: shareholders, creditors, employees, customers, and financial analysts.

f. Annual reports are public and accessible to anyone, including competitors. Discuss how this affects decisions about what information should be provided in annual reports. (*CMA Examination, adapted*)

3. United Services Automotive Association (USAA) is one of the largest diversified financial services companies in the United States, with close to $75 billion in assets under management. One reason for its success is the use of IT to lower costs and improve customer service. USAA operates one of the most advanced and successful information systems in the world. It communicates with its widely scattered customers, mostly military officers and their families, primarily by e-mail, phone, and its Web site.

Early on, USAA made a strategic choice to become one of the more technology-intensive companies in the world. It views IT as a strategic weapon and uses it in several ways, including the following:

- When customers call from their homes, offices, or cell phones, USAA personnel greet them personally by name. Unlike many diversified companies, a customer representative can handle inquires and transactions about all of USAA's products using a highly integrated database.

- USAA uses its extensive database to keep track of minute details, such as which auto parts are fixed most frequently. It also uses its database to find ways to reduce claims costs. For example, USAA discovered that repair shops would rather charge up to $300 to replace a windshield with punctures than to charge $40 to repair it. USAA began offering to waive the deductible if the owners would repair the windshield rather than replace it.

- USAA spent extensively to develop an image-processing system that digitizes all paper documents sent in by claimants (over 25 million a year). It takes only a few keystrokes for a policy service representative to retrieve pictures of all the documents in a customer's file. The system can sort and prioritize documents so that employees are always working on the most important and urgent tasks.

- USAA offers its customers remote deposit capture using scanning technology. It was the first U.S. bank to implement a remote deposit capture application for the iPhone. The iPhone application allows customers to take pictures of the front and back of each check and submit them electronically for deposit.

- USAA is a world leader in mobile banking. Customers can use their cell phones and other mobile devices to access and execute banking, investment, stock trading, and insurance applications such as filing claims. Customers can also use USAA's two-way text messaging system to send messages and receive text alerts and real-time information. They can also access person-to-person payment applications as well as social networking and personal financial management tools connected to bank accounts. Over 70% of USAA's logins are from cell phone users.

Required

a. Why should USAA collect data on which auto parts are fixed most frequently? What could it do with this data?

b. Even though USAA offered to waive the deductible, the repair shops still managed to convince 95% of the owners to replace rather than repair their damaged windshields. How could USAA use its AIS to persuade more shop owners to repair rather than replace their windows?

c. How does the image-processing system at USAA add value to the organization?

d. How do the remote deposit capture and mobile banking system at USAA add value to the organization?

e. Do an Internet search and find out what other advancements USAA has introduced. Write a brief paragraph on each new application or other newsworthy item you find (maximum limit of three applications or items).

4. Matching

Match the description listed in the right column with the information characteristic listed in the left column.

____ 1. Relevant	a. The report was carefully designed so that the data contained in the report became information to the reader.
____ 2. Reliable	b. The manager was working one weekend and needed to find some information about production requests for a certain customer. He was able to find the report on the company's network.
____ 3. Complete	c. The data in a report was checked by two clerks working independently.
____ 4. Timely	d. An accounts receivable aging report included all customer accounts.
____ 5. Understandable	e. A report was checked by three different people for accuracy.
____ 6. Verifiable	f. An accounts receivable aging report is used in credit-granting decisions.
____ 7. Accessible	g. An accounts receivable aging report was received before the credit manager had to make a decision whether to extend credit to a customer.

5. The Howard Leasing Company is a privately held, medium-sized business that purchases school busses and leases them to school districts, churches, charitable organizations, and other businesses. To better serve its customers and, more important, to protect its investment in the busses, Howard operates a large maintenance facility to maintain and repair leased vehicles. Howard's annual sales for last year were $37 million, with a net income of $2.9 million. Howard employs approximately 150 people.

You were recently hired by Howard, and you are eager to prove your worth to the company. Your supervisor just called you into her office and asked you to prepare an accounts receivable aging report as of the end of the year for use in the upcoming audit of the company's financial statements.

Required

a. What is an accounts receivable aging report?

b. Why is an accounts receivable aging report needed for an audit?

c. What is an accounts receivable aging report used for in normal company operations?

d. What data will you need to prepare the report?

e. Where will you collect the data you need to prepare the report?

f. How will you collect the necessary data for the report?

g. What will the report look like (i.e., how will you organize the data collected to create the information your supervisor needs for the audit)? Prepare an accounts receivable aging report in Excel or another spreadsheet package.

h. How will you distribute the report? How many copies will you make? Who should receive the copies? What security features will you implement?

6. Based on Walmart's success in the United States, many expected the company to quickly dominate the British market after it bought the Asda grocery chain in 1999. That has not happened; Walmart's market share in groceries is a little more than half that of its biggest competitor, Tesco. Initially, Tesco's sales and net income rose significantly while Walmart's sales and net income increased at a much slower rate. More recently, Walmart has made small gains in market share, and Tesco has had small decreases.

   Walmart found out that Tesco is a formidable worldwide competitor. Tesco operates almost 2,400 stores in Britain in four different formats. It has a very successful operation in Central Europe, and it has expanded to the United States with Fresh & Easy stores. In Korea, Tesco's 174 stores are thriving while Walmart gave up after an eight-year effort to succeed and sold its 16 stores.

   One of the biggest reasons for Tesco's success is its use of technology. In 1995, Tesco started a loyalty card program, called Clubcard, and over 80% of its shoppers are members. Shoppers fill out an application in the store and receive a plastic card and a key fob in the mail that is scanned before they make a purchase. Tesco gathers massive amounts of data about its customers' 15 million purchases each week. Sales data are analyzed and turned into information that provides Tesco with a significant competitive advantage.

   As traditional advertising loses effectiveness, these large stores of data allow Tesco to find new and creative ways to market its products.

   Required

   a. What kind of information do you think Tesco gathers?
   b. How do you think Tesco has motivated over 22 million customers to sign up for its Clubcard program?
   c. What can Tesco accomplish with the Clubcard data it collects? Think in terms of strategy and competitive advantage.
   d. What are some of the disadvantages to the Clubcard program?
   e. Do an Internet search to find out how Tesco is doing in comparison to Walmart and other grocers and retailers. Write a few paragraphs explaining your findings.

7. Have you ever imagined having one electronic device that does everything you would ever need? Mobile phone makers in Japan have gone beyond the imagining phase. Cell phones in Japan are becoming more versatile than ever. Newer models of cell phones contain a myriad of applications and can do many of the things that a personal computer (PC) can do. PCs are also able to function as phones. A small but growing number of professionals are trading in their laptops for handheld computers. Cell phone manufacturers in the United States and elsewhere are quickly catching up to their Japanese counterparts.

   Required

   a. What commercial activities can be done with a cell phone? With a cell phone/PC combination device? What do you do when you're on your cell phone? What do you expect to be doing in five years?
   b. How can businesses utilize this technology to attract more customers, sell more products, advertise their products, facilitate the sale of products, and conduct and manage their businesses more efficiently and effectively?
   c. What are some problems or drawbacks you can see with using these devices in business?

8. Classify each of the following items as belonging in the revenue, expenditure, human resources/payroll, production, or financing cycle.
   a. Purchase raw materials
   b. Pay off mortgage on a factory

c. Hire a new assistant controller
d. Establish a $10,000 credit limit for a new customer
e. Pay for raw materials
f. Disburse payroll checks to factory workers
g. Record goods received from a vendor
h. Update the allowance for doubtful accounts
i. Decide how many units to make next month
j. Complete a picking ticket for a customer order
k. Record factory employee timecards
l. Sell concert tickets
m. Draw on line of credit
n. Send new employees to a business ethics course
o. Pay utility bills
p. Pay property taxes on an office building
q. Pay federal payroll taxes
r. Sell a DVD player
s. Collect payments on customer accounts
t. Obtain a bank loan
u. Pay sales commissions
v. Send an order to a vendor
w. Put purchased goods into the warehouse

Case 1 Ackoff's Management Misinformation Systems

The Web site for this book contains an adaption of Russell L. Ackoff's classic article "Management Misinformation Systems" from *Management Science*. In the article, Ackoff identified five common assumptions about information systems and then explained why he disagreed with them.

Required

Read the five assumptions, contentions, and Ackoff's explanations. For each of the five assumptions, decide whether you agree or disagree with Ackoff's contentions. Prepare a report in which you defend your stand and explain your defense.

AIS IN ACTION SOLUTIONS

Quiz Key

1. Data differ from information in which way?
   a. Data are output, and information is input. [Incorrect. Data are facts and figures that, once organized, can become information. Therefore, data are inputs, and information is output.]
   ▶ b. Information is output, and data are input. [Correct.]
   c. Data are meaningful bits of information. [Incorrect. Information is organized and processed data that provide meaning.]
   d. There is no difference. [Incorrect. There is a difference. Data are unorganized facts and figures. Information is meaningful, organized, and processed data.]

2. Which of the following is NOT a characteristic that makes information useful?
   a. It is reliable. [Incorrect. This is one of the information characteristics listed in Table 1
   b. It is timely. [Incorrect. This is one of the information characteristics listed in Table 1

▶ c. It is inexpensive. [Correct. This is NOT one of the information characteristics listed in Table 1.]

d. It is relevant. [Incorrect. This is one of the information characteristics listed in Table 1.]

3. Which of the following is a primary activity in the value chain?
   a. purchasing [Incorrect. This is a support activity.]
   b. accounting [Incorrect. This is a firm infrastructure support activity.]
   ▶ c. post-sales service [Correct. Service is a primary activity.]
   d. human resource management [Incorrect. This is a support activity.]

4. Which transaction cycle includes interactions between an organization and its suppliers?
   a. revenue cycle [Incorrect. The revenue cycle involves interactions between an organization and its customers.]
   ▶ b. expenditure [Correct.]
   c. human resources/payroll cycle [Incorrect. The human resources/payroll cycle involves interactions between an organization and its employees, government, and potential hires.]
   d. general ledger and reporting system [Incorrect. The general ledger and reporting system receives summary information from all cycles.]

5. Which of the following is NOT a means by which information improves decision making?
   ▶ a. increases information overload [Correct. Decision makers receiving too much information have difficulty incorporating all of the information into their decision framework, and, as a result, decision quality can be reduced rather than improved.]
   b. reduces uncertainty [Incorrect. More reliable information leads to less uncertainty and thus better decisions.]
   c. provides feedback about the effectiveness of prior decisions [Incorrect. Knowledge of effective and ineffective decisions can lead to better decisions in the future.]
   d. identifies situations requiring management action [Incorrect. Identifying the need for management action can lead to improved decision making.]

6. In the value chain concept, upgrading IT is considered what kind of activity?
   a. primary activity [Incorrect. Investing in IT is a support activity.]
   b. support activity [Correct. Technology activities, including investing in IT, are considered a support activity.]
   c. service activity [Incorrect. The value chain includes only primary and support activities. A service activity is a type of primary activity.]
   d. structured activity [Incorrect. The value chain includes only primary and support activities. A structured activity is neither a primary nor a secondary activity.]

7. In which cycle does a company ship goods to customers?
   a. production cycle [Incorrect. The production cycle involves the transformation of raw materials into finished goods.]
   b. financing cycle [Incorrect. The financing cycle deals with interactions between an organization and its lenders and owners.]
   ▶ c. revenue cycle [Correct. The revenue cycle involves interactions between an organization and its customers, such as shipping them goods.]
   d. expenditure cycle [Incorrect. The expenditure cycle involves interactions between an organization and its suppliers.]

8. Which of the following is a function of an AIS?
   a. reducing the need to identify a strategy and strategic position [Incorrect. An AIS does not reduce the need to identify a strategy. It provides information to executives for the purpose of making strategic decisions.]
   ▶ b. transforming data into useful information [Correct. This is one of the primary functions of an AIS.]

    c. allocating organizational resources [Incorrect. Decision makers allocate resources, and the purpose of the AIS is to provide information to the decision makers so that they can make the allocation.]

    d. automating all decision making [Incorrect. The AIS provides information to decision makers; it is not designed to automate all decision making.]

9. A firm, its suppliers, and its customers collectively form which of the following?

   ▶ a. supply chain [Correct. The supply chain is made up of the firm, its suppliers, and customers.]

    b. value chain [Incorrect. The value chain is made up of primary and support activities within the firm.]

    c. ERP system [Incorrect. An ERP system integrates all aspects of an organization's activities into one system.]

    d. AIS [Incorrect. The AIS is made up of the human and capital resources within an organization that are responsible for collecting and processing transactions and preparing financial information.]

10. A report telling how well all approved vendors have performed in the prior 12 months is information that is MOST needed in which business process?

    a. paying vendors [Incorrect. To pay a vendor, a company needs to know whether merchandise ordered was received in good condition. They do not need a 12-month history of vendor performance.]

   ▶ b. acquiring inventory [Correct. Companies want to acquire inventory from companies that have performed well in the past. A vendor performance report would disclose whether the vendor shipped inventory on time, whether the inventory was of the requested quality, whether the prices were as agreed upon, etc.]

    c. selling merchandise [Incorrect. A 12-month history of vendor performance is usually not very helpful in trying to sell products to customers. More important would be customer tastes and preferences, customer credit status, etc.]

    d. paying employees [Incorrect. It is very rare for an employee's pay to be based on a 12-month history of vendor performance. More important are hours worked, annual salary, sales figures to calculate commissions, etc.]

Chapter 2

Overview of Transaction Processing and Enterprise Resource Planning Systems

From Chapter 2 of *Accounting Information Systems*, 12/e. Marshall B. Romney. Paul John Steinbart. Copyright © 2012 by Pearson Education. Published by Prentice Hall. All rights reserved.

Overview of Transaction Processing and Enterprise Resource Planning Systems

Learning Objectives

After studying this chapter, you should be able to:

1. Describe the four parts of the data processing cycle and the major activities in each.

2. Describe documents and procedures used to collect and process transaction data.

3. Describe the ways information is stored in computer-based information systems.

4. Discuss the types of information that an AIS can provide.

5. Discuss how organizations use enterprise resource planning (ERP) systems to process transactions and provide information.

INTEGRATIVE CASE S&S

The grand opening of S&S is two weeks away. Scott Parry and Susan Gonzalez are working long hours to make the final arrangements for the store opening. Most of the employees have already been hired; training is scheduled for next week.

Susan has ordered inventory for the first month. The store is being remodeled and will have a bright, cheery decor. All seems to be in order—all, that is, except the accounting records.

Like many entrepreneurs, Scott and Susan have not given as much thought to their accounting records as they have to other parts of their business. Recognizing they need qualified accounting help, they hired a full-time accountant, Ashton Fleming. Scott and Susan think Ashton is perfect for the job because of his three

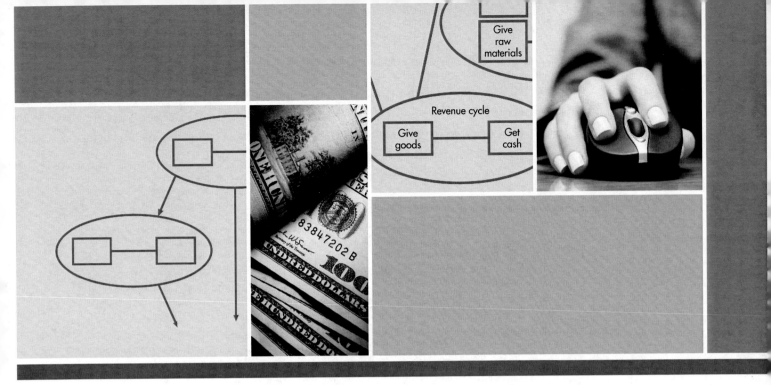

years of experience with a national CPA firm. Ashton is looking forward to working for S&S because he has always wanted to be involved in building a company from the ground up.

During Ashton's first day on the job, Susan gives him the invoices for the inventory she purchased and a folder with their bank loan documentation, with the first payment due after the grand opening. She also hands him a folder containing information on rental payments, utilities, and other expenses. Susan tells Ashton that she and Scott know little about accounting and he will run the accounting end of S&S. She adds that the only thing they have done so far is to open a checking account for S&S and that they have kept the check register updated to monitor their cash flow.

Scott explains that the sales staff is paid a fixed salary and commissions and that all other employees are paid hourly rates. Employees are paid every two weeks, with their first paychecks due next week. Ashton asks Scott what accounting software the company is using. Scott replies that he and Susan have not had time to tackle that aspect yet. Scott and Susan looked at some of the popular packages but quickly realized that they did not know enough about accounting to make an intelligent choice. Scott then tells Ashton that his first task should be to purchase whatever accounting software he thinks will be best for S&S.

After Scott leaves, Ashton feels both excited and a little nervous about his responsibility for creating an AIS for S&S. Although Ashton has audited many companies, he has never organized a company's books and is unsure how to go about it. A million questions run through his head. Here are just a few of them:

1. How should I organize the accounting records so that financial statements can be easily produced?
2. How am I going to collect and process data about all of S&S's transactions?
3. How do I organize all the data that will be collected?

27

4. How should I design the AIS so that the information provided is reliable and accurate?

5. How can I design procedures to ensure that they meet all government obligations, such as remitting sales, income, and payroll taxes?

Introduction

This chapter is divided into two major sections. The first section discusses the data processing cycle and its role in organizing business activities and providing information to users. It explains how organizations capture and enter data about business activities into their AIS and how companies process data and transform it into useful information. It also discusses basic data storage concepts, showing how data are stored for further use. Finally, information output is discussed, including the different ways information is provided to users.

The second section discusses the role of the information system in modern organizations and introduces the concept of an enterprise resource planning (ERP) system. An ERP can help integrate all aspects of a company's operations with its traditional AIS. This section also describes the significant advantages of an ERP as well as significant challenges that must be overcome to implement an ERP system.

Transaction Processing: The Data Processing Cycle

Accountants and other system users play a significant role in the data processing cycle. For example, they interact with systems analysts to help answer questions such as these: What data should be entered and stored by the organization, and who should have access to them? How should data be organized, updated, stored, accessed, and retrieved? How can scheduled and unanticipated information needs be met? To answer these and related questions, the data processing concepts explained in this chapter must be understood.

One important AIS function is to process company transactions efficiently and effectively. In manual (non-computer-based) systems, data are entered into journals and ledgers maintained on paper. In computer-based systems, data are entered into computers and stored in files and databases. The operations performed on data to generate meaningful and relevant information are referred to collectively as the *data processing cycle*. As shown in Figure 1, this process consists of four steps: data input, data storage, data processing, and information output.

Data Input

The first step in processing input is to capture transaction data and enter them into the system. The data capture process is usually triggered by a business activity. Data must be collected about three facets of each business activity:

1. Each activity of interest
2. The resource(s) affected by each activity
3. The people who participate in each activity

FIGURE 1
The Data Processing Cycle

For example, the most frequent revenue cycle transaction is a sale, either for cash or on credit. S&S may find it useful to collect the following data about a sales transaction:

- Date and time the sale occurred
- Employee who made the sale and the checkout clerk who processed the sale
- Checkout register where the sale was processed
- Item(s) sold
- Quantity of each item sold
- List price and actual price of each item sold
- Total amount of the sale
- Delivery instructions
- For credit sales: customer name, customer bill-to and ship-to addresses

Historically, most businesses used paper **source documents** to collect data about their business activities. They later transferred that data into the computer. When the data is entered using computer screens, they often retain the same name and basic format as the paper source document it replaced. Table 1 lists some common transaction cycle activities and the source document or form used to capture data about that event.

Turnaround documents are company output sent to an external party, who often adds data to the document, and then are returned to the company as an input document. They are in machine-readable form to facilitate their subsequent processing as input records. An example is a utility bill that is sent to the customer, returned with the customer's payment, and read by a special scanning device when it is returned.

Source data automation devices capture transaction data in machine-readable form at the time and place of their origin. Examples include ATMs used by banks, point-of-sale (POS) scanners used in retail stores, and bar code scanners used in warehouses.

The second step in processing input is to make sure captured data are accurate and complete. One way to do this is to use source data automation or well-designed turnaround documents and data entry screens. Well-designed documents and screens improve accuracy and completeness by providing instructions or prompts about what data to collect, grouping logically related pieces of information close together, using checkoff boxes or pull-down menus to present the available options, and using appropriate shading and borders to clearly separate data items. Data input screens usually list all the data the user needs to enter. Sometimes these screens resemble source documents, and users fill out the screen the same way they would a paper source document.

Users can improve control either by purchasing prenumbered source documents or by having the system automatically assign a sequential number to each new transaction. Prenumbering

TABLE 1 Common Business Activities and Source Documents

Business Activity	Source Document
Revenue Cycle	
Take customer order	Sales order
Deliver or ship order	Delivery ticket or bill of lading
Receive cash	Remittance advice or remittance list
Deposit cash receipts	Deposit slip
Adjust customer account	Credit memo
Expenditure Cycle	
Request items	Purchase requisition
Order items	Purchase order
Receive items	Receiving report
Pay for items	Check or electronic funds transfer
Human Resources Cycle	
Collect employee withholding data	W-4 form
Record time worked by employees	Time cards
Record time spent on specific jobs	Job time tickets or time sheet

simplifies verifying that all transactions have been recorded and that none of the documents has been misplaced. (Imagine trying to balance a checkbook if the checks were not prenumbered.)

The third step in processing input is to make sure company policies are followed, such as approving or verifying a transaction. For example, S&S would not want to sell goods to a customer who was not paying his bills or to sell an item for immediate delivery that was out of stock. These problems are prevented by programming the system to check a customer's credit limit and payment history, as well as inventory status, before confirming a customer sale.

Data Storage

A company's data are one of its most important resources. However, the mere existence of relevant data does not guarantee that they are useful. To function properly, an organization must have ready and easy access to its data. Therefore, accountants need to understand how data are organized and stored in an AIS and how they can be accessed. In essence, they need to know how to manage data for maximum corporate use.

Imagine how difficult it would be to read a textbook if it were not organized into chapters, sections, paragraphs, and sentences. Now imagine how hard it would be for S&S to find an invoice if all documents were randomly dumped into file cabinets. Fortunately, information in an AIS is organized for easy and efficient access. This section explains basic data storage concepts and definitions.

LEDGERS   Cumulative accounting information is stored in general and subsidiary ledgers. A *general ledger* contains summary-level data for every asset, liability, equity, revenue, and expense account. A *subsidiary ledger* contains detailed data for any general ledger account with many individual subaccounts. For example, the general ledger has an accounts receivable account that summarizes the total amount owed to the company by all customers. The subsidiary accounts receivable ledger has a separate record for each individual customer, with detailed information such as name, address, purchases, payments, account balance, and credit limit. Subsidiary ledgers are often used for accounts receivable, inventory, fixed assets, and accounts payable.

The general ledger account corresponding to a subsidiary ledger is called a *control account*. The relationship between the general ledger control account and the total of individual subsidiary ledger account balances helps maintain the accuracy of AIS data. Specifically, the sum of all subsidiary ledger account balances should equal the amount in the corresponding general ledger control account. Any discrepancy between them indicates that a recording error has occurred.

CODING TECHNIQUES   Data in ledgers is organized logically using coding techniques. *Coding* is the systematic assignment of numbers or letters to items to classify and organize them.

- With *sequence codes*, items are numbered consecutively to account for all items. Any missing items cause a gap in the numerical sequence. Examples include prenumbered checks, invoices, and purchase orders.
- With a *block code*, blocks of numbers are reserved for specific categories of data. For example, S&S reserved the following numbers for major product categories:

Product Code	Product Type
1000000–1999999	Electric range
2000000–2999999	Refrigerator
3000000–3999999	Washer
4000000–4999999	Dryer

  Users can identify an item's type and model using the code numbers. Other examples include ledger account numbers (blocked by account type), employee numbers (blocked by department), and customer numbers (blocked by region).
- *Group codes*, which are two or more subgroups of digits used to code items, are often used in conjunction with block codes. If S&S uses a seven-digit product code number, the group coding technique might be applied as follows.

Digit Position	Meaning
1–2	Product line, size, style
3	Color
4–5	Year of manufacture
6–7	Optional features

There are four subcodes in the product code, each with a different meaning. Users can sort, summarize, and retrieve information using one or more subcodes. This technique is often applied to general ledger account numbers.

- With *mnemonic codes*, letters and numbers are interspersed to identify an item. The mnemonic code is derived from the description of the item and is usually easy to memorize. For example, Dry300W05 could represent a low end (300), white (W) dryer (Dry) made by Whirlpool (05).

The following guidelines result in a better coding system. The code should:

- Be consistent with its intended use, which requires that the code designer determine desired system outputs prior to selecting the code.
- Allow for growth. For example, don't use a three-digit employee code for a fast-growing company with 950 employees.
- Be as simple as possible to minimize costs, facilitate memorization and interpretation, and ensure employee acceptance.
- Be consistent with the company's organizational structure and across the company's divisions.

CHART OF ACCOUNTS   A great example of coding is the *chart of accounts*, which is a list of the numbers assigned to each general ledger account. These account numbers allow transaction data to be coded, classified, and entered into the proper accounts. They also facilitate the preparation of financial statements and reports, because data stored in individual accounts can easily be summed for presentation.

However, data stored in summary accounts cannot be easily analyzed and reported in more detail. Consequently, it is important that the chart of accounts contain sufficient detail to meet an organization's information needs. To illustrate, consider the consequences if S&S were to use only one general ledger account for all sales transactions. It would be easy to produce reports showing the total amount of sales for a given time period, but it would be very difficult to prepare reports separating cash and credit sales. Indeed, the only way to produce these latter reports would be to go back to original sales records to identify the nature of each sales transaction. If S&S used separate general ledger accounts for cash and credit sales, then reports showing both types of sales could be easily produced. Total sales could also be easily reported by summing each type of sale.

Table 2 shows the chart of accounts Ashton developed for S&S. Each account number is three digits long. The first digit represents the major account category and indicates where it appears on S&S's financial statements. Thus, all current assets are numbered in the 100s, non-current assets are numbered in the 200s, and so on.

The second digit represents the primary financial subaccounts within each category. Again, the accounts are assigned numbers to match the order of their appearance in financial statements (in order of decreasing liquidity). Thus, account 120 represents accounts receivable, and account 150 represents inventory.

The third digit identifies the specific account to which the transaction data will be posted. For example, account 501 represents cash sales, and account 502 represents credit sales. Similarly, accounts 101 through 103 represent the various cash accounts used by S&S.

A chart of accounts is tailored to the nature and purpose of an organization. For example, the chart of accounts for S&S indicates that the company is a corporation. In contrast, a partnership would include separate capital and drawing accounts for each partner, instead of common stock and retained earnings. Likewise, because S&S is a retail organization, it has only one type of general ledger inventory account. A manufacturing company, in contrast,

TABLE 2 Sample Chart of Accounts for S&S

Account Code	Account Name	Account Code	Account Name
100–199	Current Assets	400–499	Equity Accounts
101	Checking Account	400	Common Stock
102	Savings Account	410	Retained Earnings
103	Petty Cash		
120	Accounts Receivable	500–599	Revenues
125	Allowance for Doubtful Accounts	501	Cash Sales
130	Notes Receivable	502	Credit Sales
150	Inventory	510	Sales Returns & Allowances
160	Supplies	511	Sales Discounts
170	Prepaid Rent	520	Interest Revenue
180	Prepaid Insurance	530	Miscellaneous Revenue
200–299	Noncurrent Assets	600–799	Expenses
200	Land	600	Cost of Goods Sold
210	Buildings	611	Wages Expense
215	Accumulated Depreciation—Buildings	612	Commissions Expense
230	Equipment	613	Payroll Tax Expense
235	Accumulated Depreciation—Equipment	620	Rent Expense
240	Furniture & Fixtures	630	Insurance Expense
245	Accumulated Depreciation—Furniture & Fixtures	640	Supplies Expense
250	Other Assets	650	Bad Debt Expense
		701	Depreciation Expense—Buildings
300–399	Liabilities	702	Depreciation Expense—Equipment
300	Accounts Payable	703	Depreciation Expense—Furniture & Fixtures
310	Wages Payable	710	Income Tax Expense
321	Employee Income Tax Payable		
322	FICA Tax Payable	900–999	
323	Federal Unemployment Tax Payable	910	Summary Accounts
324	State Unemployment Tax Payable		Income Summary
330	Accrued Interest Payable		
360	Other Liabilities		

would have separate general ledger accounts for raw materials, work in process, and finished goods inventories.

Ashton left gaps in S&S's chart of accounts to allow for additional accounts. For example, when S&S has excess cash to invest in marketable securities, a new general ledger account can be created and assigned the number 110. When S&S opens stores in the future, he will add three digits to the chart of accounts to represent each store in the chain, so that S&S can track items in each store.

Subsidiary ledger accounts often have longer account codes than general ledger accounts. At S&S, each account receivable will have a seven-digit code. The first three digits are 120, the code for accounts receivable. The next four digits identify up to 10,000 individual customers.

JOURNALS   Transaction data are often recorded in a journal before they are entered into a ledger. A journal entry shows the accounts and amounts to be debited and credited. A *general journal* is used to record infrequent or nonroutine transactions, such as loan payments and end-of-period adjusting and closing entries. A *specialized journal* records large numbers of repetitive transactions such as sales, cash receipts, and cash disbursements.

Table 3 is a sample sales journal. All transaction information is recorded in one line, with every entry a debit to accounts receivable and a credit to sales. There is no need to write an explanation of each entry, as is the case with general journal entries. Given the high number of daily sales transactions, the time saved by recording these transactions in a sales journal, rather than in the general journal, is considerable.

The Post Ref column indicates when transactions are posted to the appropriate ledger. In a manual system, ledgers are books; hence, the phrase "keeping the books" refers to the process of maintaining the ledgers.

Figure 2 shows how to journalize and post sales transactions. First, each credit sale is recorded in the sales journal. Then each sales journal entry is posted to the appropriate customer account in the accounts receivable subsidiary ledger (note the arrow linking the $1,876.50 sale to KDR Builders in the sales journal to the debit for $1,876.50 in the accounts receivable subsidiary ledger). Periodically, the total of all sales journal entries is posted to the general ledger (note the arrow showing the daily sales journal total of $15,511.00 posted to both the Accounts Receivable and the Credit Sales general ledger accounts).

AUDIT TRAIL   Figure 2 shows how the posting references and document numbers provide an audit trail. An *audit trail* is a traceable path of a transaction through a data processing system from point of origin to final output, or backwards from from final output to point of origin. It is used to check the accuracy and validity of ledger postings. Observe that the SJ5 posting reference for the $15,511 credit to the sales account in the general ledger refers to page 5 of the sales journal. By checking page 5 of the sales journal, it is possible to verify that $15,511 represents the total credit sales recorded on October 15. Similarly, the posting reference for the $1876.50 debit to the KDR Builders' account in the subsidiary accounts receivable ledger also refers to page 5 of the sales journal as the source of that entry. Furthermore, note that the sales journal lists the invoice numbers for each individual entry. This provides the means for locating and examining the appropriate source documents in order to verify that the transaction occurred and it was recorded accurately.

COMPUTER-BASED STORAGE CONCEPTS   An *entity* is something about which information is stored, such as employees, inventory items, and customers. Each entity has *attributes*, or characteristics of interest, that are stored, such as a pay rate and address. Each type of entity possesses the same set of attributes. For example, all employees possess an employee number, pay rate, and home address. The specific values for those attributes will differ. For example, one employee's pay rate might be $12.00 an hour, whereas another's might be $12.25.

TABLE 3 Sample Sales Journal

Sales Journal					Page 5
Date	Invoice Number	Account Debited	Account Number	Post Ref.	Amount
Oct. 15	151	Brown Hospital Supply	120-035	✓	798.00
15	152	Greenshadows Hotel Suites	120-122	✓	1,267.00
15	153	Heathrow Apartments	120-057	✓	5,967.00
15	154	LMS Construction	120-173	✓	2,312.50
15	155	Gardenview Apartments	120-084	✓	3,290.00
15	156	KDR Builders	120-135	✓	1,876.50
		TOTAL	120/502		15,511.00

FIGURE 2

Recording and Posting a Credit Sale

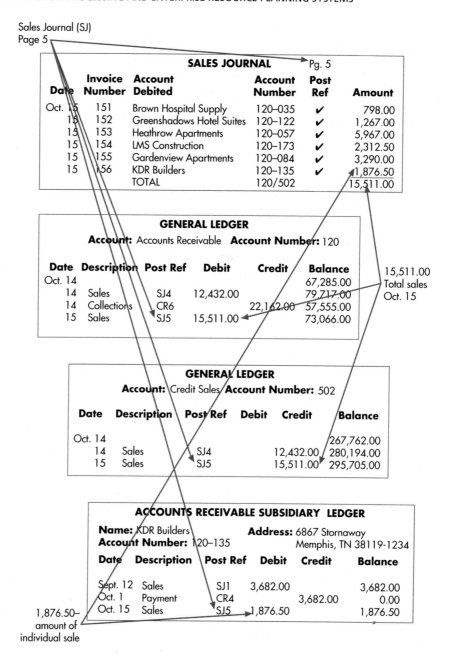

Figure 3 shows that computers store data in a *field*. The fields containing data about entity attributes constitute a *record*. In Figure 3, each row represents a different record, and each column represents an attribute. Each intersecting row and column in Figure 3 is a field within a record, the contents of which are called a *data value*.

A *file* is a group of related records. A *master file,* like a ledger in a manual AIS, stores cumulative information about an organization. The inventory and equipment master files store information about important organizational resources. The customer, supplier, and employee master files store information about important agents with whom the organization interacts.

Master files are permanent; they exist across fiscal periods. However, individual master file records may change frequently. For example, individual customer accounts balances are updated to reflect new sales transactions and payments received. Periodically, new records are added to or removed from a master file, for example, when a new customer is added or a former customer deleted.

FIGURE 3

Data Storage Elements

This accounts receivable file stores information about three separate entities: XYZ Company, ABC Company, and QRS Company. As a result, there are three records in the file. Five separate attributes are used to describe each customer: customer number, customer name, address, credit limit, and balance. There are, therefore, five separate fields in each record. Each field contains a data value that describes an attribute of a particular entity (customer). For example, the data value 19283 is the customer number for the XYZ Company.

A *transaction file* contains records of individual business transactions that occur during a specific time. It is similar to a journal in a manual AIS. For example, S&S will have a daily sales transaction file and a cash receipts file. Both files will update individual customer account balances in the customer master file. Transaction files are not permanent and may not be needed beyond the current fiscal period. However, they are usually maintained for a specified period for backup purposes.

A set of interrelated, centrally coordinated files is referred to as a *database*. For example, the accounts receivable file might be combined with customer, sales analysis, and related files to form a customer database.

Data Processing

Once business activity data have been entered into the system, they must be processed to keep the databases current. The four different types of data processing activities, referred to as CRUD, are as follows:

1. *Creating* new data records, such as adding a newly hired employee to the payroll database.
2. *Reading,* retrieving, or viewing existing data.
3. *Updating* previously stored data. Figure 4 depicts the steps required to update an accounts receivable record with a sales transaction. The two records are matched using the account number. The sale amount ($360) is added to the account balance ($1,500) to get a new current balance ($1,860).
4. *Deleting* data, such as purging the vendor master file of all vendors the company no longer does business with.

Updating done periodically, such as daily, is referred to as *batch processing*. Although batch processing is cheaper and more efficient, the data are current and accurate only immediately after processing. For that reason, batch processing is used only for applications, such as payroll, that do not need frequent updating and that naturally occur or are processed at fixed time periods.

Most companies update each transaction as it occurs, referred to as *online, real-time processing* because it ensures that stored information is always current, thereby increasing its decision-making usefulness. It is also more accurate because data input errors can be corrected in real time or refused. It also provides significant competitive advantages. For example, FedEx updated its mission statement to include the phrase "Positive control of each package will be maintained by

FIGURE 4

The Accounts Receivable File Update Process

utilizing real-time electronic tracking and tracing systems." With FedEx's system, employees and customers can track the exact location of each package and estimate its arrival time.

A combination of the two approaches is online batch processing, where transaction data are entered and edited as they occur and stored for later processing. Batch processing and online, real-time processing are summarized in Figure 5.

Information Output

The final step in the data processing cycle is information output. When displayed on a monitor, output is referred to as "soft copy." When printed on paper, it is referred to as "hard copy." Information is usually presented in one of three forms: a document, a report, or a query response.

Documents are records of transaction or other company data. Some, such as checks and invoices, are transmitted to external parties. Others, such as receiving reports and purchase requisitions, are used internally. Documents can be printed out, or they can be stored as electronic images in a computer. For example, Toys 'R' Us uses electronic data interchange to communicate with its suppliers. Every year it processes over half a million invoices electronically, thereby eliminating paper documents and dramatically reducing costs and errors. This has resulted in higher profits and more accurate information.

Reports are used by employees to control operational activities and by managers to make decisions and to formulate business strategies. External users need reports to evaluate company profitability, judge creditworthiness, or comply with regulatory requirements. Some reports, such as financial statements and sales analyses, are produced on a regular basis. Others are produced on an exception basis to call attention to unusual conditions. For example, S&S could have its system produce a report to indicate when product returns exceed a certain percentage of sales. Reports can also be produced on demand. For example, Susan could produce a report to identify the salesperson who sold the most items during a specific promotional period.

The need for reports should be periodically assessed, because they are often prepared long after they are needed, wasting time, money, and resources. For example, NCR Corporation reduced the number of reports from 1,200 to just over 100. Another company eliminated 6 million pages of reports, a stack four times higher than its 41-story headquarters building. One 25-page report took five days to prepare and sat unread.

A database *query* is used to provide the information needed to deal with problems and questions that need rapid action or answers. A user enters a request for a specific piece of information; it is retrieved, displayed, or analyzed as requested. Repetitive queries are often developed by information systems specialists. One-time queries are often developed by users. Some companies, such as Wal-Mart, allow suppliers to access their databases to help them better serve Wal-Mart's needs. Suppliers can gauge how well a product is selling in every Wal-Mart store in the world and maximize sales by stocking and promoting items that are selling well.

Batch Processing

Group source documents into batches. Generate control totals.

Enter batches at predetermined times or batch sizes. Sort file and edit data as appropriate.

Store data in temporary file.

Master File

Process all batches. Update old master files with transaction data, creating new master file.

Print desired output. Also print error reports, transaction reports, control total reports.

Online Batch Processing

Enter transactions into system as they occur.

Store data in temporary file.

Master File

Process temporary file at predetermined time. Update old master files with transaction data, creating new master file.

Print desired output.

Online Real-Time Processing

Master File

Enter transactions into system as they occur.

Process transactions as they occur. Update master files with transaction data.

Print desired output.

FIGURE 5

Batch and Online Processing

Enterprise Resource Planning (ERP) Systems

Traditionally, the AIS has been referred to as a transaction processing system because its only concern was financial data and accounting transactions. For example, when a sale took place, the AIS would record a journal entry showing only the date of the sale, a debit to either cash or accounts receivable, and a credit to sales. Other potentially useful nonfinancial information about the sale, such as the time of day that it occurred, would traditionally be collected and processed outside the AIS. Consequently, many organizations developed additional information systems to collect, process, store, and report information not contained in the AIS. Unfortunately, the existence of multiple systems creates numerous problems and inefficiencies. Often the same data must be captured and stored by more than one system, which not only results in redundancy across systems but also can lead to discrepancies if data are changed in one system but not in others. In addition, it is difficult to integrate data from the various systems.

Enterprise resource planning (ERP) systems overcome these problems as they integrate all aspects of a company's operations with a traditional AIS. Most large and many medium-sized organizations use ERP systems to coordinate and manage their data, business processes, and resources. The ERP system collects, processes, and stores data and provides the information managers and external parties need to assess the company.

As shown in Figure 6, a properly configured ERP system uses a centralized database to share information across business processes and coordinate activities. This is important because an activity that is part of one business process often triggers a complex series of activities throughout many different parts of the organization. For example, a customer order may necessitate scheduling additional production to meet the increased demand. This may trigger an order to purchase more raw materials. It may also be necessary to schedule overtime or hire temporary help. Well-designed ERP systems provide management with easy access to up-to-date information about all of these activities in order to plan, control, and evaluate the organization's business processes more effectively.

FIGURE 6
Integrated ERP System

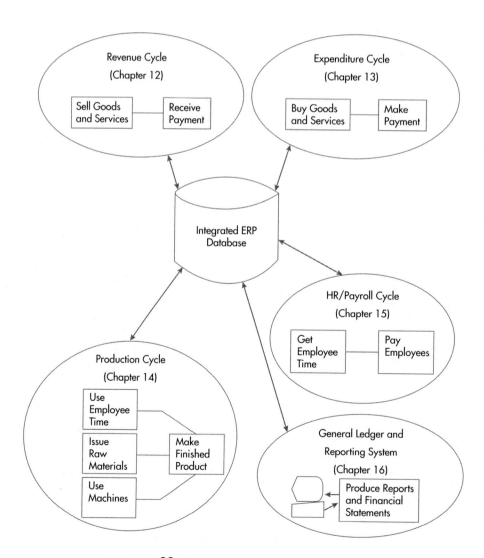

ERP systems are modular, with each module using best business practices to automate a standard business process. This modular design allows businesses to add or delete modules as needed. Typical ERP modules include:

- Financial (general ledger and reporting system)—general ledger, accounts receivable, accounts payable, fixed assets, budgeting, cash management, and preparation of managerial reports and financial statements
- Human resources and payroll—human resources, payroll, employee benefits, training, time and attendance, benefits, and government reporting
- Order to cash (revenue cycle)—sales order entry, shipping, inventory, cash receipts, commission calculation
- Purchase to pay (disbursement cycle)—purchasing, receipt and inspection of inventory, inventory and warehouse management, and cash disbursements
- Manufacturing (production cycle)— engineering, production scheduling, bill of materials, work-in-process, workflow management, quality control, cost management, and manufacturing processes and projects
- Project management—costing, billing, time and expense, performance units, activity management
- Customer relationship management—sales and marketing, commissions, service, customer contact, and call center support
- System tools—tools for establishing master file data, specifying flow of information, access controls, and so on

An ERP system, with its centralized database, provides significant advantages:

- An ERP provides an integrated, enterprise-wide, single view of the organization's data and financial situation. Storing all corporate information in a single database breaks down barriers between departments and streamlines the flow of information.
- Data input is captured or keyed once, rather than multiple times, as it is entered into different systems. Downloading data from one system to another is no longer needed.
- Management gains greater visibility into every area of the enterprise and greater monitoring capabilities. Employees are more productive and efficient because they can quickly gather data from both inside and outside their own department.
- The organization gains better access control. An ERP can consolidate multiple permissions and security models into a single data access structure.
- Procedures and reports are standardized across business units. This standardization can be especially valuable with mergers and acquisitions because an ERP system can replace the different systems with a single, unified system.
- Customer service improves because employees can quickly access orders, available inventory, shipping information, and past customer transaction details.
- Manufacturing plants receive new orders in real time, and the automation of manufacturing processes leads to increased productivity.

ERP systems also have significant disadvantages:

- Cost. ERP hardware, software, and consulting costs range from $50 to $500 million for a Fortune 500 company and upgrades can cost $50 million to $100 million. Midsized companies spend between $10 and $20 million.
- Amount of time required. It can take years to select and fully implement an ERP system, depending on business size, number of modules to be implemented, degree of customization, the scope of the change, and how well the customer takes ownership of the project. As a result, ERP implementations have a very high risk of project failure.
- Changes to business processes. Unless a company wants to spend time and money customizing modules, they must adapt to standardized business processes as opposed to adapting the ERP package to existing company processes. The failure to map current business processes to existing ERP software is a main cause of ERP project failures.
- Complexity. This comes from integrating many different business activities and systems, each having different processes, business rules, data semantics, authorization hierarchies, and decision centers.

● Resistance. Organizations that have multiple departments with separate resources, missions, profit and loss, and chains of command may believe that a single system has few benefits. It also takes considerable training and experience to use an ERP system effectively, and employee resistance is a major reason why many ERP implementations do not succeed. It is not easy to convince employees to change how they do their jobs, train them in new procedures, master the new system, and persuade them to share sensitive information. Resistance, and the blurring of company boundaries, can cause problems with employee morale, accountability, and lines of responsibility.

Reaping the potential benefits of ERP systems and mitigating their disadvantages requires conscious effort and involvement by top management. Top management's commitment to and support for the necessary changes greatly increase the chances of success.

Because ERP systems are complex and expensive, choosing one is not an easy task. In doing so, you must take great care to ensure that the ERP system has a module for every critical company process and that you are not paying for software modules that you do not need. One way to choose a suitable system is to select a package designed for your industry. Although cost is a huge concern, buying too cheaply can cost more in the long run if the system does not meet your needs, because modification costs can be quite high. You can minimize the risk of buying the wrong package by researching the best ERP vendors. There are many ERP vendors, the two largest being SAP and Oracle. Other leading vendors are The Sage Group, Microsoft, and Infor.

Because it is too difficult for most companies to implement ERP software by themselves, they often hire an ERP vendor or a consulting company to do it for them. These firms usually provide three types of services: consulting, customization, and support. For most midsized companies, implementation costs range from the list price of the ERP user licenses to twice that amount. Large companies with multiple sites often spend three to five times the cost of the user license.

Because many processes automatically trigger additional actions in other modules, proper configuration is essential. This requires a sound understanding of all major business processes and their interactions so they can be defined. Examples include setting up cost/profit centers, credit approval policies, and purchase approval rules. In the configuration process, companies balance the way they want the system to operate with the way it lets them operate. If the way an ERP module operates is unacceptable, the company can modify the module. Alternatively, it can use an existing system and build interfaces between it and the ERP system. Both options are time consuming, costly, and result in fewer system integration benefits. In addition, the more customized a system becomes, the more difficult it is to communicate with suppliers and customers. To make configuration easier, ERP vendors are developing built-in "configuration" tools to address most customers' needs for system changes.

The importance of sound internal controls in an ERP cannot be overstated. The integrated nature of ERP systems means that unless every data item is validated and checked for accuracy at the time of initial entry, errors will automatically propagate throughout the system. Thus, data entry controls and access controls are essential. Most managers and employees see and have access to only a small portion of the system. This segregation of duties provides sound internal control. It is important to separate responsibility for custody of assets, authorization of activities that affect those assets, and recording information about activities and the status of organizational assets.

Summary and Case Conclusion

Ashton is aware that Scott and Susan plan to open additional stores in the near future and want to develop a Web site to conduct business over the Internet. Based on this information, Ashton will select an accounting package that will satisfy S&S's current and anticipated future needs. The software should be able to take care of all data processing and data storage tasks. Ashton will also make sure that the software can interface with the source data automation devices he wants to use to capture most data input. The software must be capable of producing a full set of financial reports and be flexible enough to produce other useful information the company will need to be successful. Finally, Ashton realized his next step would be to select the software and produce some documentation of how the system worked.

Key Terms

data processing cycle	mnemonic code	master file
source documents	chart of accounts	transaction file
turnaround documents	general journal	database
source data automation	specialized journal	batch processing
general ledger	audit trail	online, real-time
subsidiary ledger	entity	processing
control account	attribute	document
coding	field	report
sequence code	record	query
block code	data value	enterprise resource planning
group code	file	(ERP) system

AIS IN ACTION

Chapter Quiz

1. Which of the following is NOT a step in the data processing cycle?
   a. data collection
   b. data input
   c. data storage
   d. data processing

2. All of the information (name, GPA, major, etc.) about a particular student is stored in the same _____.
   a. file
   b. record
   c. attribute
   d. field

3. Which of the following would contain the total value of all inventory owned by an organization?
   a. source document
   b. general ledger
   c. cash budget

4. Which of the following is most likely to be a general ledger control account?
   a. accounts receivable
   b. petty cash
   c. prepaid rent
   d. retained earnings

5. Which of the following documents is most likely to be used in the expenditure cycle?
   a. sales orders
   b. credit memo
   c. receiving report
   d. job time ticket

6. Which of the following is LEAST likely to be a specialized journal?
   a. sales journal
   b. cash receipts journal
   c. prepaid insurance journal
   d. cash disbursements journal

7. How does the chart of accounts list general ledger accounts?
   a. alphabetical order
   b. chronological order
   c. size order
   d. the order in which they appear in financial statements

8. Which of the following is NOT an advantage of an ERP system?
   a. better access control
   b. standardization of procedures and reports
   c. improved monitoring capabilities
   d. simplicity and reduced costs

9. Records of company data sent to an external party and then returned to the system as input are called _____.
   a. turnaround documents
   b. source data automation documents
   c. source documents
   d. external input documents

41

10. Recording and processing information about a transaction at the time it takes place is referred to as which of the following?
    a. batch processing
    b. online, real-time processing
    c. captured transaction processing
    d. chart of accounts processing

Discussion Questions

1. Table 1 lists some of the documents used in the revenue, expenditure, and human resources cycle. What kinds of input or output documents or forms would you find in the production (also referred to as the conversion) cycle?

2. With respect to the data processing cycle, explain the phrase "garbage in, garbage out." How can you prevent this from happening?

3. What kinds of documents are most likely to be turnaround documents? Do an Internet search to find the answer and to find example turnaround documents.

4. The data processing cycle in Figure 1 is an example of a basic process found throughout nature. Relate the basic input/process/store/output model to the functions of the human body.

5. Some individuals argue that accountants should focus on producing financial statements and leave the design and production of managerial reports to information systems specialists. What are the advantages and disadvantages of following this advice? To what extent should accountants be involved in producing reports that include more than just financial measures of performance? Why?

Problems

1. The chart of accounts must be tailored to an organization's specific needs. Discuss how the chart of accounts for the following organizations would differ from the one presented for S&S in Table 2.
   a. university
   b. bank
   c. government unit (city or state)
   d. manufacturing company
   e. expansion of S&S to a chain of two stores

2. Ollie Mace is the controller of SDC, an automotive parts manufacturing firm. Its four major operating divisions are heat treating, extruding, small parts stamping, and machining. Last year's sales from each division ranged from $150,000 to $3,000,000. Each division is physically and managerially independent, except for the constant surveillance of Sam Dilley, the firm's founder.
   The AIS for each division evolved according to the needs and abilities of its accounting staff. Mace is the first controller to have responsibility for overall financial management. Dilley wants Mace to improve the AIS before he retires in a few years so that it will be easier to monitor division performance. Mace decides to redesign the financial reporting system to include the following features:

   - It should give managers uniform, timely, and accurate reports of business activity. Monthly reports should be uniform across divisions and be completed by the fifth day of the following month to provide enough time to take corrective actions to affect the next month's performance. Company-wide financial reports should be available at the same time.
   - Reports should provide a basis for measuring the return on investment for each division. Thus, in addition to revenue and expense accounts, reports should show assets assigned to each division.

- The system should generate meaningful budget data for planning and decision-making purposes. Budgets should reflect managerial responsibility and show costs for major product groups.

Mace believes that a new chart of accounts is required to accomplish these goals. He wants to divide asset accounts into six major categories, such as current assets and plant and equipment. He does not foresee a need for more than 10 control accounts within each of these categories. From his observations to date, 100 subsidiary accounts are more than adequate for each control account.

No division has more than five major product groups. Mace foresees a maximum of six cost centers within any product group, including both the operating and nonoperating groups. He views general divisional costs as a non-revenue-producing product group. Mace estimates that 44 expense accounts plus 12 specific variance accounts would be adequate.

Required

Design a chart of accounts for SDC. Explain how you structured the chart of accounts to meet the company's needs and operating characteristics. Keep total account code length to a minimum, while still satisfying all of Mace's desires. *(CMA Examination, adapted)*

3. An audit trail enables a person to trace a source document to its ultimate effect on the financial statements or work back from financial statement amounts to source documents. Describe in detail the audit trail for the following:
   a. Purchases of inventory
   b. Sales of inventory
   c. Employee payroll

4. Your nursery sells various types and sizes of trees, bedding plants, vegetable plants, and shrubs. It also sells fertilizer and potting soil. Design a coding scheme for your nursery.

5. Match the following terms with their definitions.

Term	Definition
____ a. data processing cycle	1. Contains summary-level data for every asset, liability, equity, revenue, and expense account
____ b. source documents	2. Items are numbered consecutively to account for all items; missing items cause a gap in the numerical sequence
____ c. turnaround documents	3. Path of a transaction through a data processing system from point of origin to final output, or backwards from final output to point of origin
____ d. source data automation	4. List of general ledger account numbers; allows transaction data to be coded, classified, and entered into proper accounts; facilitates preparation of financial statements and reports
____ e. general ledger	5. Contents of a specific field, such as "George" in a name field
____ f. subsidiary ledger	6. Portion of a data record that contains the data value for a particular attribute, like a cell in a spreadsheet
____ g. control account	7. Company data sent to an external party and then returned to the system as input
____ h. coding	8. Used to record infrequent or nonroutine transactions

_____ **i.** sequence code

_____ **j.** block code

_____ **k.** group code

_____ **l.** mnemonic code

_____ **m.** chart of accounts

_____ **n.** general journal

_____ **o.** specialized journal

_____ **p.** audit trail

_____ **q.** entity

_____ **r.** attribute

_____ **s.** field

_____ **t.** record

_____ **u.** data value

_____ **v.** master file

_____ **w.** transaction file

_____ **x.** database

_____ **y.** batch processing

_____ **z.** online, real-time processing

9. Characteristics of interest that need to be stored

10. The steps a company must follow to efficiently and effectively process data about its transactions

11. Something about which information is stored

12. Stores cumulative information about an organization; like a ledger in a manual AIS

13. Contains detailed data for any general ledger account with many individual subaccounts

14. Contains records of individual business transactions that occur during a specific time period

15. Updating each transaction as it occurs

16. Devices that capture transaction data in machine-readable form at the time and place of their origin

17. Used to record large numbers of repetitive transactions

18. Set of interrelated, centrally coordinated files

19. Two or more subgroups of digits are used to code items

20. Updating done periodically, such as daily

21. Systematic assignment of numbers or letters to items to classify and organize them

22. Letters and numbers, derived from the item description, are interspersed to identify items; usually easy to memorize

23. Initial record of a transaction that takes place; usually recorded on preprinted forms or formattted screens

24. Fields containing data about entity attributes; like a row in a spreadsheet

25. Sets of numbers are reserved for specific categories of data

26. The general ledger account corresponding to a subsidiary ledger, where the sum of all subsidiary ledger entries should equal the amount in the general ledger account

6. For each of the following scenarios, identify which data processing method (batch or online, real-time) would be the most appropriate.
   a. Make an airline reservation
   b. Register for a university course
   c. Prepare biweekly payroll checks
   d. Process an order through an e-commerce Web site
   e. Prepare a daily bank deposit
   f. Preparation of customer bills by a local utility
   g. Accumulate daily costs from a production run of a single automobile part
   h. Identify the replacement drill bit size for a bit broken during a recent production run

7. On the following Web sites, you will find several online demonstrations for the SAP and Oracle ERP systems. Visit these Web sites and explore their content by doing the following:
   a. The SAP Web site is www.sap.com/solutions. Search the site for corporate videos, and watch two of them. Explore the industries, services, solutions, and platforms that SAP offers. Read several of the articles, such as the ones about customer successes.
   b. The Oracle Web site is www.oracle.com/solutions/mid/demo.html. Explore the Web site just as you explored the SAP site.

Required

After viewing the Web sites, and based on your reading of the chapter, write a two-page paper that describes how an ERP can connect and integrate the revenue, expenditure, human resources/payroll, and financing cycles of a business.

8. Which of the following actions update a master file and which would be stored as a record in a transaction file?
   a. Update customer address change
   b. Update unit pricing information
   c. Record daily sales
   d. Record payroll checks
   e. Change employee pay rates
   f. Record production variances
   g. Record sales commissions
   h. Change employee office location
   i. Update accounts payable balance
   j. Change customer credit limit
   k. Change vendor payment discount terms
   l. Record purchases

9. You were hired to assist Ashton Fleming in designing an accounting system for S&S. Ashton has developed a list of the journals, ledgers, reports, and documents that he thinks S&S needs (see Table 4). He asks you to complete the following tasks:
   a. Specify what data you think should be collected on each of the following four documents: sales invoice, purchase order, receiving report, employee time card.

TABLE 4 Documents, Journals, and Ledgers for S&S

Title	Purpose
Documents	
Sales Invoice	Record cash and credit sales of merchandise
Service Invoice	Record sales of repair services
Delivery Ticket	Record delivery of merchandise to customers
Monthly Statement	Inform customers of outstanding account balances
Credit Memo	Support adjustments to customer accounts for sales returns and allowances and sales discounts; also support write-off of uncollectible accounts
Purchase Order	Order merchandise from vendors
Receiving Report	Record receipt of merchandise from vendors, indicating both quantity and condition of items received
Time Card	Record time worked by employees
Specialized Journals	
Sales	Record all credit sales
Cash Receipts	Record cash sales, payments from customers, and other cash receipts
Purchases	Record all purchases from vendors
Cash Disbursements	Record all cash disbursements
General Journal	Record infrequent, nonroutine transactions; also record adjusting and closing entries
Subsidiary Ledgers	
Accounts Receivable	Maintain details about amounts due from customers
Accounts Payable	Maintain details about amounts due to vendors
Inventory	Maintain details about each inventory item
Fixed Assets	Maintain details about each piece of equipment and other fixed assets
General Ledger	Maintain details about all major asset, liability, equity, revenue, and expense accounts

b. Design a report to manage inventory.
c. Design a report to assist in managing credit sales and cash collections.
d. Visit a local office supply store and identify what types of journals, ledgers, and blank forms for various documents (sales invoices, purchase orders, etc.) are available. Describe how easily they could be adapted to meet S&S's needs.

Case 1 Bar Harbor Blueberry Farm

The Bar Harbor Blueberry Farm is a family-owned, 200-acre farm that grows and sells blueberries to grocery stores, blueberry wholesalers, and small roadside stands. Bar Harbor has 25 full-time employees and hires 150 to 200 seasonal workers for the harvest.

For the past six summers, you have picked berries for Bar Harbor. When you graduated, you were hired full-time as the accountant/office manager. Until now, Bar Harbor kept most of its accounting records in a big file box. Jack Phillips, the owner, would like a more organized approach to the farm's accounting records. He asked you to establish a proper set of books. You decide to start by establishing appropriate journals and ledgers for these transactions.

Presented below are a set of vendor invoices and a few partially completed journals and ledgers. Your job is to record these transactions and update the appropriate ledgers. Be sure to leave a proper audit trail. You may also use Excel, Great Plains, Peachtree, QuickBooks, or another accounting software package of your choosing to complete this problem.

Vendor Invoices

Date	Supplier Invoice	Supplier Name	Supplier Address	Amount
March 7	AJ34	Bud's Soil Prep	PO Box 34	$2,067.85
March 11	14568	Osto Farmers Supply	45 Main	$ 67.50
March 14	893V	Whalers Fertilizer	Route 34	$5,000.00
March 21	14699	Osto Farmers Supply	45 Main	$3,450.37
March 21	10102	IFM Wholesale	587 Longview	$4,005.00
March 24	10145	IFM Wholesale	587 Longview	$ 267.88

Purchases Journal

Page 1

Date	Supplier	Supplier Invoice	Account Number	Post Ref	Amount
March 7	Bud's Soil Prep	AJ34			$2,067.85

General Ledger

Accounts Payable   Account Number: 300

Date	Description	Post Ref	Debit	Credit	Balance
March 1	Balance Forward				$18,735.55

General Ledger

Purchases					Account Number: 605
Date	Description	Post Ref	Debit	Credit	Balance
March 1	Balance Forward				$54,688.49

Accounts Payable Subsidiary Ledger

Account No: 23	Bud's Soil Prep		PO Box 34	Terms: 2/10, Net 30
Date	Description	Debit	Credit	Balance

Account No: 24				Terms: 2/10, Net 30
Date	Description	Debit	Credit	Balance

Account No: 36				Terms: 2/10, Net 30
Date	Description	Debit	Credit	Balance

Account No: 38				Terms: 2/10, Net 30
Date	Description	Debit	Credit	Balance

AIS IN ACTION SOLUTIONS

Quiz Key

1. Which of the following is NOT a step in the data processing cycle?
   ▶ a. data collection [Correct. Data collection is a part of data input and is therefore not a step in the data processing cycle.]
   b. data input [Incorrect. Data input is the first step in the data processing cycle. This is the step where data is captured, collected, and entered into the system.]
   c. data storage [Incorrect. Data storage is the data processing cycle step where data is stored for future use by the company.]
   d. data processing [Incorrect. Data processing is the data processing cycle step where stored data is updated with new input data.]

2. All of the information (name, GPA, major, etc.) about a particular student is stored in the same _____.
   a. file [Incorrect. A file is designed to include information about many students.]
   ▶ b. record [Correct. A record should include all information maintained by the system about a particular entity, such as a student.]
   c. attribute [Incorrect. An attribute is a descriptor or a characteristic of an entity—in this example, the student's major is an attribute.]
   d. field [Incorrect. A field represents a data storage space—in this example, an accounting student would have "Accounting" stored in the major field.]

3. Which of the following would contain the total value of all inventory owned by an organization?
   a. source document [Incorrect. A source document contains data about a particular event or transaction.]
   ▶ b. general ledger [Correct. The general ledger maintains summary information on inventory and every other general ledger account.]
   c. cash budget [Incorrect. A cash budget provides information only on projected cash inflows and outflows.]

4. Which of the following is most likely to be a general ledger control account?
   ▶ a. accounts receivable [Correct. Accounts receivable is typically made up of many individual customer accounts maintained in a subsidiary ledger. The total of all individual customer accounts in the subsidiary ledger is maintained in the accounts receivable control account in the general ledger.]
   b. petty cash [Incorrect. Petty cash is made up of only one account.]
   c. prepaid rent [Incorrect. A subsidiary ledger containing multiple prepaid rent accounts is usually not necessary.]
   d. retained earnings [Incorrect. Retained earnings is typically comprised of only one account.]

5. Which of the following documents is most likely to be used in the expenditure cycle?
   a. sales order [Incorrect. The sales order is a revenue cycle document that captures the information about a customer's order.]
   b. credit memo [Incorrect. A credit memo is a revenue cycle document that is used to give a credit to a customer for damaged or returned goods.]
   ▶ c. receiving report [Correct. A receiving report is an expenditure cycle document that is used to record the receipt of goods from suppliers. Companies pay their suppliers based on the goods received and recorded on the receiving report.]
   d. job time ticket [Incorrect. A job time ticket is a production cycle document that is used to record time spent on specific jobs.]

6. Which of the following is LEAST likely to be a specialized journal?
    a. sales journal [Incorrect. A specialized journal is used to record large numbers of repetitive transactions. Most companies have a large number of sales.]
    b. cash receipts journal [Incorrect. A specialized journal is used to record large numbers of repetitive transactions. Most companies have a large number of cash receipts.]
    ▶ c. prepaid insurance journal [Correct. A specialized journal is used to record large numbers of repetitive transactions, and most companies have very few prepaid insurance transactions.]
    d. cash disbursements journal [Incorrect. A specialized journal is used to record large numbers of repetitive transactions. Most companies have a large number of cash disbursements.]

7. How does the chart of accounts list general ledger accounts?
    a. alphabetical order [Incorrect. General ledger accounts are listed in the order in which they appear in the financial statements, not in alphabetical order.]
    b. chronological order [Incorrect. General ledger accounts are listed in the order in which they appear in the financial statements, not according to the date they were created.]
    c. size order [Incorrect. General ledger accounts are listed in the order in which they appear in the financial statements, not according to their size.]
    ▶ d. the order in which they appear in financial statements [Correct.]

8. Which of the following is NOT an advantage of an ERP system?
    a. better access control [Incorrect. Better access control is an advantage because an ERP can consolidate multiple permissions and security models into a single data access structure.]
    b. standardization of procedures and reports [Incorrect. Standardization of procedures and reports is an advantage because procedures and reports can be standardized across business units and in mergers and acquisitions they can replace the different systems with a single, unified system.]
    c. improved monitoring capabilities [Incorrect. Improved monitoring capabilities are an advantage because management gains greater visibility into every area of the enterprise that allows them to better monitor the organization.]
    ▶ d. simplicity and reduced costs [Correct. ERP systems are quite complex and costly; they do not offer the advantages of simplicity and reduced costs.]

9. Records of company data sent to an external party and then returned to the system as input are called _____.
    ▶ a. turnaround documents [Correct. For example, a utility bill is sent to a customer, who then returns the bill with payment.]
    b. source data automation documents [Incorrect. Source data automation is the capturing of input data in machine-readable form.]
    c. source documents [Incorrect. Source documents collect data about business activities.]
    d. external input documents [Incorrect. These documents originate from external sources.]

10. Recording and processing information about a transaction at the time it takes place is referred to as which of the following?
    a. batch processing [Incorrect. Batch processing involves processing transactions in groups or batches all at the same time.]
    ▶ b. online, real-time processing [Correct. Online, real-time processing involves processing transactions as they occur.]
    c. captured transaction processing [Incorrect. This is not a recognized transaction processing method.]
    d. chart of accounts processing [Incorrect. The chart of accounts, although typically updated every so often, is not a transaction processing method.]

Chapter 3

Systems Documentation Techniques

From Chapter 3 of *Accounting Information Systems*, 12/e. Marshall B. Romney. Paul John Steinbart. Copyright © 2012 by Pearson Education. Published by Prentice Hall. All rights reserved.

Systems Documentation Techniques

Learning Objectives

After studying this chapter, you should be able to:

1. Prepare and use data flow diagrams to understand, evaluate, and document information systems.
2. Prepare and use flowcharts to understand, evaluate, and document information systems.

INTEGRATIVE CASE S&S

What a hectic few months it has been for Ashton Fleming! He helped S&S get started, helped get S&S through its weeklong grand opening, and was swamped with processing all the transactions from the highly successful grand opening. Because of its rapid growth, S&S has outgrown the initial rudimentary AIS that Ashton selected. Lacking time and expertise, Ashton has engaged Computer Applications (CA), a systems consulting firm, to help S&S select and install a new and more powerful AIS.

During Ashton's first meeting with Kimberly Sierra, CA's manager, she asked about S&S's system requirements and management's expectations. Ashton had yet to think through these issues, so he could not answer her specifically. When she asked how S&S's system worked, Ashton plunged into a discussion about the use of various company documents, but Kimberly seemed unable to absorb his detailed explanations. Ashton thought that part of his discussion was helpful, but overall it was irrelevant to the issue at hand.

Ashton came away impressed by CA and Kimberly. He also realized the need to understand S&S's information requirements more clearly. From his days as an auditor, Ashton knew the value of good system documentation in helping unfamiliar users both understand and evaluate a system. Good system documentation would be a big help to him and Kimberly, as well as to Scott and Susan as they evaluate the current and proposed systems.

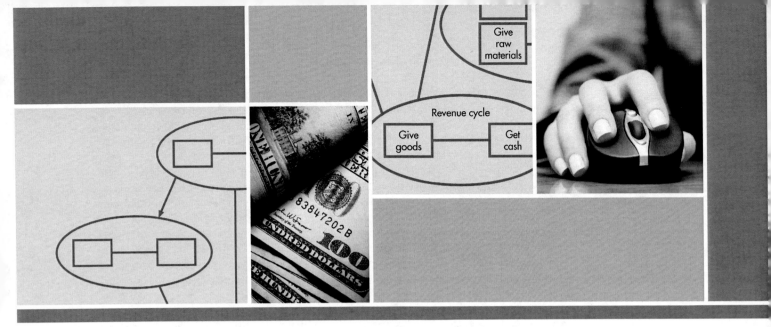

After sharing his conclusions with Susan and Scott, they enthusiastically approved Ashton's plan to document the current and proposed systems. They supported his taking a leadership role in moving toward a new system and were especially interested in diagrams or charts that would document the existing system and help them understand and evaluate it.

Introduction

Documentation encompasses the narratives, flowcharts, diagrams, and other written materials that explain how a system works. This information covers the who, what, when, where, why, and how of data entry, processing, storage, information output, and system controls. Popular means of documenting a system include diagrams, flowcharts, tables, and other graphical representations of information. These are supplemented by a ***narrative description*** of the system, a written step-by-step explanation of system components and interactions. In this chapter, we explain two common systems documentation tools: data flow diagrams and flowcharts.

Documentation tools are important on the following levels:

1. At a minimum, you must be able to *read* documentation to determine how a system works.
2. You may need to *evaluate* internal control systems documentation to identify strengths and weaknesses and recommend improvements. Or, you may need to evaluate documentation for a proposed system to determine whether it meets the company's needs.
3. More skill is needed to *prepare* internal control documentation or documentation that shows how an existing or proposed system operates.

This chapter discusses the following documentation tools:

1. *Data flow diagram (DFD),* a graphical description of data sources, flows, processes, storage, and destinations
2. *Document flowchart,* a graphical description of the flow of documents and information between departments or areas of responsibility
3. *System flowchart,* a graphical description of the relationship among the input, processing, and output in an information system
4. *Program flowchart,* a graphical description of the sequence of logical operations a computer performs as it executes a program

Accountants use documentation techniques extensively. Auditing standards require that independent auditors understand the automated and manual internal control procedures an entity uses.

One good way to gain this understanding is to use flowcharts to document the internal control system, because such graphic portrayals more readily reveal weaknesses and strengths.

The Sarbanes-Oxley Act (SOX) of 2002 requires an internal control report in public company annual reports that (1) states that management is responsible for establishing and maintaining an adequate internal control structure and (2) assesses the effectiveness of the company's internal controls. SOX also specifies that a company's auditor must evaluate management's assessment of the company's internal control structures and attest to its accuracy. The auditor's attestation should include a specific notation about significant defects or material noncompliance found during internal control tests. This means that both the company and its auditors have to document and test the company's internal controls. To do so, they must be able to prepare, evaluate, and read different types of documentation, such as flowcharts.

Documentation tools are also used extensively in the systems development process. In addition, the team members who develop information systems applications often change, and documentation tools help the new team members get up to speed quickly.

According to one study, 62.5% of information systems professionals use DFDs and 97.6% use flowcharts. Over 92% of users were satisfied with the use of both DFDs and flowcharts and use both.

Documentation is easier to prepare and revise when a software package is used. Once a few basic commands are mastered, users can quickly and easily prepare, store, revise, and print presentation-quality documentation.

The documentation tools in this chapter are used throughout the book. They are also tested on professional examinations, and learning about them better prepares you for these examinations.

Data Flow Diagrams

A *data flow diagram (DFD)* graphically describes the flow of data within an organization. It uses the symbols shown in Figure 1 to represent four basic elements: data sources and destinations, data flows, transformation processes, and data stores. For example, Figure 2 shows that the input to process C is data flow B, which comes from data source A. The outputs of process C are data flows D and E. Data flow E is sent to data destination J. Process F uses data flows D and G as input and produces data flows I and G as output. Data flow G comes from and returns to data store H. Data flow I is sent to data destination K.

Figure 3 assigns specific titles to each of the processes depicted in Figure 2. Figures 2 and 3 will be used to examine the four basic elements of a DFD in more detail.

A *data source* and a *data destination* are entities that send or receive data that the system uses or produces. An entity can be both a source and a destination. They are represented by squares, as illustrated by items A (customer), J (bank), and K (credit manager) in Figure 3.

FIGURE 1
Data Flow Diagram Symbols

Symbol	Name	Explanation
□	Data sources and destinations	The people and organizations that send data to and receive data from the system are represented by square boxes. Data destinations are also referred to as *data sinks*.
⟋→	Data flows	The flow of the data into or out of a process is represented by curved or straight lines with arrows.
○	Transformation processes	The processes that transform data from inputs to outputs are represented by circles. They are often referred to as *bubbles*.
═	Data stores	The storage of data is represented by two horizontal lines.

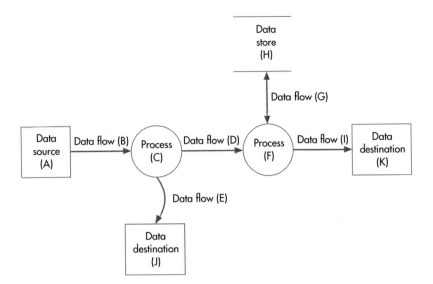

FIGURE 2

Basic Data Flow Diagram Elements

A *data flow* is the movement of data among processes, stores, sources and destinations. Data that pass between data stores and a source or destination must go through a data transformation process. Data flows are labeled to show what information is flowing. The only exception is data flow between a process and a data store, such as data flow G in Figure 3, because the data flow is usually obvious. In data flow G, data from the accounts receivable file is retrieved, updated, and stored back in the file. Other data flows in Figure 3 are B (customer payment), D (remittance data), E (deposit), and I (receivables information).

If two or more data flows move together, a single line is used. For example, data flow B (customer payment) consists of a payment and remittance data. Process 1.0 (process payment) splits them and sends them in different directions. The remittance data (D) is used to update accounts receivable records, and the payment (E) is deposited in the bank. If the data flow separately, two lines are used. For example, Figure 4 shows two lines because customer inquiries (L) do not always accompany a payment (B). If represented by the same data flow, the separate elements and their different purposes are obscured, and the DFD is more difficult to interpret.

Processes represent the transformation of data. Figure 3 shows that process payment (C) splits the customer payment into the remittance data and the check, which is deposited in the bank. The update receivables process (F) uses remittance (D) and accounts receivable (H) data to update receivable records and send receivables information to the credit manager.

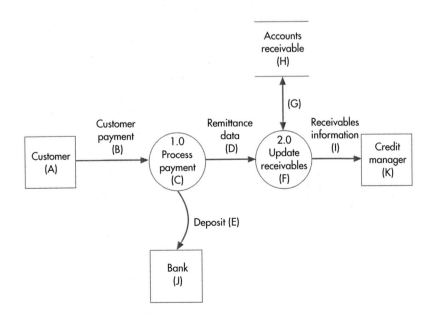

FIGURE 3

Data Flow Diagram of Customer Payment Process

FIGURE 4

Splitting Customer Payments and Inquiries

A *data store* is a repository of data. DFDs do not show the physical storage medium (such as a server or paper) used to store the data. As shown in Figure 3, data stores (H) are represented by horizontal lines, with the name of the file written inside the lines.

Subdividing the DFD

DFDs are subdivided into successively lower levels to provide ever-increasing amounts of detail, because few systems can be fully diagrammed on one sheet of paper. Also, users have differing needs, and a variety of levels can better satisfy differing requirements.

The highest-level DFD is referred to as a *context diagram* because it provides the reader with a summary-level view of a system. It depicts a data processing system and the entities that are the sources and destinations of system inputs and outputs. For example, Ashton drew Figure 5 to document payroll processing procedures at S&S. The payroll processing system receives time card data from different departments and employee data from human resources. The system processes these data and produces (1) tax reports and payments for governmental agencies, (2) employee paychecks, (3) a payroll check deposited in the payroll account at the bank, and (4) payroll information for management.

Ashton used the description of S&S's payroll processing procedures in Table 1 to decompose the context diagram into successively lower levels, each with an increasing amount of detail. Read this description and determine the following:

● How many major data processing activities are involved?
● What are the data inputs and outputs of each activity (ignoring all references to people, departments, and document destinations)?

The narrative in Table 1 describes five data processing activities:

1. Updating the employee/payroll master file (first paragraph).
2. Handling employee compensation (second, fifth, and sixth paragraphs). Later in this chapter, you will see a breakdown of this activity into smaller parts in a lower-level DFD.
3. Generating management reports (third paragraph).

FIGURE 5

Context Diagram for S&S Payroll Processing

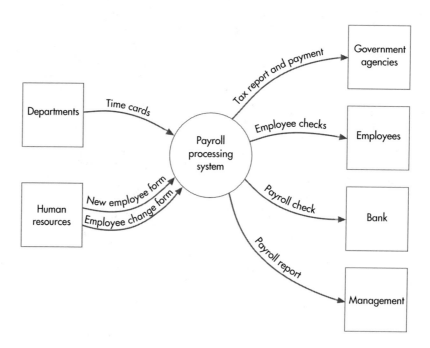

TABLE 1 Narrative Description of Payroll Processing at S&S

When employees are hired, they complete a new-employee form. When a change to an employee's payroll status occurs, such as a raise or a change in the number of exemptions, the human resources department completes an employee change form. A copy of these forms is sent to payroll. These forms are used to create or update the records in the employee/payroll file and are then stored in the file. Employee records are stored alphabetically.

Some S&S employees are paid a salary, but most are hourly workers who record their time on time cards. At the end of each pay period, department managers send the time cards to the payroll department. The payroll clerk uses the time card data, data from the employee file (such as pay rate and annual salary), and the appropriate tax tables to prepare a two-part check for each employee. The clerk also prepares a two-part payroll register showing gross pay, deductions, and net pay for each employee. The clerk updates the employee file to reflect each employee's current earnings. The original copy of the employee paychecks is forwarded to Susan. The payroll register is forwarded to the accounts payable clerk. The time cards and the duplicate copies of the payroll register and paychecks are stored by date in the payroll file.

Every pay period, the payroll clerk uses the data in the employee/payroll file to prepare a payroll summary report for Susan so that she can control and monitor labor expenses. This report is forwarded to Susan, with the original copies of the employee paychecks.

Every month, the payroll clerk uses the data in the employee/payroll file to prepare a two-part tax report. The original is forwarded to the accounts payable clerk, and the duplicate is added to the tax records in the payroll file. The accounts payable clerk uses the tax report to prepare a two-part check for taxes and a two-part cash disbursements voucher. The tax report and the original copy of each document are forwarded to Susan. The duplicates are stored by date in the accounts payable file.

The accounts payable clerk uses the payroll register to prepare a two-part check for the total amount of the employee payroll and a two-part disbursements voucher. The original copy of each document is forwarded to Susan, and the payroll register and the duplicates are stored by date in the accounts payable file.

Susan reviews each packet of information she receives, approves it, and signs the checks. She forwards the cash disbursements vouchers to Ashton, the tax reports and payments to the appropriate governmental agency, the payroll check to the bank, and the employee checks to the employees. She files the payroll report chronologically.

Ashton uses the payroll tax and the payroll check cash disbursement vouchers to update the general ledger. He then cancels the journal voucher by marking it "posted" and files it numerically.

4. Paying taxes (fourth paragraph).
5. Posting entries to the general ledger (last paragraph).

The five activities and all data inflows and outflows are shown in Table 2.

Ashton exploded his context diagram and created the Level 0 DFD (called level 0 because there are zero meaningful decimal points—1.0, 2.0, etc.) shown in Figure 6. Notice that some data inputs and outputs have been excluded from this DFD. For example, in process 2.0, the data inflows and outflows that are not related to an external entity or to another process are not depicted (tax tables and payroll register). These data flows are internal to the "pay employees" activity and are shown on the next DFD level.

TABLE 2 Activities and Data Flows in Payroll Processing at S&S

Activities	Data Inputs	Data Outputs
Update employee/payroll file	New employee form Employee change form	Updated employee/payroll file
Pay employees	Time cards Employee/payroll file Tax rates table	Employee checks Payroll register Updated employee/payroll file Payroll check Payroll cash disbursements voucher
Prepare reports	Employee/payroll file	Payroll report
Pay taxes	Employee/payroll file	Tax report Tax payment Payroll tax cash disbursements voucher Updated employee/payroll file
Update general ledger	Payroll tax cash disbursements voucher Payroll cash disbursements voucher	Updated general ledger

FIGURE 6
Level 0 DFD for S&S payroll processing

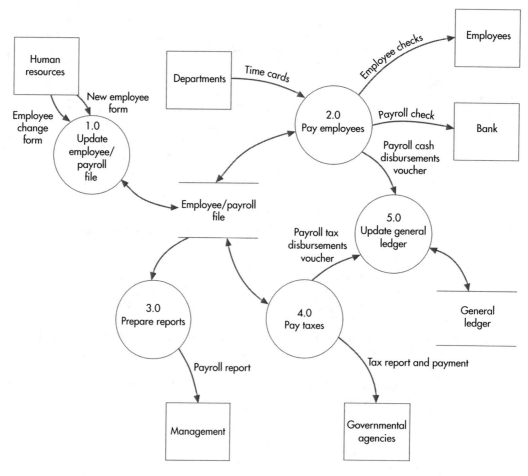

Ashton exploded process 2.0 (pay employees) to create a Level 1 DFD (it has one meaningful decimal place—2.1, 2.2, etc.). Figure 7 provides more detail about the data processes involved in paying employees, and it includes the tax rates table and the payroll register data flow omitted from Figure 6. In a similar fashion, each of the Figure 6 processes could be exploded, using a Level 1 DFD, to show a greater level of detail.

Some general guidelines for developing DFDs are shown in Focus 1.

FIGURE 7
Level 1 DFD for Process 2.0 in S&S Payroll Processing

Guidelines for Drawing a DFD

1. **Understand the system.** Observe organization information flows, and interview the individuals who use and process the data.
2. **Ignore certain aspects of the system.** A DFD is a diagram of the origins, flow, transformation, storage, and destinations of data. All control processes and actions are ignored. Only very important error paths are included; unimportant error paths are ignored. Determining how the system starts and stops is not shown.
3. **Determine system boundaries.** Determine what to include and exclude. Include all relevant data elements in the DFD, because excluded items will not be considered during system development.
4. **Develop a context diagram.** A context diagram depicts system boundaries. In the diagram's center is a circle with the name of the system. Outside entities the system interacts with directly are in boxes on either side, connected by data flows depicting the data passed between them. DFDs in successively more detail depict data flows in the system.
5. **Identify data flows.** Identify all data flows entering or leaving the system's boundary, including where the data originate and its final destination. A significant movement of information is usually a data flow. All data flows come from and go to a transformation process, a data store (file), or a source or destination. Data flows can move in two directions, shown as a line with arrows on both ends (see G in Figure 3).
6. **Group data flows.** A data flow can consist of one or more pieces of datum. Data elements that always flow together should be grouped together and shown as one data flow until they are separated. If the data do not always flow together, show them as separate data flows.
7. **Identify transformation processes.** Place a circle wherever work is required to transform one data flow into another. All transformation processes should have one or more incoming and outgoing data flows.
8. **Group transformation processes.** Transformation processes that are logically related or occur at the same time and place should be grouped together. Never combine unrelated items into a single transformation process. If data are not processed together, or are sometimes processed differently, then separate them.
9. **Identify all files or data stores.** Identify each temporary or permanent data repository, and identify each data flow into and out of it.
10. **Identify all data sources and destinations.** Include them on the DFD.
11. **Name all DFD elements.** Except for data flows into or out of data stores (the data store name is usually sufficient to identify the data flow), data elements should be given unique and descriptive names representing what is known about them. Naming data flows first forces you to concentrate on the all-important data flows, rather than on the processes or stores. Processes and data stores typically take their names from the data inflows or outflows. Choose active and descriptive names, such as "update inventory" and "validate transaction," rather than "input data" or "update process." Process names should include action verbs such as *update, edit, prepare, reconcile,* and *record.*
12. **Subdivide the DFD.** A cluttered DFD is hard to read and understand. If you have more than five to seven processes on a page, decompose the context diagram into high-level processes. Explode these high-level processes into successively lower-level processes.
13. **Give each process a sequential number.** Giving each process a sequential number (lower to higher) helps readers navigate among the DFD levels.
14. **Repeat the process.** Work through data flows several times. Each subsequent pass helps refine the diagram and identify the fine points. Organize the DFD to flow from top to bottom and from left to right.
15. **Prepare a final copy.** Do not allow data flow lines to cross over each other; if necessary, repeat a data store or destination. Place the name of the DFD, the date prepared, and the preparer's name on each page.

Flowcharts

A *flowchart* is an analytical technique used to describe some aspect of an information system in a clear, concise, and logical manner. Flowcharts use a standard set of symbols to describe pictorially the transaction processing procedures a company uses and the flow of data through a system. The symbols used to create flowcharts are shown in Figure 8.

Flowcharting was introduced by industrial engineers in the 1950s as a way of (1) recording how business processes are performed and documents flow and (2) analyzing how to improve processes and document flows. Soon internal auditors began using flowcharts in operational audits to better understand their company's business processes. Later, external auditors began using flowcharts to evaluate their clients' internal controls. Flowcharts became even more important when the Sarbanes-Oxley Act required companies to document their business processes and internal controls.

Flowcharts have significant advantages. A pictorial representation is much easier to understand than a narrative description. Both the auditor and the business owner can use the flowchart as a working tool during discussions. For an experienced flowcharter using a computerized drawing tool, flowcharts provide an easy way to capture and record data during interviews, and they can be easily and quickly revised.

Flowcharts do have some disadvantages. Some people do not like or understand them. Many are poorly drawn and therefore not as helpful as they should be. They are time-consuming to prepare if the flowcharter is not trained properly.

Early flowcharts were drawn using a flowcharting template, a piece of hard, flexible plastic on which symbols have been die cut. Most flowcharts are now drawn using a software program such as Visio. Flowcharts can also be drawn using Microsoft Word, Excel, or PowerPoint.

Flowcharting symbols are divided into four categories, as shown in Figure 8:

1. *Input/output symbols* represent devices or media that provide input to or record output from processing operations.
2. *Processing symbols* show what types of devices are used to process data or indicate when processing is performed manually.
3. *Storage symbols* represent the devices used to store data.
4. *Flow and miscellaneous symbols* indicate the flow of data, where flowcharts begin or end, where decisions are made, and when to add explanatory notes to flowcharts.

FIGURE 8
Common flowcharting symbols

Symbol	Name	Explanation
Input/Output Symbols		
	Document	A document or report.
	Multiple copies of one document	Illustrated by overlapping the document symbol and printing the document number on the face of the document in the upper right corner
	Input/output; Journal/ledger	Any input or output function on a program flowchart. Also used to represent accounting journals and ledgers in a document flowchart
	Display	Information displayed by an online output device such as a terminal, monitor, or screen
	Online keying	Data entry by online devices, such as a terminal or personal computer
	Terminal or personal computer	The display and online keying symbols are used together to represent terminals, personal computers, and other electronic devices capable of both input and output
	Transmittal tape	Manually prepared control totals; used for control purposes to compare to computer-generated totals
Processing Symbols		
	Computer processing	A computer-performed processing function; usually results in a change in data or information
	Manual operation	A processing operation performed manually

FIGURE 8
(*continued*)

Symbol	Name	Explanation
	Auxiliary operation	A processing function performed by a device that is not a computer
	Off-line keying	An operation utilizing an off-line keying device (e.g., key to disk, off-line cash register)

Storage Symbols

Symbol	Name	Explanation
	Magnetic disk/drive	Data stored on a magnetic disk or drive
	Magnetic tape	Data stored on a magnetic tape
N	File	File of documents manually stored and retrieved; following letters indicate file-ordering sequence: N = numerically, A = alphabetically, D = by date

Flow and Miscellaneous Symbols

Symbol	Name	Explanation
	Document or processing flow	Direction of processing or document flow; normal flow is down and to the right
	Data/ information flow	Direction of data/information flow; often used to show data copied from one document to another
	Communication link	Transmission of data from one geographic location to another via communication lines
	On-page connector	Connects the processing flow on the same page; its usage avoids lines crisscrossing a page
	Off-page connector	An entry from, or an exit to, another page
	Terminal	A beginning, end, or point of interruption in a process or program; also used to indicate an external party
	Decision	A decision-making step; used in a program flowchart to show branching to alternative paths
	Annotation	Addition of descriptive comments or explanatory notes as clarification

Document Flowcharts

A *document flowchart* illustrates the flow of documents and information among areas of responsibility within an organization. They trace a document from its cradle to its grave, showing where each document originates, its distribution, its purpose, its disposition, and everything that happens as it flows through the system.

A document flowchart is particularly useful in analyzing internal control procedures. Document flowcharts that describe and evaluate internal controls are often referred to as *internal control flowcharts*. They can reveal system weaknesses or inefficiencies, such as inadequate communication flows, unnecessary complexity in document flows, or procedures responsible for causing wasteful delays. Document flowcharts prepared as part of the systems design process should be included in system documentation.

The document flowchart that Ashton developed for the payroll process at S&S, as described in Table 1 and 2, is shown in Figure 9.

General guidelines for preparing flowcharts that are readable, clear, concise, consistent, and understandable are presented in Focus 2.

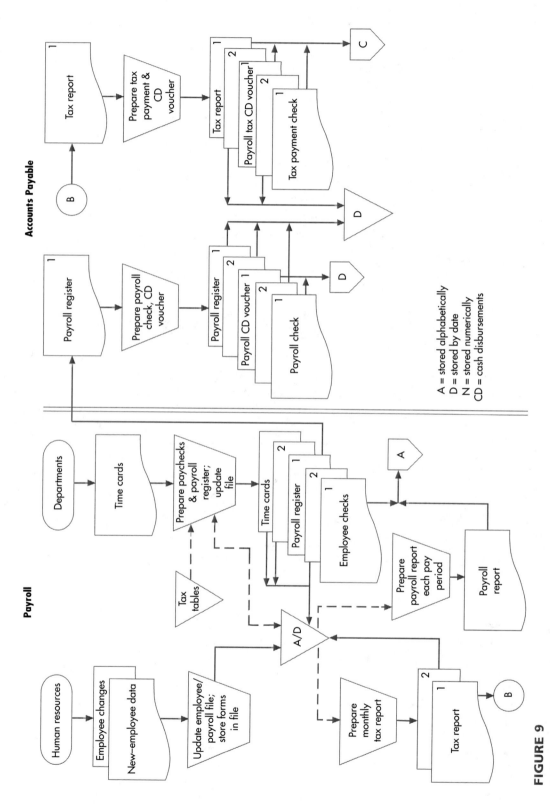

FIGURE 9

Document Flowchart of Payroll Processing at S&S

62

General Ledger (Ashton)

Management (Susan)

FIGURE 9
(continued)

63

Guidelines for Preparing Flowcharts

1. **Understand a system before flowcharting it.** Interview users, developers, auditors, and management, or have them complete a questionnaire. Read a narrative description of the system, or walk through system transactions.
2. **Identify the entities to be flowcharted.** Identify departments, job functions, and external parties. Identify documents and information flows, as well as the activities or processes performed on the data.
3. **Divide the flowchart into columns.** When several departments or functions need to be shown, divide the flowchart into columns and label each one. Flowchart the activities of each entity in its respective column.
4. **Flowchart the normal flow of operations.** Ensure that all procedures and processes are in proper order. Identify exception procedures using the annotation symbol.
5. **Organize flowchart.** Design the flowchart so that information flows from top to bottom and from left to right.
6. **Give the flowchart a clear beginning and ending.** Designate where each document originates, and show the final disposition of all documents so that there are no loose ends that leave the reader dangling.
7. **Use standard flowcharting symbols drawn with a template or a computer.**
8. **Clearly label all symbols.** Write a description of the input, process, or output inside the symbol. If the description will not fit, use the annotation symbol.
9. **Multiple copies of documents.** For multiple copies of a document, place document numbers in the top right-hand corner of the symbol. The number should accompany the symbol as it moves through the system.
10. **Manual processing symbol.** Each manual processing symbol should have an input and an output. Do not directly connect two documents, except when moving from one column to another. When a document is moved to another column, it is often best to show the document in both.
11. **Page connectors.** Use off-page connectors to move from one flowchart page to another. Consider using on-page connectors to avoid excess flow lines and thereby produce a neat-looking page. Clearly label all connectors to avoid confusion.
12. **Use arrowheads on all flow lines.** Do not assume the reader will know the direction of the flow.
13. **Multiple pages.** If a flowchart cannot fit on a single page, clearly label the pages as follows: 1 of 3, 2 of 3, and so on.
14. **Show documents or reports in the column where they are created.** Then show them moving to another column for further processing.
15. **Files.** Show data entered into or retrieved from a computer file as passing through a processing operation (a computer program) first. Draw a line from a document to a file to indicate that it is being filed. A manual process is not needed to show a document entering a file.
16. **Draw a rough sketch of the flowchart.** Be more concerned with capturing content than with making a perfect drawing. Few systems can be flowcharted in a single draft.
17. **Redesign the flowchart.** Avoid clutter and a large number of crossed lines.
18. **Verify the flowchart's accuracy.** Review it with the people familiar with the system. Be sure all uses of flowcharting conventions are consistent.
19. **Draw a final copy of the flowchart.** Place the flowchart name, date, and preparer's name on each page.

System Flowcharts

System flowcharts depict the relationships among system input, processing, and output. A system flowchart begins by identifying system inputs and their origins. The input is followed by the processing performed on the data. The resulting new information is the output component, which can be stored for later use, displayed on a screen, or printed on paper. In many instances, the output from one process is an input to another.

The sales processing system flowchart in Figure 10 represents Ashton's proposal to capture sales data using state-of-the-art sales terminals. These terminals will edit the sales data and print a customer receipt. All sales data will be stored in a sales data file on a disk. At the end of each day, the data will be forwarded to S&S's computers, where it will be summarized and batch totals will be printed. A batch total is the sum of a numerical item contained in each transaction being processed. An example is total sales for all sales transactions. The summary data will then be processed, and batch totals will again be generated and printed. These amounts will be compared with the batch totals generated prior to processing, and all errors and exceptions will be reconciled. The accounts receivable, inventory, and sales marketing databases and the general ledger will be updated. Users can access the files at any time by using an inquiry processing

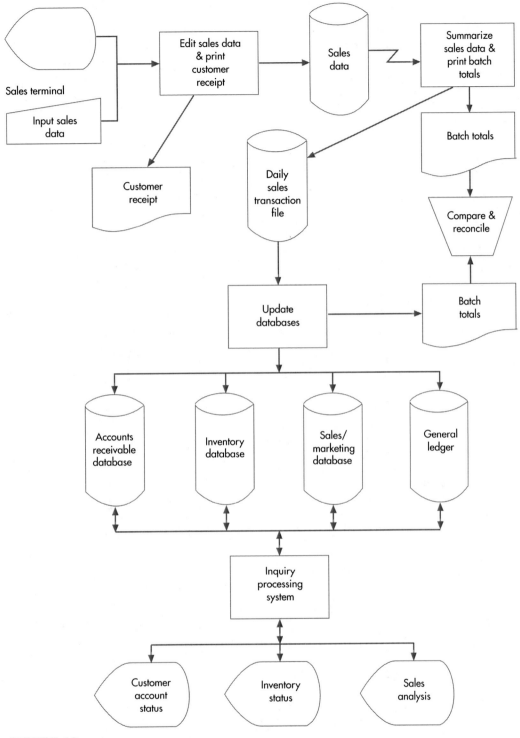

FIGURE 10

System Flowchart of Sales Processing at S&S

system. This system will produce standard reports and allow users to access the data needed for special analyses.

System flowcharts are an important systems analysis, design, and evaluation tool. They are universally employed in systems work and provide an immediate form of communication among workers. The system flowchart is an excellent vehicle for describing information flows and procedures within an AIS.

Program Flowcharts

A *program flowchart* illustrates the sequence of logical operations performed by a computer in executing a program. The relationship between system and program flowcharts is shown in Figure 11. A program flowchart describes the specific logic used to perform a process shown on a system flowchart.

Program flowcharts employ a subset of the symbols shown in Figure 8. Once designed and approved, the program flowchart serves as the blueprint for coding the computer program.

Summary and Case Conclusion

Ashton prepared the DFDs and flowcharts of S&S's payroll processing system (Figures 6, 7, and 9) to document and explain the operation of the existing system. He was pleased to see that Scott and Susan were able to grasp the essence of the system from this documentation. The DFDs indicated the logical flow of data, and the flowcharts illustrated the physical dimensions of the system: The origin and final disposition and the interworkings of the documents in each department were clear.

Susan and Scott agreed that Ashton should document the remainder of the system. The documentation would help all of them understand the current system. It would also help Ashton and the consultants design the new system. In fact, the payroll documentation had already helped them identify a few minor changes they wanted to make in their system. Using the information from Figure 9, Susan now understands why the payroll clerk sometimes had to borrow the only copy of the payroll report that was prepared. She thus recommended that a second copy be made and kept in the payroll department. Susan also questioned the practice of keeping all the payroll records in one employee/payroll file. To keep the file from becoming unwieldy, she recommended that it be divided into three files: personal employee data, pay period documentation, and payroll tax data. A discussion with the payroll clerk verified that this approach would make payroll processing easier and more efficient.

Over the next few weeks, Ashton documented the remaining accounting cycles. This process helped him identify inefficiencies and unneeded reports. He also found that some system documents were inadequately controlled. In addition, he got several ideas about how an automated system could help him reengineer the business processes at S&S. By substituting technology for human effort, outdated processes and procedures could be eliminated to make the system more effective.

FIGURE 11

Relationship Between System and Program Flowcharts

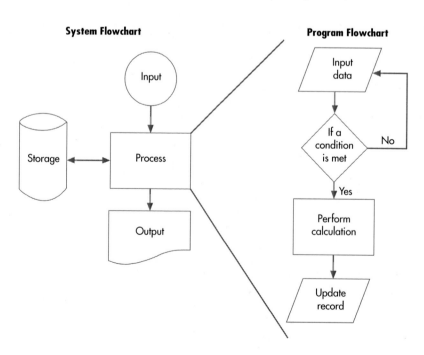

When Ashton completed his analysis and documentation of the current system, Susan and Scott asked him to continue his work in designing a new system. To do that, Ashton must thoroughly understand the information needs of the various employees in the company. Then he can design a new system using the tools that were explained in this chapter.

Key Terms

documentation	data flow	document flowchart
narrative description	process	internal control flowchart
data flow diagram (DFD)	data store	system flowchart
data source	context diagram	program flowchart
data destination	flowchart	

AIS IN ACTION

Chapter Quiz

1. A DFD is a representation of which of the following?
   a. relationship among modules, data, and programs of an AIS
   b. flow of data in an organization
   c. decision rules in a computer program
   d. computer hardware configuration

2. Documentation methods such as DFDs and flowcharts save both time and money, adding value to an organization.
   a. True   b. False

3. Which of the following statements is FALSE?
   a. Flowcharts make use of many symbols.
   b. A flowchart emphasizes the flow of documents or records containing data.
   c. DFDs help convey the timing of events.
   d. Both a and b are false.

4. A DFD consists of the following four basic elements: data sources and destinations, data flows, transformation processes, and data stores. Each is represented on a DFD by a different symbol.
   a. True   b. False

5. Which of the following is NOT one of the guidelines that should be followed in naming DFD data elements?
   a. Process names should include action verbs such as *update, edit, prepare,* and *record.*
   b. Make sure the names describe all the data or the entire process.
   c. Name only the most important DFD elements.
   d. Choose active and descriptive names.

6. The documentation skills that accountants require vary with their job function. However, they should at least be able to do which of the following?
   a. Read documentation to determine how the system works.
   b. Critique and correct documentation that others prepare.
   c. Prepare documentation for a newly developed information system.
   d. Teach others how to prepare documentation.

7. Which of the following statements is FALSE?
    a. A flowchart is an analytical technique used to describe some aspect of an information system in a clear, concise, and logical manner.
    b. Flowcharts use a standard set of symbols to describe pictorially the flow of documents and data through a system.
    c. Flowcharts are easy to prepare and revise when the designer utilizes a flowcharting software package.
    d. A system flowchart is a narrative representation of an information system.
    e. A program flowchart shows the logic used in computer programs.

8. Which of the following flowcharts illustrates the flow of information among areas of responsibility in an organization?
    a. program flowchart   c. system flowchart
    b. computer configuration chart d. document flowchart

9. Which of the following is NOT one of the recommended guidelines for making flowcharts more readable, clear, concise, consistent, and understandable?
    a. Divide the flowchart into columns with labels.
    b. Flowchart all information flows, especially exception procedures and error routines.
    c. Design the flowchart so that flow proceeds from top to bottom and from left to right.
    d. Show the final disposition of all documents to prevent loose ends that leave the reader dangling.
    e. Make sure that each manual processing symbol has an input and an output.

10. How are data sources and destinations represented in a data flow diagram?
    a. as a square   d. as two parallel lines
    b. as a curved arrow   e. none of the above
    c. as a circle

Comprehensive Problem

Accuflow Cash Disbursements Process

SoftData, a vendor, sends an invoice to Accuflow for data warehousing support services. The invoice is sent directly to Megan Waters, the accounts payable clerk, who manually records the invoice in the accounts payable subsidiary ledger. Once the invoice is recorded, it is forwarded to Stan Phillips, the cash disbursements clerk, for processing. Stan prepares a check to pay the invoice and sends the check and invoice to John Sterling, the company treasurer. John approves and signs the check and cancels the invoice. John then mails the check back to SoftData and returns the canceled invoice to Stan for recording in the cash disbursements journal and filing. Once a week, Megan manually posts disbursements from the cash disbursements journal to the accounts payable subsidiary ledger.

Required

Prepare a document flowchart, a context diagram, a level 0 data flow diagram, and a level 1 data flow diagram for the Accuflow cash disbursement process. To maximize learning from this problem, do your best to solve it before looking at the solution at the end of the chapter.

Discussion Questions

1. Identify the DFD elements in the following narrative: A customer purchases a few items from a local grocery store. Jill, a salesclerk, enters the transaction in the cash register and takes the customer's money. At closing, Jill gives both the cash and the register tape to her manager.

2. Do you agree with the following statement: "Any one of the systems documentation procedures can be used to adequately document a given system"? Explain.

3. Compare the guidelines for preparing flowcharts and DFDs. What general design principles and limitations are common to both documentation techniques?

4. Your classmate asks you to explain flowcharting conventions using real-world examples. Draw each of the major flowchart symbols from memory, placing them into one of four categories: input/output, processing, storage, and flow and miscellaneous. For each symbol, suggest several uses.

Problems

1. Prepare flowcharting segments for each of the following operations:
   a. processing transactions stored on magnetic tape to update a master file stored on magnetic tape
   b. processing transactions stored on magnetic tape to update a database stored on a magnetic disk
   c. converting source documents to magnetic tape using a computer-based optical character reader (OCR)
   d. processing OCR documents online to update a database on magnetic disk
   e. reading data from a magnetic disk into the computer to be printed on a report
   f. using a computer or terminal to key data from source documents to a file stored on a magnetic disk
   g. manually sorting and filing invoices numerically
   h. using a terminal to enter source document data and send it to a remote location where an online processing system records it in a database stored on magnetic disk
   i. a scheduled automatic backup of an internal hard drive to an external hard drive
   j. using a terminal to query customer sales data maintained on a magnetic disk
   k. entering employee hours recorded on time cards in the payroll transaction file maintained on disk and updating wage data maintained on the payroll master file
   l. using a terminal to access a price list maintained on disk to complete a purchase order. An electronic copy of the purchase order is sent to the vendor and a backup copy is printed and filed by vendor name
   m. updating an airline reservation on a Web-based airline reservation system from a home computer

2. The Happy Valley Utility Company uses turnaround documents in its computerized customer accounting system. Meter readers are provided with preprinted computer forms, each containing the account number, name, address, and previous meter readings. Each form also contains a formatted area in which the customer's current meter reading can be marked in pencil. After making their rounds, meter readers turn in batches of these documents to the computer data preparation department, where they are processed by a mark-sense document reader that transfers their contents to magnetic tape.

   This magnetic tape file is used as input for two computer runs. The first run sorts the transaction records on the tape into sequential order by customer account number. On the second run, the sorted transaction tape is processed against the customer master file, which is stored on a magnetic disk. Second-run outputs are (1) a printed report listing summary information and any erroneous transactions detected by the computer and (2) customer bills printed in a special OCR-readable font. Bills are mailed, and customers are requested to return the stub portion along with payment.

   Customer payments are received in the mailroom and checked for consistency against the returned remittance stubs. Checks are then sent to the cashier's office. The mailroom provides the computer data preparation department with three sets of records: (1) stubs with compatible amounts, (2) stubs with differing amounts, and (3) a list of amounts received from customers, without stubs. For the latter two types of records, data preparation personnel use a special off-line keying device to prepare corrected stubs. An

OCR document reader reads all the stubs and sends the data to the company's computer. The computer updates the customer master file to post the payment amounts. Two printed outputs from this second process are (1) reports listing erroneous transactions and summary information and (2) past-due customer balances.

Required

a. Draw a system flowchart of the billing operations, commencing with the computer preparation of the meter reading forms and ending with the mailing of customer bills.
b. Draw a system flowchart depicting customer payments processing, starting with the mailroom operations and ending with the two printed reports.

3. The Dewey Construction Company processes its payroll transactions to update both its payroll master file and its work-in-process master file in the same computer run. Both files are stored on magnetic disk.

   Job time tickets are keyed onto a tape using an off-line key-to-tape encoder. The tape is then processed to update the files. The processing run also produces a payroll register on magnetic tape, employee paychecks and earnings statements, and a printed report listing error transactions and summary information.

Required

Prepare a system flowchart of the process described.

4. Prepare a document flowchart to reflect how ANGIC Insurance Company processes its casualty claims. The process begins when the claims department receives a notice of loss from a claimant. The claims department prepares and sends the claimant four copies of a proof-of-loss form on which the claimant must detail the cause, amount, and other aspects of the loss. The claims department also initiates a record of the claim, which is sent with the notice of loss to the data processing department, where it is filed by claim number.

   The claimant must fill out the proof-of-loss forms with an adjuster's assistance. The adjuster must concur with the claimant on the estimated amount of loss. The claimant and adjuster each keep one copy of the proof-of-loss form. The adjustor files his copy numerically. The adjustor sends the first two copies to the claims department. Separately, the adjuster submits a report to the claims department, confirming the estimates on the claimant's proof-of-loss form.

   The claims department authorizes a payment to the claimant, forwards a copy of the proof-of-loss form to data processing, and files the original proof-of-loss form and the adjuster's report alphabetically. The data processing department prepares payment checks and mails them to the customers, files the proof-of-loss form with the claim record, and prepares a list of cash disbursements, which it transmits to the accounting department.

5. Beccan Company is a discount tire dealer operating 25 retail stores in the metropolitan area. The company operates a centralized purchasing and warehousing facility and employs a perpetual inventory system. All purchases of tires and related supplies are placed through the company's central purchasing department to optimize quantity discounts. The tires and supplies are received at the central warehouse and distributed to the retail stores as needed. The perpetual inventory system at the central facility maintains current inventory records, designated reorder points, and optimum order quantities for each type and size of tire and other related supplies. Beccan uses the following five documents in its inventory control system.

   - **Retail stores requisition.** The retail stores submit a retail store requisition to the central warehouse when they need tires or supplies. The warehouse shipping clerks fill the orders from inventory and authorize store deliveries.
   - **Purchase requisition.** The inventory control clerk prepares a purchase requisition when the quantity on hand for an item falls below the designated reorder point and forwards it to the purchasing department.
   - **Purchase order.** The purchasing department prepares a purchase order when items need to be ordered and submits it to an authorized vendor.

- **Receiving report.** The warehouse department prepares a receiving report when ordered items are received from vendors. The receiving clerk indicates the vendor's name and the date and quantity of the shipment received.
- **Invoice.** An invoice is received from vendors, specifying the amounts Beccan owes.

The following departments are involved in Beccan's inventory control system:

- **Inventory control department.** Responsible for the maintenance of all perpetual inventory records, including quantity on hand, reorder point, optimum order quantity, and quantity on order for each item carried.
- **Warehouse department.** Maintains the physical inventory of all items carried in stock. All orders from vendors are received (receiving clerk) and all distributions to retail stores are filled (shipping clerks) in this department.
- **Purchasing department.** Places all orders for items needed by the company.
- **Accounts payable department.** Maintains all open accounts with vendors and other creditors, in addition to processing payments.

Required

a. Prepare a document flowchart that indicates the interaction and use of these documents among all departments at Beccan Company's central facility. It should provide adequate internal control over the receipt, issuance, replenishment, and payment of tires and supplies. You may assume that there are a sufficient number of document copies to ensure that the perpetual inventory system has the necessary basic internal controls.

b. Using the flowcharting conventions discussed in Focus 2, critique the instructor provided CMA solution. List all the ways the CMA solution violates those flowcharting guidelines. (*CMA Examination, adapted*)

6. As the internal auditor for No-Wear Products, you have been asked to document the company's payroll processing system. Based on your documentation, No-Wear hopes to develop a plan for revising the current system to eliminate unnecessary delays in paycheck processing. The head payroll clerk explained the system:

> The payroll processing system at No-Wear Products is fairly simple. Time data are recorded in each department using time cards and clocks. It is annoying, however, when people forget to punch out at night, and we have to record their time by hand. At the end of the period, our payroll clerks enter the time card data into a payroll file for processing. Our clerks are pretty good—though I've had to make my share of corrections when they mess up the data entry.
>
> Before the payroll file is processed for the current period, human resources sends us personnel changes, such as increases in pay rates and new employees. Our clerks enter this information into the payroll file. Usually, when mistakes get back to us, it's because human resources is recording the wrong pay rate or an employee has left and the department forgets to remove the record.
>
> The data are processed and individual employee paychecks are generated. Several reports are generated for management—though I don't know what they do with them. In addition, the government requires regular federal and state withholding reports for tax purposes. Currently, the system generates these reports automatically, which is nice.

Required

a. Prepare a context diagram and level 0 DFD to document the payroll processing system at No-Wear Products.

b. Prepare a document flowchart to document the payroll processing system at No-Wear Products.

7. Ashton Fleming has decided to document and analyze the accounts payable process at S&S so the transition to a computerized system will be easier. He also hopes to improve

any weaknesses he discovers in the system. In the following narrative, Ashton explains what happens at S&S:

> Before S&S pays a vendor invoice, the invoice must be matched against the purchase order used to request the goods and the receiving report that the receiving department prepares. Because all three of these documents enter the accounts payable department at different times, a separate alphabetical file is kept for each type of document. The purchase orders that are forwarded from purchasing are stored in a purchase order file. The receiving reports are stored in a receiving report file. When vendor invoices are received, the accounts payable clerk records the amount due in the accounts payable file and files the invoices in the vendor invoice file.

> S&S pays all accounts within 10 days to take advantage of early-payment discounts. When it is time to pay a bill, the accounts payable clerk retrieves the vendor invoice, attaches the purchase order and the receiving report, and forwards the matched documents to Ashton Fleming.

> Ashton reviews the documents to ensure they are complete, prepares a two-part check, forwards all the documents to Susan, and records the check in the cash disbursements journal.

> Susan reviews the documents to ensure that they are valid payables and signs the checks. She forwards the check to the vendor and returns the documents and the check copy to the accounts payable clerk. The clerk files the documents alphabetically in a paid invoice file. At the end of every month, the accounts payable clerk uses the accounts payable ledger to prepare an accounts payable report that is forwarded to Susan. After she is finished with the report, Susan files it chronologically.

Required

a. Prepare a context diagram and a level 0 DFD to document accounts payable processing at S&S.
b. Prepare a document flowchart to document accounts payable processing at S&S.

8. Since opening its doors in Hawaii two years ago, Oriental Trading has enjoyed tremendous success. Oriental Trading purchases textiles from Asia and resells them to local retail shops. To keep up with the strong demand, Oriental Trading is expanding its local operations, including a new information system to handle the tremendous increase in purchases.

   The following is a summary of your interviews with department supervisors who interact with the acquisition/payment system:

> A purchase requisition is sent from the inventory system to Sky Ishibashi, a purchasing department clerk . Sky prepares a purchase order using the vendor and inventory files and mails it to the vendor. The vendor returns a vendor acknowledgment to Sky indicating receipt of the purchase order. Sky then sends a purchase order notification to Elei Mateaki, an accounts payable clerk.

> When the receiving department accepts vendor goods, the inventory system sends Elei a receiving report. Elei also receives invoices from the various vendors. He matches the invoices with the purchase order notification and the receiving report and updates the accounts payable master file. Elei then sends a payment authorization to the accounting department. There, Andeloo Nonu prepares and mails a check to the vendor. When the check is issued, the system automatically updates the accounts payable master file and the general ledger.

Required

a. Develop a context diagram and a level 0 DFD of the acquisition/payment system at Oriental Trading.
b. Prepare a document flowchart to document the acquisition/payment system at Oriental Trading.

9. Ashton Fleming has asked you to develop a comprehensive DFD for the cash receipts system. Ashton's narrative of the system follows:

> Customer payments include cash received at the time of purchase and payments received in the mail. At day's end, the treasurer endorses all checks and prepares a

deposit slip for the checks and the cash. A clerk deposits the checks, cash, and deposit slip at the local bank each day. When checks are received as payment for accounts due, a remittance slip is included with the payment. The remittance slips are used to update the accounts receivable file at the end of the day. The remittance slips are stored in a file drawer by date.

Every week, a cash receipts report and an aged trial balance are generated using the accounts receivable ledger. The cash receipts report is sent to Scott and Susan. A copy of the aged trial balance is sent to the credit and collections department.

Required

a. Develop a context diagram and a level 0 DFD for the cash receipts system at S&S.
b. Prepare a document flowchart for the cash receipts system at S&S.

10. A mail-order skin and body care company advertises in magazines. Magazine subscribers initiate most orders by completing and sending coupons directly to the company. The firm also takes orders by phone, answers inquiries about products, and handles payments and cancellations of orders. Products that have been ordered are sent either directly to the customer or to the company's regional offices that handle the required distribution. The mail-order company has three basic data files, which contain customer mailing information, product inventory information, and billing information based on invoice number. During the next few years, the company expects to become a multimillion-dollar operation. Recognizing the need to computerize much of the mail-order business, the company has begun the process by calling you.

Required

Draw a context diagram and at least two levels of DFDs for the preceding operations.

11. The local college requires that each student complete a registration request form and mail or deliver it to the registrar's office. A clerk enters the request into the system. The system checks the accounts receivable subsystem to ensure that no fees are owed. Next, for each course, the system checks the student transcript to ensure that he or she has completed the course prerequisites. Then the system checks class position availability and adds the student's Social Security number to the class list.

The report back to the student shows the result of registration processing: If the student owes fees, a bill is sent and the registration is rejected. If prerequisites for a course are not fulfilled, the student is notified and that course is not registered. If the class is full, the student request is annotated with "course closed." If a student is accepted into a class, then the day, time, and room are printed next to the course number. Student fees and total tuition are computed and printed on the form. Student fee information is interfaced to the accounts receivable subsystem. Course enrollment reports are prepared for the instructors.

Required

a. Prepare a context diagram and at least two levels of DFDs for this operation.
b. Prepare a document flowchart for this operation.

12. Charting, Inc., a new audit client of yours, processes its sales and cash receipts documents in the following manner:

1. *Payment on account.* Each morning a mail clerk in the sales department opens the mail and prepares a remittance advice (showing customer and amount paid) if one is not received. The checks and remittance advices are forwarded to the sales department supervisor, who reviews each check and forwards the checks and remittance advices to the accounting department supervisor.

The accounting department supervisor, who also functions as credit manager (approving new credit and credit limits), reviews all checks for payments on past-due accounts. He forwards the checks and remittance advices to the accounts receivable clerk, who arranges the advices in alphabetical order. The remittance advices are posted directly to the accounts receivable ledger. The checks are endorsed and the total is posted to the cash receipts journal. The remittance advices are filed chronologically. After receiving the cash from the previous day's cash sales, the accounts receivable clerk prepares the daily deposit slip in triplicate. The third copy of the deposit slip is filed by date, and the second copy and the original accompany the bank deposit.

2. *Sales.* Sales clerks prepare sales invoices in triplicate. The original and the second copy are presented to the cashier. The sales clerk retains the third copy in the sales book. When a sale is for cash, the customer pays the sales clerk, who gives the money to the cashier with the invoice copies.

The cashier approves a credit sale from an approved credit list after the sales clerk prepares the three-part invoice. After receiving the cash or approving the invoice, the cashier validates the original copy of the sales invoice and gives it to the customer. At the end of each day, the cashier recaps the sales and cash received and forwards the cash and the second copy of the sales invoices to the accounts receivable clerk.

The accounts receivable clerk balances the cash received with cash sales invoices and prepares a daily sales summary. The credit sales invoices are posted to the accounts receivable ledger, and then all invoices are sent to the inventory control clerk in the sales department for posting to the inventory control cards. After posting, the inventory control clerk files all invoices numerically. The accounts receivable clerk posts the daily sales summary to the cash receipts and sales journals and files the sales summaries by date.

The cash from cash sales is combined with the cash received on account to make up the daily bank deposit.

3. *Bank deposits.* The bank validates the deposit slip and returns the second copy to the accounting department, where the accounts receivable clerk files it by date.

Monthly bank statements are reconciled promptly by the accounting department supervisor and filed by date.

Required

You recognize weaknesses in the existing system and believe a document flowchart would be beneficial in evaluating the client's internal control in preparing for your examination of the financial statements.

a. Complete the flowchart given in Figure 12, for sales and cash receipts of Charting, Inc., by labeling the appropriate symbols and indicating information flows.
b. Using the guidelines for preparing flowcharts in Focus 2 and the flowcharting symbols shown in Figure 8, critique the flowchart shown in Figure 12. List the ways the flowchart violates the guidelines or uses improper symbols. (*CPA Examination, adapted*)

13. A partially completed flowchart appears in Figure 13. The flowchart depicts the credit sales activities of the Bottom Manufacturing Corporation.

When a customer's purchase order is received, a six-part sales order is prepared and distributed as follows:

Copy 1—Billing copy, to billing department

Copy 2—Shipping copy, to shipping department

Copy 3—Credit copy, to credit department

Copy 4—Stock request copy, to credit department

Copy 5—Customer copy, to customer

Copy 6—Sales order copy, filed in sales order department

When each copy of the sales order reaches the appropriate department or destination, it calls for specific internal control procedures and related documents. Some procedures and related documents are indicated on the flowchart; others are labeled by the letters *a* to *r*.

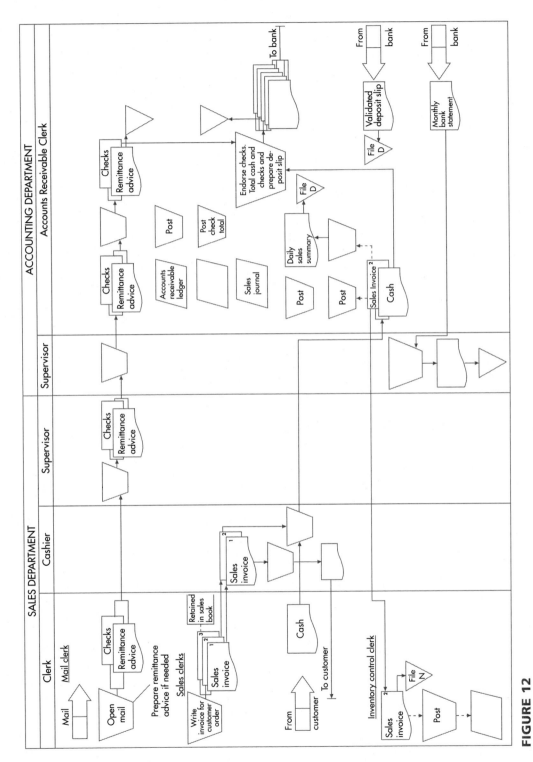

FIGURE 12

Charting, Inc., Flowchart for Sales and Cash Receipts

FIGURE 13
Bottom Manufacturing Corporation Flowchart of Credit Sales Activities

Required

a. List the procedures or the internal documents that are labeled letters *c* to *r* in the flow-chart of Bottom Manufacturing Corporation's charge sales system. Organize your answer as follows (Note that the explanations of the letters *a* and *b* in the flowchart are entered as examples):

Flowchart Symbol Letter	Procedures or Internal Document
a	Prepare six-part sales order.
b	File by order number.

b. Using the guidelines for preparing flowcharts in Focus 2 and the flowcharting symbols shown in Figure 8, critique the flowchart shown in Figure 13. List the ways the flow-chart violates the guidelines or uses improper symbols. *(CPA Examination, adapted)*

14. Prepare a context diagram and a level 0 data flow diagram for each of the following situations.
    a. Prepare and file a tax return with the tax owed to the Internal Revenue Service.
    b. A customer pays an invoice with a check. Accounts receivable is updated to reflect the payment. The check is recorded and deposited into the bank.
    c. A customer places an online order to purchase merchandise. The order is approved, filled, and sent to the customer with an invoice.
    d. An inventory request is received by the purchasing department. The purchasing depart-ment prepares and sends a purchase order to the appropriate vendor.
    e. A vendor invoice is received, reviewed, and compared against the appropriate purchase order, then paid and filed.
    f. A bill of lading for ordered inventory is received from a vendor, recorded, checked against the appropriate purchase order, and filed.

15. Melanie is doing a study on various weight-loss plans and needs to determine an individ-ual's weight status by calculating his body mass index. To calculate a person's body mass index, height must be measured in meters and weight measured in kilograms. The index is calculated by dividing a person's weight by the square of his height. The result is then compared to the following scale to determine the person's weight status: Below 18.5 = underweight; 18.5–24.5 = normal weight; over 25.0 = overweight. Five hundred people have agreed to participate in Melanie's study. With so many calculations to perform, she would like a computer program that will do this calculation for her. She decides to prepare a flowchart to help her properly design the computer program.

Required

Prepare a program flowchart to help Melanie program this process.

16. Match the flowchart, context diagram, or data flow diagram segments in the right column to an appropriate description in the left column.

1. Statements are prepared and sent to customers from data contained in the accounts receivable data store.

A.

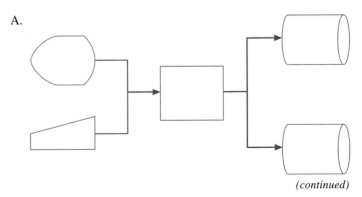

(continued)

2. A customer sends a sales invoice to the accounts payable process.

B.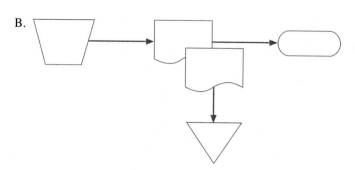

3. A check is manually prepared from data on a vendor invoice.

C.

4. The cash receipt process updates the cash receipts data store.

D.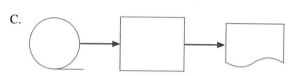

5. A sales invoice is manually prepared and sent to a customer.

E.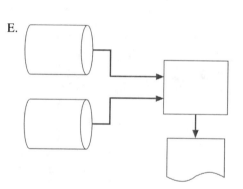

6. A report is prepared from data stored on magnetic tape.

F.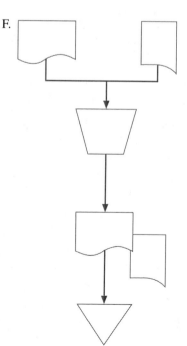

7. Billing data are entered online and used to update the sales order file and the customer master file.

G.

8. Data from a cancelled invoice are used to update the cash disbursements ledger.

H.

9. A sales order is prepared manually. Copy 1 is sent to the warehouse, and copy 2 is filed.

I.

10. An accounts receivable aging report is prepared from the accounts receivable master file and the cash receipts master file, both stored on disk.

J.

11. An error listing and batch total are compared and filed.

K.

17. Replicate the following flowchart in Visio, Microsoft Word, Microsoft Excel, or some other documentation software package.

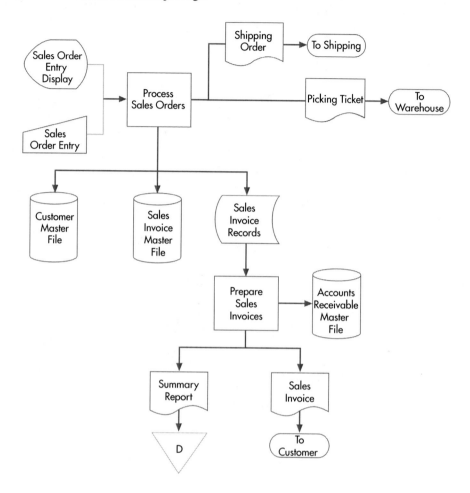

18. Replicate the following data flow diagram in Visio, Microsoft Word, Microsoft Excel, or some other documentation software package.

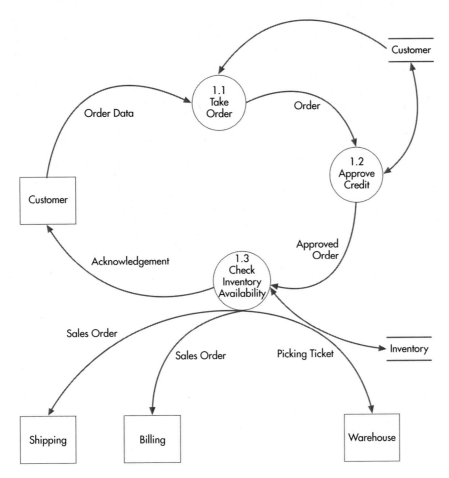

Case 1   Dub 5

You are the systems analyst for the Wee Willie Williams Widget Works (also known as Dub 5, which is a shortened version of 5 Ws). Dub 5 has been producing computer keyboard components for more than 20 years and has recently signed an exclusive 10-year contract to provide the keyboards for all Dell personal computers. As the systems analyst, you have been assigned the task of developing a level 0 DFD for Dub 5's order processing system. You have finished gathering all the information you need to develop the first-pass DFD and now want to complete the diagram.

Customer orders, which are all credit sales, arrive via e-mail and by phone. When an order is processed, a number of other documents are prepared. You have diagrammed the overall process and the documents produced, as shown in the context diagram shown below.

The following documents are created:

- Order processing creates a packing slip, which the warehouse uses to fill the order.
- A customer invoice is prepared and sent once the goods have been shipped.
- When orders are not accepted, an order rejection is sent to the customer, explaining why the order cannot be filled.
- A receivables notice, which is a copy of the customer invoice, is sent to the accounting department so accounts receivable records can be updated.

After reviewing your notes, you write the following narrative summary:

When an order comes in, the order processing clerk checks the customer's credit file to confirm credit approval and

ensure that the amount falls within the credit limit. If either of these conditions is not met, the order is sent to the credit department. If an order meets both conditions, the order-processing clerk enters it into the system on a standard order form. The information on the form is used to update the company's customer file (in which the name, address, and other information are stored), and the form is placed in the company's open order file.

When the credit department receives a rejected order, the credit clerk determines why the order has been rejected. If the credit limit has been exceeded, the customer is notified that the merchandise will be shipped as soon as Dub 5 receives payment. If the customer has not been approved for credit, a credit application is sent to the customer along with a notification that the order will be shipped as soon as credit approval is granted.

Before preparing a packing slip, the system checks the inventory records to determine whether the company has the products ordered on hand. If the items are in stock, a packing slip is prepared and sent to the warehouse.

Once notification of shipped goods has been received from the warehouse, a customer invoice is prepared. A copy is filed by the order processing department, another is sent to the customer, and another is sent to the accounting department so that accounts receivables can be updated. A note is placed in the customer file indicating that the invoice has been sent.

From the information presented, complete a Level 0 DFD for order processing and a Level 1 DFD for the credit review process for Dub 5.

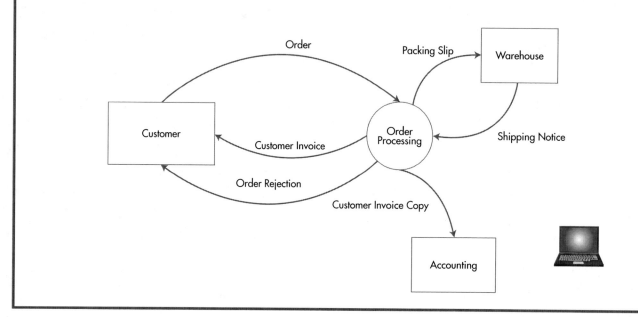

AIS IN ACTION SOLUTIONS

Quiz Key

1. A DFD is a representation of which of the following?
   a. relationship among modules, data, and programs of an AIS [Incorrect. A flowchart represents the relationship among modules, data, and programs.]
   ▶ b. flow of data in an organization [Correct.]
   c. decision rules in a computer program [Incorrect. A DFD is a graphical representation of how data move through an organization. Decision rules are objective statements specific to computer programs.]
   d. computer hardware configuration [Incorrrect. This relates to how various parts of a computer fit together.]

2. Documentation methods such as DFDs and flowcharts save both time and money, adding value to an organization.
   ▶ a. True [Correct. A picture is worth a thousand words: An individual may learn more and learn it more quickly by studying the DFD or flowchart of a system than by reading a narrative description of the same system.]
   b. False [Incorrect]

3. Which of the following statements is FALSE?
   a. Flowcharts make use of many symbols. [Incorrect. The statement is true. See Figure 8 for an illustration of the many symbols used in flowcharts.]
   b. A document flowchart emphasizes the flow of documents or records containing data. [Incorrect. The statement is true. The reason it is called a document flowchart is that it shows the flow of documents or records containing data.]
   ▶ c. DFDs help convey the timing of events. [Correct. DFDs show data movement, but not necessarily the timing of the movement.]
   d. Both a and b are false. [Incorrect. As explained above, a and b are true statements.]

4. A DFD consists of the following four basic elements: data sources and destinations, data flows, transformation processes, and data stores. Each is represented on a DFD by a different symbol.
   ▶ a. True [Correct. The four elements of DFDs are illustrated in Figure 1.]
   b. False [Incorrect]

5. Which of the following is NOT one of the guidelines that should be followed in naming DFD data elements?
   a. Process names should include action verbs such as *update*, *edit*, *prepare*, and *record*. [Incorrect. Action verbs should be used to name process data elements. See item 11 in Focus 1.]
   b. Make sure the names describe all the data or the entire process. [Incorrect. Data element names should reflect what is known about the element. See item 11 in Focus 1.]
   ▶ c. Name only the most important DFD elements. [Correct. All data elements should be named, with the exception of data flows into data stores, when the inflows and outflows make naming the data store redundant. See item 11 in Focus 1.]
   d. Choose active and descriptive names. [Incorrect. Active and descriptive names should be used in naming data elements. See item 11 in Focus 1.]

6. The documentation skills that accountants require vary with their job function. However, all accountants should at least be able to do which of the following?
   ▶ a. Read documentation to determine how the system works. [Correct. All accountants should at least be able to read and understand system documentation.]
   b. Critique and correct documentation that others prepare. [Incorrect. Although senior accountants may critique and correct documentation prepared by junior accountants, at a minimum all accountants need to be able to read and understand documentation.]

c. Prepare documentation for a newly developed information system. [Incorrect. Some accountants may need to develop internal control documentation, but system developers and analysts normally prepare systems documentation.]

d. Teach others how to prepare documentation. [Incorrect. Most accountants will not be asked to teach documentation skills.]

7. Which of the following statements is FALSE?

a. A flowchart is an analytical technique used to describe some aspect of an information system in a clear, concise, and logical manner. [Incorrect. This is the definition of a flowchart given previously in the text.]

b. Flowcharts use a standard set of symbols to describe pictorially the flow of documents and data through a system. [Incorrect. The symbols used for flowcharting are shown in Figure 8.]

c. Flowcharts are easy to prepare and revise when the designer utilizes a flowcharting software package. [Incorrect. There are a number of good flowcharting software packages that make it easy to draw and modify flowcharts.]

▶ d. A system flowchart is a narrative representation of an information system. [Correct. A flowchart is a graphical rather than a narrative representation of an information system.]

e. A program flowchart shows the logic used in computer programs. [Incorrect. A program flowchart illustrates program logic and the structure of the program.]

8. Which of the following flowcharts illustrates the flow of information among areas of responsibility in an organization?

a. program flowchart [Incorrect. A program flowchart documents a computer program.]

b. computer configuration chart [Incorrect. A computer configuration chart illustrates how computer hardware is arranged and implemented.]

c. system flowchart [Incorrect. A system flowchart illustrates the relationship among inputs, processes, and outputs of a system, not areas of responsibility.]

▶ d. document flowchart [Correct. A document flowchart traces the life of a document from its cradle to its grave as it works its way through the areas of responsibility within an organization.]

9. Which of the following is NOT one of the recommended guidelines for making flowcharts more readable, clear, concise, consistent, and understandable?

a. Divide the flowchart into columns with labels. [Incorrect. Dividing the flowchart into columns helps make it more readable, clear, concise, consistent, and understandable. See item 3 in Focus 2.]

▶ b. Flowchart all information flows, especially exception procedures and error routines. [Correct. Including all exception procedures and error routines clutters the flowchart and makes it difficult to read and understand. See item 4 in Focus 2.]

c. Design the flowchart so that flow proceeds from top to bottom and from left to right. [Incorrect. Flowcharts should be prepared so that they are read like a book. See item 5 in Focus 2.]

d. Show the final disposition of all documents to prevent loose ends that leave the reader dangling. [Incorrect. All documents should be placed either in a file or sent to another entity. See item 6 in Focus 2.]

e. Make sure that each manual processing symbol has an input and an output. [Incorrect. A manual process must have an input and an output. Without an input, nothing can be processed; and without an output, there is no evidence of processing. See item 10 in Focus 2.]

10. How are data sources and destinations represented in a data flow diagram?

▶ a. as a square [Correct. See Figure 1.]

b. as a curved arrow [Incorrect. A curved arrow represents a data flow. See Figure 1.]

c. as a circle [Incorrect. A circle represents a process. See Figure 1.]

d. as two parallel lines [Incorrect. Two parallel lines represent a data store. See Figure 1.]

e. as none of the above [Incorrect. Option a is correct.]

Comprehensive Problem Solution

Flowchart

The first step in preparing a document flowchart is to become familiar with the problem. The next step is to identify the primary actors or major players. In this problem there are three major players: Megan Waters (accounts payable clerk), Stan Phillips (cash disbursement clerk), and John Sterling (treasurer). Since we are documenting Accuflow's cash disbursement process, we are not interested in the internal workings of the vendor, SoftData. As a result, we do not include it as one of our major players. Now that we have identified the major players, we can list their functions in Table 3. Note that forwarding to and receiving from the next major player are not considered functions in preparing document flowcharts.

We will now explain, step by step, how to create the document flowchart solution for Accuflow shown in Figure 14. To document the functions of the three major players, divide the document flowchart into three columns, one for each player. It is usually best to arrange the columns in the order in which they occur and to use the primary function of the major player as the column name. Because the accounts payable clerk receives the invoice from the vendor, we place her in the first column. After the accounts payable clerk records the invoice, she sends it to the cash disbursements clerk, who prepares a check and sends it to the treasurer. Therefore, the cash disbursements clerk should be in the second column, and the treasurer should be in the last column, as illustrated in Figure 14.

Because the process begins with an invoice from an external party (a vendor), a terminal symbol with the term "From Vendor" is placed in the upper left portion of the Accounts Payable Clerk column. Next, a document symbol with the words "Vendor Invoice" printed inside it is placed below the terminal symbol. An arrow representing the document's flow and the order of operations connects the two symbols.

According to the narrative, Megan manually records the invoice in the accounts payable subsidiary ledger. Thus, a manual process symbol with the words "Record Invoice" is placed below the invoice document symbol, and the two symbols are connected with an arrow. Then, a journal/ledger symbol, also called an input/output symbol, is placed to the side of the manual process. Because only information from the invoice is used to update the accounts payable subsidiary ledger, a dotted arrow is used to connect the two symbols. A new vendor invoice symbol is drawn below the record invoice symbol.

Because the vendor invoice moves from the accounts payable clerk to the cash disbursements clerk, the vendor invoice symbol is placed at the top of the cash disbursements column with an arrow connecting the two representations of the same document. We redraw the vendor invoice symbol in the cash disbursements clerk column to make the flowchart easier to read.

To show that the cash disbursement clerk prepares a check to pay the vendor invoice, a manual process symbol with "Prepare Check" inside it is placed next to the vendor invoice. We could have placed it below the invoice symbol but put it beside it to save space. Two document symbols are placed below the manual process for the vendor invoice and the newly prepared check.

The cash disbursements clerk then sends the invoice and check to the treasurer. As a result, the vendor invoice and check appear in the Treasurer column. A manual symbol with "Approve & Sign Check; Cancel Invoice" inside is used to show that the check is signed and the invoice is cancelled. The documents are again shown in the flowchart, this time with new titles (Cancelled Invoice and Signed Check) to show the changed nature of the documents. The treasurer sends the signed check to the vendor, which is illustrated using a terminal symbol with words "To Vendor" written in it.

TABLE 3 Accuflow's Table of Functions

Accounts Payable Clerk (Megan Waters)	Cash Disbursements Clerk (Stan Phillips)	Treasurer (John Sterling)
Receives invoice	Prepares check	Approves and signs check
Records invoice	Records cash disbursement	Cancels invoice
Posts cash disbursement	Files cancelled invoice	Mails check

FIGURE 14
Accuflow's Document Flowchart

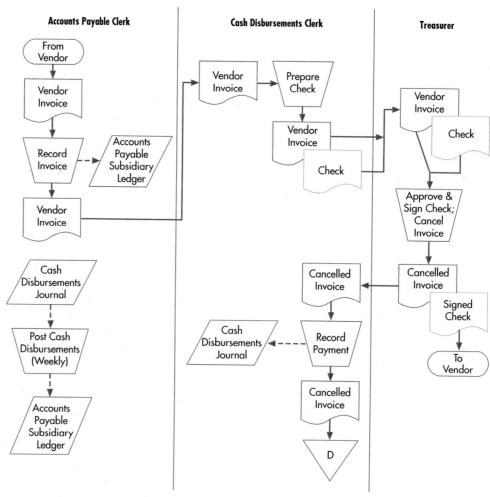

The cancelled invoice is used to record the cash disbursement in the cash disbursements journal, so it is sent back to the middle column (Cash Disbursements). A manual process symbol with "Record Payment" inside it and a dotted arrow are used to show that the disbursement is recorded in the cash disbursements journal, represented by a journal/ledger symbol. To illustrate that the cancelled invoice is filed by date, it is shown, using appropriate arrows, as exiting the record payment manual process and entering a file. A "D" is placed in the file symbol to indicate that the documents are filed by date.

Each week, the accounts payable clerk manually posts entries from the cash disbursements journal to the accounts payable subsidiary ledger. To show this, the cash disbursements journal symbol is reproduced in the accounts payable clerk column, and a manual process symbol with the words "Post Cash Disbursements (Weekly)" is placed under it. Dotted arrows show information from this journal being entered into the accounts payable subsidiary ledger.

This completes the document flowchart for the Accuflow Company's cash disbursements process.

Context Diagram

A context diagram is an overview of the information process being documented. As such, a context diagram includes a single transformation process (circle or bubble) and the data sources and data destinations that send or receive data directly from the transformation process. Thus, the first step in preparing a context diagram is to draw a single circle or bubble and then label it with a name that best describes the process being documented. In this case, "Cash Disbursements System" effectively describes the process (see Figure 15).

The next step is to draw and label squares for the entities that either send data to the cash disbursements process or receive data from the cash disbursements process. In this example, there is

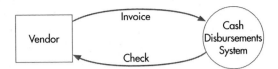

FIGURE 15

Accuflow's Context Diagram

a single entity—the vendor that acts as both a source and a destination of data to/from the cash disbursements process. In other processes, an outside entity could be just a source or a destination of data, and there could be more than one source or destination of data.

The last step is to connect the process (circle) with the source/destination (square) with arrows representing data flows. In this case, we have two arrows representing an invoice sent to Accuflow's cash disbursement process and a check sent to the vendor from Accuflow.

Level 0 Data Flow Diagram

In the context diagram, we saw the entire cash disbursements process in one bubble. In a level 0 DFD, we break down the cash disbursements process into its major functions. In reading the narrative, we find the following five primary steps in the cash disbursements process at Accuflow:

1. Receive vendor invoice and record payable
2. Prepare the check
3. Sign and send the check and cancel the invoice
4. Record the cash disbursement
5. Post the cash disbursements to the accounts payable ledger

Each of these processes is represented by a circle or bubble in Figure 16. Since this is the level 0 DFD, we assign each of these processes a real number, with the first digit after the decimal point being a zero. We also place the circles in the order that the data should flow in the process. As a result, "Receive and Record Invoice" is assigned process 1.0, "Prepare Check" is assigned process 2.0, "Approve and Sign Check" is 3.0, "Record Cash Disbursement" is 4.0, and "Post Cash Disbursement to Accounts Payable Ledger" is 5.0. This numbering system allows us to

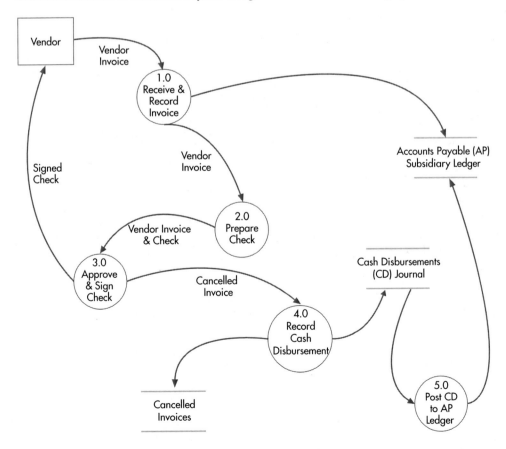

FIGURE 16

Accuflow's Level 0 Data Flow Diagram

decompose these processes into more detailed subprocesses and still keep a consistent numbering system. Thus, if we needed to decompose process 3.0 to a more detailed level, we could assign subprocess bubbles as 3.1, 3.2, 3.3, etc. We can even provide greater detail by decomposing process 3.1 into subprocesses 3.1.1, 3.1.2, 3.1.3, etc.

Next, we place the data sources and data destinations on the level 0 DFD. Because we had only one data source and destination (i.e., the vendor), we draw a square and label it "Vendor." It is very important that we reconcile back to the context diagram when we prepare the different levels of DFDs. That is, the same data sources and destinations that appeared on the context diagram must also appear on the level 0 DFD. No new data sources and destinations may appear on the level 0 DFD. If, when preparing the level 0 DFD, you discover that a data source/destination is necessary to document the system properly, then you must revise the context diagram with the new data source/destination, because the context diagram should represent the entire process.

Once the data source/destinations and processes are drawn, we then connect them by drawing the arrows between the appropriate symbols. These arrows represent the data moving or flowing from one process to another and from one source or destination to or from a particular process. Accordingly, we have a vendor invoice moving from the vendor to the "Receive and Record Invoice" process and from that process to the "Prepare Check" process. The vendor invoice and a check move from the "Prepare Check" process to the "Approve and Sign Check" process. We also have arrows leaving process 3.0 to represent the signed check being sent to the vendor and the cancelled invoice going to process 4.0, "Record Cash Disbursements."

Some processes require that data be stored. As a result, we also draw any necessary files or data stores. The level 0 DFD is the first time data stores appear in a DFD set. (Note: Data stores should not be represented on a context diagram.) Data store labels should identify the data being sent to or from it. As a result, labeling the data flows to or from data stores is normally unnecessary. Data stores are prepared by drawing two parallel lines and inserting the name of the data store between the parallel lines.

In Figure 16 we have three data stores: the cash disbursements journal, accounts payable subsidiary ledger, and the cancelled invoices data store. Because the cash disbursements journal is updated in process 4.0, a data flow is sent from the process 4.0 circle to the cash disbursements journal data store. To show that the accounts payable ledger is updated when invoices are received (process 1.0), an arrow is drawn from that process to the accounts payable ledger. To show that accounts payable is updated with data from the cash disbursements journal (process 5.0), a data flow arrow is drawn from the cash disbursements data store to process 5.0, and another data flow arrow is drawn from process 5.0 to the accounts payable subsidiary ledger data store. The update takes place weekly, but unlike document flowcharts, a DFD does not indicate the timing of data flows.

Level 1 Data Flow Diagram

When additional detail is needed to document data flows, a process bubble may be decomposed further. As indicated in Focus 1, to be clear, understandable, and easy to read, a DFD should contain no more than seven process bubbles. In the Accuflow example, we broke the company's data flows into five main processes. Each of these five processes can be further decomposed. To illustrate this, we will decompose process 3.0. The narrative indicates that the treasurer approves and signs the prepared check, sends it to the vendor, and cancels the invoice to prevent duplicate payments. Therefore, we will break down process 3.0 into process 3.1 (approve and sign check), 3.2 (send check to vendor), and 3.3 (cancel invoice). To display the three processes, we draw three circles and label them as shown on Figure 17. We also draw the data flows and label them. Notice that the vendor data source/destination is not needed on the level 1 DFD since it is already shown on level 0. Since it would clutter the DFD, and because we are showing greater detail on the level 1 than on the level 0 for one particular process, we do not replicate all of the processes and data stores in the level 0 DFD.

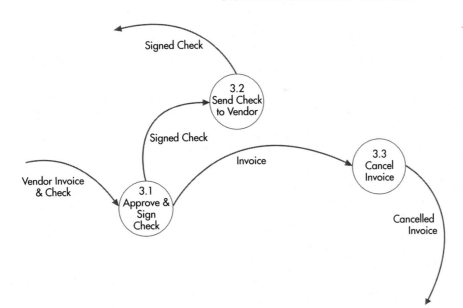

FIGURE 17
Accuflow's Level 1 Data Flow Diagram

Chapter 4

Relational Databases

From Chapter 4 of *Accounting Information Systems*, 12/e. Marshall B. Romney. Paul John Steinbart. Copyright © 2012 by Pearson Education.
Published by Prentice Hall. All rights reserved.

Relational Databases

Learning Objectives

After studying this chapter, you should be able to:

1. Explain the importance and advantages of databases, as well as the difference between database systems and file-based legacy systems.

2. Explain the difference between logical and physical views of a database.

3. Explain fundamental concepts of database systems such as DBMS, schemas, the data dictionary, and DBMS languages.

4. Describe what a relational database is and how it organizes data.

5. Create a set of well-structured tables to store data in a relational database.

6. Perform simple queries using the Microsoft Access database.

INTEGRATIVE CASE S&S

S&S is very successful and operates five stores and a popular Web site. Ashton Fleming believes that it is time to upgrade S&S's AIS so that Susan and Scott can easily access the information they need to run their business. Most new AISs are based on a relational database. Since Ashton knows that Scott and Susan are likely to have questions, he prepared a brief report that explains why S&S's new AIS should be a relational database system. His report addresses the following questions:

1. What is a database system, and how does it differ from file-oriented systems?
2. What is a *relational* database system?
3. How do you design a well-structured set of tables in a relational database?
4. How do you query a relational database system?

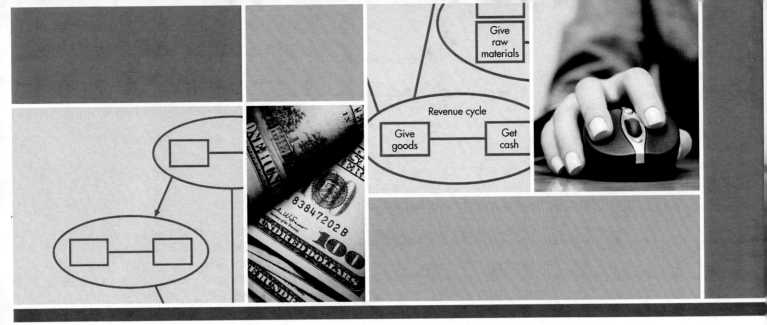

Introduction

Relational databases underlie most modern integrated AISs. This chapter explains how to participate in the design and implementation of a database. This chapter defines a database, with the emphasis on understanding the relational database structure.

Files versus Databases

To appreciate the power of databases, it is important to understand how data are stored in computer systems. Figure 1 shows a data hierarchy. Information about the attributes of a customer, such as name and address, are stored in fields. All the fields containing data about one entity (e.g., one customer) form a record. A set of related records, such as all customer records, forms a file (e.g., the customer file). A set of interrelated, centrally coordinated files forms a *database*.

FIGURE 1

Basic Elements of Data Hierarchy

Databases were developed to address the proliferation of master files. For many years, companies created new files and programs each time a need for information arose. Bank of America once had 36 million customer accounts in 23 separate systems. This proliferation created problems such as storing the same data in two or more master files, as shown in Figure 2. This made it difficult to integrate and update data and to obtain an organization-wide view of data. It also created problems because the data in the different files were inconsistent. For example, a customer's address may have been correctly updated in the shipping master file but not the billing master file.

Figure 2 illustrates the differences between file-oriented systems and database systems. In the database approach, data is an organizational resource that is used by and managed for the entire organization, not just the originating department. A *database management system (DBMS)* is the interface between the database and the various application programs. The database, the DBMS, and the application programs that access the database through the DBMS are referred to as the *database system*. The *database administrator (DBA)* is responsible for the database.

Using Data Warehouses for Business Intelligence

In today's fast-paced global economy, management must constantly reevaluate financial and operating performance in light of strategic goals and quickly alter plans as needed. Since strategic decision making requires access to large amounts of historical data, organizations are building separate databases called data warehouses. A *data warehouse* contains both detailed and summarized data for a number of years and is used for analysis rather than transaction processing. It is not unusual for data warehouses to contain hundreds of terabytes of data.

Data warehouses do not replace transaction processing databases; they complement them by providing support for strategic decision making. Since data warehouses are not used for transaction processing, they are usually updated periodically rather than in real time. Whereas transaction processing databases minimize redundancy and maximize the efficiency of updating them to reflect the results of current transactions, data warehouses are purposely redundant to maximize query efficiency.

Using a data warehouse for strategic decision making is often referred to as *business intelligence*. There are two main techniques used in business intelligence: online analytical processing (OLAP) and data mining. *Online analytical processing (OLAP)* is using queries to guide the investigation of hypothesized relationships in data. For example, a manager may analyze

FIGURE 2
File-Oriented Systems Versus Database Systems

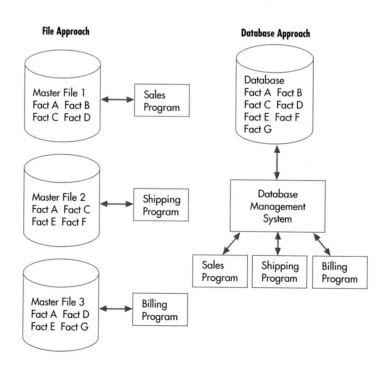

94

supplier purchases for the last three years. This may be followed by additional queries that "drill down" to lower levels by, for example, grouping purchases by different items and by fiscal periods. *Data mining* is using sophisticated statistical analysis, including artificial intelligence techniques such as neural networks, to "discover" unhypothesized relationships in the data. For example, credit card companies use data mining to identify usage patterns indicative of fraud. Similarly, data mining techniques can identify previously unknown relationships in sales data that can be used in future promotions.

Proper controls are needed to reap significant benefits from data warehousing. Data validation controls are needed to ensure that data warehouse input is accurate. Verifying the accuracy, called scrubbing the data, is often one of the most time-consuming and expensive steps in creating a data warehouse. It is also important to control access to the data warehouse as well as to encrypt the data stored in the data warehouse. Finally, it is important to regularly backup copies of the data warehouse and store them securely.

Bank of America created a customer information database to provide customer service, marketing analysis, and managerial information. It was the largest in the banking industry, with over 600 billion characters of data. It contained all bank data on checking and savings accounts; real estate, consumer, and commercial loans; ATMs; and bankcards. Although the bank spends $14 million a year to maintain the data warehouse, it is worth the cost. Queries that formerly averaged two hours took only five minutes. Minutes after Los Angeles suffered an earthquake, the bank sorted its $28 billion mortgage loan portfolio by Zip code, identified loans in the earthquake area, and calculated its potential loan loss.

The Advantages of Database Systems

Virtually all mainframes and servers use database technology, and database use in personal computers is growing rapidly. Most accountants are involved with databases through data entry, data processing, querying, or auditing. They also develop, manage, or evaluate the controls needed to ensure database integrity. Databases provide organizations with the following benefits:

- *Data integration.* Master files are combined into large "pools" of data that many application programs access. An example is an employee database that consolidates payroll, personnel, and job skills master files.
- *Data sharing.* Integrated data are more easily shared with authorized users. Databases are easily browsed to research a problem or obtain detailed information underlying a report. The FBI, which does a good job of collecting data but a poor job of sharing it, is spending eight years and $400 million to integrate data from their different systems.
- *Minimal data redundancy and data inconsistencies.* Because data items are usually stored only once, data redundancy and data inconsistencies are minimized.
- *Data independence.* Because data and the programs that use them are independent of each other, each can be changed without changing the other. This facilitates programming and simplifies data management.
- *Cross-functional analysis.* In a database system, relationships, such as the association between selling costs and promotional campaigns, can be explicitly defined and used in the preparation of management reports.

The Importance of Good Data

Incorrect database data can lead to bad decisions, embarrassment, and angry users. For example:

- A company sent half its mail-order catalogs to incorrect addresses. A manager finally investigated the large volume of returns and customer complaints. Correcting customer address in the database saved the company $12 million a year.
- Valparaiso, Indiana, used the county database to develop its tax rates. After the tax notices were mailed, a huge error was discovered: A $121,900 home was valued at $400 million and caused a $3.1 million property tax revenue shortfall. As a result, the city, the school district, and governmental agencies had to make severe budget cuts.

The Data Warehousing Institute estimates that bad data cost businesses over $600 billion a year in unnecessary postage, marketing costs, and lost customer credibility. It is estimated that over

25% of business data is inaccurate or incomplete. In a recent survey, 53% of 750 information technology (IT) professionals said their companies experienced problems due to poor-quality data.

Managing data gets harder every year: The quantity of data generated and stored doubles every 18 months. To avoid outdated, incomplete, or erroneous data, management needs policies and procedures that ensure clean, or scrubbed, data. The Sarbanes-Oxley Act states that top executives face prosecution and jail time if a company's financial data are not in order.

Database Systems

Logical and Physical Views of Data

In file-oriented systems, programmers must know the physical location and layout of records. Figure 3 shows a *record layout* of an accounts receivable file. Suppose a programmer wants a report showing customer number, credit limit, and current balance. To write the program, she must understand the location and length of the fields needed (i.e., record positions 1 through 10 for customer number) and the format of each field (alphanumeric or numeric). The process becomes more complex if data from several files are used.

Database systems overcome this problem by separating the storage of the data from the use of data elements. The database approach provides two separate views of the data: the physical view and the logical view. The *logical view* is how people conceptually organize and understand the data. For example, a sales manager views all customer information as being stored in a table. The *physical view* refers to how and where data are physically arranged and stored in the computer system.

As shown in Figure 4, database management (DBMS) software links the way data are physically stored with each user's logical view of the data. The DBMS allows users to access, query, or update the database without reference to how or where data are physically stored. Separating the logical and physical views of data also means that users can change their logical view of data without changing the way data are physically stored. Likewise, the database administrator can change physical storage to improve system performance without affecting users or application programs.

Schemas

A *schema* describes the logical structure of a database. There are three levels of schemas: the conceptual, the external, and the internal. Figure 5 shows the relationships among these three levels. The *conceptual-level schema*, the organization wide view of the *entire* database, lists all data elements and the relationships among them. The *external-level schema* consists of individual user views of portions of the database, each of which is referred to as a *subschema*. The *internal-level schema*, a low-level view of the database, describes how the data are stored and accessed, including record layouts, definitions, addresses, and indexes. Figure 5 connects each of the levels with bidirectional arrows to represent schema mappings. The DBMS uses the mappings to translate a user's or a program's request for data (expressed in terms of logical names and relationships) into the indexes and addresses needed to physically access the data.

At S&S, the conceptual schema for the revenue cycle database contains data about customers, sales, cash receipts, sales personnel, cash, and inventory. External subschemas are derived from this schema, each tailored to the needs of different users or programs. Each subschema can prevent access to those portions of the database that do not apply to it. For example,

FIGURE 3
Accounts Receivable File Record Layout

Customer Number N	Customer Name A		Address A	Credit Limit N	Balance N
1 10	11 30	31	60	61 68	69 76

A = alphanumeric field
N = numeric field

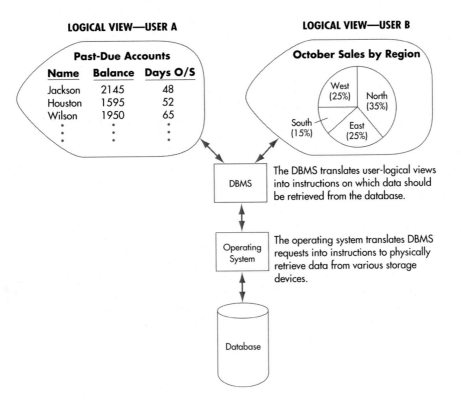

LOGICAL VIEW—USER A

Past-Due Accounts

Name	Balance	Days O/S
Jackson	2145	48
Houston	1595	52
Wilson	1950	65

LOGICAL VIEW—USER B

October Sales by Region

West (25%)
North (35%)
South (15%)
East (25%)

DBMS

The DBMS translates user-logical views into instructions on which data should be retrieved from the database.

Operating System

The operating system translates DBMS requests into instructions to physically retrieve data from various storage devices.

Database

FIGURE 4

Function of the DBMS: To Support Multiple Logical Views of Data

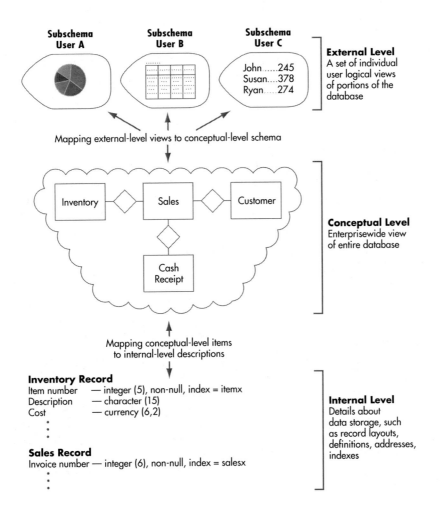

Subschema User A

Subschema User B

Subschema User C

John 245
Susan....378
Ryan.....274

External Level
A set of individual user logical views of portions of the database

Mapping external-level views to conceptual-level schema

Inventory — Sales — Customer

Cash Receipt

Conceptual Level
Enterprisewide view of entire database

Mapping conceptual-level items to internal-level descriptions

Inventory Record
Item number — integer (5), non-null, index = itemx
Description — character (15)
Cost — currency (6,2)

Sales Record
Invoice number — integer (6), non-null, index = salesx

Internal Level
Details about data storage, such as record layouts, definitions, addresses, indexes

FIGURE 5

Three Levels of Schemas

the sales order entry subschema includes data about customer credit limits, current balances, and inventory quantities and prices. It would not include the cost of inventory or bank account balances.

The Data Dictionary

A *data dictionary* contains information about the structure of the database. As shown in Table 1, for each data element stored in the database, there is a record in the dictionary describing it. The DBMS maintains the data dictionary, whose inputs include new or deleted data elements and changes in data element names, descriptions, or uses. Outputs include reports for programmers, designers, and users such as (1) programs or reports using a data item, (2) synonyms for the data elements in a file, and (3) data elements used by a user. These reports are used for system documentation, for database design and implementation, and as part of the audit trail.

DBMS Languages

A DBMS has several languages. The *data definition language (DDL)* builds the data dictionary, creates the database, describes logical views for each user, and specifies records or field security constraints. The *data manipulation language (DML)* changes database content, including data element updates, insertions, and deletions. The *data query language (DQL)* contains powerful, easy-to-use commands that enable users to retrieve, sort, order, and display data. A *report writer* simplifies report creation. Users specify the data elements they want printed, and the report writer searches the database, extracts the data elements, and prints them in the user-specified format. The DQL and report writer are available to users. The DDL and DML should be restricted to authorized administrators and programmers.

Relational Databases

A DBMS is characterized by the logical *data model*, or abstract representation of database contents, upon which it is based. As most new DBMSs are relational databases, this chapter focuses primarily on them. The *relational data model* represents conceptual- and external-level schemas as if data are stored in tables like the one shown in Table 2. The data are actually stored not in tables, but in the manner described in the internal-level schema.

Each row in a table, called a *tuple* (rhymes with *couple*), contains data about a specific occurrence of the type of entity represented by that table. Each column contains data about an attribute of that entity. For example, each row in Table 2 contains data about a particular inventory item that S&S carries, and each column contains data about specific inventory attributes, such as description, color, and price. Similarly, each row in a customer table contains data about a specific customer, and each column contains data about customer attributes, such as name and address.

Types of Attributes

A *primary key* is the database attribute, or combination of attributes, that uniquely identifies a specific row in a table. The primary key in Table 2 is Item Number as it uniquely identifies each merchandise item that S&S sells. Usually, the primary key is a single attribute. In some tables, two or more attributes are needed to identify uniquely a specific row in a table. The primary key of the Sales-Inventory table in Table 5 is the combination of Sales Invoice # and Item #.

A *foreign key, which* is an attribute that is a primary key in another table, is used to link tables. Customer # in Table 5 is the primary key in the Customer table and a foreign key in the Sales table. In the Sales table, Customer # links a sale to data about the customer who made the purchase, as contained in the Customer table (see arrows connecting tables).

Other nonkey attributes in a table store important information about that entity. The inventory table in Table 2 contains information about the description, color, vendor number, quantity on hand, and price of each item S&S carries.

TABLE 1 Example of a Data Dictionary

Data Element Name	Description	Records in Which Contained	Source	Field Length	Field Type	Programs in Which Used	Outputs in Which Contained	Authorized Users	Other Data Names
Customer number	Unique identifier of each customer	A/R record, customer record, sales analysis record	Customer number listing	10	Numeric	A/R update, customer file update, sales analysis update, credit analysis	A/R aging report, customer status report, sales analysis report, credit report	No restrictions	None
Customer name	Complete name of customer	Customer record	Initial customer order	20	Alphanumeric	Customer file update, statement processing	Customer status report, monthly statement	No restrictions	None
Address	Street, city, state, and Zip code	Customer record	Credit application	30	Alphanumeric	Customer file update, statement processing	Customer status report, monthly statement	No restrictions	None
Credit limit	Maximum credit that can be extended to customer	Customer record, A/R record	Credit application	8	Numeric	Customer file update, A/R update, credit analysis	Customer status report, A/R aging report, credit report	D. Dean R. Dalebout H. Heaton	CR_limit
Balance	Balance due from customer on credit purchases	A/R record, sales analysis record	Various sales and payment transactions	8	Numeric	A/R update, sales analysis update, statement processing, credit analysis	A/R aging report, sales analysis report, monthly statement, credit report	G. Burton B. Heninger S. Summers	Cust_bal

TABLE 2 Sample Inventory Table for S&S

Item Number	Description	Color	Vendor Number	Quantity on Hand	Price
1036	Refrigerator	White	10023	12	1199
1038	Refrigerator	Almond	10023	7	1299
1039	Refrigerator	Hunter Green	10023	5	1499
2061	Range	White	10011	6	799
2063	Range	Black	10011	5	999
3541	Washer	White	10008	15	499
3544	Washer	Black	10008	10	699
3785	Dryer	White	10019	12	399
3787	Dryer	Almond	10019	8	499

Record: 10 of 10

Designing a Relational Database for S&S, Inc.

In a manual accounting system, S&S would capture sales information on a preprinted sales invoice that provides both a logical and physical view of the data collected. Physical storage of sales invoice data is simple; S&S stores a copy of the invoice in a file cabinet.

Storing the same data in a computer is more complex. Suppose S&S wanted to store five sales invoices (numbered 101 to 105) electronically. On several invoices, a customer buys more than one item. Let us look at the effects of several ways of storing this information.

1: Store All Data in One Uniform Table.   S&S could store sales data in one table, as illustrated in Table 3. This approach has two disadvantages. First, it stores lots of redundant data. Examine invoice 102 in Table 3. Because three inventory items are sold, invoice and customer data (columns 1–9) are recorded three times. Likewise, inventory descriptions and unit prices are repeated each time an item is sold. Because sales volumes are high in a retail store (remember, Table 3 represents only five invoices), such redundancy makes file maintenance unnecessarily time-consuming and error-prone.

Second, problems occur when invoice data are stored in one table. The first is called an *update anomaly*, because data value updates are not correctly recorded. Changing a customer's address involves searching the entire table and changing every occurrence of that customer's address. Overlooking even one row creates an inconsistency, because multiple addresses would exist for the same customer. This could result in unnecessary duplicate mailings and other errors.

An *insert anomaly* occurs in our example because there is no way to store information about prospective customers until they make a purchase. If prospective customer data is entered before a purchase is made, the Sales Invoice # column would be blank. However, the sales invoice number is the primary key for Table 3 and cannot be blank, as it uniquely identifies the record.

A *delete anomaly* occurs when deleting a row has unintended consequences. If a customer had one purchase of a single item, deleting that row erases all data about that customer.

2: Vary the Number of Columns.   An alternative to Table 3 is to record sales invoice and customer data once and add additional columns to record each item sold. Table 4 illustrates this approach. Although this reduces data redundancy and eliminates some anomalies associated with Table 3, it has drawbacks. S&S would have to decide in advance how many item numbers to leave room for in each row (that is, how many columns to put in the table; note in Table 4 that to store each additional item requires five additional columns—Item, Quantity, Description, Unit Price, and Extended Amount). If room is left for four items (20 columns), how would data about a sale involving eight items (40 columns) be stored? If room is left for eight items, however, there will be a great deal of wasted space, as is the case for sales invoices 103 and 104.

TABLE 3 Example of Storing All Sales Data for S&S in One Table

Sales : Table

Sales Invoice #	Date	Salesperson	Customer #	Invoice Total	Customer Name	Street	City	State	Item #	Quantity	Description	Unit Price	Extended Amount
101	10/15/2015	J. Buck	151	1447	D. Ainge	123 Lotus Lane	Phoenix	AZ	10	2	Television	499	998
101	10/15/2015	J. Buck	151	1447	D. Ainge	123 Lotus Lane	Phoenix	AZ	50	1	Microwave	449	449
102	10/15/2015	S. Knight	152	4394	G. Kite	40 Quatro Road	Mesa	AZ	10	1	Television	499	499
102	10/15/2015	S. Knight	152	4394	G. Kite	40 Quatro Road	Mesa	AZ	20	3	Freezer	699	2097
102	10/15/2015	S. Knight	152	4394	G. Kite	40 Quatro Road	Mesa	AZ	30	2	Refrigerator	899	1798
103	10/15/2015	S. Knight	151	898	D. Ainge	123 Lotus Lane	Phoenix	AZ	50	2	Microwave	449	898
104	10/15/2015	J. Buck	152	789	G. Kite	40 Quatro Road	Mesa	AZ	40	1	Range	789	789
105	11/14/2015	J. Buck	153	3994	F. Roberts	401 Excel Way	Chandler	AZ	10	3	Television	499	1497
105	11/14/2015	J. Buck	153	3994	F. Roberts	401 Excel Way	Chandler	AZ	20	1	Freezer	699	699
105	11/14/2015	J. Buck	153	3994	F. Roberts	401 Excel Way	Chandler	AZ	30	2	Refrigerator	899	1798

Record: 11 of 11

TABLE 4 Example of Storing S&S Sales Data by Adding Columns for Each Additional Item Sold

Sales Invoice #	Columns 2-9	Item #	Quantity	Description	Unit Price	Extended Amount	Item #2	Quantity2
101	Same 8	10	2	Television	499	998	50	1
102	columns	10	1	Television	499	499	20	3
103	as in	50	2	Microwave	449	898		
104	Table 4-3	40	1	Range	789	789		
105	above	10	3	Television	499	1497	20	1

Record: 6 of 6

3. The Solution: A Set of Tables. The storage problems in Tables 3 and 4 are solved using a *relational database*. The set of tables in Table 5 represent a well-structured relational database.

Basic Requirements of a Relational Database

We now turn to the guidelines used to develop a properly structured relational database.

1. *Every column in a row must be single valued.* In a relational database, there can only be one value per cell. At S&S, each sale can involve more than one item. On invoice 102, the customer bought a television, a freezer, and a refrigerator. If Item # were an attribute in the Sales table, it would have to take on three values (item numbers 10, 20, and 30). To solve this problem, a Sales-Inventory table was created that lists each item sold on an invoice. The third line in the Sales-Inventory table in Table 5 shows invoice 102 and item number 10 (television). The fourth line shows invoice 102 and item 20 (freezer). The fifth line shows invoice 102 and item 30 (refrigerator). This table repeats the invoice number as often as needed to show all the items purchased on a sales invoice.

2. *Primary keys cannot be null.* A primary key cannot uniquely identify a row in a table if it is null (blank). A non-null primary key ensures that every row in a table represents something and that it can be identified. This is referred to as the *entity integrity rule*. In the Sales-Inventory table in Table 5, no single field uniquely identifies each row. However, the first two columns, taken together, do uniquely identify each row and constitute the primary key.

3. *Foreign keys, if not null, must have values that correspond to the value of a primary key in another table.* Foreign keys link rows in one table to rows in another table. In Table 5, Customer # can link each sales transaction with the customer who participated in that event only if the Sales table Customer # value corresponds to an actual customer number in the Customer table. This constraint, called the *referential integrity rule*, ensures database consistency. Foreign keys can contain null values. For example, when customers pay cash, Customer # in the sales table can be blank.

4. *All nonkey attributes in a table must describe a characteristic of the object identified by the primary key.* Most tables contain other attributes in addition to the primary and foreign keys. In the Customer table in Table 5, Customer # is the primary key, and customer name, street, city, and state are important facts that describe the customer.

These four constraints produce a well-structured (normalized) database in which data are consistent and redundancy is minimized and controlled. In Table 5, having a table for each entity of interest avoids the anomaly problems discussed previously and minimizes redundancy. Redundancy is not eliminated, as certain items, such as Sales Invoice #, appear in more than one table when they are foreign keys. The referential integrity rule ensures that there are no update anomaly problems with the foreign keys.

When data about objects of interest are stored in separate database tables, it is easy to add new data by adding another row to the table. For example, adding a new customer is as simple as adding a new row to the Customer table. Thus, the tables depicted in Table 5 are free from insert anomalies.

Relational databases also simplify data deletion. Deleting sales invoice 105, the only sale to customer 153, does not erase all data about that customer, because it is stored in the Customer table. This avoids delete anomalies.

Description2	Unit Price2	Extended Amou	Item #3	Quantity3	Description3	Unit Price3	Extended Amount3
Microwave	449	449					
Freezer	699	2097	30	2	Refrigerator	899	1798
Freezer	699	699	30	2	Refrigerator	899	1798

of 6

Another benefit of the schema shown in Table 5 is that space is used efficiently. The Sales-Inventory table contains a row for each item sold on each invoice. There are no blank rows, yet all sales data are recorded. In contrast, the schema in Table 4 results in much wasted space.

Two Approaches to Database Design

One way to design a relational database, called **normalization**, assumes that everything is initially stored in one large table. Rules are followed to decompose that initial table into a set of tables in what is called *third normal form (3NF)*, because they are free of update, insert, and delete anomalies. The details of the normalization process can be found in any database textbook.

In an alternative design approach, called **semantic data modeling**, the designer uses knowledge of business processes and information needs to create a diagram that shows what to include in the database. This diagram is used to create a set of relational tables that are already in 3NF.

Semantic data modeling has significant advantages. First, using a system designer's knowledge of business processes facilitates the efficient design of transaction processing databases. Second, the graphical model explicitly represents the organization's business processes and policies and, by facilitating communication with system users, helps ensure that the new system meets users' actual needs.

Creating Relational Database Queries

To retrieve stored data, users query databases. This section of the chapter shows you how to query databases using Microsoft Access. If you want to follow along by creating the queries illustrated in this section, download the S&S In-Chapter Database from the text's Web site. When you open the database and select the Create ribbon, the ribbon in the top half of Table 6 appears. There are two ways to query the database: create a query in Design view (the "Query Design" button) or use the wizard (the "Query Wizard" button). These options are highlighted in the top half of Table 6. In the example shown in Table 6, the Design view is used. Clicking on the "Query Design" button produces the Show Table window shown in Table 6. The user selects the tables needed to produce the desired information; if more tables than necessary are selected, the query may not run properly.

We will use the tables in Table 5 to walk through the steps needed to create and run five queries. This will not make you an expert in querying an Access database, but it will show you how to produce useful information.

Query 1

Query 1 answers two questions: What are the invoice numbers of all sales made to D. Ainge, and who was the salesperson for each sale?

The Sales and Customer tables contain the three items needed to answer this query: Sales Invoice #, Salesperson, and Customer Name. Click the "Query Design" button (see Table 6), and select the Sales and Customer tables by double-clicking on their names or by single-clicking

TABLE 5 Set of Relational Tables for Storing S&S Sales Data

TABLE 6 Creating Queries in the Microsoft Access Database

on the name and clicking the Add button. The selected tables appear as shown in Table 7. A line between the two tables connects the Customer # fields (the Customer table primary key and the Sales table foreign key). Click on Close to make the Show Table window disappears.

To populate the bottom half of the screen shown in Table 7, double-click on Sales Invoice #, Salesperson, and Customer Name or drag and drop them into the Field row. Access automatically checks the box in the Show line, so the item will be shown when the query is run.

Since we only want sales to D. Ainge, enter that in the criteria line of the Customer Name column. Run the query by clicking on the red ! (exclamation) mark on the Query Tools Design ribbon. Table 8 shows the tables used, the relationship of the primary and foreign keys between tables, and the query answer. The query answer does not automatically have the title "Ainge Sales." To assign the query a name, save it by selecting File from the Access menu, then Save Object As, and then enter "Ainge Sales" in the first line of the Save As window, making sure the Object select box is set to "Query," and then clicking OK. When the query is rerun, the title shown in Table 8 will appear.

TABLE 7 Completed Query 1

TABLE 8 Query 1 Relationships and Query Answer

Query Answer

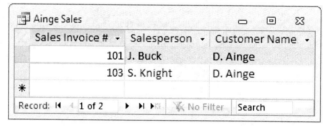

Query 2

Query 2 answers this question: How many televisions were sold in October?

The Sales, Inventory, and Sales-Inventory tables contain the three items needed to answer this query: Date, Inventory Description, and Quantity. Click on the "Query Design" button in the Create ribbon and select the three tables and the three fields, as shown in Table 9. Since we want the quantity of televisions sold in October, we add the criteria "Between #10/1/2015# And #10/31/2015#" to the Date field and "Television" to the Description field.

To specify criteria, Access uses operators such as "And" "Or" and "Between." An "And" operator returns the data that meets *all* the criteria linked by "And" operators. The "Between" operator selects all the data in October of 2015; that is, between and including the first and last days of the month. If the "Between" operator was not used and "Or" replaced "And," all televisions sold either on 10/1/2015 or on 10/31/2015 would be selected. The "#" symbol tells Access to look for a date rather than some other type of text.

Since we are only looking for total television sales in October, we uncheck the "Show" box in the Date and Description columns. To generate total sales, click the "Totals" button in the Show/Hide portion of the Query Tools Design ribbon. A new line, called Total, appears (compare Tables 7 and 9). Click on the Totals line in the Quantity column, then click on the down-arrow symbol, and select Sum from the drop-down menu that appears. The remaining two fields in the Total line will stay as Group By. Running the query in Table 9 produces the answer shown.

TABLE 9 Completed Query 2 and Answer

Query Answer

Query 3

Query 3 answers this question: What are the names and addresses of customers buying televisions in October?

This query needs these fields: Date (to select October sales), Description (to select televisions), and Customer Name, Street, City, and State (the information requested). All four tables are used because the Sales-Inventory table is used to move between the Sales and Inventory tables. The query uses the same criteria as Query 2. The date and description data do not need to be displayed, so the boxes in the Show line are unchecked. Running the query produces the answer shown in Table 10.

Query 4

Query 4 answers this question: What are the sales invoice numbers, dates, and invoice totals for October sales, arranged in descending order by sale amount?

Since the database does not contain an Invoice Total column, it is calculated as follows:

1. For each invoice, calculate the total sales price of each item sold by multiplying the Quantity field in the Sales-Inventory table by the Unit Price field in the Inventory table. The Sales-Inventory table in Table 5 shows that three items were sold on Sales Invoice 102. For item 20, we multiply the quantity (3) by the Unit Price (699), producing 2,097. The same calculation is made for items 10 and 30.
2. Sum the three item totals to get an invoice total.

TABLE 10 Completed Query 3 and Answer

Query Answer

Customer Name	Street	City	State
D. Ainge	124 Lotus Lane	Phoenix	AZ
G. Kite	40 Quatro Road	Mesa	AZ

Record: 1 of 2   No Filter   Search

Query 4 requires the Sales table (Date, Sales Invoice #), Sales-Inventory table (Quantity), and the Inventory table (Unit Price). However, some fields will not appear in columns on the Select Query window. As shown in Table 11, three columns are displayed: Sales Invoice #, Date, and Invoice Total, which we will calculate. The other fields are used in the Invoice Total calculations.

To calculate Invoice Total, type "Invoice Total:" in the first blank Field cell, right-click in the cell, and select Build from the pop-up menu that appears. An Expression Builder window (see Table 12) appears, where the formula to calculate the invoice total is entered by typing "Sum( )". Between the parentheses, click on the + sign in front of the S&S In-Chapter Database folder in the Expressions Elements box. Then clicking on the + sign in the Tables folder causes the four database tables to appear. Click on the Sales-Inventory table, and the fields in the Sales-Inventory table appear. Double-click on Quantity to put this field in the expression. Note in Table 12 that the expression shows the table name and the field name, separated by an exclamation point. To multiply Quantity by Unit Price, type * (the multiplication symbol) and select the Inventory table and the Unit Price field. The formula is now complete, and the screen will appear as shown. To enter the expression into the Select Query window, click on OK.

To complete Query 4, click the Totals button in the Query Tools Design ribbon. Click on the down arrow in the Total row of the Invoice Totals column, and select Expression from the pop-up menu. This tells Access to calculate the indicated expression for all items with the same sales invoice number and date. In the same column, click on the down arrow in the Sort row, and select Descending so that the answer is show in descending Invoice Total order. In the criteria section of the Date column, use the "Between" operator to specify the month of October. Running Query 4 produces the answer shown in Table 11.

TABLE 11 Completed Query 4 and Answer

Query Answer

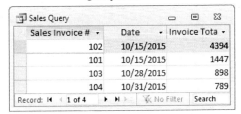

TABLE 12 Expression Builder for Query 4

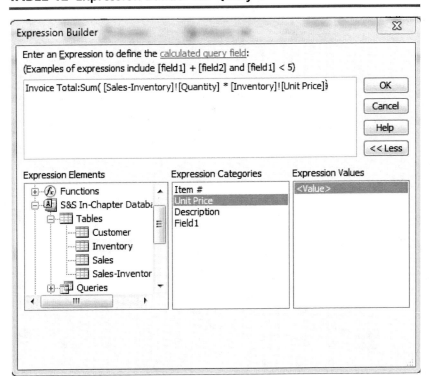

Query 5

Query 5 will answer this question: What are total sales by salesperson?

This query is similar to Query 4, except that we total invoices by salesperson rather than by invoice number. We are also not confining our query to the month of October. Try coming up with the query by yourself. The completed query and the answer are shown in Table 13.

Database Systems and the Future of Accounting

Database systems have the potential to alter external reporting significantly. Considerable time and effort are currently invested in defining how companies should summarize and report accounting information to external users. In the future, companies may make a copy of the company's financial database available to external users in lieu of the traditional financial statements. Users would be free to analyze the raw data however they see fit. Focus 1 discusses this possibility in more detail.

A significant advantage of database systems is the ability to create ad hoc queries to provide the information needed for decision making. No longer is financial information available only in predefined formats and at specified times. Instead, powerful and easy-to-use relational

TABLE 13 Query 5

Query Answer

FOCUS 1 Databases or Financial Statements?

Although information technology has dramatically changed the way business is conducted, it has had less effect on external reporting. Companies still produce highly aggregated, periodic (quarterly and annual) financial reports of past activities based on historical costs. It is estimated that the average financial database of a large company is over 100 gigabytes. Yet annual reports contain only 100 kilobytes of data. Consequently, users see only a small portion of company data presented in a predefined financial statement format.

Why not replace the annual report with a copy of the company's financial database? Many companies already give suppliers and customers limited access to their databases. Suppliers are given access to inventory data to plan production and deliveries. However, they are not given access to payroll data. Companies could similarly exclude data too

sensitive to fall into competitors' hands. This database view could be placed on the Internet for investors, creditors, and other external users. The computing power of PCs makes processing such a database feasible, and external users would get a fuller and timelier picture of the organization's performance.

In such a system, the company's primary financial reporting function would be defining data elements and database structure. Users would be free to aggregate and classify that information using whatever decision model they believed to be appropriate.

Source: Robert K. Elliot, "Confronting the Future: Choices for the Attest Function," *Accounting Horizons* (September 1994): 106–124.

database query languages can find and prepare the information management needs, when they want it.

Relational DBMSs can also accommodate multiple views of the same underlying phenomenon. For example, tables storing information about assets can include columns not only for historical costs but also for current replacement costs and market values. Thus, managers will no longer be forced to look at data in ways predefined by accountants.

Finally, relational DBMSs are capable of integrating financial and operational data. For example, customer satisfaction data could be stored in the database, giving managers a richer set of data for decision making.

Relational DBMSs have the potential to increase the use and value of accounting information. Accountants must understand database systems so they can help design and use the AISs of the future. Such participation is important for ensuring that adequate controls are included in those systems to safeguard the data and ensure the reliability of the information produced.

Summary and Case Conclusion

Ashton prepared a report for Scott and Susan summarizing what he knew about databases. He explained that a database management system (DBMS), the software that makes a database system work, is based on a logical data model that shows how users perceive the way the data are stored. Many DBMSs are based on the relational data model that represents data as being stored in tables. Every row in a relational table has only one data value in each column. Neither row nor column position is significant. These properties support the use of simple, yet powerful, query languages for interacting with the database. Users only need to specify the data they want and do not need to be concerned with how the data are retrieved. The DBMS functions as an intermediary between the user and the database, thereby hiding the complex addressing schemes actually used to retrieve and update the information stored in the database.

After reading Ashton's report, Scott and Susan agreed that it was time to upgrade S&S's AIS and to hire a consulting firm to help select and install the new system. They asked Ashton to oversee the design process to ensure that the new system meets their needs.

Key Terms

database
database management system
   (DBMS)
database system
database administrator
   (DBA)
data warehouse
business intelligence
online analytical processing
   (OLAP)
data mining
record layout
logical view
physical view

schema
conceptual-level schema
external-level schema
subschema
internal-level schema
data dictionary
data definition language
   (DDL)
data manipulation language
   (DML)
data query language
   (DQL)
report writer
data model

relational data model
tuple
primary key
foreign key
update anomaly
insert anomaly
delete anomaly
relational database
entity integrity rule
referential integrity rule
normalization
semantic data modeling

AIS IN ACTION

Chapter Quiz

1. The relational data model portrays data as being stored in _____.
   a. hierarchies
   b. tables
   c. objects
   d. files

2. How a user conceptually organizes and understands data is referred to as the _____.
   a. physical view
   b. logical view
   c. data model view
   d. data organization view

3. What is each row in a relational database table called?
   a. relation
   b. attribute
   c. anomaly
   d. tuple

4. Which of the following is an individual user's view of the database?
   a. conceptual-level schema
   b. external-level schema
   c. internal-level schema
   d. logical-level schema

5. Which of the following would managers most likely use to retrieve information about sales during the month of October?
   a. DML
   b. DSL
   c. DDL
   d. DQL

6. Which of the following attributes would most likely be a primary key?
   a. supplier name
   b. supplier number
   c. supplier Zip code
   d. supplier account balance

7. Which of the following is a software program that runs a database system?
   a. DQL
   b. DBMS
   c. DML
   d. DDL

8. The constraint that all primary keys must have non-null data values is referred to as which of the following?
   a. referential integrity rule
   b. entity integrity rule
   c. normalization rule
   d. relational data model rule

9. The constraint that all foreign keys must have either null values or the value of a primary key in another table is referred to as which of the following?
   a. referential integrity rule
   b. entity integrity rule
   c. foreign key value rule
   d. null value rule

10. Which of the following attributes in the Cash Receipts table (representing payments received from customers) would most likely be a foreign key?
   a. cash receipt number
   b. customer check number
   c. customer number
   d. cash receipt date

Comprehensive Problem

The Butler Financing Company runs a mortgage brokerage business that matches lenders and borrowers. Table 14 lists some of the data that Butler maintains on its borrowers and lenders. The data are stored in a spreadsheet that must be manually updated for each new

TABLE 14 Butler Financing Company Spreadsheet

Borrower Number	Last Name	First Name	Current Address	Requested Mortgage Amount	Lender Number	Lender Name	Lender Office Address	Property Appraiser Number	Property Appraiser Name
450	Adams	Jennifer	450 Peachtree Rd.	$245,000	13	Excel Mortgage	6890 Sheridan Dr.	8	Advent Appraisers
451	Adamson	David	500 Loop Highway	$124,688	13	Excel Mortgage	6890 Sheridan Dr.	9	Independent Appraisal Service
452	Bronson	Paul	312 Mountain View Dr.	$345,000	14	CCY	28 Buckhead Way	10	Jones Property Appraisers
453	Brown	Marietta	310 Loop Highway	$ 57,090	15	Advantage Lenders	3345 Lake Shore Dr.	10	Jones Property Appraisers
454	Charles	Kenneth	3 Commons Blvd.	$ 34,000	16	Capital Savings	8890 Coral Blvd.	8	Advent Appraisers
455	Coulter	Tracey	1367 Peachtree Rd.	$216,505	13	Excel Mortgage	6890 Sheridan Dr.	8	Advent Appraisers
456	Foster	Harold	678 Loop Highway	$117,090	12	National Mortgage	750 16 St.	9	Independent Appraisal Service
457	Frank	Vernon	210 Bicayne Blvd.	$ 89,000	12	National Mortgage	750 16 St.	10	Jones Property Appraisers
458	Holmes	Heather	1121 Bicayne Blvd.	$459,010	16	Capital Savings	8890 Coral Blvd.	10	Jones Property Appraisers
459	Johanson	Sandy	817 Mountain View Dr.	$ 67,900	15	Advantage Lenders	3345 Lake Shore Dr.	9	Independent Appraisal Service
460	Johnson	James	985 Loop Highway	$ 12,000	12	National Mortgage	750 16 St.	10	Jones Property Appraisers
461	Jones	Holly	1650 Washington Blvd.	$ 67,890	15	Advantage Lenders	3345 Lake Shore Dr.	9	Independent Appraisal Service

borrower, lender, or mortgage. This updating is error-prone, which has harmed the business. In addition, the spreadsheet has to be sorted in many different ways to retrieve the necessary data.

Create a database from Butler's spreadsheet that does not have any of the data anomalies explained in the chapter. To test the database, prepare a query to show which borrowers (both borrower number and name) took out loans from Excel Mortgage and who the appraiser was for each loan.

Discussion Questions

1. Contrast the logical and the physical views of data, and discuss why separate views are necessary in database applications. Describe which perspective is most useful for each of the following employees: a programmer, a manager, and an internal auditor. How will understanding logical data structures assist you when designing and using database systems?

2. The relational data model represents data as being stored in tables. Spreadsheets are another tool that accountants use to employ a tabular representation of data. What are some similarities and differences in the way these tools use tables? How might an accountant's familiarity with the tabular representation of spreadsheets facilitate or hinder learning how to use a relational DBMS?

3. Some people believe database technology may eliminate the need for double-entry accounting. This creates three possibilities: (1) the double-entry model will be abandoned; (2) the double-entry model will not be used directly, but an external-level schema based on the double-entry model will be defined for accountants' use; or (3) the double-entry model will be retained in database systems. Which alternative do you think is most likely to occur? Why?

4. Relational DBMS query languages provide easy access to information about the organization's activities. Does this mean that online, real-time processing should be used for all transactions? Does an organization need real-time financial reports? Why or why not?

5. Why is it so important to have good data?

6. What is a data dictionary, what does it contain, and how is it used?

7. Compare and contrast the file-oriented approach and the database approach. Explain the main advantages of database systems.

Problems

1. The following data elements comprise the conceptual-level schema for a database:
   billing address
   cost
   credit limit
   customer name
   customer number
   description
   invoice number

item number
price
quantity on hand
quantity sold
shipping address
terms

Required

a. Identify three potential users and design a subschema for each. Justify your design by explaining why each user needs access to the subschema data elements.

b. Use Microsoft Access or some other relational database product to create the schema tables. Specify the primary key(s), foreign key(s), and other data for each table. Test your model by entering sample data in each table.

2. Most DBMS packages contain data definition, data manipulation, and data query languages. For each of the following, indicate which language would be used and why.

a. A database administrator defines the logical structure of the database.

b. The controller requests a cost accounting report containing a list of all employees being paid for more than 10 hours of overtime in a given week.

c. A programmer develops a program to update the fixed-assets records stored in the database.

d. The human resources manager requests a report noting all employees who are retiring within five years.

e. The inventory serial number field is extended in the inventory records to allow for recognition of additional inventory items with serial numbers containing more than 10 digits.

f. A user develops a program to print out all purchases made during the past two weeks.

g. An additional field is added to the fixed-asset records to record the estimated salvage value of each asset.

3. Ashton wants to store the following data about S&S's purchases of inventory:

item number
date of purchase
vendor number
vendor address
vendor name
purchase price
quantity purchased
employee number
employee name
purchase order number
description
quantity on hand
extended amount
total amount of purchase

Required

a. Design a set of relational tables to store this data. Do all of the data items need to be stored in a table? If not, which ones do not need to be stored, and why do they not need to be stored?

b. Identify the primary key for each table.

c. Identify the foreign keys needed in the tables to implement referential integrity.

d. Implement your tables using any relational database product to which you have access.

e. Test your specification by entering sample data in each table.

f. Create a few queries to retrieve or analyze the data you stored.

4. Retrieve the S&S In-Chapter Database (in Microsoft Access format) from the text's Web site (or create the tables in Table 5 in a relational DBMS product). Write queries to answer the following questions. *Note*: For some questions, you may have to create two queries—one to calculate an invoice total and the second to answer the question asked.
   a. How many different kinds of inventory items does S&S sell?
   b. How many sales were made during October?
   c. What were total sales in October?
   d. What was the average amount of a sales transaction?
   e. Which salesperson made the largest sale?
   f. How many units of each product were sold?
   g. Which product was sold most frequently?

5. Enter the tables in Table 15 into a relational DBMS package. Write queries to answer the following questions. *Note*: For some questions, you may have to create two queries— one to calculate a total and the second to answer the question asked.
   a. Which customers (show their names) made purchases from Martinez?
   b. Who has the largest credit limit?
   c. How many sales were made in October?
   d. What were the item numbers, price, and quantity of each item sold on invoice number 103?
   e. How much did each salesperson sell?
   f. How many customers live in Arizona?
   g. How much credit does each customer still have available?
   h. How much of each item was sold? (Include the description of each item in your answer.)
   i. Which customers still have more than $1,000 in available credit?
   j. For which items are there at least 100 units on hand?

TABLE 15

6. The BusyB Company wants to store data about its employee skills. Each employee may possess one or more specific skills, and several employees may have the same skill. Include the following facts in the database:
date hired
date of birth
date skill acquired
employee name
employee number
pay rate
skill name

TABLE 16 Database That Needs to Be Extended

Item Number	Description	Quantity on Hand	List Price
10573	19" Monitor	13	$495.00
10574	21" Monitor	8	$949.00
10622	Laser Printer	22	$395.00
10623	Color Laser Printer	5	$699.00
10624	Multi-functional Printer	12	$799.00
0			

Inventory Table (Item # is primary key)

Customer Number	Name	Street	City	State	Zip Code	Credit Limit	Account Balance
11255	G. Hwang	2993 Main	Mesa	AZ	85281	$4,000.00	$875.00
12971	J. Jackson	466 W. Oak	Tempe	AZ	85286	$5,000.00	$2,588.00
13629	P. Szabo	246 E. Palm	Mesa	AZ	85281	$6,000.00	$3,955.00
15637	S. Martinez	2866 Spring	Tempe	AZ	85287	$5,000.00	$250.00
18229	B. Adams	1744 Apache	Tempe	AZ	85287	$3,000.00	$1,675.00
0							

Customer Table (Customer # is primary key)

Invoice Number	Date	Salesperson #	Customer #	Amount
10001	9/8/2015	25	15637	$399.00
10002	9/10/2015	22	12971	$1,748.00
10003	9/25/2015	24	13629	$1,185.00
10004	10/2/2015	25	11255	$399.00
10005	10/11/2015	22	15637	$1,098.00
10006	10/25/2015	25	18229	$990.00
0			0	

Sales Table (Invoice # is primary key)

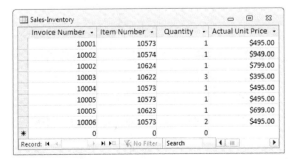

Invoice Number	Item Number	Quantity	Actual Unit Price
10001	10573	1	$495.00
10002	10574	1	$949.00
10002	10624	1	$799.00
10003	10622	3	$395.00
10004	10573	1	$495.00
10005	10573	1	$495.00
10005	10623	1	$699.00
10006	10573	2	$495.00
0	0	0	

Sales-Inventory Line Items Table (Combination of Invoice # and Item # forms primary key)

117

skill number
supervisor

Required

a. Design a set of relational tables to store these data.
b. Identify the primary key for each table, and identify any needed foreign keys.
c. Implement your schema using any relational DBMS. Specify primary and foreign keys, and enforce referential integrity. Demonstrate the soundness of your design by entering sample data in each table.

7. You want to extend the schema shown in Table 16 to include information about customer payments. Some customers make installment payments on each invoice. Others write a check to pay for several different invoices. You want to store the following information:
amount applied to a specific invoice
cash receipt number
customer name
customer number
date of receipt
employee processing payment
invoice payment applies to
total amount received

Required

a. Modify the set of tables in Table 16 to store this additional data.
b. Identify the primary key for each new table you create.
c. Implement your schema using any relational DBMS package. Indicate which attributes are primary and foreign keys, and enter sample data in each table you create.

8. Create relational tables that solve the update, insert, and delete anomalies in Table 17.

TABLE 17 Invoice Table

Invoice #	Date	Order Date	Customer ID	Customer Name	Item #	Description	Quantity
52	6-19-2015	5-25-2015	201	Johnson	103	Trek 9000	5
52	6-19-2015	5-25-2015	201	Johnson	122	Nimbus 4000	8
52	6-19-2015	5-25-2015	201	Johnson	10	Izzod 3000	11
52	6-19-2015	5-25-2015	201	Johnson	71	LD Trainer	12
57	6-20-2015	6-01-2015	305	Henry	535	TR Standard	18
57	6-20-2015	6-01-2015	305	Henry	115	NT 2000	15
57	6-20-2015	6-01-2015	305	Henry	122	Nimbus 4000	5

9. Create relational tables that solve the update, insert, and delete anomalies in Table 18.

TABLE 18 Purchase Order (PO) Table

Purchase Order #	Purchase Date	Order Part #	Description	Unit Price	Quantity Ordered	Vendor #	Vendor Name	Vendor Address
2	3/9/2015	334	XYZ	$30	3	504	KL Supply	75 Stevens Dr.
2	3/9/2015	231	PDQ	$50	5	504	KL Supply	75 Stevens Dr.
2	3/9/2015	444	YYM	$80	6	504	KL Supply	75 Stevens Dr.
3	4/5/2015	231	PDQ	$50	2	889	Oscan Inc	55 Cougar Cir.

TABLE 19 Selected Query Screen for Chapter Comprehensive Problem

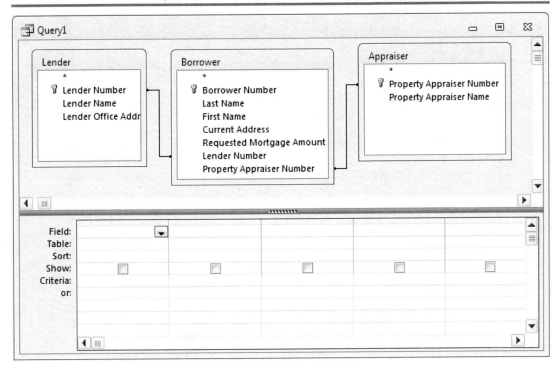

10. From the database created in the comprehensive problem, perform queries based on the tables and query grid shown in Table 19.
   a. Which borrowers use Advent Appraisers?
   b. What is the average amount borrowed from National Mortgage?
   c. List all of the property appraisers.
   d. List all of the lenders.
   e. List the lenders that lent more than $100,000.
   f. Which borrower requested the largest mortgage?
   g. Which borrower requested the smallest mortgage?

Case 1 Research Project

As in all areas of information technology, DBMSs are constantly changing and improving. Research how businesses are using DBMSs, and write a report of your findings. Address the following issues:

1. Which popular DBMS products are based on the relational data model?

2. Which DBMS products are based on a logical model other than the relational data model?

3. What are the relative strengths and weaknesses of the different types (relational versus other logical models) of DBMSs?

AIS IN ACTION SOLUTIONS

Quiz Key

1. The relational data model portrays data as being stored in _____.
   a. hierarchies (Incorrect. A hierarchical database portrays data as being stored in hierarchies.)
   ▶ b. tables (Correct. The relational data model portrays data as being stored in a table or relation format.)
   c. objects (Incorrect. An object-oriented database portrays data as being stored as objects.)
   d. files (Incorrect. The file-based data model portrays data as being stored in files.)

2. How a user conceptually organizes and understands data is referred to as the _____.
   a. physical view (Incorrect. The physical view shows how and where data are physically stored.)
   ▶ b. logical view (Correct. The logical view shows how a user conceptually organizes and understands data.)
   c. data model view (Incorrect. This is not a typical database view.)
   d. data organization view (Incorrect. This is not a typical database view.)

3. What is each row in a relational database table called?
   a. relation (Incorrect. A relation is a table in a relational database.)
   b. attribute (Incorrect. Each column in a relational database is an attribute that describes some characteristic of the entity about which data are stored.)
   c. anomaly (Incorrect. An anomaly is a problem in a database, such as an insert anomaly or a delete anomaly.)
   ▶ d. tuple (Correct. A tuple is also called a row in a relational database.)

4. Which of the following is an individual user's view of the database?
   a. conceptual-level schema (Incorrect. A conceptual-level schema is the organization-wide view of the entire database.)
   ▶ b. external-level schema (Correct. The external-level schema represents an individual user's view of the database.)
   c. internal-level schema (Incorrect. The internal-level schema represents how the data are actually stored and accessed.)
   d. logical-level schema (Incorrect. This is not a schema mentioned in the text.)

5. Which of the following would managers most likely use to retrieve information about sales during the month of October?
   a. DML (Incorrect. DML—data manipulation language—is used for data maintenance.)
   b. DSL (Incorrect. DSL is not a DBMS language.)
   c. DDL (Incorrect. DDL—data definition language—is used to build the data dictionary, create a database, describe logical views, and specify any limitations or constraints on security.)
   ▶ d. DQL (Correct. DQL—data query language—is used to retrieve information from a database.)

6. Which of the following attributes would most likely be a primary key?
   a. supplier name (Incorrect. The primary key must be unique. The same name could be used by multiple entities.)
   ▶ b. supplier number (Correct. A unique number can be assigned as a primary key for each entity.)
   c. supplier Zip code (Incorrect. The primary key must be unique. More than one supplier could reside in the same Zip code.)
   d. supplier account balance (Incorrect. The primary key must be unique. The same account balance, such as a $0.00 balance, could be maintained by multiple entities.)

7. Which of the following is a software program that runs a database system?
   a. DQL (Incorrect. DQL—data query language—is used to retrieve information from a database.)
   ▶ b. DBMS (Correct. A DBMS—database management system—is a software program that acts as an interface between a database and various application programs.)
   c. DML (Incorrect. DML—data manipulation language—is used for data maintenance.)
   d. DDL (Incorrect. DDL—data definition language—is used to build the data dictionary, create a database, describe logical views, and specify any limitations or constraints on security.)

8. The constraint that all primary keys must have non-null data values is referred to as which of the following?
   a. referential integrity rule (Incorrect. The referential integrity rule stipulates that foreign keys must have values that correspond to the value of a primary key in another table or be empty.)
   ▶ b. entity integrity rule (Correct. Every primary key in a relational table must have a non-null value.)
   c. normalization rule (Incorrect. The text does not discuss a normalization rule.)
   d. relational data model rule (Incorrect. The text does not discuss a relational data model rule.)

9. The constraint that all foreign keys must have either null values or the value of a primary key in another table is referred to as which of the following?
   ▶ a. referential integrity rule (Correct. The referential integrity rule stipulates that foreign keys must have values that correspond to the value of a primary key in another table or be empty.)
   b. entity integrity rule (Incorrect. This rule states that every primary key in a relational table must have a non-null value.)
   c. foreign key value rule (Incorrect. The text does not discuss a foreign key value rule.)
   d. null value rule (Incorrect. The text does not discuss a null value rule.)

10. Which of the following attributes in the Cash Receipts table (representing payments received from customers) would most likely be a foreign key?
    a. cash receipt number (Incorrect. A cash receipt number is a good candidate for the primary key of the Cash Receipts table.)
    b. customer check number (Incorrect. Because there is no reason to store customer check numbers in a separate table, it is not a good candidate for a foreign key.)
    ▶ c. customer number (Correct. Customer number would be a foreign key in the Cash Receipts table and would link the Cash Receipts table to the Customer Table.)
    d. cash receipt date (Incorrect. Dates usually are not good candidates for foreign keys. The cash receipt date would likely be an attribute in the Cash Receipts table.)

Comprehensive Problem Solution

Since lender and appraiser data are repeated throughout Table 14, the spreadsheet contains update, insert, and delete anomalies. To eliminate anomaly problems and reduce redundancy, we break the spreadsheet into three smaller tables: borrowers (Table 20), lenders (Table 21), and appraisers (Table 22).

TABLE 20 Borrower Table

Borrower Number (Primary Key)	Last Name	First Name	Current Address	Requested Mortgage Amount	Lender Number (Foreign Key to Lender Table)	Property Appraiser Number (Foreign Key to Appraiser Table)
450	Adams	Jennifer	450 Peachtree Rd.	$245,000	13	8
451	Adamson	David	500 Loop Highway	$124,688	13	9
452	Bronson	Paul	312 Mountain View Dr.	$345,000	14	10
453	Brown	Marietta	310 Loop Highway	$ 57,090	15	10
454	Charles	Kenneth	3 Commons Blvd.	$ 34,000	16	8
455	Coulter	Tracey	1367 Peachtree Rd.	$216,505	13	8
456	Foster	Harold	678 Loop Highway	$117,090	12	9
457	Frank	Vernon	210 Bicayne Blvd.	$ 89,000	12	10
458	Holmes	Heather	1121 Bicayne Blvd.	$459,010	16	10
459	Johanson	Sandy	817 Mountain View Dr.	$ 67,900	15	9
460	Johnson	James	985 Loop Highway	$ 12,000	12	10
461	Jones	Holly	1650 Washington Blvd.	$ 67,890	15	9

TABLE 21 Lender Table

Lender Number (Primary Key)	Lender Name	Lender Office Address
12	National Mortgage	750 16 St.
13	Excel Mortgage	6890 Sheridan Dr.
14	CCY	28 Buckhead Way
15	Advantage Lenders	3345 Lake Shore Dr.
16	Capital Savings	8890 Coral Blvd.

TABLE 22 Appraiser Table

Property Appraiser Number (Primary Key)	Property Appraiser Name
8	Advent Appraisers
9	Independent Appraisal Service
10	Jones Property Appraisers

Borrower number, lender number, and appraiser number are the primary keys because each uniquely identifies the rows in their respective tables. The primary keys from the Lender and Appraiser tables are added to the Borrower table as foreign keys so that the Lender and Appraiser tables will have a direct link to the Borrower table.

Creating smaller tables with primary and foreign keys solves the three anomaly problems.

- The insert anomaly is solved because a new lender and appraiser can be added without requiring a borrower.
- The delete anomaly is solved because deleting a borrower that decides not to pursue a mortgage does not delete information about the lender and appraiser.
- The update anomaly is solved because there is only one row in one table to update when a lender moves and changes its address, instead of changing all spreadsheet rows that store the lender address.

After the data are entered into the Microsoft Access tables, we can query the database. The query in Table 23, which finds the borrowers and appraisers associated with loans from Excel Mortgage, is created as follows:

- From the Query menu option, select "Create Query in Design view."
- Add all three tables to your Query Design. Access automatically links the primary and foreign keys.
- Select the following fields: Borrower Number, Last Name, First Name, Lender Name, and Property Appraiser Name.
- Specify "Excel Mortgage" as the criteria in the Lender Name column.
- Run the query.

TABLE 23 Borrowers with Loans from Excel Mortgage

Query Answer

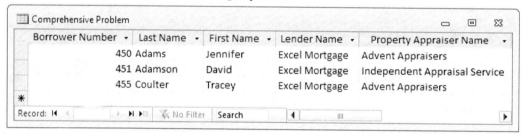

Chapter 5

Computer Fraud

From Chapter 5 of *Accounting Information Systems*, 12/e. Marshall B. Romney. Paul John Steinbart. Copyright © 2012 by Pearson Education. Published by Prentice Hall. All rights reserved.

Computer Fraud

Learning Objectives

After studying this chapter, you should be able to:

1. Explain the threats faced by modern information systems.
2. Define *fraud* and describe the process one follows to perpetuate a fraud.
3. Discuss who perpetrates fraud and why it occurs, including the pressures, opportunities, and rationalizations that are present in most frauds.
4. Define *computer fraud* and discuss the different computer fraud classifications.
5. Explain how to prevent and detect computer fraud and abuse.

INTEGRATIVE CASE NORTHWEST INDUSTRIES

Jason Scott is an internal auditor for Northwest Industries, a forest products company. On March 31, he reviewed his completed tax return and noticed that the federal income tax withholding on his final paycheck was $5 more than the amount indicated on his W-2 form. He used the W-2 amount to complete his tax return and made a note to ask the payroll department what happened to the other $5. The next day, Jason was swamped, and he dismissed the $5 difference as immaterial.

On April 16, a coworker grumbled that the company had taken $5 more from his check than he was given credit for on his W-2. When Jason realized he was not the only one with the $5 discrepancy, he investigated and found that all 1,500 employees had the same $5 discrepancy. He also discovered that the W-2 of Don Hawkins, the payroll programmer, had thousands of dollars more in withholdings reported to the IRS than had been withheld from his paycheck.

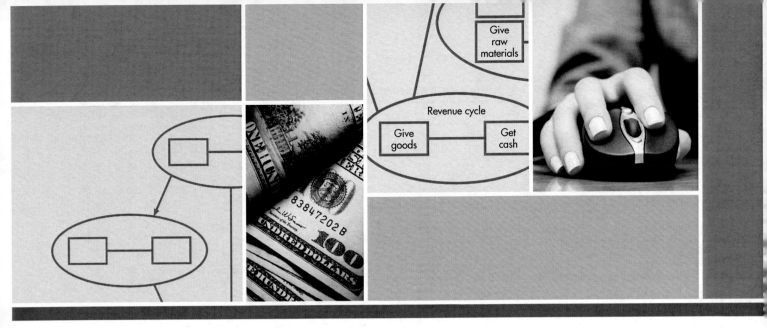

Jason knew that when he reported the situation, management was going to ask questions, such as:

1. What constitutes a fraud, and is the withholding problem a fraud?
2. How was the fraud perpetrated? What motivated Don to commit it?
3. Why did the company not catch these mistakes? Was there a breakdown in controls?
4. How can the company detect and prevent fraud?
5. How vulnerable is the company's computer system to fraud?

Introduction

As accounting information systems grow more complex to meet our escalating needs for information, companies face the growing risk that their systems may be compromised. Recent surveys show that 67% of companies had a security breach, over 45% were targeted by organized crime, and 60% reported financial losses.

The four types of AIS threats a company faces are summarized in Table 1.

AIS Threats

Natural and political disasters—such as fires, floods, earthquakes, hurricanes, tornadoes, blizzards, war, and attacks by terrorists—can destroy an information system and cause many companies to fail. For example:

- Terrorist attacks on the World Trade Center in New York City and on the Federal Building in Oklahoma City destroyed or disrupted all the systems in those buildings.
- A flood in Chicago destroyed or damaged 400 data processing centers. Hurricanes on the East coast of the United States have destroyed many computer systems.
- The Mississippi and Missouri rivers overflowed and flooded parts of eight states. Many organizations lost their systems, including the city of Des Moines, Iowa, whose computers were buried under eight feet of water.

TABLE 1 Threats to Accounting Information Systems

Threats	Examples
Natural and political disasters	Fire or excessive heat
	Floods, earthquakes, landslides, hurricanes, tornadoes, blizzards, snowstorms, and freezing rain
	War and attacks by terrorists
Software errors and equipment malfunctions	Hardware or software failure
	Software errors or bugs
	Operating system crashes
	Power outages and fluctuations
	Undetected data transmission errors
Unintentional acts	Accidents caused by human carelessness, failure to follow established procedures, and poorly trained or supervised personnel
	Innocent errors or omissions
	Lost, erroneous, destroyed, or misplaced data
	Logic errors
	Systems that do not meet company needs or cannot handle intended tasks
Intentional acts (computer crimes)	Sabotage
	Misrepresentation, false use, or unauthorized disclosure of data
	Misappropriation of assets
	Financial statement fraud
	Corruption
	Computer fraud—attacks, social engineering, malware, etc.

- Earthquakes in Los Angeles and San Francisco destroyed numerous computer systems and severed communication lines. Other systems were damaged by falling debris, water from ruptured sprinkler systems, and dust.
- Attacks on government information systems by foreign countries, espionage agents, and terrorists are widespread. Military contractors and businesses are also targets.

Software errors, operating system crashes, hardware failures, power outages and fluctuations, and undetected data transmission errors constitute a second type of threat. Of special concern are vulnerabilities in Microsoft Windows; in a recent survey, 30% of companies had moved systems off Windows to reduce security risks.

A federal study estimated yearly economic losses due to software bugs at almost $60 billion. More than 60% of companies studied had significant software errors in. For example:

- As a result of tax system bugs, California failed to collect $635 million in business taxes.
- Defective software caused massive power failures that left hundreds of thousands of people and businesses without power.
- A bug in Burger King's software resulted in a $4,334.33 debit card charge for four hamburgers. The cashier accidentally keyed in the $4.33 charge twice, resulting in the overcharge.

A third type of threat, unintentional acts such as accidents or innocent errors and omissions, is the greatest risk to information systems and causes the greatest dollar losses. The Computing Technology Industry Association estimates that human errors cause 80% of security problems. Forrester Research estimates that employees unintentionally create legal, regulatory, or financial risks in 25% of their outbound e-mails.

Unintentional acts are caused by human carelessness, failure to follow established procedures, and poorly trained or supervised personnel. Users lose or misplace data and accidentally erase or alter files, data, and programs. Computer operators and users enter the wrong input or erroneous input, use the wrong version of a program or the wrong data files, or misplace data files. Systems analysts develop systems that do not meet company needs, that leave them vulnerable to attack, or that are incapable of handling their intended tasks. Programmers make logic errors. Examples of unintentional acts include the following:

- A data entry clerk at Mizuho Securities mistakenly keyed in a sale for 610,000 shares of J-Com for 1 yen instead of the sale of 1 share for 610,000 yen. The error cost the company $250 million.
- A programmer made a one-line-of-code error that priced all goods at Zappos, an online retailer, at $49.95—even though some of the items it sells are worth thousands of dollars. The change went into effect at midnight, and by the time it was detected at 6:00 A.M., the company had lost $1.6 million on goods sold far below cost.
- A bank programmer mistakenly calculated interest for each month using 31 days. Before the mistake was discovered, over $100,000 in excess interest was paid.
- A Fannie Mae spreadsheet error misstated earnings by $1.2 billion.
- UPS lost a box of computer tapes containing sensitive information on 3.9 million Citigroup customers.
- Jefferson County, West Virginia released a new online search tool that exposed the personal information of 1.6 million people.
- McAfee, the antivirus software vendor, mistakenly identified svchost.exe, a crucial part of the Windows operating system, as a malicious program in one of its updates. Hundreds of thousands of PCs worldwide had to be manually rebooted—a process that took 30 minutes per machine. A third of the hospitals in Rhode Island were shut down by the error. One company reported that the error cost them $2.5 million.

A fourth threat is an intentional act such as a computer crime, a fraud, or **sabotage**, which is deliberate destruction or harm to a system. Information systems are increasingly vulnerable to attack. Symantec estimates that hackers attack computers more than 8.6 million times per day. It is estimated that Internet fraud cost its victims over $600 million a year. In a recent three-year period, the number of networks that were compromised rose 700%. That is just the tip of the iceberg: Experts believe the actual number of incidents is six times higher because companies tend not to report security breaches.

Consider the case of OpenTable, a restaurant reservation service that did not properly design its **cookie** (data a Web site stores on your computer to identify the Web site to your computer so that you do not have to log on each time you visit the site). An experienced programmer opened an account at OpenTable and, in less than an hour, wrote a program that downloaded most of the company's database. Many other companies have had problems with the same type of system vulnerability.

Introduction to Fraud

Fraud is gaining an unfair advantage over another person. Legally, for an act to be fraudulent there must be:

1. A *false statement, representation, or disclosure*
2. A *material fact*, which is something that induces a person to act
3. An *intent to deceive*
4. A *justifiable reliance;* that is, the person relies on the misrepresentation to take an action
5. An *injury or loss* suffered by the victim

No one knows the total losses to fraud each year. Income tax fraud (the difference between what taxpayers owe and what they pay) is estimated to be almost $400 billion a year. Fraud in the health care industry is estimated to exceed $100 billion a year. The Association of Certified Fraud Examiners estimates that:

- Fraud and abuse costs the United States $994 billion a year.
- The average organization loses 7% of its annual revenues to fraud.
- The median fraud loss is $175,000. Financial statement fraud is the most costly fraud, with a median loss of $2 million.
- The average fraud lasted two years.
- The most common frauds are corruption and fraudulent billing schemes.
- Small businesses are especially vulnerable, with check tampering and fraudulent billings the most common frauds.
- Frauds are more likely to be detected by a tip than by audits, controls, or other means.
- The industries most commonly victimized were banking and financial services, government, and health care. The largest median losses occurred in manufacturing ($441,000), banking ($250,000), and insurance ($216,000).
- People in accounting departments committed 29% of frauds; executives or upper management committed 18%. Frauds committed by executives were particularly costly, resulting in a median loss of $853,000.
- Most fraudsters are first-time offenders. Only 7% had prior convictions, and only 12% had been previously terminated by an employer for fraud-related conduct.
- Fraud perpetrators often display behavioral traits related to living beyond their means or struggling to overcome financial difficulties. In financial statement fraud, excessive organizational pressure to perform is a particularly strong warning sign.

An estimated 75% to 90% of computer fraud perpetrators are knowledgeable insiders with the requisite access, skills, and resources. Because employees understand a company's system and its weaknesses, they are better able to commit and conceal a fraud. The controls used to protect corporate assets make it more difficult for an outsider to steal from a company. Fraud perpetrators are often referred to as **white-collar criminals.**

Fraud takes two forms: misappropriation of assets and fraudulent financial reporting.

Misappropriation of Assets

Misappropriation of assets is the theft of company assets. Examples include the following:

- Albert Milano, a manager at *Reader's Digest* responsible for processing bills, embezzled $1 million over a five-year period. He forged a superior's signature on invoices for services never performed, submitted them to accounts payable, forged the endorsement on the check, and deposited it in his account. Milano used the stolen funds to buy an expensive home, five cars, and a boat.
- A bank vice president approved $1 billion in bad loans in exchange for $585,000 in kickbacks. The loans cost the bank $800 million and helped trigger its collapse.
- A manager at a Florida newspaper went to work for a competitor after he was fired. The first employer soon realized its reporters were being scooped. An investigation revealed the manager still had an active account and password and regularly browsed its computer files for information on exclusive stories.

The most significant contributing factor in most misappropriations is the absence of internal controls and/or the failure to enforce existing internal controls. A typical misappropriation has the following important elements or characteristics. The perpetrator:

- Gains the trust or confidence of the entity being defrauded.
- Uses trickery, cunning, or false or misleading information to commit fraud.
- Conceals the fraud by falsifying records or other information.
- Rarely terminates the fraud voluntarily.
- Sees how easy it is to get extra money, need or greed impels the person to continue. Some frauds are self-perpetuating; if perpetrators stop, their actions are discovered.
- Spends the ill-gotten gains. Rarely does the perpetrator save or invest the money. Some perpetrators come to depend on the "extra" income, and others adopt a lifestyle that

requires even greater amounts of money. For these reasons, there are no small frauds—only large ones that are detected early.

- Gets greedy and takes ever-larger amounts of money at intervals that are more frequent, exposing the perpetrator to greater scrutiny and increasing the chances the fraud is discovered. The sheer magnitude of some frauds leads to their detection. For example, the accountant at an auto repair shop, a lifelong friend of the shop's owner, embezzled ever-larger sums of money over a seven-year period. In the last year of the fraud, the embezzler took over $200,000. Facing bankruptcy, the owner eventually laid off the accountant and had his wife take over the bookkeeping. When the company immediately began doing better, the wife investigated and uncovered the fraud.
- Grows careless or overconfident as time passes. If the size of the fraud does not lead to its discovery, the perpetrator eventually makes a mistake that does lead to the discovery.

Fraudulent Financial Reporting

The National Commission on Fraudulent Financial Reporting (the Treadway Commission) defined **fraudulent financial reporting** as intentional or reckless conduct, whether by act or omission, that results in materially misleading financial statements. Financial statements are falsified to deceive investors and creditors, increase a company's stock price, meet cash flow needs, or hide company losses and problems. The Treadway Commission studied 450 lawsuits against auditors and found undetected fraud to be a factor in half of them.

Through the years, many highly publicized financial statement frauds have occurred. In each case, misrepresented financial statements led to huge financial losses and a number of bankruptcies. The most frequent "cook the books" schemes involve fictitiously inflating revenues, holding the books open (recognizing revenues before they are earned), closing the books early (delaying current expenses to a later period), overstating inventories or fixed assets, and concealing losses and liabilities.

The Treadway Commission recommended four actions to reduce fraudulent financial reporting:

1. Establish an organizational environment that contributes to the integrity of the financial reporting process.
2. Identify and understand the factors that lead to fraudulent financial reporting.
3. Assess the risk of fraudulent financial reporting within the company.
4. Design and implement internal controls to provide reasonable assurance of preventing fraudulent financial reporting.

The Association of Certified Fraud Examiners found that an asset misappropriation is 17 times more likely than fraudulent financial reporting but that the amounts involved are much smaller. As a result, auditors and management are more concerned with fraudulent financial reporting even though they are more likely to encounter misappropriations. The following section discusses an auditors' responsibility for detecting material fraud.

SAS No. 99: The Auditor's Responsibility to Detect Fraud

Statement on Auditing Standards (SAS) No. 82, *Consideration of Fraud in a Financial Statement Audit*, was adopted in 1997 to clarify the auditor's responsibility to detect fraud. It was revised as SAS No. 99, with the same title, and became effective in December 2002. SAS No. 99 requires auditors to:

- *Understand fraud.*   Because auditors cannot effectively audit something they do not understand, they must understand fraud and how and why it is committed.
- *Discuss the risks of material fraudulent misstatements.*   While planning the audit, team members discuss among themselves how and where the company's financial statements are susceptible to fraud.
- *Obtain information.*   The audit team gathers evidence by looking for fraud risk factors; testing company records; and asking management, the audit committee of the board of

directors, and others whether they know of past or current fraud. Because many frauds involve revenue recognition, special care is exercised in examining revenue accounts.

- *Identify, assess, and respond to risks.* The evidence is used to identify, assess, and respond to fraud risks by varying the nature, timing, and extent of audit procedures and by evaluating carefully the risk of management overriding internal controls.
- *Evaluate the results of their audit tests.* Auditors must evaluate whether identified misstatements indicate the presence of fraud and determine its impact on the financial statements and the audit.
- *Document and communicate findings.* Auditors document and communicate their findings to management and the audit committee.
- *Incorporate a technology focus.* SAS No. 99 recognizes the impact technology has on fraud risks and provides commentary and examples recognizing this impact. It also notes the opportunities auditors have to use technology to design fraud-auditing procedures.

Who Perpetrates Fraud and Why

When researchers compared the psychological and demographic characteristics of white-collar criminals, violent criminals, and the public, they found significant differences between violent and white-collar criminals. They found few differences between white-collar criminals and the public. Their conclusion: Fraud perpetrators look just like you and me.

Some fraud perpetrators are disgruntled and unhappy with their jobs and seek revenge against employers. Others are dedicated, hard-working, and trusted employees. Most have no previous criminal record; they were honest, valued, and respected members of their community.

Computer fraud perpetrators are younger and possess more computer experience and skills. Some are motivated by curiosity, a quest for knowledge, the desire to learn how things work, and the challenge of beating the system. Some view their actions as a game rather than as dishonest behavior. Others commit computer fraud to gain stature in the hacking community.

A large and growing number of computer fraud perpetrators seek to turn their actions into money. Malicious software is a big business and a huge profit engine for the criminal underground, especially for digitally savvy hackers in Eastern Europe. They break into financial accounts and steal money. They sell data to spammers, organized crime, hackers, and the intelligence community. They market malware, such as virus-producing software, to others. Some work with organized crime. A recently convicted hacker was paid $150 for every 1,000 computers he infected with his adware and earned hundreds of thousands of dollars a year.

Cyber-criminals are a top FBI priority because they have moved from isolated and uncoordinated attacks to organized fraud schemes targeted at specific individuals and businesses. They use online payment companies to launder their ill-gotten gains. To hide their money, they take advantage of the lack of coordination between international law enforcement organizations.

The Fraud Triangle

Three conditions are present when fraud occurs: a pressure, an opportunity, and a rationalization. This is referred to as the fraud triangle, and is the middle triangle in Figure 1.

PRESSURES   A **pressure** is a person's incentive or motivation for committing fraud. Three types of pressures that lead to misappropriations are shown in the Employee Pressure Triangle in Figure 1 and are summarized in Table 2.

Financial pressures often motivate misappropriation frauds by employees. Examples of such pressures include living beyond one's means, heavy financial losses, or high personal debt. Often, the perpetrator feels the pressure cannot be shared and believes fraud is the best way out of a difficult situation. For example, Raymond Keller owned a grain elevator where he stored grain for local farmers. He made money by trading in commodities and built a lavish house overlooking the Des Moines River. Heavy financial losses created a severe cash shortage and high debt. He asked some farmers to wait for their money, gave others bad checks, and sold grain that did not belong to him. Finally, the seven banks to which he owed over $3 million began to call their loans. When a state auditor showed up unexpectedly, Raymond took his life rather than face the consequences of his fraud.

132

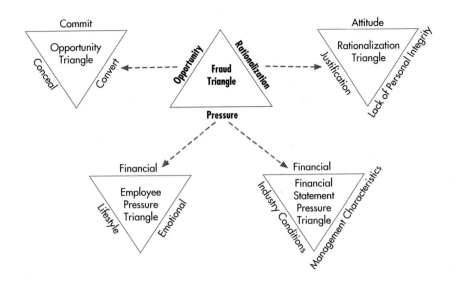

FIGURE 1
Fraud Triangles

TABLE 2 Pressures That Can Lead to Employee Fraud

Financial	Emotional	Lifestyle
Living beyond one's means	Greed	Gambling habit
High personal debt/expenses	Performance not recognized	Drug or alcohol addiction
"Inadequate" salary/income	Job dissatisfaction	Sexual relationships
Poor credit ratings	Fear of losing job	Family/peer pressure
Heavy financial losses	Need for power or control	
Bad investments	Excessive pride or ambition	
Tax avoidance	Overt, deliberate nonconformity	
Unreasonable quotas/goals	Inability to abide by or respect rules	
	Challenge of beating the system	
	Envy or resentment against others	

A second type of pressure is emotional. Many employee frauds are motivated by greed. Some employees turn to fraud because they have strong feelings of resentment or believe they have been treated unfairly. They may feel their pay is too low, their contributions are not appreciated, or the company is taking advantage of them. A California accountant, passed over for a raise, increased his salary by 10%, the amount of the average raise. He defended his actions by saying he was only taking what was rightfully his. When asked why he did not increase his salary by 11%, he responded that he would have been stealing 1%.

Other people are motivated by the challenge of "beating the system" or subverting system controls and breaking into a system. When a company boasted that its new system was impenetrable, a team of individuals took less than 24 hours to break into the system and leave a message that the system had been compromised.

A third type of employee pressure is a person's lifestyle. The person may need funds to support a gambling habit or support a drug or alcohol addiction. Some people commit fraud to keep pace with other family members. A plastic surgeon, making $800,000 a year, defrauded his clinic of $200,000 to compete in the family "game" of financial one-upmanship.

Three types of organizational pressures that motivate management to misrepresent financial statements are shown in the Financial Statement Pressure triangle in Figure 1 and summarized in Table 3. A prevalent financial pressure is a need to meet or exceed earnings expectations to keep a stock price from falling. Managers create significant pressure with unduly aggressive earnings forecasts or unrealistic performance standards or with incentive programs that motivate employees to falsify financial results to keep their jobs or to receive stock options and other incentive payments. Industry conditions such as new regulatory requirements or significant market saturation with declining margins can motivate fraud.

TABLE 3 Pressures That Can Lead to Financial Statement Fraud

Management Characteristics	Industry Conditions	Financial
Questionable management ethics, management style, and track record	Declining industry	Intense pressure to meet or exceed earnings expectations
Unduly aggressive earnings forecasts, performance standards, accounting methods, or incentive programs	Industry or technology changes leading to declining demand or product obsolescence	Significant cash flow problems; unusual difficulty collecting receivables, paying payables
Significant incentive compensation based on achieving unduly aggressive goals	New regulatory requirements that impair financial stability or profitability	Heavy losses, high or undiversified risk, high dependence on debt, or unduly restrictive debt covenants
Management actions or transactions with no clear business justification	Significant competition or market saturation, with declining margins	Heavy dependence on new or unproven product lines
Oversensitivity to the effects of alternative accounting treatments on earnings per share	Significant tax changes or adjustments	Severe inventory obsolescence or excessive inventory buildup
Strained relationship with past auditors		Economic conditions (inflation, recession)
Failure to correct errors on a timely basis, leading to even greater problems		Litigation, especially management vs. shareholders
High management/employee turnover		Impending business failure or bankruptcy
Unusual/odd related-party relationships		Problems with regulatory agencies
		High vulnerability to rise in interest rates
		Poor or deteriorating financial position
		Unusually rapid growth or profitability compared to companies in same industry
		Significant estimates involving highly subjective judgments or uncertainties

OPPORTUNITIES   As shown in the Opportunity Triangle in Figure 1, **opportunity** is the condition or situation that allows a person or organization to do three things:

1. *Commit the fraud.*   The theft of assets is the most common type of misappropriation. Most instances of fraudulent financial reporting involve overstatements of assets or revenues, understatements of liabilities, or failures to disclose information.
2. *Conceal the fraud.*   To prevent detection when assets are stolen or overstated, perpetrators must keep the accounting equation in balance by inflating other assets or decreasing liabilities or equity. Concealment often takes more effort and time and leaves behind more evidence than the theft or misrepresentation. Taking cash requires only a few seconds; altering records to hide the theft is more challenging and time-consuming.

    One way to hide a theft is to charge the stolen item to an expense account. The perpetrator's exposure is limited to a year or less, because expense accounts are zeroed out at the end of each year. Perpetrators who hide a theft in a balance sheet account must continue the concealment. In a **lapping** scheme, a perpetrator steals the cash or checks customer A mails in to pay its accounts receivable. Later, funds from customer B are used to pay off customer A's balance. Funds from customer C are used to pay off customer B's balance, and so forth. Because the theft involves two asset accounts (cash and accounts receivable), the cover-up must continue indefinitely unless the money is replaced.

    In check **kiting**, cash is created using the lag between the time a check is deposited and the time it clears the bank. Suppose a fraud perpetrator opens accounts in banks A, B, and C. The perpetrator "creates" cash by depositing a $1,000 check from bank B in bank C and withdrawing the funds. If it takes two days for the check to clear bank B, he has created $1,000 for two days. After two days, the perpetrator deposits a $1,000 check from bank A in bank B to cover the created $1,000 for two more days. At the appropriate time, $1,000 is deposited from bank C in bank A. The scheme continues—writing checks and making deposits as needed to keep the checks from bouncing.
3. *Convert the theft or misrepresentation to personal gain.*   In a misappropriation, fraud perpetrators who do not steal cash or use the stolen assets personally must convert them to

a spendable form. For example, employees who steal inventory or equipment sell the items or otherwise convert them to cash. In cases of falsified financial statements, perpetrators convert their actions to personal gain through indirect benefits; that is, they keep their jobs, their stock rises, they receive pay raises and promotions, or they gain more power and influence.

Table 4 lists frequently mentioned opportunities. Many opportunities are the result of a deficient system of internal controls, such as deficiencies in proper segregation of duties, authorization procedures, clear lines of authority, proper supervision, adequate documents and records, safeguarding assets, or independent checks on performance. Management permits fraud by inattention or carelessness. Management commits fraud by overriding internal controls or using a position of power to compel subordinates to perpetrate it. The most prevalent opportunity for fraud results from a company's failure to design and *enforce* its internal control system.

Companies who do not perform a background check on potential employees risk hiring a "phantom controller." In one case, the company president stopped by the office one night, saw a light on in the controller's office, and went to see why he was working late. The president was surprised to find a complete stranger at work. An investigation showed that the controller was not an accountant and had been fired from three jobs over the prior eight years. Unable to do the accounting work, he hired someone to do his work for him at night. What he was good at was stealing money—he had embezzled several million dollars.

Other factors provide an opportunity to commit and conceal fraud when the company has unclear policies and procedures, fails to teach and stress corporate honesty, and fails to prosecute those who perpetrate fraud. Examples include large, unusual, or complex transactions; numerous adjusting entries at year-end; questionable accounting practices; pushing accounting principles to the limit; related-party transactions; incompetent personnel, inadequate staffing, rapid turnover of key employees, lengthy tenure in a key job, and lack of training.

Frauds occur when employees build mutually beneficial personal relationships with customers or suppliers, such as a purchasing agent buying goods at an inflated price in exchange for a vendor kickback. Fraud can also occur when a crisis arises and normal control procedures are ignored. A Fortune 500 company had three multimillion-dollar frauds the year it disregarded standard internal control procedures while trying to resolve a series of crises.

TABLE 4 Opportunities Permitting Employee and Financial Statement Fraud

Internal Control Factors	Other Factors
Failure to enforce/monitor internal controls	Large, unusual, or complex transactions
Management's failure to be involved in the control system	Numerous adjusting entries at year-end
Management override of controls	Related-party transactions
Managerial carelessness, inattention to details	Accounting department that is understaffed, overworked
Dominant and unchallenged management	Incompetent personnel
Ineffective oversight by board of directors	Rapid turnover of key employees
No effective internal auditing staff	Lengthy tenure in a key job
Infrequent third-party reviews	Overly complex organizational structure
Insufficient separation of authorization, custody, and record-keeping duties	No code of conduct, conflict-of-interest statement, or definition of unacceptable behavior
Too much trust in key employees	Frequent changes in auditors, legal counsel
Inadequate supervision	Operating on a crisis basis
Unclear lines of authority	Close association with suppliers/customers
Lack of proper authorization procedures	Assets highly susceptible to misappropriation
No independent checks on performance	Questionable accounting practices
Inadequate documents and records	Pushing accounting principles to the limit
Inadequate system for safeguarding assets	Unclear company policies and procedures
No physical or logical security system	Failing to teach and stress corporate honesty
No audit trails	Failure to prosecute dishonest employees
Failure to conduct background checks	Low employee morale and loyalty
No policy of annual vacations, rotation of duties	

RATIONALIZATIONS   A **rationalization** allows perpetrators to justify their illegal behavior. As shown in the Rationalization Triangle in Figure 1, this can take the form of a justification ("I only took what they owed me"), an attitude ("The rules do not apply to me"), or a lack of personal integrity ("Getting what I want is more important than being honest"). In other words, perpetrators rationalize that they are not being dishonest, that honesty is not required of them, or that they value what they take more than honesty and integrity. Some perpetrators rationalize that they are not hurting a real person, but a faceless and nameless computer system or an impersonal company that will not miss the money. One such perpetrator stole no more than $20,000, the maximum loss the insurance company would reimburse.

The most frequent rationalizations include the following:

- I am only "borrowing" it, and I will repay my "loan."
- You would understand if you knew how badly I needed it.
- What I did was not that serious.
- It was for a good cause. (The Robin Hood syndrome: robbing the rich to give to the poor)
- In my very important position of trust, I am above the rules.
- Everyone else is doing it.
- No one will ever know.
- The company owes it to me; I am taking no more than is rightfully mine.

Fraud occurs when people have high pressures; an opportunity to commit, conceal, and convert; and the ability to rationalize away their personal integrity. Fraud is less likely to occur when people have few pressures, little opportunity, and high personal integrity. Usually all three elements of the fraud triangle must be present to some degree before a person commits fraud.

Likewise, fraud can be prevented by eliminating or minimizing one or more fraud triangle elements. Although companies can reduce or minimize some pressures and rationalizations, their greatest opportunity to prevent fraud lies in reducing or minimizing opportunity by implementing a good system of internal controls.

Computer Fraud

Computer fraud is any fraud that requires computer technology knowledge to perpetrate, investigate, or prosecute it.. Examples include the following:

- Unauthorized theft, use, access, modification, copying, or destruction of software or data
- Theft of assets by altering computer records
- Theft of computer time
- Theft or destruction of hardware or software
- Use of computer resources to commit a felony
- Intent to obtain information or tangible property illegally using computers

Millions of dollars can be stolen in less than a second, leaving little or no evidence. Therefore, computer fraud can be much more difficult to detect than other types of fraud.

The Rise in Computer Fraud

Computer systems are particularly vulnerable for the following reasons:

- People who break into corporate databases can steal, destroy, or alter massive amounts of data in very little time. One bank lost $10 million in cash in a single day.
- Perpetrators can steal many more assets with much less time and effort.
- Some organizations grant employees, customers, and suppliers access to their system. The number and variety of these access points significantly increase the risks.
- Computer programs need to be modified illegally only once for them to operate improperly for as long as they are in use.
- Personal computers (PCs) are vulnerable to security risks. It is difficult to control physical access to each PC that accesses the network. The more legitimate users there are, the greater the risk of an attack on the network. PC users are generally less aware of the

importance of security and control. Segregation of systems duties is difficult because PCs are located in user departments, and one person may be responsible for both development and operations. PCs and their data can be lost, stolen, or misplaced.

● Computer systems face a number of unique challenges: reliability, equipment failure, environmental dependency (i.e., power, damage from water or fire), vulnerability to electromagnetic interference and interruption, eavesdropping, and misrouting.

As early as 1979, *Time* magazine labeled computer fraud a "growth industry." Most businesses have been victimized by computer fraud. During a one-year period, the estimated dollar losses from unauthorized employee computer fraud and abuse in the United States increased 15-fold, from $181,400 to $2.81 million per incident. A few years ago, it was estimated that U.S. Defense Department computers were attacked more than a half million times per year, with the number of incidents increasing 50% to 100% per year. Defense Department staffers and outside consultants made 38,000 "friendly hacks" on their networks to evaluate security. Almost 70% were successful, and the Defense Department detected only 4% of the attacks; the others went unnoticed. The Pentagon, which has the U.S. government's most advanced hacker-awareness program, detected and reported only 1 in 500 break-ins. The Defense Department estimates that more than 100 foreign spy agencies are working to gain access to U.S. government computers as well as an unknown number of criminal organizations. Recently, a spy network in China hacked into 1,300 government and corporate computers in 103 countries.

The number of incidents, the total dollar losses, and the sophistication of the perpetrators and the schemes used to commit computer fraud are increasing rapidly for several reasons:

1. *Not everyone agrees on what constitutes computer fraud.* Many people, for example, do not believe that copying software constitutes computer fraud. Software publishers think otherwise and prosecute those who make illegal copies. Some people do not think it is a crime to browse someone else's computer files if they do no harm, whereas companies whose data are browsed feel much differently.

2. *Many instances of computer fraud go undetected.* At one time, the FBI estimated that only 1% of computer crime is detected; other estimates are between 5% and 20%.

3. *A high percentage of frauds is not reported.* Many companies believe the adverse publicity would result in copycat fraud and a loss of customer confidence, which could cost more than the fraud itself.

4. *Many networks are not secure.* Dan Farmer, who wrote SATAN (a network security testing tool), tested 2,200 high-profile Web sites at government institutions, banks, and newspapers. Only three sites detected and contacted him.

5. *Internet sites offer step-by-step instructions on how to perpetrate computer fraud and abuse.* For instance, an Internet search found thousands of sites telling how to conduct a "denial of service" attack, a common form of computer abuse.

6. *Law enforcement cannot keep up with the growth of computer fraud.* Because of lack of funding and skilled staff, the FBI investigates only 1 in 15 computer crimes.

7. *Calculating losses is difficult.* It is difficult to calculate total losses when information is stolen, Web sites are defaced, and viruses shut down entire computer systems.

This increase in computer fraud created the need for the cyber sleuths discussed in Focus 1.

Computer Fraud Classifications

As shown in Figure 2, computer fraud can be categorized using the data processing model.

INPUT FRAUD   The simplest and most common way to commit a computer fraud is to alter or falsify computer input. It requires little skill; perpetrators need only understand how the system operates so they can cover their tracks. For example:

● A man opened a bank account in New York and had blank bank deposit slips printed that were similar to those available in bank lobbies, except that his account number was encoded on them. He replaced the deposit slips in the bank lobby with his forged ones. For three days, bank deposits using the forged slips went into his account. The perpetrator withdrew the money and disappeared. He was never found.

FOCUS 1   Cyber Sleuths

Two forensic experts, disguised as repair people, entered an office after hours. They took a digital photograph of three employee desks, made a copy of each employee's hard drive, and used the photo to leave everything as they found it. When the hard drive copy was analyzed, they found evidence of a fraud and notified the company who had hired them. The company turned the case over to law enforcement for investigation and prosecution.

The forensic experts breaking into the company and copying the data worked for a Big Four accounting firm. The accountants, turned cyber sleuths, specialize in catching fraud perpetrators. Cyber sleuths come from a variety of backgrounds, including accounting, information systems, government, law enforcement, military, and banking.

Cyber sleuths need the following skills:

- **Ability to follow a trail, think analytically, and be thorough.** Fraud perpetrators leave tracks, and a cyber sleuth must think analytically to follow paper and electronic trails and uncover fraud. They must be thorough so they do not miss or fail to follow up on clues.
- **Good understanding of information technology (IT).** Cyber sleuths need to understand data storage, data communications, and how to retrieve hidden or deleted files and e-mails.
- **Ability to think like a fraud perpetrator.** Cyber sleuths must understand what motivates perpetrators,

how they think, and the schemes they use to commit and conceal fraud.
- **Ability to use hacking tools and techniques.** Cyber sleuths need to understand the tools computer criminals use to perpetrate fraud and abuse.

Another way to fight crime is to develop software to examine bank or accounting records for suspicious transactions. Pattern recognition software searches millions of bank, brokerage, and insurance accounts and reviews trillions of dollars worth of transactions each day. Some companies, such as PayPal, use the software to lower their fraud rates significantly.

This software is based on a mathematical principle known as Benford's Law. In 1938, Frank Benford discovered that one can predict the first or second digit in a set of naturally occurring numerical data with surprising accuracy. Benford found that the number 1 is the first digit 31% of the time, compared to only 5% for the number 9. Pattern recognition software uses Benford's Law to examine company databases and transaction records to root out accounting fraud.

Students seeking to find their niche in life should be aware that if playing James Bond sounds appealing, then a career as a computer forensics expert might be the way to go.

- A man used desktop publishing to prepare bills for office supplies that were never ordered or delivered and mailed them to companies across the country. The perpetrator kept the invoice total below $300, an amount that in many companies does not require purchase orders or approvals. A high percentage of the companies paid the bills.
- A Milwaukee woman electronically filed over $13,000 of federal and state income tax refunds for 10 fictitious people.
- An employee at the Veteran's Memorial Coliseum sold customers full-price tickets, entered them as half-price tickets, and pocketed the difference.

FIGURE 2

Computer Fraud Classifications

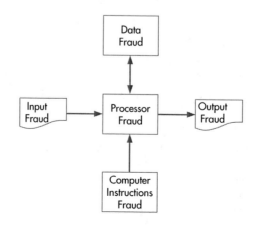

- Railroad employees entered data to scrap over 200 railroad cars. They removed the cars from the railway system, repainted them, and sold them.
- A company providing on-site technical support created exact duplicates of the checks used to pay them, using off-the-shelf scanners, graphics software, and printers. If the double payments were caught, the bank checked their microfiche copies of the two identical checks, assumed a clerical error had occurred, and wrote off the loss as a gesture of maintaining good customer relations.

PROCESSOR FRAUD   Processor fraud includes unauthorized system use, including the theft of computer time and services. For example:

- An insurance company installed software to detect abnormal system activity and found that employees were using company computers to run an illegal gambling Web site.
- Two accountants without the appropriate access rights hacked into Cisco's stock option system, transferred over $6.3 million of Cisco stock to their brokerage accounts, and sold the stock. They used part of the funds to support an extravagant lifestyle, including a $52,000 Mercedes-Benz, a $44,000 diamond ring, and a $20,000 Rolex watch.

COMPUTER INSTRUCTIONS FRAUD   Computer instruction fraud includes tampering with company software, copying software illegally, using software in an unauthorized manner, and developing software to carry out an unauthorized activity. This approach used to be uncommon because it required specialized programming knowledge. Today, it is more frequent because of the many Web pages that tell users how to create them.

DATA FRAUD   Illegally using, copying, browsing, searching, or harming company data constitutes data fraud. It is estimated that, on average, it costs a company $6.6 million, including lost business, to recover from a data breach. The biggest cause of data breaches is employee negligence.

Company employees are much more likely to perpetrate data fraud than outsiders are. A recent study shows that 59% of employees who lost or left a job admitted to stealing confidential company information. Almost 25% of them had access to their former employer's computer system.

In the absence of controls, it is not hard for an employee to steal data. For example, an employee using a small flash drive or an iPod can steal large amounts of data and remove it without being detected. In today's world, you can even buy wristwatches with a USB port and internal memory.

The following are some recent examples of stolen data:

- The office manager of a Wall Street law firm sold information about prospective mergers and acquisitions found in Word files to friends and relatives, who made several million dollars trading the securities.
- A 22-year old Kazakh man broke into Bloomberg's network and stole account information, including that of Michael Bloomberg, the mayor of New York and the founder of the financial news company. He demanded $200,000 in exchange for not using or selling the information. He was arrested in London when accepting the ransom.
- A software engineer tried to steal Intel's new microprocessor plans. Because he could view but not copy or print the plans, he photographed them screen by screen late at night in his office. Unbeknownst to him, one of Intel's controls was to notify security when the plans were viewed after business hours. He was caught red-handed and arrested.
- Cyber-criminals used sophisticated hacking and identity theft techniques to hack into seven accounts at a major online brokerage firm. They sold the securities in those accounts and used the cash to pump up the price of low-priced, thinly traded companies they already owned. Then they sold the stocks in their personal accounts for huge gains. E-trade lost $18 million and Ameritrade $4 million in similar pump-and-dump schemes.
- The U.S. Department of Veterans Affairs was sued because an employee laptop containing the records of 26.5 million veterans was stolen, exposing them to identity theft. Soon thereafter, a laptop with the records of 38,000 people disappeared from a subcontractor's office.

Data can also be changed, damaged, destroyed, or defaced, especially by disgruntled employees and hackers. Vandals broke into the NCAA's Web site before basketball tournament pairings were announced and posted swastikas, racial slurs, and a white-power logo. The Air Force, CIA, and NASA have also been the victims of high-profile Web site attacks. A Computer Security Institute analyst described the problem as "cyberspace vandals with digital spray cans."

Data can be lost as a result of negligence or carelessness. Particularly good sources of confidential data are the hard drives of used computers donated to charity or resold. A professor at a major university bought 10 used computers for his computer forensics class. Using commercially available software, his students found highly confidential data on 8 of the 10 hard drives.

Deleting files does not erase them. Even reformatting a hard drive may not wipe it clean. To erase a hard drive completely, special software must be used. When used computers are to be disposed of, the best way to protect data is to destroy the hard drive.

OUTPUT FRAUD   Unless properly safeguarded, displayed or printed output can be stolen, copied, or misused. A Dutch engineer showed that some monitors emit television-like signals that, with the help of some inexpensive electronic gear, can be displayed on a television screen. Under ideal conditions, the signals can be picked up from monitors two miles away. One engineer set up equipment in the basement of an apartment building and read a monitor on the eighth floor.

Fraud perpetrators use computers to forge authentic-looking outputs, such as a paycheck. A fraud perpetrator can scan a company paycheck, use desktop publishing software to erase the payee and amount, and print fictitious paychecks. Losses to check fraud in the United States total more than $20 billion a year.

Preventing and Detecting Fraud and Abuse

To prevent fraud, organizations must create a climate that makes fraud less likely, increases the difficulty of committing it, improves detection methods, and reduces the amount lost if a fraud occurs. These measures are summarized in Table 5.

TABLE 5 Summary of Ways to Prevent and Detect Fraud

Make Fraud Less Likely to Occur

- Create an organizational culture that stresses integrity and commitment to ethical values and competence.
- Adopt an organizational structure, management philosophy, operating style, and risk appetite that minimizes the likelihood of fraud.
- Require oversight from an active, involved, and independent audit committee of the board of directors.
- Assign authority and responsibility for business objectives to specific departments and individuals, encourage them to use initiative to solve problems, and hold them accountable for achieving those objectives.
- Identify the events that lead to increased fraud risk, and take steps to prevent, avoid, share, or accept that risk.
- Develop a comprehensive set of security policies to guide the design and implementation of specific control procedures, and communicate them effectively to company employees.
- Implement human resource policies for hiring, compensating, evaluating, promoting, and discharging employees that send messages about the required level of ethical behavior and integrity.
- Effectively supervise employees, including monitoring their performance and correcting their errors.
- Train employees in integrity and ethical considerations, as well as security and fraud prevention measures.
- Require annual employee vacations and signed confidentiality agreements; periodically rotate duties of key employees.
- Implement formal and rigorous project development and acquisition controls, as well as change management controls.
- Increase the penalty for committing fraud by prosecuting fraud perpetrators more vigorously.

Increase the Difficulty of Committing Fraud

- Develop a strong system of internal controls.
- Segregate the accounting functions of authorization, recording, and custody.
- Implement a proper segregation of duties between systems functions.
- Restrict physical and remote access to system resources to authorized personnel.

TABLE 5 Continued

- Require transactions and activities to be authorized by appropriate supervisory personnel. Have the system authenticate the person, and their right to perform the transaction, before allowing the transaction to take place.
- Use properly designed documents and records to capture and process transactions.
- Safeguard all assets, records, and data.
- Require independent checks on performance, such as reconciliation of two independent sets of records, where practical.
- Implement computer-based controls over data input, computer processing, data storage, data transmission, and information output.
- Encrypt stored and transmitted data and programs to protect them from unauthorized access and use.
- When disposing of used computers, destroy the hard drive to keep criminals from mining recycled hard drives.
- Fix software vulnerabilities by installing operating system updates, as well as security and application programs.

Improve Detection Methods

- Create an audit trail so individual transactions can be traced through the system to the financial statements and financial statement data can be traced back to individual transactions.
- Conduct periodic external and internal audits, as well as special network security audits.
- Install fraud detection software.
- Implement a fraud hotline.
- Employ a computer security officer, computer consultants, and forensic specialists as needed.
- Monitor system activities, including computer and network security efforts, usage and error logs, and all malicious actions. Use intrusion detection systems to help automate the monitoring process.

Reduce Fraud Losses

- Maintain adequate insurance.
- Develop comprehensive fraud contingency, disaster recovery, and business continuity plans.
- Store backup copies of program and data files in a secure off-site location.
- Use software to monitor system activity and recover from fraud.

Summary and Case Conclusion

Needing evidence to support his belief that Don Hawkins had committed a fraud, Jason Scott expanded the scope of his investigation. A week later, Jason presented his findings to the president of Northwest. To make his case hit close to home, Jason presented her with a copy of her IRS withholding report and pointed out her withholdings. Then he showed her a printout of payroll withholdings and pointed out the $5 difference, as well as the difference of several thousand dollars in Don Hawkins's withholdings. This got her attention, and Jason explained how he believed a fraud had been perpetrated.

During the latter part of the prior year, Don had been in charge of a payroll program update. Because of problems with other projects, other systems personnel had not reviewed the update. Jason asked a former programmer to review the code changes. She found program code that subtracted $5 from each employee's withholdings and added it to Don's withholdings. Don got his hands on the money when the IRS sent him a huge refund check.

Don apparently intended to use the scheme every year, as he had not removed the incriminating code. He must have known there was no reconciliation of payroll withholdings with the IRS report. His simple plan could have gone undetected for years if Jason had not overheard someone in the cafeteria talk about a $5 difference.

Jason learned that Don had become disgruntled when he was passed over the previous year for a managerial position. He made comments to coworkers about favoritism and unfair treatment and mentioned getting even with the company somehow. No one knew where he got the money, but Don purchased an expensive sports car in April, boasting that he had made a sizable down payment.

When the president asked how the company could prevent this fraud from happening again, Jason suggested the following guidelines:

1. Review internal controls to determine their effectiveness in preventing fraud. An existing control—reviewing program changes—could have prevented Don's scheme had it been followed. As a result, Jason suggested a stricter enforcement of the existing controls.

2. Put new controls into place to detect fraud. For example, Jason suggested a reconciliation of the IRS report and payroll record withholdings.
3. Train employees in fraud awareness, security measures, and ethical issues.

Jason urged the president to prosecute the case. She was reluctant to do so because of the adverse publicity and the problems it would cause Don's wife and children. Jason's supervisor tactfully suggested that if other employees found out that Don was not prosecuted, it would send the wrong message to the rest of the company. The president finally conceded to prosecute if the company could prove that Don was guilty. The president agreed to hire a forensic accountant to build a stronger case against Don and try to get him to confess.

Key Terms

sabotage	fraudulent financial	rationalization
cookie	reporting	computer fraud
fraud	pressure	
white-collar criminal	opportunity	
misappropriation of	lapping	
assets	kiting	

AIS IN ACTION

Chapter Quiz

1. Which of the following is a fraud in which later payments on account are used to pay off earlier payments that were stolen?
   a. lapping
   b. kiting
   c. Ponzi scheme
   d. salami technique

2. Which type of fraud is associated with 50% of all auditor lawsuits?
   a. kiting
   b. fraudulent financial reporting
   c. Ponzi schemes
   d. lapping

3. Which of the following statements is FALSE?
   a. The psychological profiles of white-collar criminals differ from those of violent criminals.
   b. The psychological profiles of white-collar criminals are significantly different from those of the general public.
   c. There is little to no difference between computer fraud perpetrators and other types of white-collar criminals.
   d. Computer fraud perpetrators often do not view themselves as criminals.

4. Which of the following conditions is/are usually necessary for a fraud to occur? (Select all correct answers.)
   a. pressure
   b. opportunity
   c. explanation
   d. rationalization

5. Which of the following is NOT an example of computer fraud?
   a. theft of money by altering computer records
   b. obtaining information illegally using a computer
   c. failure to perform preventive maintenance on a computer
   d. unauthorized modification of a software program

6. Which of the following causes the majority of computer security problems?
   a. human errors
   b. software errors
   c. natural disasters
   d. power outages

7. Which of the following is NOT one of the responsibilities of auditors in detecting fraud according to SAS No. 99?
   a. Evaluate the results of their audit tests.
   b. Incorporate a technology focus.
   c. Discuss the risks of material fraudulent misstatements.
   d. Catch the perpetrators in the act of committing the fraud.

8. Which of the following control procedures is most likely to deter lapping?
   a. encryption
   b. continual update of the access control matrix
   c. background check on employees
   d. periodic rotation of duties

9. Which of the following is the most important, basic, and effective control to deter fraud?
   a. enforced vacations
   b. logical access control
   c. segregation of duties
   d. virus protection controls

10. Once fraud has occurred, which of the following will reduce fraud losses? (Select all correct answers.)
    a. insurance
    b. regular backup of data and programs
    c. contingency plan
    d. segregation of duties

Discussion Questions

1. Do you agree that the most effective way to obtain adequate system security is to rely on the integrity of company employees? Why or why not? Does this seem ironic? What should a company do to ensure the integrity of its employees?

2. You are the president of a multinational company in which an executive confessed to kiting $100,000. What is kiting, and what can your company do to prevent it? How would you respond to the confession? What issues must you consider before pressing charges?

3. Discuss the following statement by Roswell Steffen, a convicted embezzler: "For every foolproof system, there is a method for beating it." Do you believe a completely secure computer system is possible? Explain. If internal controls are less than 100% effective, why should they be employed at all?

4. Revlon hired Logisticon to install a real-time invoice and inventory processing system. Seven months later, when the system crashed, Revlon blamed the Logisticon programming bugs they discovered and withheld payment on the contract. Logisticon contended that the software was fine and that it was the hardware that was faulty. When Revlon again refused payment, Logisticon repossessed the software using a telephone dial-in feature to disable the software and render the system unusable. After a three-day standoff, Logisticon reactivated the system. Revlon sued Logisticon, charging them with trespassing, breach of contract, and misappropriation of trade secrets (Revlon passwords). Logisticon countersued for breach of contract. The companies settled out of court.

   Would Logisticon's actions be classified as sabotage or repossession? Why? Would you find the company guilty of committing a computer crime? Be prepared to defend your position to the class.

5. Because improved computer security measures sometimes create a new set of problems—user antagonism, sluggish response time, and hampered performance—some people believe the most effective computer security is educating users about good moral conduct. Richard Stallman, a computer activist, believes software licensing is antisocial because it

prohibits the growth of technology by keeping information away from the neighbors. He believes high school and college students should have unlimited access to computers without security measures so that they can learn constructive and civilized behavior. He states that a protected system is a puzzle and, because it is human nature to solve puzzles, eliminating computer security so that there is no temptation to break in would reduce hacking.

Do you agree that software licensing is antisocial? Is ethical teaching the solution to computer security problems? Would the removal of computer security measures reduce the incidence of computer fraud? Why or why not?

Problems

1. You were asked to investigate extremely high, unexplained merchandise shortages at a department store chain. You found the following:
   a. The receiving department supervisor owns and operates a boutique carrying many of the same labels as the chain store. The general manager is unaware of the ownership interest.
   b. The receiving supervisor signs receiving reports showing that the total quantity shipped by a supplier was received and then diverts 5% to 10% of each shipment to the boutique.
   c. The store is unaware of the short shipments because the receiving report accompanying the merchandise to the sales areas shows that everything was received.
   d. Accounts Payable paid vendors for the total quantity shown on the receiving report.
   e. Based on the receiving department supervisor's instructions, quantities on the receiving reports were not counted by sales personnel.

   Required

   Classify each of the five situations as a fraudulent act, a fraud symptom, an internal control weakness, or an event unrelated to the investigation. Justify your answers.
   (*CIA Examination, adapted*)

2. A client heard through its hot line that John, the purchases journal clerk, periodically enters fictitious acquisitions. After John creates a fictitious purchase, he notifies Alice, the accounts payable ledger clerk, so she can enter them in her ledger. When the payables are processed, the payment is mailed to the nonexistent supplier's address, a post office box rented by John. John deposits the check in an account he opened in the nonexistent supplier's name.

   Required

   a. Define *fraud, fraud deterrence, fraud detection*, and *fraud investigation*.
   b. List four personal (as opposed to organizational) fraud symptoms, or red flags, that indicate the possibility of fraud. Do not confine your answer to this example.
   c. List two procedures you could follow to uncover John's fraudulent behavior.
      (*CIA Examination, adapted*)

3. The computer frauds that are publicly revealed represent only the tip of the iceberg. Although many people perceive that the major threat to computer security is external, the more dangerous threats come from insiders. Management must recognize these problems and develop and enforce security programs to deal with the many types of computer fraud.

   Required

   Explain how each of the following six types of fraud is committed. Using the format provided, identify a different method of protection for each, and describe how it works.
   (*CMA Examination, adapted*)

Type of Fraud	Explanation	Identification and Description of Protection Methods
a. Input manipulation		
b. Program alteration		
c. File alteration		
d. Data theft		
e. Sabotage		
f. Theft of computer time		

4. Environmental, institutional, or individual pressures and opportune situations, which are present to some degree in all companies, motivate individuals and companies to engage in fraudulent financial reporting. Fraud prevention and detection require that pressures and opportunities be identified and evaluated in terms of the risks they pose to a company.

   Required
   a. Identify two company pressures that would increase the likelihood of fraudulent financial reporting.
   b. Identify three corporate opportunities that make fraud easier to commit and detection less likely.
   c. For each of the following, identify the external environmental factors that should be considered in assessing the risk of fraudulent financial reporting:
      ● The company's industry
      ● The company's business environment
      ● The company's legal and regulatory environment
   d. What can top management do to reduce the possibility of fraudulent financial reporting? *(CMA Examination, adapted)*

5. For each of the following independent cases of employee fraud, recommend how to prevent similar problems in the future.
   a. Abnormal inventory shrinkage in the audiovisual department at a retail chain store led internal auditors to conduct an in-depth audit of the department. They learned that one customer frequently bought large numbers of small electronic components from a certain cashier. The auditors discovered that they had colluded to steal electronic components by not recording the sale of items the customer took from the store.
   b. During an unannounced audit, auditors discovered a payroll fraud when they, instead of department supervisors, distributed paychecks. When the auditors investigated an unclaimed paycheck, they discovered that the employee quit four months previously after arguing with the supervisor. The supervisor continued to turn in a time card for the employee and pocketed his check.
   c. Auditors discovered an accounts payable clerk who made copies of supporting documents and used them to support duplicate supplier payments. The clerk deposited the duplicate checks in a bank account she had opened using a name similar to that of the supplier. *(CMA Examination, adapted)*

6. An auditor found that Rent-A-Wreck management does not always comply with its stated policy that sealed bids be used to sell obsolete cars. Records indicated that several vehicles with recent major repairs were sold at negotiated prices. Management vigorously assured the auditor that performing limited repairs and negotiating with knowledgeable buyers resulted in better sales prices than the sealed-bid procedures. Further investigation revealed that the vehicles were sold to employees at prices well below market value. Three managers and five other employees pleaded guilty to criminal charges and made restitution.

   Required
   a. List the fraud symptoms that should have aroused the auditor's suspicion.
   b. What audit procedures would show that fraud had in fact occurred? *(CIA Examination, adapted)*

7. A bank auditor met with the senior operations manager to discuss a customer's complaint that an auto loan payment was not credited on time. The customer said the payment was made on May 5, its due date, at a teller's window using a check drawn on an account in the bank. On May 10, when the customer called for a loan pay-off balance so he could sell the car, he learned that the payment had not been credited to the loan. On May 12, the customer went to the bank to inquire about the payment and meet with the manager. The manager said the payment had been made on May 11. The customer was satisfied because no late charge would have been assessed until May 15. The manager asked whether the auditor was comfortable with this situation.

The auditor located the customer's paid check and found that it had cleared on May 5. The auditor traced the item back through the computer records and found that the teller had processed the check as being cashed. The auditor traced the payment through the entry records of May 11 and found that the payment had been made with cash instead of a check.

Required

What type of embezzlement scheme is this, and how does it work?

(CIA Examination, adapted)

8. Jamison Cardstock did not spend much time or money on internal controls for its cash transactions. The following information reflects Jamison's cash position as of June 30:
- The accounting records show a cash balance of $18,901.62, including undeposited cash receipts.
- A $100 bank statement credit was not recorded in the company's accounting records.
- The bank statement balance was $15,550.
- There were six outstanding checks:

Check Number	Amount
62	$116.25
183	$150.00
284	$253.25
8621	$190.71
8623	$206.80
8632	$145.28

The company cashier embezzled all undeposited cash receipts in excess of the $3,794.41 listed on the following bank reconciliation:

Balance per books, June 30		$18,901.62
Add: Outstanding Checks:		
No. 8621	$190.71	
No. 8623	$206.80	
No. 8632	$145.28	442.79
		$19,344.41
Subtract: Undeposited Receipts		3,794.41
Balance per bank, June 30		$15,550.00
Subtract: Unrecorded Credit		100.00
True Cash, June 30		$15,450.00

Required

a. Prepare a schedule showing how much the cashier embezzled.
b. Describe how the cashier attempted to hide the theft. *(AICPA, adapted)*

9. An accountant with the Atlanta Olympic Games was charged with embezzling over $60,000 to purchase a Mercedes-Benz and to invest in a certificate of deposit. Police alleged that he created fictitious invoices from two companies that had contracts with the Olympic Committee: International Protection Consulting and Languages Services. He then wrote checks to pay the fictitious invoices and deposited them into a bank account he had opened under the name of one of the companies. When he was apprehended, he cooperated with

police to the extent of telling them of the bogus bank account and the purchase of the Mercedes-Benz and the CD. The accountant was a recent honors graduate from a respected university who, supervisors stated, was a very trusted and loyal employee.

   a. How does the accountant fit the profile of a fraudster? How does he not fit the profile?

   b. What fraud scheme did he use to perpetrate his fraud?

   c. What controls could have prevented his fraud?

   d. What controls could have detected his fraud?

10. Lexsteel, a manufacturer of steel furniture, has facilities throughout the United States. Problems with the accounts payable system have prompted Lexsteel's external auditor to recommend a detailed study to determine the company's exposure to fraud and to identify ways to improve internal control. Lexsteel's controller assigned the study to Dolores Smith. She interviewed Accounts Payable employees and created the flowchart of the current system shown in Figure 3.

     Lexsteel's purchasing, production control, accounts payable, and cash disbursements functions are centralized at corporate headquarters. The company mainframe at corporate headquarters is linked to the computers at each branch location by leased telephone lines.

     The mainframe generates production orders and the bills of material needed for the production runs. From the bills of material, purchase orders for raw materials are generated and e-mailed to vendors. Each purchase order tells the vendor which manufacturing plant to ship the materials to. When the raw materials arrive, the manufacturing plants produce the items on the production orders received from corporate headquarters.

     The manufacturing plant checks the goods received for quality, counts them, reconciles the count to the packing slip, and e-mails the receiving data to Accounts Payable. If raw material deliveries fall behind production, each branch manager can send emergency purchase orders directly to vendors. Emergency order data and verification of materials received are e-mailed to Accounts Payable. Since the company employs a computerized perpetual inventory system, periodic physical counts of raw materials are not performed.

     Vendor invoices are e-mailed to headquarters and entered by Accounts Payable when received. This often occurs before the branch offices transmit the receiving data. Payments are due 10 days after the company receives the invoices. Using information on the invoice, Data Entry calculates the final day the invoice can be paid, and it is entered as the payment due date.

     Once a week, invoices due the following week are printed in chronological entry order on a payment listing, and the corresponding checks are drawn. The checks and payment listing are sent to the treasurer's office for signature and mailing to the payee. The check number is printed by the computer, displayed on the check and the payment listing, and validated as the checks are signed. After the checks are mailed, the payment listing is returned to Accounts Payable for filing. When there is insufficient cash to pay all the invoices, the treasurer retains certain checks and the payment listing until all checks can be paid. When the remaining checks are mailed, the listing is then returned to Accounts Payable. Often, weekly check mailings include a few checks from the previous week, but rarely are there more than two weekly listings involved.

     When Accounts Payable receives the payment listing from the treasurer's office, the expenses are distributed, coded, and posted to the appropriate cost center accounts. Accounts Payable processes weekly summary performance reports for each cost center and branch location.

   1. Discuss three ways Lexsteel is exposed to fraud, and recommend improvements to correct these weaknesses.

   2. Describe three ways in which management information could be distorted, and recommend improvements to correct these weaknesses.

   3. Identify and explain three strengths in Lexsteel's procedures. *(CMA Examination, adapted)*

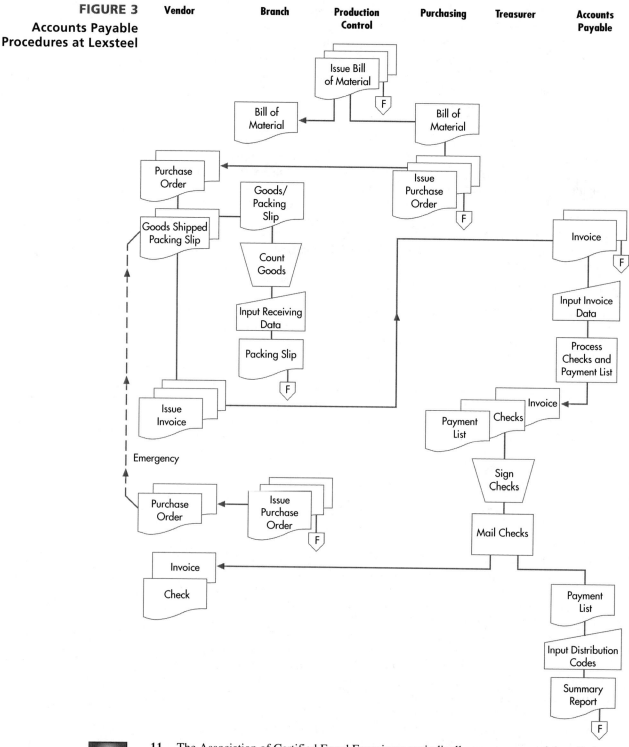

FIGURE 3
Accounts Payable Procedures at Lexsteel

| Vendor | Branch | Production Control | Purchasing | Treasurer | Accounts Payable |

11. The Association of Certified Fraud Examiners periodically prepares an article called "What Is Your Fraud IQ?" It consists of 10 or more multiple choice questions dealing with various aspects of fraud. The answers, as well as an explanation of each answer, are provided at the end of the article. Visit the *Journal of Accountancy* site (http://www.journalofaccountancy.com) and search for the articles. Read and answer the questions in three of these articles, and then check your answers.

12. Explore the Anti-Fraud and Forensic Accounting portion of the AICPA Web site (www.aicpa.org/InterestAreas/ForensicAndValuation/Resources/ForensicAcctg/Pages/default.aspx), and write a two-page report on the three most interesting things you found on the site.

Case 1 David L. Miller: Portrait of a White-Collar Criminal

There is an old saying: Crime doesn't pay. However, for David Miller crime paid for two Mercedes-Benz sedans; a lavish suburban home; a condominium at Myrtle Beach; expensive suits; tailored and monogrammed shirts; diamond, sapphire, ruby, and emerald rings for his wife; and a new car for his father-in-law. Though Miller confessed to embezzling funds from six different employers over a 20-year period, he has never been prosecuted or incarcerated—in large part because his employers never turned him in.

Miller was fired from his first employer for stealing $200. After an assortment of odd jobs, he worked as an accountant for a local baker. Miller was caught embezzling funds and paid back the $1,000 he stole. Again, law enforcement was not notified, and he was quietly dismissed.

Several months after Miller started work at Wheeling Bronze, his third victim, the president discovered a $30,000 cash shortfall and several missing returned checks. An extensive search found the canceled checks, with forged signatures, in an outdoor sand pile. Miller confessed to the scheme and was given the choice of repaying the stolen funds or being prosecuted. When Miller's parents mortgaged their home and repaid the stolen money, he escaped prosecution.

Miller's fourth victim was Robinson Pipe Cleaning. When Miller was caught embezzling funds, he again avoided prosecution by promising to repay the $20,000 he stole.

Miller's fifth victim was Crest Industries, where he worked as accountant. He was an ideal employee—dedicated and hard working, doing outstanding work. He was quickly promoted to office manager and soon purchased a new home, car, and wardrobe. Two years later, Crest auditors discovered that $31,000 was missing. Miller had written several checks to himself, recorded them as payments to suppliers, and intercepted and altered the monthly bank statements. With the stolen money, he financed his lifestyle and repaid Wheeling Bronze and Robinson Pipe Cleaning. Once again, Miller tearfully confessed, claiming he had never embezzled funds previously. Miller showed so much remorse that Crest hired a lawyer for him. He promised to repay the stolen money, gave Crest a lien on his house, and was quietly dismissed. Because Crest management did not want to harm Miller's wife and three children, Crest never pressed charges.

Miller's sixth victim was Rustcraft Broadcasting Company. When Rustcraft was acquired by Associated Communications, Miller moved to Pittsburgh to become Associated's new controller. Miller immediately began dipping into Associated's accounts. Over a six-year period, Miller embezzled $1.36 million, $450,000 of that after he was promoted to CFO. Miller circumvented the need for two signatures on checks by asking executives leaving on vacation to sign several checks "just in case" the company needed to disburse funds while he was gone. Miller used the checks to siphon funds to his personal account. To cover the theft, Miller removed the canceled check from the bank reconciliation and destroyed it. The stolen amount was charged to a unit's expense account to balance the company's books.

While working at Associated, Miller bought a new house, new cars, a vacation home, and an extravagant wardrobe. He was generous with tips and gifts. His $130,000 salary could not have supported this lifestyle, yet no one at Associated questioned the source of his conspicuous consumption. Miller's lifestyle came crashing down while he was on vacation and the bank called to inquire about a check written to Miller. Miller confessed and, as part of his out-of-court settlement, Associated received most of Miller's personal property.

Miller cannot explain why he was never prosecuted. His insistence that he was going to pay his victims back usually satisfied his employers and got him off the hook. He believes these agreements actually contributed to his subsequent thefts; one rationalization for stealing from a new employer was to pay back the former one. Miller believes his theft problem is an illness, like alcoholism or compulsive gambling, that is driven by a subconscious need to be admired and liked by others. He thought that by spending money, others would like him. Ironically, he was universally well liked and admired at each job, for reasons that had nothing to do with money. In fact, one Associated coworker was so surprised by the thefts that he said it was like finding out that your brother was an ax murderer. Miller claims he is not a bad person; he never intended to hurt anyone, but once he got started, he could not stop.

After leaving Associated, Miller was hired by a former colleague, underwent therapy, and now believes he has resolved his problem with compulsive embezzlement.

1. How does Miller fit the profile of the average fraud perpetrator? How does he differ? How did these characteristics make him difficult to detect?
2. Explain the three elements of the opportunity triangle (commit, conceal, convert), and discuss how Miller accomplished each when embezzling funds from Associated Communications. What specific concealment techniques did Miller use?
3. What pressures motivated Miller to embezzle? How did Miller rationalize his actions?
4. Miller had a framed T-shirt in his office that said, "He who dies with the most toys wins." What does this tell you about Miller? What lifestyle red flags could have tipped off the company to the possibility of fraud?
5. Why do companies hesitate to prosecute white-collar criminals? What are the consequences of not prosecuting? How could law enforcement officials encourage more prosecution?
6. What could the victimized companies have done to prevent Miller's embezzlement?

Source: Based on Bryan Burrough, "David L. Miller Stole from His Employer and Isn't in Prison," *The Wall Street Journal* (September 19, 1986): 1.

Case 2   Heirloom Photo Plans

Heirloom Photos sells a $900 photography plan to rural customers using a commissioned sales force. Rather than pay the price up front, most customers pay $250 down and make 36 monthly payments of $25 each. The $900 plan includes the following:

1. A coupon book good for one free sitting every 6 months for the next 5 years (10 sittings) at any Heirloom-approved photo studio. The customer receives one free 11-by-14-inch black-and-white print. Additional photos or color upgrades can be purchased at the photographer's retail prices.
2. To preserve the 11-by-14-inch photos, the family name is embossed in 24-carat gold on a leather-bound photo album.

The embossed leather album, with a retail value of $300, costs Heirloom $75. Each sitting and free 11-by-14-inch print, with a retail value of $150, costs Heirloom only $50 because photographers are given exclusive rights to all Heirloom customers in a geographic region and have the opportunity to offer customers upgrades to color and/or more pictures.

The commissioned sales staff is paid on the 10th of each month, based upon the prior month's sales. The commission rates are as follows:

Number of plans sold	Commission	Quantity bonus
Fewer than 100	$100 per plan	
101 to 200	$125 per plan	On sale of plan #101, $2,500 is paid to cover the extra $25 on the first 100 sales
More than 200	$150 per plan	On sale of plan #201, $5,000 is paid to cover the extra $25 on the first 200 sales

Over 70% of all agents sell at least 101 plans per year; 40% sell over 200. There is a strong sales surge before year-end as customers purchase plans to give as holiday gifts. About 67% of all agents reach their highest incentive level in late November or December. Heirloom treats the sales staff and the photographers as independent contractors and does not withhold any income or payroll taxes on amounts paid to them.

Salespeople send Heirloom's accounting department the order form, the total payment or the down payment, and the signed note for $650 if the customer finances the transaction. Often, the payment is a hand-written money order. Because many customers live in rural areas, the return address is often a Post Office box, and some customers do not have phones. Heirloom does not perform any credit checks of customers.

Heirloom makes the following entries at the time a new contract is recorded:

To record sale of the contract (assumes contract financed)

Cash	250	
Note Receivable	650	
Sales of Photo Plans		900

To record expenses related to the sale

Album Expense	65	
Embossing/shipping	10	
Sales Expense	130	
Album Inventory		65
Accounts Payable		10
Commissions Payable		130

(Sales expense is estimated using the average cost paid to salespersons in the prior year.)

To record the liability for Photographer Sittings Expense

Photographer Expense	500	
Accrued Liabilities		500

Because the entire cost of the photographer is accrued, the company points to the last entry to show how conservative its accounting is.

After waiting 10 days for the check or money order to clear, Heirloom embosses and ships the album, the photo coupon book, and a payment coupon book with 36 payments of $25. Customers mail a payment coupon and a check or money order to a three-person Receivables Department at headquarters. The Receivables employees open the envelopes, post the payments to the receivables records, and prepare the bank deposit.

The photo coupon book has 10 coupons for photographer sessions, each good for a specific 6-month period. If not used within the 6-month period, the coupon expires.

Each month, the credit manager sends letters and makes phone calls to collect on delinquent accounts. Between 35% and 40% of all customers eventually stop paying on their notes, usually either early in the contract (months 4 to 8) or at the 2-year point (months 22 to 26).

Notes are written off when they are 180 days delinquent. Heirloom's CFO and credit manager use their judgment to adjust the Allowance for Bad Debts monthly. They are confident they can accurately predict the Allowance balance needed at any time, which historically has been about 5% of outstanding receivables.

Agricultural product prices in the area where Heirloom sells its plans have been severely depressed for the second straight year.

Heirloom has been growing quickly and finds that it is continually running short of cash, partly because of the large salaries paid to the two equal owners and their wives. (The wives each receive $100,000 to serve as the treasurer and the secretary; very little, if any, time is required in these duties.) In addition, Heirloom spent large amounts of cash to buy its headquarters, equipment and furnishings, and expensive automobiles for the two owners, their wives, and the four vice presidents.

Heirloom needs to borrow from a local bank for corporate short-term operating purposes. It is willing to pledge unpaid contracts as collateral for a loan. A local bank president is willing to lend Heirloom up to 70% of the value of notes receivable that are not more than 60 days overdue. Heirloom must also provide, by the fifth day of each month, a note receivable aging list for the preceding month and a calculation showing the maximum amount Heirloom may borrow under the agreement.

1. **Figure 4** shows the employees and external parties that deal with Heirloom. Explain how Heirloom could defraud the bank and how each internal and external party, except the bank, could defraud Heirloom.

2. What risk factor, unusual item, or abnormality would alert you to each fraud?

3. What control weaknesses make each fraud possible?

4. Recommend one or more controls to prevent or detect each means of committing fraud.

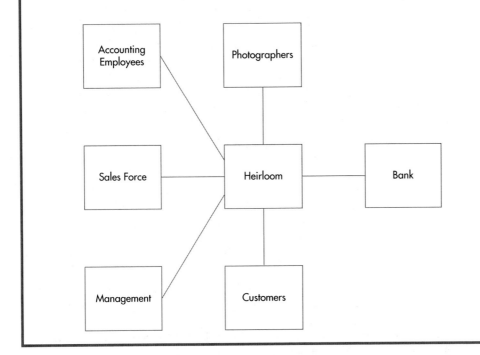

FIGURE 4

Internal and External Relationships at Heirloom Photos

AIS IN ACTION SOLUTIONS

Quiz Key

1. Which of the following is a fraud in which later payments on account are used to pay off earlier payments that were stolen?
   ▶ a. lapping (Correct.)
   b. kiting (Incorrect. In a kiting scheme, the perpetrator creates cash by transferring money between banks.)
   c. Ponzi scheme (Incorrect. In a Ponzi scheme, money from new investors is used to pay off earlier investors.)
   d. salami technique (Incorrect. The salami technique involves stealing tiny slices of money over a period of time.)

2. Which type of fraud is associated with 50% of all auditor lawsuits?
   a. kiting (Incorrect. Losses from kiting, a scheme involving bank transfers, are not large enough to be associated with 50% of auditor lawsuits.)

► b. fraudulent financial reporting (Correct. Attesting to fraudulent financial statements is the basis of a large percentage of lawsuits against auditors.)

c. Ponzi schemes (Incorrect. Ponzi schemes, in which money from new investors is used to pay off earlier investors, are investment frauds that often do not involve auditors.)

d. lapping (Incorrect. Losses from lapping, in which later payments on account are used to pay off earlier payments that were stolen, are not large enough to be associated with 50% of auditor lawsuits.)

3. Which of the following statements is FALSE?

a. The psychological profiles of white-collar criminals differ from those of violent criminals. (Incorrect. This is a true statement. Psychologically, white-collar criminals are very different than violent criminals.)

► b. The psychological profiles of white-collar criminals are significantly different from those of the general public. (Correct. This is false; the psychological profile of white-collar criminals is similar to that of the general public.)

c. There is little to no difference between computer fraud perpetrators and other types of white-collar criminals. (Incorrect. This is a true statement. Although different things can motivate perpetrators of computer fraud, they share many similarities with other types of white-collar criminals.)

d. Computer fraud perpetrators often do not view themselves as criminals. (Incorrect. This is a true statement. Computer fraud perpetrators often do not view what they do as wrong.)

4. Which of the following conditions is/are usually necessary for a fraud to occur? (See the Fraud Triangle in Figure 1.)

► a. pressure (Correct.)

► b. opportunity (Correct.)

c. explanation (Incorrect. An explanation is not one of the three elements of the fraud triangle, as shown in Figure 1.)

► d. rationalization (Correct.)

5. Which of the following is NOT an example of computer fraud? (See the "Computer Fraud Classifications" section of the chapter.)

a. theft of money by altering computer records (Incorrect. The simplest and most common way to commit a computer fraud is to alter or falsify computer input, such as altering computer records.)

b. obtaining information illegally using a computer (Incorrect. One type of data fraud is using a computer to acquire information illegally.)

► c. failure to perform preventive maintenance on a computer (Correct. This is poor management of computer resources, but it is not computer fraud.)

d. unauthorized modification of a software program (Incorrect. Tampering with company software is a type of computer instructions fraud.)

6. Which of the following causes the majority of computer security problems?

► a. human errors (Correct. The Computing Technology Industry Association estimates that human errors cause 80% of security problems. These unintentional acts usually are caused by human carelessness, failure to follow established procedures, and poorly trained or supervised personnel.)

b. software errors (Incorrect. Although a federal study estimated yearly economic losses due to software bugs at almost $60 billion a year and revealed that more than 60% of companies studied had significant software errors in the previous year, it is not the main cause of computer security issues.)

c. natural disasters (Incorrect. Natural disasters—such as fires, floods, earthquakes, hurricanes, tornadoes, and blizzards—can destroy an information system and cause a company to fail. When a disaster strikes, many companies are affected at the same time. However, this is not a frequent occurrence and is not the main cause of computer security problems.)

    d. power outages (Incorrect. Massive power failures caused by defective software occasionally occur and leave hundreds of thousands of people and businesses without power, but this is not the main cause of computer security issues.)

7. Which of the following is NOT one of the responsibilities of auditors in detecting fraud according to SAS No. 99?
   - **a.** Evaluate the results of their audit tests. (Incorrect. When an audit is completed, auditors must evaluate whether any identified misstatements indicate the presence of fraud. If they do, the auditor must determine the impact of this on the financial statements and the audit.)
   - **b.** Incorporate a technology focus. (Incorrect. SAS No. 99 recognizes the impact technology has on fraud risks and provides commentary and examples specifically recognizing this impact. It also notes the opportunities the auditor has to use technology to design fraud-auditing procedures.)
   - **c.** Discuss the risks of material fraudulent misstatements. (Incorrect.While planning the audit, team members should discuss among themselves how and where the company's financial statements might be susceptible to fraud.)
   - ▶ **d.** Catch the perpetrators in the act of committing the fraud. (Correct. SAS No. 99 does not require auditors to witness the perpetrators committing fraud.)

8. Which of the following control procedures is most likely to deter lapping?
   - **a.** encryption (Incorrect. Encryption is used to code data in transit so it cannot be read unless it is decoded. It does not stop employees from lapping accounts receivable payments.)
   - **b.** continual update of the access control matrix (Incorrect. The access control matrix specifies what computer functions employees can perform and what data they can access with a computer. It does not stop employees from lapping accounts receivable payments.)
   - **c.** background check on employees (Incorrect. A background check can help screen out dishonest job applicants, but it does not stop employees from lapping accounts receivable payments.)
   - ▶ **d.** periodic rotation of duties (Correct. Lapping requires a constant and ongoing cover-up to hide the stolen funds. Rotating duties such that the perpetrator does not have access to the necessary accounting records will most likely result in the fraud's discovery.)

9. Which of the following is the most important, basic, and effective control to deter fraud?
   - **a.** enforced vacations (Incorrect. Enforced vacations will prevent or deter some, but not all, fraud schemes.)
   - **b.** logical access control (Incorrect. Logical access controls will prevent or deter some, but not all, fraud schemes.)
   - ▶ **c.** segregation of duties (Correct. Segregating duties among different employees is the most effective control for the largest number of fraud schemes, because it makes it difficult for any single employee to both commit and conceal a fraud.)
   - **d.** virus protection controls (Incorrect. Virus protection controls will help prevent some computer-related abuses, but they are unlikely to deter much fraud.)

10. Once fraud has occurred, which of the following will reduce fraud losses? (Select all correct answers.)
    - ▶ **a.** insurance (Correct. The right insurance will pay for all or a portion of fraud losses.)
    - ▶ **b.** regular backup of data and programs (Correct. Regular backup helps the injured party recover lost or damaged data and programs.)
    - ▶ **c.** contingency plan (Correct. A contingency plan helps the injured party restart operations on a timely basis.)
    - **d.** segregation of duties (Incorrect. Segregation of duties is an effective method of deterring fraud but does not help a company recover from fraud once it occurs.)

Chapter 6

Computer Fraud and Abuse Techniques

From Chapter 6 of *Accounting Information Systems*, 12/e. Marshall B. Romney. Paul John Steinbart. Copyright © 2012 by Pearson Education. Published by Prentice Hall. All rights reserved.

Computer Fraud and Abuse Techniques

Learning Objectives

After studying this chapter, you should be able to:

1. Compare and contrast computer attack and abuse tactics.

2. Explain how social engineering techniques are used to gain physical or logical access to computer resources.

3. Describe the different types of malware used to harm computers.

INTEGRATIVE CASE NORTHWEST INDUSTRIES

Northwest Industries wants to expand its service area and has been negotiating to buy Remodeling Products Centers (RPC), a competitor that operates in an area contiguous to Northwest. Jason Scott was part of a team sent to look over RPC's books before the deal was finalized. At the end of their first day, RPC's computer system crashed. The team decided to finish up what work they could and to let RPC's information technology (IT) people get the system up that night.

The next day, RPC's system was still down, so Jason tried to log into Northwest's computer system. It seemed to take forever to access, and then Jason found that system response was rather slow. His manager called the corporate office and found that there was something wrong with Northwest's system. It was assumed that the problem had something to do with communications with RPC's computers.

Jason's team was assigned to do a computer fraud and abuse evaluation of RPC's system while they waited. Since Jason had never participated in such a review, he was told to go back to the hotel where he could get on the Internet and spend the day researching the different ways computer systems could be attacked.

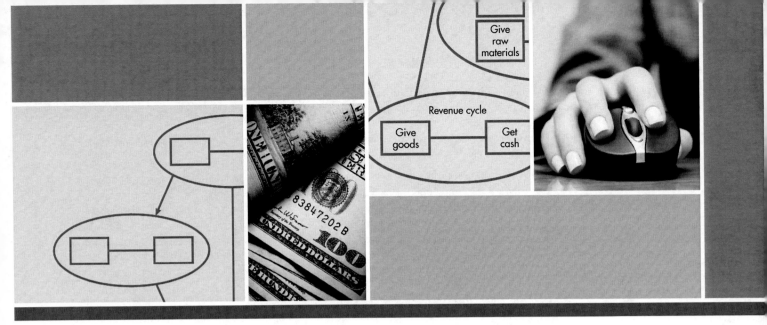

Introduction

Cyber criminals have devised an ever-increasing number of ways to commit computer fraud and abuse. This chapter discusses some of the more common techniques in three sections: computer attacks and abuse, social engineering, and malware. These classifications are not distinct; there is a lot of overlap among the categories. For example, social engineering methods are often used to launch computer attacks.

Computer Attacks and Abuse

All computers connected to the Internet, especially those with important trade secrets or valuable IT assets, are under constant attack from hackers, foreign governments, terrorist groups, disaffected employees, industrial spies, and competitors. These people attack computers looking for valuable data or to harm the computer system. Preventing attacks is a constant battle. On a busy day, large Web hosting farms suffer millions of attack attempts. This section describes some of the more common attack techniques.

Hacking is the unauthorized access, modification, or use of an electronic device or some element of a computer system. Most hackers break into systems using known flaws in operating systems or application programs, or as a result of poor access controls. One software-monitoring company estimates there are over 7,000 known flaws in software released in any given year. The following examples illustrate hacking attacks and the damage they cause:

- Russian hackers broke into Citibank's system and stole $10 million from customer accounts.
- Acxiom manages customer information for credit card issuers, banks, automotive manufacturers, and retailers. Daniel Baas, a systems administrator for a company doing business with Acxiom, exceeded his authorized access, downloaded an encrypted password file, and used a password-cracking program to access confidential identification information. The intrusion cost Acxiom over $5.8 million.
- During the Iraq war, Dutch hackers stole confidential information, including troop movements and weapons information, from 34 military sites. Their offer to sell the information to Iraq was declined, probably because Iraq feared it was a setup.
- A 17-year-old hacker, nicknamed Shadow Hawk, hacked the Bell Laboratories national network, destroyed files valued at $174,000, and copied 52 proprietary software programs worth $1.2 million. He published confidential information—such as telephone numbers, passwords, and instructions on how to breach AT&T's computer security

system—on underground bulletin boards. He was sentenced to nine months in prison and fined $10,000. Like Shadow Hawk, many hackers are young, some as young as 12 and 13.

- A hacker penetrated a software supplier's computer and used its "open pipe" to a bank customer to install a powerful Trojan horse in the bank's computer.

A *botnet*, short for robot network, is a network of powerful and dangerous hijacked computers. *Hijacking* is gaining control of a computer to carry out illicit activities without the user's knowledge. *Bot herders* install software that responds to the hacker's electronic instructions onto unwitting PCs. Bot software is delivered in a variety of ways, including Trojans, e-mails, instant messages, Tweets, or an infected Web site. Bot herders use the combined power of the hijacked computers, called *zombies*, to mount a variety of Internet attacks. Worldwide, there are over 2,000 botnets containing over 10 million computers (10% of online computers), many of them for rent. Bot toolkits and easy-to-use software are available on the Internet showing hackers how to create their own botnets; hacking is now almost as simple as picking and choosing features and clicking on a checkbox. The Mariposa botnet, containing almost 13 million computers in 190 countries, was created by three men without any advanced hacker skills.

Botnets are used to perform a *denial-of-service (DoS) attack*, which is designed to make a resource unavailable to its users. In an e-mail attack, so many e-mails (thousands per second) are received, often from randomly generated false addresses, that the Internet service provider's e-mail server is overloaded and shuts down. Another attack involves sending so many Web page requests that the Web server crashes. An estimated 5,000 denial-of-service attacks occur per week. The Web sites of online merchants, banks, governmental agencies, and news agencies are frequent victims. The following examples illustrate denial-of-service attacks and the damage they cause:

- A DoS attack shut down 3,000 Web sites for 40 hours on one of the busiest shopping weekends of the year.
- CloudNine, an Internet service provider, went out of business after DoS attacks prevented its subscribers and their customers from communicating.
- An estimated 1 in 12 e-mails carried the MyDoom virus at its peak. The virus turned its host into a zombie that attacked Microsoft. Other companies, such as Amazon, Yahoo, CNN, and eBay, have all suffered similar DoS attacks.

Spamming is e-mailing or texting an unsolicited message to many people at the same time, often in an attempt to sell something. An estimated 250 billion e-mails are sent every day (2.8 million per second); 80% are spam and viruses. The Federal Trade Commission estimates that 80% of spam is sent from botnets. Spams are annoying and costly, and 10% to 15% offer products or services that are fraudulent. In retaliation, some spammers are spammed in return with thousands of messages, causing their e-mail service to fail. Such retaliation affects innocent users and can result in the closure of an e-mail account. Spammers scan the Internet for addresses posted online, hack into company databases, and steal or buy mailing lists. An AOL employee stole the names and e-mail addresses of 92 million people and sold them to spammers.

Spammers also stage *dictionary attacks* (also called *direct harvesting attacks*). Spammers use special software to guess addresses at a company and send blank e-mail messages. Messages not returned usually have valid e-mail addresses and are added to spammer e-mail lists. Dictionary attacks are a major burden to corporate e-mail systems and Internet service providers. Some companies receive more dictionary attack e-mail than valid e-mail messages. One day 74% of the e-mail messages that Lewis University received were for nonexistent addresses. Companies use e-mail filtering software to detect dictionary attacks; unfortunately, spammers continue to find ways around the rules used in e-mail filtering software.

A blog (short for W*eb log*) is a Web site containing online journals or commentary. Hackers create *splogs* (combination of *sp*am and b*log*) with links to Web sites they own to increase their Google PageRank, which is how often a Web page is referenced by other Web pages. Since Web sites with high PageRanks appear first in search results pages, splogs are created to artificially inflate paid-ad impressions from visitors, to sell links, or to get new sites indexed. Splogs are annoying, waste valuable disk space and bandwidth, and pollute search engine results.

Spoofing is making an electronic communication look as if someone else sent it to gain the trust of the recipient. Spoofing can take various forms, including the following:

- *E-mail spoofing* is making an e-mail appear as though it originated from a different source. Many spam and phishing attacks use special software to create random sender addresses. A former Oracle employee was charged with breaking into the company's computer network, falsifying evidence, and committing perjury for forging an e-mail message to support her charge that she was fired for ending a relationship with the company CEO. Using cell phone records, Oracle lawyers proved that the supervisor who had supposedly fired her and written the e-mail was out of town when the e-mail was written and could not have sent it. The employee was found guilty of forging the e-mail message and faced up to six years in jail.

- *Caller ID spoofing* is displaying an incorrect number (any number the attacker chooses) on a caller ID display to hide the caller's identity.

- *IP address spoofing* is creating Internet Protocol (IP) packets with a forged source IP address to conceal the identity of the sender or to impersonate another computer system. IP spoofing is most frequently used in denial-of-service attacks.

- *Address Resolution Protocol (ARP) spoofing* is sending fake ARP messages to an Ethernet LAN. ARP is a networking protocol for determining a network host's hardware address when only its IP or network address is known. ARP is critical for local area networking as well as for routing internet traffic across gateways (routers). ARP spoofing allows an attacker to associate his *MAC address* (*M*edia *A*ccess *C*ontrol address, a hardware address that uniquely identifies each node on a network) with the IP address of another node. Any traffic meant for the intended IP address is mistakenly sent to the attacker instead. The attacker can sniff the traffic and forward it to its intended target, modify the data before forwarding it (called a man-in-the-middle attack), or launch a denial of service attack.

- *SMS spoofing* is using the short message service (SMS) to change the name or number a text message appears to come from. In Australia, a woman got a call asking why she had sent the caller multiple adult message texts every day for the past few months. Neither she nor her mobile company could explain the texts, as her account showed that they were not coming from her phone. When she realized there was no way of blocking the messages, she changed her mobile number to avoid any further embarrassment by association.

- *Web-page spoofing*, also called phishing, is discussed later in the chapter.

- *DNS spoofing* is sniffing the ID of a Domain Name System (the "phone book" of the Internet that converts a domain, or Web site name, to an IP address) request and replying before the real DNS server can.

A *zero-day attack* (or *zero-hour attack*) is an attack between the time a new software vulnerability is discovered and the time a software developer releases a *patch* that fixes the problem. When hackers detect a new vulnerability, they "release it into the wild" by posting it on underground hacker sites. Word spreads quickly, and the attacks begin. It takes companies time to discover the attacks, study them, develop an antidote, release the patch to fix the problem, install the patch on user systems, and update antivirus software. One way software developers minimize the vulnerability window is to monitor known hacker sites so they know about the vulnerability when the hacker community does.

Vulnerability windows last anywhere from hours to forever if users do not patch their system. A national retailing firm employee used the server that clears credit card transactions to download music from an infected Web site. The music contained Trojan horse software that allowed Russian hackers to take advantage of an unpatched, known vulnerability to install software that collected and sent credit card data to 16 different computers in Russia every hour for four months until it was detected.

Cybercrooks take advantage of Microsoft's security update cycle by timing new attacks right before or just after "Patch Tuesday"—the second Tuesday of each month, when the software maker releases its fixes. The term "zero-day Wednesday" describes this strategy.

Cross-site scripting (XSS) is a vulnerability in dynamic Web pages that allows an attacker to bypass a browser's security mechanisms and instruct the victim's browser to execute code thinking it came from the desired Web site. Most attacks use executable JavaScript, although HTML, Flash, or other codes the browser can execute are also used. XSS flaws are the most prevalent flaws in Web applications today and occur anywhere a Web application uses input from a user in the output it generates without validating or encoding it. The likelihood that a site contains XSS vulnerabilities is extremely high. Finding these flaws is not difficult for attackers; there are many free tools available that help hackers find them, create the malicious code, and inject it into a target site. Many prominent sites have had XSS attacks, including Google, Yahoo, Facebook, MySpace, and MediaWiki. In fact, MediaWiki has had to fix over 30 XSS weaknesses to protect Wikipedia.

An example of how XSS works follows. Luana hosts a Web site that Christy frequently uses to store all her financial data. To use the Web site, Christy logs on using her username and password. While searching for vulnerable Web sites, Miles finds that Luana's Web site has an XSS vulnerability. Miles creates a URL to exploit it and sends it to Christy in an e-mail that motivates Christy to click on it while logged into Luana's Web site. The XSS vulnerability is exploited when the malicious script embedded in Miles's URL executes in Christy's browser, as if it came directly from Luana's server. The script sends Christy's session cookie to Miles, who hijacks Christy's session. Miles can now do anything Christy can do. Miles can also send the victim's cookie to another server, inject forms that steal Christy's confidential data, disclose her files, or install a Trojan horse program on her computer. Miles can also use XSS to send a malicious script to her husband Jeremy's computer. Jeremy's browser has no way of knowing that the script should not be trusted; it thinks it came from a trusted source and executes the script.

Miles could also execute XSS by posting a message with the malicious code to a social network. When Brian reads the message, Miles's XSS will steal his cookie, allowing Miles to hijack Brian's session and impersonate him.

Attempting to filter out malicious scripts is unlikely to succeed, as attackers encode the malicious script in hundreds of ways so it looks less suspicious to the user. The best way to protect against XSS is HTML sanitization, which is a process of validating input and only allowing users to input predetermined characters. Companies also try to identify and remove XSS flaws from a Web application. To find flaws, companies review their code, searching for all the locations where input from an HTTP request could enter the HTML output.

A *buffer overflow attack* happens when the amount of data entered into a program is greater than the amount of the memory (the input buffer) set aside to receive it. The input overflow usually overwrites the next computer instruction, causing the system to crash. Hackers exploit this buffer overflow by carefully crafting the input so that the overflow contains code that tells the computer what to do next. This code could open a back door into the system, provide the attacker with full control of the system, access confidential data, destroy or harm system components, slow system operations, and carry out any number of other inappropriate acts. Buffer overflow exploits can occur with any form of input, including mail servers, databases, Web servers, and ftps. Many exploits have been written to cause buffer overflows. The Code Red worm used a buffer overflow to exploit a hole in Microsoft's Internet Information Services.

In an *SQL injection (insertion)* attack, malicious code in the form of an SQL query is inserted into input so it can be passed to and executed by an application program. The idea is to convince the application to run SQL code that it was not intended to execute by exploiting a database vulnerability. It is one of several vulnerabilities that can occur when one programming language is embedded inside another. A successful SQL injection can read sensitive data from the database; modify, disclose, destroy, or limit the availability of the data; allow the attacker to become a database administrator; spoof identity; and issue operating system commands. An SQL injection attack can have a significant impact that is limited only by the attacker's skill and imagination and system controls.

Albert Gonzalez used SQL injection techniques to create a back door on corporate systems. He then used packet sniffing and ARP spoofing attacks to steal data on more than 170 million credit cards. His $200 million fraud was the largest such fraud in history. He was sentenced to 20 years in prison, the harshest computer crime sentence in American history. Like most fraud perpetrators, he spent his ill-gotten gains on a Miami condominium, an expensive car, Rolex watches, and a Tiffany ring for his girlfriend. He threw himself a $75,000 birthday party and stayed in lavish hotels and resorts. He even complained about having to count $340,000 by hand after his currency-counting machine broke.

As shown in Figure 1, a *man-in-the-middle (MITM) attack* places a hacker between a client and a host and intercepts network traffic between them. An MITM attack is often called a

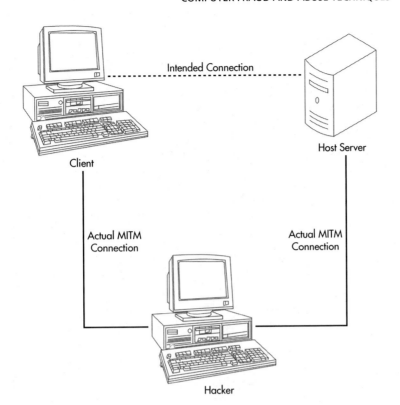

FIGURE 1

A Man-in-the Middle
Cyber Attack

session hijacking attack. MITM attacks are used to attack public-key encryption systems where sensitive and valuable information is passed back and forth. For example, Linda sniffs and eavesdrops on a network communication and finds David sending his public key to Teressa so that they can communicate securely. Linda substitutes her forged public key for David's key and steps in the middle of their communications. If Linda can successfully impersonate both David and Teressa by intercepting and relaying the messages to each other, they believe they are communicating securely. Once an MITM presence is established, the hacker can read and modify client messages, mislead the two parties, manipulate transactions, and steal confidential data. To prevent MITM attacks, most cryptographic protocols authenticate each communication endpoint. Many of the spoofing techniques discussed in the chapter are used in MITM attacks.

Masquerading or *impersonation* is pretending to be an authorized user to access a system. This is possible when the perpetrator knows the user's ID number and password or uses her computer after she has logged in (while the user is in a meeting or at lunch).

Piggybacking has several meanings:

1. The clandestine use of a neighbor's Wi-Fi network; this can be prevented by enabling the security feature in the wireless network.
2. Tapping into a telecommunications line and electronically latching onto a legitimate user before the user enters a secure system; the legitimate user unknowingly carries the perpetrator into the system.
3. An unauthorized person following an authorized person through a secure door, bypassing physical security controls such as keypads, ID cards, or biometric identification scanners.

Password cracking is penetrating a system's defenses, stealing the file containing valid passwords, decrypting them, and using them to gain access to programs, files, and data. A police officer suspected his wife of an affair and believed the lovers communicated by e-mail. He asked a former police officer to break into his wife's password-protected corporate e-mail account and print her e-mails. The hacker used a wireless access point to penetrate the network and download her e-mail. It took three days to crack her password and confirm the husband's suspicions.

War dialing is programming a computer to dial thousands of phone lines searching for dial-up modem lines. Hackers hack into the PC attached to the modem and access the network to which it is connected. This approach got its name from the movie *War Games*. Much more problematic in today's world is *war driving*, which is driving around looking for unprotected wireless networks. One enterprising group of researchers went *war rocketing*. They used rockets to let loose wireless access points attached to parachutes that detected unsecured wireless networks in a 50-square-mile area.

Phreaking is attacking phone systems to obtain free phone line access or using phone lines to transmit viruses and to access, steal, and destroy data. One telephone company lost $4.5 million in three days when details on how to use its phone lines for free were published on the Internet. Phreakers also break into voice mail systems, as the New York Police Department learned. The hackers changed the voice mail greeting to say that officers were too busy drinking coffee and eating doughnuts to answer the phone and to call 119 (not 911) in case of an emergency. The owner of two small voice-over-IP (VoIP) phone companies hacked into a larger VoIP provider and routed over $1 million of calls through one of his systems. To keep the rerouting from being discovered, they broke into a New York firm's system, set up a server, and made it look like the calls came from many third parties. Other hackers have hijacked calls, rerouted them to their own call centers, and asked callers to identify themselves by divulging confidential information. To protect a system from phreakers, companies use a voice firewall that scans inbound and outbound voice traffic, terminates any suspicious activity, and provides real-time alerts.

Data diddling is changing data before, during, or after it is entered into the system in order to delete, alter, add, or incorrectly update key system data. A clerk for a Denver brokerage altered a transaction to record 1,700 shares of Loren Industries stock worth $2,500 as shares in Long Island Lighting worth more than $25,000.

Data leakage is the unauthorized copying of company data. Ten Social Security employees stole 11,000 Social Security numbers and other identifying information and sold them to identity theft fraudsters. Acxiom suffered a data loss when, over a year and a half, an individual used a company's ftp client to steal 8.2 GB of data. *Podslurping* is using a small device with storage capacity, such as an iPod or Flash drive, to download unauthorized data. Security expert Abe Usher created slurp.exe and copied all document files from his computer in 65 seconds. Usher now makes a version of his program for security audits that does not copy files but generates a report of the information that could have been stolen in a real attack.

The *salami technique* is used to embezzle money a "salami slice" at a time from many different accounts. A disgruntled employee programmed the company computer to increase all production costs by a fraction of a percent and place the excess in the account of a dummy vendor he controlled. Every few months, the fraudulent costs were raised another fraction of a percent. Because all expenses were rising together, no single account would call attention to the fraud. The perpetrator was caught when a teller failed to recognize the payee name on a check the perpetrator was trying to cash. The salami scheme was part of the plot line in several films, including *Superman III, Hackers,* and *Office Space.*

One salami technique has been given a name. In a *round-down fraud*, all interest calculations are truncated at two decimal places and the excess decimals put into an account the perpetrator controls. No one is the wiser, since all the books balance. Over time, these fractions of a cent add up to a significant amount, especially when interest is calculated daily.

Economic espionage is the theft of information, trade secrets, and intellectual property. Losses are estimated to total $250 billion a year, with losses increasing by 323% during one five-year period. Almost 75% of losses are to an employee, former employee, contractor, or supplier. The FBI is investigating about 800 separate incidents of economic espionage at any point in time. Reuters Analytics allegedly broke into the computers of Bloomberg, a competitor, and stole code that helps financial institutions analyze stock market data. Toshiba paid $465 million to Lexar Media as compensation for trade secrets provided by a member of Lexar's board of directors.

Cyber-extortion is threatening to harm a company or a person if a specified amount of money is not paid. The owner of a credit card processor received an e-mail listing his clients as well as their credit card numbers. The e-mail told him to pay $50,000 in six payments, or the data would be sent to his clients. An investigation showed that his system had been successfully penetrated and that customer data had been copied. Not believing the attacker, the owner did nothing. The extortionists released the data, and he spent weeks trying to reassure his irate customers. His efforts were futile; his customers abandoned him, and within six months, he shut down his business. Diana DeGarmo, the runner-up from the third season of *American Idol*, was stalked by an obsessive fan who wanted to "become" Diana. The fan broke into Diana's MySpace account, stole her identity, and sent e-mails to her friends and fans. The fan phoned, e-mailed, and texted Diana more than a hundred times a day. When Diana finally asked her what she wanted, she replied that she wanted $1 million.

Cyber-bullying is using the Internet, cell phones, or other communication technologies to support deliberate, repeated, and hostile behavior that torments, threatens, harasses, humiliates, embarrasses, or otherwise harms another person. Cyber-bullying is especially prevalent among young people; research shows that almost half of all teens and preteens report some form of cyber-bullying. *Sexting* is exchanging explicit text messages and revealing pictures. One particularly degrading form of cyber-bullying is posting or sharing these pictures and messages with people who were never intended to see or read them. Anyone involved in transmitting nude pictures of someone under the age of 18 can be charged with dealing in child pornography. Legislation penalizing cyber-bullying has been passed in many states.

Internet terrorism is the act of disrupting electronic commerce and harming computers and communications. A Massachusetts man hired hackers to attack the WeaKnees.com Web site because WeaKnees turned down a business deal with him. The six-week-long attack used a botnet of 10,000 hijacked computers and caused $2 million in damage.

Internet misinformation is using the Internet to spread false or misleading information. McDonald's spent seven years fighting false accusations on Web sites. After 313 days of testimony and a cost of $16 million, McDonald's won and was awarded $94,000. A Web site mocked the verdict, called its campaign "unstoppable," and set up shop under a new name. Another form of Internet misinformation is pretending to be someone else and posting Web-based messages that damage the reputation of the impersonated person. Even subtler is entering bogus information in legitimate news stories. One young man broke into Yahoo's news pages and replaced the name of an arrested hacker with that of Bill Gates.

Perpetrators also send unsolicited *e-mail threats*. Global Communications sent messages threatening legal action if an overdue amount was not paid within 24 hours. The court action could be avoided by calling an 809 area code (the Caribbean). Callers got a clever recording that responded to the caller's voice. The responses were designed to keep callers on the phone as long as possible because they were being billed at $25 per minute.

Internet auction fraud is using an Internet auction site to defraud another person. According to the FBI, 45% of the complaints they receive are about Internet auction fraud. Internet auction fraud can take several forms. For example, a seller can use a false identity or partner with someone to drive up the bid price. A person can enter a very high bid to win the auction and then cancel his bid, allowing his partner, who has the next highest, and much lower, bid to win. The seller can fail to deliver the merchandise, or the buyer can fail to make the agreed-upon payment. The seller can deliver an inferior product or a product other than the one sold. In a recent case, three art dealers were convicted of casting bids in over 1,100 of each other's eBay auctions to drive up the price of their merchandise over a five-year period. Many of the 120 defrauded consumers paid thousands of dollars more than they would have without the fake bids.

Internet pump-and-dump fraud is using the Internet to pump up the price of a stock and then selling it. Pump-and-dump fraudsters do three things. First, they buy a significant number of shares in small, low-priced, thinly traded penny stocks without driving up their price. Second, they use spam e-mails, texts, Tweets, and Internet postings to disseminate overly optimistic or false information about the company to create a buying frenzy that drives up the stock price. Third, they sell their shares to unsuspecting investors at inflated prices and pocket a handsome profit. Once they stop touting the stock, its price crumbles, and investors lose their money. In a recent fraud, fraudsters quietly acquired shares in 15 thinly traded public companies. They used sophisticated hacking and identity fraud techniques, such as installing keystroke-logging software on computers in hotel business centers and Internet cafes, to gain access to online brokerage accounts. The hackers sold the securities in those accounts, used the money to purchase large quantities of stock of the 15 companies to pump up the share prices of those companies, and sold their stock for a $732,941 profit. The pump-and-dump operation, which was perpetrated in a few hours, cost U.S. brokerage firms an estimated at $2 million.

Companies advertising online pay from a few cents to over $10 for each click on their ads. *Click fraud* is manipulating click numbers to inflate advertising bills. Examples include

(1) companies clicking on a competitor's ad to drive up their advertising costs, (2) Web page owners who get a commission to host a pay-per-click ad clicking to boost commissions, and (3) ad agencies inflating the number of clicks to make an ad campaign appear more effective. Most click fraudsters are cyber criminals who create Web sites with nothing on them but ads and use their botnets to repeatedly click on the ads. As many as 30% of all clicks are not legitimate. That is no small sum, given that total revenues from online advertising exceed $15 billion dollars a year.

Web cramming is offering a free Web site for a month, developing a worthless Web site, and charging the phone bill of the people who accept the offer for months, whether they want to continue using the Web site or not. Web cramming has been in the top ten of online scams for the past few years, and there are no signs that it is going away. Law enforcement has cracked down on this for the past few years with no apparent permanent success.

Software piracy is the unauthorized copying or distribution of copyrighted software. Software piracy usually takes one of three forms: (1) selling a computer with pre-loaded illegal software, (2) installing a single-license copy on multiple machines, and (3) loading software on a network server and allowing unrestricted access to it in violation of the software license agreement.

It is estimated that for every legal software sale, between seven and eight illegal copies are made. Within days of being released, most new software is on the Internet and available free to those who want to download it illegally. An estimated 43% of software is pirated; in some countries, over 90% is pirated. The software industry estimates the economic losses due to software piracy exceed $50 billion a year.

The Business Software Alliance, which files lawsuits against software pirates, found 1,400 copies of unlicensed software at an adult vocational school in Los Angeles and claimed $5 million in damages. Individuals convicted of software piracy are subject to fines of up to $250,000 and jail terms of up to five years. However, they are often given more creative punishments. A Puget Sound student was required to write a 20-page paper on the evils of software piracy and copyright infringement and perform 50 hours of community service wiring schools for Internet usage. Failure to comply would subject him to a $10,000 fine and a copyright infringement lawsuit.

Social Engineering

Social engineering refers to techniques or psychological tricks used to get people to comply with the perpetrator's wishes in order to gain physical or logical access to a building, computer, server, or network—usually to get the information needed to access a system for the purpose of obtaining confidential data. Often, the perpetrator has a conversation with someone to trick, lie to, or otherwise deceive the victim. Often the perpetrator has information, knowledge, authority, or confidence that makes it appear that he belongs or knows what he is doing.

Establishing the following policies and procedures—and training people to follow them—can help minimize social engineering:

1. Never let people follow you into a restricted building.
2. Never log in for someone else on a computer, especially if you have administrative access.
3. Never give sensitive information over the phone or through e-mail.
4. Never share passwords or user IDs.
5. Be cautious of anyone you do not know who is trying to gain access through you.

The remainder of this section discusses various social engineering issues and techniques.

Identity theft is assuming someone's identity, usually for economic gain, by illegally obtaining and using confidential information, such as a Social Security number or a bank account or credit card number. Identity thieves empty bank accounts, apply for credit cards, run up large debts, and take out mortgages and loans. By carefully covering his tracks and having all bills sent to an address he controls, the identity thief can prolong the scheme because the victim will not know what is happening until considerable damage has been caused. Victims can usually prove they are not responsible for the debts or missing funds, but it takes significant time to clean up credit records and restore reputations.

A convicted felon incurred $100,000 of credit card debt, took out a home loan, purchased homes and consumer goods, and filed for bankruptcy in the victim's name. He phoned and mocked his victim because the victim could not do anything, because identity theft was not a crime at the time. The victim spent four years and $15,000 to restore his credit and reputation. The identity thief served a brief sentence for lying while buying a gun and did not have to make restitution. This and similar cases resulted in Congress making identity theft a federal offense in 1998.

Pretexting is using an invented scenario (the pretext) to increase the likelihood that a victim will divulge information or do something. The pretext is more than a just simple lie; it usually involves creating legitimacy in the target's mind that makes impersonation possible. Pretexters conduct a security survey and lull the victim into disclosing confidential information by asking 10 innocent questions before asking the confidential ones. They call help desks and claim to be an employee who has forgotten a password. They call users and say they are testing the system and need a password. They pose as buyers, prospective employees, or salespeople to get plant tours and obtain information that may help them break into the system. They use voice-changing devices to make a male voice sound like a female voice or use spoofing devices to make it appear they are phoning from the intended victim's phone.

The chairwoman of Hewlett-Packard was forced to resign after H-P hired a private investigator to catch H-P directors who had leaked confidential information to reporters. The private investigator pretended to be someone he was not to get private phone records and other confidential information of directors and journalists. As a result, Congress passed a bill making the use of pretexting to obtain a person's phone records illegal.

A hacker tricked a T-Mobile employee into disclosing the information needed to hack into Paris Hilton's phone by answering the question "What is your favorite pet's name?" Tinkerbell, the name of her dog, was well known. The hacker accessed her phone and posted the contents of her address book, notes, and some very embarrassing photos on the Internet.

Posing is creating a seemingly legitimate business (often selling new and exciting products), collecting personal information while making a sale, and never delivering the product. Fraudsters also create Internet job listing sites to collect confidential information.

Phishing is sending an electronic message pretending to be a legitimate company, usually a financial institution, and requesting information or verification of information and often warning of some dire consequence if it is not provided. The recipient is asked to respond to the bogus request or visit a Web page and submit data. The message usually contains a link to a Web page that appears legitimate. The Web page has company logos, familiar graphics, phone numbers, and Internet links that appear to be those of the victimized company. It also has a form requesting everything from a home address to an ATM card's PIN. Phishers are becoming more sophisticated. Early phishing scams sent messages to everyone. Targeted versions of phishing, called spear phishing, have emerged that target known customers of a specific company.

In the early days, each phishing e-mail resulted in tens of thousands of calls to bank call centers, disrupted business, and cost hundreds of thousands of dollars to handle the deluge of calls. An estimated 2 million Americans have been fooled by phishing scams, with yearly losses exceeding $3.2 billion.

It is easy to launch a phishing attack because hackers sell kits that lead people through the process. Some phishing e-mails secretly install software that spies on or hijacks the user's computer. The software captures log-on names or takes pictures of the user's screen when he logs into his financial institution.

The IRS has set up a Web site and an e-mail address (phishing@irs.gov) where people can forward suspicious e-mails that purport to be from the IRS. In a recent IRS phishing attack, e-mail recipients were told that they were due a refund and were directed to a Website that looked just like the IRS Web site and contained forms that looked just like IRS forms. To claim the refund, the taxpayer had to enter confidential information that facilitated identity theft.

Voice phishing, or *vishing*, is like phishing except that the victim enters confidential data by phone. Perpetrators use Voice over Internet Protocol (VoIP) to spoof the legitimate phone number (caller ID shows they are calling their financial institution) and to detect the telephone keystrokes.

To avoid being phished or vished, be highly skeptical of any message that suggests you are the target of illegal activity. Ignore e-mails that request confidential information, and do not call a number given in an unsolicited message. If you are concerned, call the institution using a number you know is valid to ensure that account information has not been tampered with.

Carding refers to activities performed on stolen credit cards, including making a small online purchase to determine whether the card is still valid and buying and selling stolen credit card numbers. Scores of underground Web sites facilitate carding, with some rating the reliability of sellers the same way eBay does. Cyber-criminal gangs run many of the carding sites.

Pharming is redirecting Web site traffic to a spoofed Web site. If you could change XYZ Company's number in the phone book to your phone number, people using the phone book to call XYZ Company would reach you instead. Similarly, each Web site has a unique IP (Internet) address (four groupings of numbers separated by three periods). There is a Domain Name System (think phone book) that converts a domain (Web site) name to an IP address. Pharmers change the IP address in the Domain Name System (DNS) to an IP address they control. Compromised DNS servers are referred to as "poisoned."

Malware can also be used to change a computer's host file (internal DNS) or an Internet service provider's IP addresses. Because most PCs are not as well controlled, they are better targets for pharming than Internet servers. Once these files are poisoned, all subsequent requests to visit that Web site are directed to the spoofed site.

Pharming is a very popular social engineering tool for two reasons. First, it is difficult to detect because the user's browser shows the correct Web site. Antivirus and spyware removal software are currently ineffective protections against pharming. Instead, complicated anti-pharming techniques are required. Second is the ability to target many people at a time through domain spoofing rather than one at a time with phishing e-mails.

A recent pharming attack targeted 65 financial firms, including PayPal, eBay, Discover Card, and American Express. The sophisticated and multi-pronged attack involved thousands of computers, multiple IP addresses in multiple countries, and a flood of fraudulent spam. The two-and-a-half-day pharming attack was so successful, resilient, and hard to correct that it was evident that a professional team planned it. The first e-mail spam contained bogus news that the Australia Prime Minister was struggling for his life after a heart attack. The e-mail contained a link to a newspaper story from *The Australian*. The second e-mail lure had a link to news of a cricket match in Australia. When people clicked on the links, they were redirected to one of five malicious Web sites that infected their computers with pharming malware.

An *evil twin* is a wireless network with the same name (called *Service Set Identifier*, or *SSID*) as a legitimate wireless access point. The hacker produces a wireless signal that is stronger than the legitimate signal or disrupts or disables the legitimate access point by disconnecting it, directing a denial-of-service against it, or creating radio frequency interference around it. Users are unaware that they connect to the evil twin. The perpetrator monitors the traffic looking for confidential information. Hackers also use evil twins to unleash a wide variety of malware and to install software to attack other computers. After a small coffee shop advertised free wireless Internet, there was an increase in identity thefts. The police discovered that a man living next to the coffee shop had set up an evil twin and was stealing confidential information.

Typosquatting, or *URL hijacking*, is setting up similarly named Web sites so that users making typographical errors when entering a Web site name are sent to an invalid site. For example, typing goggle.com instead of google.com might lead to a cyber-squatter site that:

- Tricks the user into thinking she is at the real site because of a copied or a similar logo, Web site layout, or content. These sites often contain advertising that appeals to the person looking for the real domain name. The typosquatter might also be a competitor.
- Is very different from what was wanted. One typosquatter sent people looking for a children's site to a pornographic Web site.
- Distributes malware such as viruses, spyware, and adware.

To stop typosquatting, companies send a cease-and-desist letter to the offender, purchase the Web site address, or file a lawsuit. Google won a case against a Russian typosquatter who registered domain names such as googkle.com and gooigle.com. The lawsuit was decided on three criteria: The domain names were obvious misspellings of google.com, the Russian had no independent claims or interest in the names, and he used the Web sites to infect computers with malware. Google was given possession of the domain names.

To prevent typosquatting, a company (1) tries to obtain all the Web names similar to theirs to redirect people to the correct site, or (2) uses software to scan the Internet and find domains that appear to be typosquatting. Parents can use the same software to restrict access to sites that squat on typos of children's Web sites.

Tabnapping is secretly changing an already open browser tab. Tabnapping begins when a victim is tricked into opening an e-mail link or visiting an infected Web site. The site uses JavaScript to identify a frequently visited site and secretly change the label and contents of the open, but inactive, browser tab. When the victim clicks on the altered tab, it shows that the site has been timed out. When the victim logs back in, the user ID and password are captured and forwarded to the identity thief.

Scavenging, or *dumpster diving*, is gaining access to confidential information by searching documents and records. Some identity thieves search garbage cans, communal trash bins, and city dumps to find information. Oracle Corporation was embarrassed a few years ago when investigators it hired were caught going through the trash of companies that supported its rival, Microsoft. The investigators had paid building janitors $1,200 for the trash. In another instance, Jerry Schneider discovered Pacific Telephone computer operating guides in a trash bin on his way home from high school. Over time, his scavenging activities resulted in a technical library that allowed him to steal $1 million worth of electronic equipment.

In *shoulder surfing*, as its name suggests, perpetrators look over a person's shoulders in a public place to get information such as ATM PIN numbers or user IDs and passwords. Fraudsters also surf from a distance using binoculars or cameras. In South America, a man hid a video camera in some bushes and pointed it at a company president's computer, which was visible through a first-floor window. A significant business acquisition almost fell through because of the information on the videotape. Shoulder surfers can be foiled by blocking the surfer's view of the input device.

In *Lebanese looping*, the perpetrator inserts a sleeve into an ATM that prevents the ATM from ejecting the card. When it is obvious that the card is trapped, the perpetrator approaches the victim and pretends to help, tricking the person into entering her PIN again. Once the victim gives up, the thief removes the card and uses the card and PIN to withdraw as much money as the ATM allows. Lebanese looping is common in any country with a large number of ATMs.

Skimming is double-swiping a credit card in a legitimate terminal or covertly swiping a credit card in a small, hidden, handheld card reader that records credit card data for later use. Commonly committed in retail outlets such as restaurants and carried out by employees with a legitimate reason to possess the victim's cards, skimming losses exceed $1 billion per year. A part-time employee at a gas station skimmed the cards of 80 customers, including the owner, who was a relative, and stole over $200,000.

Chipping is posing as a service engineer and planting a small chip that records transaction data in a legitimate credit card reader. The chip is later removed to access the data recorded on it.

Eavesdropping is listening to private communications or tapping into data transmissions. The equipment needed to set up a wiretap on an unprotected communications line is readily available at local electronics stores. One alleged wiretapping fraud involved Mark Koenig, a 28-year-old telecommunications consultant, and four associates. Federal agents say they pulled crucial data about Bank of America customers from telephone lines and used it to make 5,500 fake ATM cards. Koenig and his friends allegedly intended to use the cards over a long weekend to withdraw money from banks across the country. Authorities were tipped off, and they were apprehended before they could use the cards.

Malware

This section describes *malware*, which is any software that can be used to do harm. A recent study shows that malware is spread using several simultaneous approaches, including file sharing (used in 72% of attacks), shared access to files (42%), e-mail attachments (25%), and remote access vulnerabilities (24%).

Spyware software secretly monitors and collects personal information about users and sends it to someone else. The information is gathered by logging keystrokes, monitoring Web sites visited, and scanning documents on the computer's hard drive. Spyware can also hijack a browser, replacing a computer's home page with a page the spyware creator wants you to visit. Unless the spyware is removed, resetting a browser home page lasts only until the computer is rebooted. Spyware can also hijack search requests, returning results chosen by the spyware rather than the results desired. Spyware infections, of which users are usually unaware, come from the following:

- Downloads such as file-sharing programs, system utilities, games, wallpaper, screensavers, music, and videos.
- Web sites that secretly download spyware. This is called *drive-by downloading*.
- A hacker using security holes in Web browsers and other software.
- Malware masquerading as anti-spyware security software.
- A worm or virus.
- Public wireless networks. At Kinko's in Manhattan, an employee gathered the data needed to open bank accounts and apply for credit cards in the names of the people using Kinko's wireless network.

Spyware is especially problematic for companies with employees who telecommute or remotely access the network. Spyware on these computers record the user's network interactions, copy corporate data, and introduce spyware to the entire organization. A main source of spyware is adult-oriented sites. The computers of people who visit those sites are infected, and when they log onto their corporate systems those infections are passed to their employer's internal network.

Adware is spyware that pops banner ads on a monitor, collects information about the user's Web-surfing and spending habits, and forwards it to the adware creator. Adware companies charge for each computer showing its ads. They increase the number of computers with adware by paying shareware developers to bundle the adware with their software. This allows shareware developers to make money without charging for their software. One company that engages in digital media content sharing offers users a $30 version or a free version. The license agreement for the free software discloses the adware (hence making it "legal" spyware), but most users do not read the agreement and are not aware it is installed. Reputable adware companies claim sensitive or identifying data are not collected. However, there is no way for users to effectively control or limit the data collected and transmitted.

A recent AOL study found that 80% of inspected computers were infected with spyware, each machine containing on average 93 spyware or adware components. Another study estimated that 90% of computers connected to the Internet had spyware, with 90% of the owners unaware of the infection. The best protection against spyware and adware is a good antispyware software package that neutralizes or eliminates it and prevents its installation. One downside is that after the spyware or adware is erased, the free software that was its host may not work. Use multiple anti-spyware programs; unlike antivirus software and firewalls, they won't conflict.

Some malware developers intentionally make their software difficult to uninstall. Malware companies sometimes battle each other over whose software will infect a computer. Some of them have developed *torpedo software* that destroys competing malware, resulting in "malware warfare" between competing developers.

Scareware is software that is often malicious and of little or no benefit that is sold using scare tactics. The most common scare tactic is a dire warning that most computers are infected with viruses, spyware, and other catastrophic problems. Some scareware even warns that a user's job, career, or marriage is at risk. The scareware creators offer a solution—a free computer scan using their fake antivirus software. Accepting the free scan does several things. First, it does not perform a scan. Second, it claims to find dozens of problems and again warns of dire consequences if the computer is not cleaned up. Third, it often introduces into the consumer's computer the very problems that scared the consumer into trying the software. Fourth, it encourages the consumer to buy the fake antivirus software to clean the computer and keep it clean.

Scareware is marketed using spam e-mail and pop-up windows or banners on Web sites, some of which look as though they were placed by big-name corporations. To deceive consumers, the software looks and feels like legitimate security software, the e-mails look like they come from legitimate security software companies, and the pop-ups look like they come from the user's operating system. Scareware scammers also create Web pages about celebrity news and other hot topics that appear at the top of Google search results; clicking on any of the many links on the Web page launches the scareware. Scammers also steal Facebook and Twitter account logons, send messages carrying a tainted Web link to the victim's contacts, and rely on the high trust common to social networks to trick users into launching scareware.

There are tens of thousands of different scareware packages, with the number rising almost 600% in one recent six-month period. In another growth comparison, Microsoft reported that its free Malicious Software Removal Tool cleaned scareware off 7.8 million PCs in one six-month period compared to 5.3 million in the prior six months.

Scareware can be spotted several ways, First, the scare tactics are a big giveaway; legitimate companies will not try to scare you into using their products. A second giveaway is bad English; most scareware comes from countries where English is not the creator's first language.

The Federal Trade Commission sued the perpetrators of a massive scareware scheme that offered fake computer scans that falsely claimed to detect viruses, spyware, system errors, and illegal pornography. They tricked over a million people into spending $1.9 million to buy fake computer security products, including DriveCleaner, XP Antivirus, WinAntivirus, ErrorSafe, and WinFixer.

Like scareware, *ransomware* comes in the form of fake antivirus software. When activated, well-written ransomware locks you out of all your programs and data by encrypting them. That means you can't run your installed security programs and, if it disables your USB ports and DVD drives, you can't load new security programs to combat it. It directs Internet Explorer to the perpetrator's Web site, where the victim is informed that a monetary payment made directly to a bank must be made to have the software removed. Since payments can be traced, ransomware is not as common as other malware. Most ransomware is delivered via a spam e-mail that motivates the recipient to open an infected file. It can also be delivered by Web sites. Keeping Windows updated is crucial to blocking these downloads.

Key logging software records computer activity, such as a user's keystrokes, e-mails sent and received, Web sites visited, and chat session participation. Parents use the software to monitor their children's computer usage, and businesses use it to monitor employee activity. Law enforcement uses it to detect or prevent crime. A Drug Enforcement Administration agent persuaded a federal judge to authorize him to sneak into an Escondido, California, office believed to be a front for manufacturing the drug Ecstasy. Copying the contents of all hard drives and installing keystroke loggers successfully thwarted their plans to distribute Ecstasy.

Fraud perpetrators use key loggers to capture and send confidential information. Over 10,000 unique key logging software programs are available in underground chat rooms; most are free or very cheap. Computers are infected with key logging software when they visit corrupt Web sites or download free software. One enterprising student installed key logging software on his teacher's computer, recorded her typed exams answers, and decoded the keystrokes. He was caught trying to sell exam answers to other students.

A *Trojan horse* is a set of malicious computer instructions in an authorized and otherwise properly functioning program. Unlike viruses and worms, the code does not try to replicate itself. Some Trojan horses give the creator the power to control the victim's computer remotely. Most Trojan horse infections occur when a user runs an infected program received in an e-mail, visits a malicious Web site, or downloads software billed as helpful add-ons to popular software programs. In Israel, companies were sent business proposals on a disk that contained the Trojan. In another case, visitors to an adult site were told to download a special program to see the pictures. This program disconnected them from their Internet service providers and connected them to a service that billed them $2 a minute until they turned off their computers. Over 800,000 minutes were billed, with some phone bills as high as $3,000, before the scam was detected. The HotLan Trojan caused infected computers to sign up for Microsoft Hotmail and Google Gmail accounts and used them for spamming. Over 514,000 Hotmail accounts and 49,000 Gmail accounts were created in a single day. One type of Trojan horse relies on the curiosity of the victim. The attacker creates a malware-infected CD ROM or USB flash drive, gives it a legitimate looking and curiosity piquing label (company logo, accompanied by 4Q Evaluation and Salary Data), leaves it where it can be found (bathroom, desktop, hallway), and waits for a curious employee to try to read the file. The file installs the Trojan on the employee's computer, likely giving the attacker access to the company's internal computer network.

Time bombs and *logic bombs* are Trojan horses that lie idle until triggered by a specified date or time, by a change in the system, by a message sent to the system, or by an event that does not occur. Once triggered, the bomb goes off, destroying programs, data, or both. Disgruntled company insiders who want to get even with their company write many bombs. Anticipating that he would not receive a bonus or new contract, Roger Duronio planted a Trojan horse time bomb at USB PaineWebber. Several weeks after he left the firm, the trigger date of March 4 arrived. His 60 lines of malicious code attacked the company's 2,000 servers and deleted company files just as the stock market opened. The effects were catastrophic. Broker computers were out of commission for days or weeks, depending on how badly the machines were damaged and the existence of branch backup tapes. Some 20% of the computers had no backup tapes, and some servers were never fully restored. Over 400 employees and 200 IBM consultants worked feverishly, at a cost of $3.1 million, to restore the system. Duronio cashed out his IRA and sold UBS stock short, figuring to make a killing when the stock plunged. It never did, and he lost money on his short sale. Duronio was sentenced to eight years in prison.

There are legal uses of time and logic bombs, such as in trial versions of software. The software becomes unusable after a certain amount of time passes or after the software has been used a certain number of times.

A *trap door*, or *back door*, is a way into a system that bypasses normal authorization and authentication controls. Programmers create trap doors so they can modify programs during systems development and then remove them before the system is put into operation. The back door can also be created by a virus or worm or by a disgruntled programmer. Anyone who discovers a trap door can enter the program. Security consultants claim that back doors are frequently discovered in organizations. BackOrifice, Netbus, and SubSeven are tools intruders use to gain remote, back door access to systems with Windows software. Jonathan James, the first juvenile sent to prison for hacking, installed a back door into a Department of Defense server, accessed sensitive e-mails, and captured employee usernames and passwords.

Packet sniffers capture data from information packets as they travel over networks. Captured data are examined to find confidential or proprietary information. In Sweden, Dan Egerstad's packet sniffer looked for key words such as *government*, *military*, *war*, *passport*, and *visa*. He intercepted e-mails from embassies and governments, many with visa and passport data.

Steganography is writing hidden messages in such a way that no one, apart from the sender and intended recipient, suspects their existence. Steganography messages do not attract attention to themselves, whereas an encrypted message arouses suspicion. *Steganography programs* hide data files inside a host file, such as a large image or sound file. The software merges the two files by removing scattered bytes from the host file and replacing them with data from the hidden file. The steganography program password protects the merged file, and the only way to reassemble the hidden file is to key the password into the same steganography program. The host file can still be heard or viewed because human visual and auditory senses are not sensitive enough to pick up the slight decrease in image or sound quality that the hidden file causes. Company employees can merge confidential information with a seemingly harmless file and send it anywhere in the world, where the confidential information is reassembled.

Steganography is used by terrorists, as it is an effective way for a spy to transmit information and receive orders. Some experts believe steganography was one way terrorists communicated in planning the September 11 terrorist attack on the United States. A *USA Today* article alleged that Al-Qaeda operatives sent hundreds of messages hidden in digital photographs sold on eBay.

A *rootkit* conceals processes, files, network connections, memory addresses, systems utility programs, and system data from the operating system and other programs. Rootkits often modify the operating system or install themselves as drivers. A rootkit is used to hide the presence of trap doors, sniffers, and key loggers; conceal software that originates a denial-of-service or an e-mail spam attack; and access user names and log-in information. Unlike viruses and worms, rootkits do not spread to other systems. Rootkit software is readily available on the Internet. Several vendors sell programs that detect rootkits, and security vendors include rootkit detection in their antivirus products. When a rootkit is detected, it is better to reinstall the operating system from scratch rather than spend the time and effort to delete it from the system. In a famous instance of rootkit use, Sony music CDs secretly placed a copy-protection rootkit on Windows computers. The software inadvertently opened security holes that allowed viruses to break in. Sony had to recall all CDs that included the software.

Superzapping is the unauthorized use of special system programs to bypass regular system controls and perform illegal acts, all without leaving an audit trail. The technique derives its name from Superzap, a software utility developed by IBM to handle emergencies. The manager of computer operations at a bank was told to use a Superzap program to correct a problem affecting account balances caused by unanticipated problems in changing from one computer system to another. When he discovered he could use the program to make account changes without the usual controls, audits, or documentation, he moved $128,000 into the accounts of several friends. Because the Superzap program left no evidence of data file changes, he was not detected until a customer complained about a shortage in his account.

A computer *virus* is a segment of self-replicating, executable code that attaches itself to a file or program. During its replication phase, the virus spreads to other systems when the infected file or program is downloaded or opened by the recipient. Newer viruses can mutate each time they infect a computer, making them more difficult to detect and destroy. Many viruses lie dormant for extended periods without causing damage, except to propagate themselves. In one survey, 90% of respondents said their company was infected with a virus during the prior 12 months.

During the attack phase, triggered by some predefined event, viruses destroy or alter data or programs, take control of the computer, destroy the hard drive's file allocation table, delete or rename files or directories, reformat the hard drive, change the content of files, or keep users from booting the system or accessing data on the hard drive. A virus can intercept and change transmissions, display disruptive images or messages, or cause the screen image to change color or disappear. Many viruses automatically send e-mails, faxes, or text messages with the victim's name as the source. As the virus spreads, it takes up space, clogs communications, and hinders system performance. Computer virus symptoms include computers that will not start or execute; unexpected read or write operations; an inability to save files; long program load times; abnormally large file sizes; slow systems operation; incessant pop-ups; and unusual screen activity, error messages, or file names.

A bad virus attack shut down a bank with 200 servers and 10,000 desktop computers for four days. During the downtime, the bank was locked out of its system, and customer accounts could not be accessed. A firm that specializes in fixing virus attacks eventually restored the system. The Sobig virus, written by Russian hackers, infected an estimated 1 of every 17 e-mails several years ago. The virus took months to write and was released in ever-improving versions. A year later, the MyDoom virus infected 1 in 12 e-mails and did $4.75 billion in damages.

Every day, virus creators send an estimated 1 billion virus-infected e-mail messages. The creators are getting good at making them look authentic. One recent virus came in an e-mail that appeared to come from Microsoft—the Microsoft logo and copyright were included in the message window launched by the virus. The e-mail told the recipient to use the attached patch to fix a security flaw in either Microsoft Internet Explorer or Outlook. Instead, opening the attachment downloaded malicious software that installed a back door allowing the perpetrator to control the computer.

It is estimated that viruses and worms cost businesses over $20 billion a year. A computer system can be protected from viruses by following the guidelines listed in Focus 1.

A computer *worm* is a self-replicating computer program similar to a virus, with some exceptions:

1. A virus is a segment of code hidden in or attached to a host program or executable file, whereas a worm is a stand-alone program.
2. A virus requires a human to do something (run a program, open a file, etc.) to replicate itself, whereas a worm does not and actively seeks to send copies of itself to other network devices.
3. Worms harm networks (if only by consuming bandwidth), whereas viruses infect or corrupt files or data on a targeted computer.

Worms often reside in e-mail attachments and reproduce by mailing themselves to the recipient's mailing list, resulting in an electronic chain letter. Some recent worms have completely shut down e-mail systems. Worms are not confined to personal computers; thousands of worms infect cell phones each year by jumping from phone to phone over wireless networks.

A worm usually does not live very long, but it is quite destructive while alive. It takes little technical knowledge to create a worm or virus. Many Web sites provide applications that enable unsophisticated users to create worms. One application has been downloaded over 25,000 times.

Focus 2 describes an early and destructive worm that affected 6,000 computers in a very short time. More recently, MySpace had to go offline to disable a worm that added over 1 million friends to the hacker's site in less than a day. MySpace profiles were also infected by a worm after viewing

Keeping Your Computers Virus-Free

Here are some practical suggestions for protecting computers from viruses:

- Install reputable and reliable antivirus software that scans for, identifies, and destroys viruses. Use only one antivirus program; multiple programs conflict with each other.
- Do not fall for ads touting free antivirus software; much of it is fake and contains malware. Some hackers create Web sites stuffed with content about breaking news so that the site appears on the first page of search results. Anyone clicking on the link is confronted with a pop-up with a link to fake antivirus software.
- Do not fall for pop-up notices that warn of horrible threats and offer a free scan of your computer. Although no scan actually takes place, the program reports dozens of dangerous infections and tells you to purchase and download their fake antivirus program to clean it up.
- Make sure that the latest versions of the antivirus programs are used. National City Bank in Cleveland, Ohio, installed some new laptops. The manufacturer and the bank checked the laptops for viruses but did not use the latest antivirus software. A virus spread from the laptop hard drives to 300 network servers and 12,000 workstations. It took the bank over two days to eradicate the virus from all bank systems.
- Scan all incoming e-mail for viruses at the server level as well as at users' desktops.

- Do not download anything from an e-mail that uses noticeably bad English, such as terrible grammar and misspelled words. Real companies hire people to produce quality writing. Many viruses come from overseas perpetrators whose first language is not English.
- All software should be certified as virus-free before you load it into the system. Be wary of software from unknown sources: They may be virus bait—especially if their prices or functionality sound too good to be true.
- Deal only with trusted software retailers.
- Some software suppliers use electronic techniques to make tampering evident. Ask whether the software you are purchasing has such protection.
- Check new software on an isolated machine with virus-detection software. Software direct from the publisher has been known to have viruses.
- Have two backups of all files. Data files should be backed up separately from programs to avoid contaminating backup data.
- If you use flash drives or CDs, do not put them in strange machines; they may become infected. Do not let others use those storage devices on your machine. Scan all new files with antiviral software before any data or programs are copied to your machine.

A Worm Run Amok

Within minutes, a rash of unknown users trying to log on crashed Berkeley's computer system. Within hours, computer experts discovered it was invading the *entire* Internet. While scientists attempted to stop the worm, law enforcement and the press investigated it. Information on the perpetrator was scarce until an unidentified phone caller tipped off a *New York Times* writer by inadvertently referring to him as "RTM."

Robert T. Morris acquired a passion for computer security while working with his father, a scientist at Bell Labs. At Harvard, he was recognized for projects that improved Bell Systems' Internet operations and its UNIX operating system. At age 20, Robert's skills in UNIX security were so extensive that he gave an address on computer security to both the National Security Agency and the Naval Research Laboratory.

While Robert was in graduate school at Cornell, the first computer viruses sparked his interest in developing an

undetectable worm that would reach as many computers as possible. Using a bug in the UNIX Sendmail subprogram, Robert developed a worm capable of entering a system without authorization. From his system at Cornell, Robert illegally logged on to an artificial intelligence lab computer at MIT and released his creation. After dinner, Robert attempted to log on, but the computer did not respond. He immediately knew something was wrong. After several attempts to remedy the problem, Robert realized he had made a fatal programming error that allowed the worm to replicate out of control throughout the Internet. Cleaning out the Internet system and recreating the files that the worm destroyed took several months.

Robert was arrested, charged with a felony, convicted, and sentenced to three years' probation, 400 hours of community service, and a $10,000 fine.

a QuickTime video containing malicious software that replaced the links in the user's page with links to a phishing site. The devastating Conficker worm infected 25% of enterprise Window PCs.

Many viruses and worms exploit known software vulnerabilities than can be corrected with a software patch. Therefore, a good defense against them is making sure that all software patches are installed as soon as they are available.

Recent viruses and worms have attacked cell phones and personal electronic devices using text messages, Internet page downloads, and Bluetooth wireless technology. Flaws in Bluetooth applications open the system to attack. *Bluesnarfing* is stealing (snarfing) contact lists, images, and other data using Bluetooth. A reporter for TimesOnline accompanied Adam Laurie, a security expert, around London scanning for Bluetooth-compatible phones. Before a Bluetooth connection can be made, the person contacted must agree to accept the link. However, Laurie has written software to bypass this control and identified vulnerable handsets at an average rate of one per minute. He downloaded entire phonebooks, calendars, diary contents, and stored pictures. Phones up to 90 meters away were vulnerable.

Bluebugging is taking control of someone else's phone to make or listen to calls, send or read text messages, connect to the Internet, forward the victim's calls, and call numbers that charge fees. These attacks will become more popular as phones are used to pay for items purchased. When a hacker wants something, all he has to do is bluebug a nearby phone and make a purchase. To prevent these attacks, a bluetooth device can be set to make it hard for other devices to recognize it. Antivirus software for phones is being developed to deal with such problems.

In the future, many other devices—such as home security systems, home appliances, automobiles, and elevators—will be connected to the Internet and will be the target of viruses and worms.

Table 1 summarizes, in alphabetical order, the computer fraud and abuse techniques discussed in the chapter.

TABLE 1 Computer Fraud and Abuse Techniques

Technique	Description
Address Resolution Protocol (ARP) spoofing	Sending fake ARP messages to an Ethernet LAN. ARP is a computer networking protocol for determining a network host's hardware address when only its IP or network address is known.
Adware	Software that collects and forwards data to advertising companies or causes banner ads to pop up as the Internet is surfed.
Bluebugging	Taking control of a phone to make calls, send text messages, listen to calls, or read text messages.
Bluesnarfing	Stealing contact lists, images, and other data using Bluetooth.
Botnet, bot herders	A network of hijacked computers. Bot herders use the hijacked computers, called zombies, in a variety of Internet attacks.
Buffer overflow attack	Inputting so much data that the input buffer overflows. The overflow contains code that takes control of the computer.
Caller ID spoofing	Displaying an incorrect number on the recipient's caller ID display to hide the identity of the caller.
Carding	Verifying credit card validity; buying and selling stolen credit cards.
Chipping	Planting a chip that records transaction data in a legitimate credit card reader.
Cross-site scripting (XSS) attack	Exploits Web page security vulnerabilities to bypass browser security mechanisms and create a malicious link that injects unwanted code into a Web site.
Cyber-bullying	Using computer technology to harm another person.
Cyber-extortion	Requiring a company to pay money to keep an extortionist from harming a computer or a person.
Data diddling	Changing data before, during, or after it is entered into the system.
Data leakage	Unauthorized copying of company data.
Denial-of-service attack	An attack designed to make computer resources unavailable to its users. For example, so many e-mail messages that the Internet service provider's e-mail server is overloaded and shuts down.
Dictionary attack	Using software to guess company addresses, send employees blank e-mails, and add unreturned messages to spammer e-mail lists.
DNS spoofing	Sniffing the ID of a Domain Name System (server that converts a Web site name to an IP address) request and replying before the real DNS server.
Eavesdropping	Listening to private voice or data transmissions.

(Continued)

TABLE 1 Continued

Technique	Description
Economic espionage	The theft of information, trade secrets, and intellectual property.
E-mail threats	Sending a threatening message asking recipients to do something that makes it possible to defraud them.
E-mail spoofing	Making a sender address and other parts of an e-mail header appear as though the e-mail originated from a different source.
Evil twin	A wireless network with the same name as another wireless access point. Users unknowingly connect to the evil twin; hackers monitor the traffic looking for useful information.
Hacking	Unauthorized access, modification, or use of computer systems, usually by means of a PC and a communications network.
Hijacking	Gaining control of someone else's computer for illicit activities.
IP address spoofing	Creating Internet Protocol packets with a forged IP address to hide the sender's identity or to impersonate another computer system.
Identity theft	Assuming someone's identity by illegally obtaining confidential information such as a Social Security number.
Internet auction fraud	Using an Internet auction site to commit fraud.
Internet misinformation	Using the Internet to spread false or misleading information.
Internet terrorism	Using the Internet to disrupt communications and ecommerce.
Internet pump-and-dump fraud	Using the Internet to pump up the price of a stock and then sell it.
Key logger	Using spyware to record a user's keystrokes.
Lebanese looping	Inserting a sleeve into an ATM so that it will not eject the victim's card, pretending to help the victim as a means to discover his or her PIN, and then using the card and PIN to drain the account.
Logic bombs and time bombs	Software that sits idle until a specified circumstance or time triggers it, destroying programs, data, or both.
Malware	Software that can be used to do harm.
Man-in-the-middle (MITM) attack	A hacker placing himself between a client and a host to intercept network traffic; also called *session hijacking*.
Masquerading/impersonation	Accessing a system by pretending to be an authorized user. The impersonator enjoys the same privileges as the legitimate user.
Packet sniffing	Inspecting information packets as they travel the Internet and other networks.
Password cracking	Penetrating system defenses, stealing passwords, and decrypting them to access system programs, files, and data.
Pharming	Redirecting traffic to a spoofed Web site to obtain confidential information.
Phishing	Communications that request recipients to disclose confidential information by responding to an e-mail or visiting a Web site.
Phreaking	Attacking phone systems to get free phone access; using phone lines to transmit viruses and to access, steal, and destroy data.
Piggybacking	1. Clandestine use of someone's Wi-Fi network. 2. Tapping into a communications line and entering a system by latching onto a legitimate user. 3. Bypassing physical security controls by entering a secure door when an authorized person opens it.
Podslurping	Using a small device with storage capacity (iPod, Flash drive) to download unauthorized data from a computer.
Posing	Creating a seemingly legitimate business, collecting personal data while making a sale, and never delivering items sold.
Pretexting	Acting under false pretenses to gain confidential information.
Rootkit	Software that conceals processes, files, network connections, and system data from the operating system and other programs.
Round-down fraud	Truncating interest calculations at two decimal places and placing truncated amounts in the perpetrator's account.
Ransomware	Software that encrypts programs and data until a ransom is paid to remove it.
Salami technique	Stealing tiny slices of money over time.
Scareware	Malicious software of no benefit that is sold using scare tactics.

TABLE 1 Continued

Technique	Description
Scavenging/dumpster diving	Searching for confidential information by searching for documents and records in garbage cans, communal trash bins, and city dumps
Sexting	Exchanging explicit text messages and pictures.
Shoulder surfing	Watching or listening to people enter or disclose confidential data.
Skimming	Double-swiping a credit card or covertly swiping it in a card reader that records the data for later use.
SMS spoofing	Using short message service (SMS) to change the name or number a text message appears to come from.
Social engineering	Techniques that trick a person into disclosing confidential information.
Software piracy	Unauthorized copying or distribution of copyrighted software.
Spamming	E-mailing an unsolicited message to many people at the same time.
Splog	A spam blog that promotes Web sites to increase their Google PageRank (how often a Web page is referenced by other pages).
Spyware	Software that monitors computing habits and sends that data to someone else, often without the user's permission.
Spoofing	Making electronic communications look like someone else sent it.
SQL injection attack	Inserting a malicious SQL query in input in such a way that it is passed to and executed by an application program.
Steganography	Hiding data from one file inside a host file, such as a large image or sound file.
Superzapping	Using special software to bypass system controls and perform illegal acts.
Tabnapping	Secretly changing an already open browser tab using JavaScript.
Trap door	A back door into a system that bypasses normal system controls.
Trojan horse	Unauthorized code in an authorized and properly functioning program.
Typosquatting/URL hijacking	Web sites with names similar to real Web sites; users making typographical errors are sent to a site filled with malware.
Virus	Executable code that attaches itself to software, replicates itself, and spreads to other systems or files. Triggered by a predefined event, it damages system resources or displays messages.
Vishing	Voice phishing, in which e-mail recipients are asked to call a phone number that asks them to divulge confidential data.
War dialing	Dialing phone lines to find idle modems to use to enter a system, capture the attached computer, and gain access to its network(s).
War driving/rocketing	Looking for unprotected wireless networks using a car or a rocket.
Web cramming	Developing a free and worthless trial-version Web site and charging the subscriber's phone bill for months even if the subscriber cancels.
Web-page spoofing	Also called *phishing*.
Worm	Similar to a virus; a program rather than a code segment hidden in a host program. Actively transmits itself to other systems. It usually does not live long but is quite destructive while alive.
Zero-day attack	Attack between the time a software vulnerability is discovered and a patch to fix the problem is released.

Summary and Case Conclusion

It took RPC two days to get its system back up to the point that the audit team could continue their work. RPC had been hit with multiple problems at the same time. Hackers had used packet sniffers and eavesdropping to intercept a public key RPC had sent to Northwest. That led to a man-in-the-middle attack, which allowed the hacker to intercept all communications about the pending merger. It also opened the door to other attacks on both systems.

Law enforcement was called into investigate the problem, and they were following up on three possibilities. The first was that hackers had used the intercepted information to purchase stock in both companies, leak news of the purchase to others via Internet chat rooms, and, once the stock price had been pumped up, to dump the stock of both companies. There did seem to be significant, unusual trading in the two companies' stock in the last few months. The second possibility was hackers exploiting system weaknesses they had found, stealing confidential data on RPC's customers, and causing considerable harm when they were done to cover their tracks. The third possibility was economic espionage and Internet terrorism. They received an anonymous tip that one of Northwest's competitors was behind the attack. It would take weeks or even months to track down all the leads and determine who had caused the problem and why.

Jason's research helped him understand the many ways outside hackers and employees attack systems. He never knew there were so many different things that could be spoofed in systems. He was also intrigued by some of the more technical attacks, such as cross-site scripting, buffer overflow attacks, man-in-the middle attacks, zero-day attacks, and SQL injection. He also found it interesting to learn about all the ways that people use computers to defraud other individuals and companies: Internet terrorism, misinformation, and auction fraud as well as cyber-bullying and cyber-extortion.

Jason was familiar with some of the social engineering techniques he read about, such as pretexting, posing, pharming, and phishing. However, he was unfamiliar with many of the techniques such as Lebanese looping, evil twin, chipping, and typosquatting. He had a similar experience when learning about malware. He was familiar with spyware, adware, Trojan horses, viruses, and key loggers. He learned many new things when he read about scareware, ransomware, steganography, rootkits, and bluebugging.

Jason's research also gave him a perspective on past and future uses of computer fraud and abuse techniques. He learned that many hacker attacks use more than one technique. For example, hackers often send spam e-mails that lure the victim to a Web site that downloads either a keylogger software or code that hijacks the computer and turns it into a botnet zombie or tries to trick the user into disclosing confidential information.

He also learned that hackers take advantage of people who share personal information on social networking sites. For example, a recent worm-based phishing attack targeted Twitter and Facebook users. Users received a message from a friend telling them they could accumulate more friends by clicking on a link. They were prompted to enter their account information, which was used to send the same message to all their friends.

With the harvested personal information that makes them more targeted than before, cyber attacks are increasingly successful in tricking even savvy users into making a mistake. For example, past phishing attacks used a generic spam e-mail message that was obviously bogus. Newer attacks use current-events issues or hot-button topics. Clicking on the accompanying links automatically downloads botware software. Attacks that are even more sophisticated use information about the intended target to make them look legitimate. For example, the e-mail may use stolen information, such as the victim's employer or a friend of family member, to induce them to open an attachment or visit a Web site.

Lastly, Jason learned there is a plethora of fraud software on the market and that hackers compete to make the most easy-to-use tools. In a recent month, six different Web exploit vendors released new products at the same time. As a result, hackers do not need to be programmers; they just need to know to whom they want to target and check a few boxes. For example, with Zeus, one of the most popular and successful data-stealing toolkits, cyber criminals can generate detailed reports on each Web site visited. They can also use the program's powerful search engine to browse through their victims' machines and find detailed information, such as which banks they use. Conversely, the best hackers are more knowledgeable than in the past and use sophisticated technologies. For example, zombies on a botnet used an automated SQL injection attack to compromise over 500,000 Web sites last year, stealing sensitive information and injecting malware into the site.

Key Terms

hacking	zombie	dictionary attack
botnet	denial-of-service (DoS)	splog
hijacking	attack	spoofing
bot herder	spamming	e-mail spoofing

caller ID spoofing
IP address spoofing
Address Resolution Protocol
    (ARP) spoofing
MAC address
SMS spoofing
Web-page spoofing
DNS spoofing
zero-day attack
patch
cross-site scripting
    (XSS)
buffer overflow attack
SQL injection
    (insertion)
man-in-the-middle (MITM)
    attack
masquerading/impersonation
piggybacking
password cracking
war dialing
war driving
war rocketing
phreaking
data diddling
data leakage

podslurping
salami technique
round-down fraud
economic espionage
cyber-extortion
cyber-bullying
sexting
Internet terrorism
Internet misinformation
e-mail threats
Internet auction fraud
Internet pump-and-dump
    fraud
click fraud
Web cramming
software piracy
social engineering
identity theft
pretexting
posing
phishing
vishing
carding
pharming
evil twin
typosquatting/URL
    hijacking

tabnapping
scavenging/dumpster
    diving
shoulder surfing
Lebanese looping
skimming
chipping
eavesdropping
malware
spyware
adware
torpedo software
scareware
ransomware
key logging software
Trojan horse
time bomb/logic bomb
trap door/back door
packet sniffers
steganography
    programs
rootkit
superzapping
virus
worm
bluesnarfing
bluebugging

AIS IN ACTION

Chapter Quiz

1. A set of instructions to increase a programmer's pay rate by 10% is hidden inside an authorized program. It changes and updates the payroll file. What is this computer fraud technique called?
   a. virus
   b. worm
   c. trap door
   d. Trojan horse

2. Which computer fraud technique involves a set of instructions hidden inside a calendar utility that copies itself each time the utility is enabled until memory is filled and the system crashes?
   a. logic bomb
   b. trap door
   c. virus
   d. Trojan horse

3. Interest calculations are truncated at two decimal places, and the excess decimals are put into an account the perpetrator controls. What is this fraud called?
   a. typosquatting
   b. URL hijacking
   c. chipping
   d. round-down fraud

4. A perpetrator attacks phone systems to obtain free phone line access or uses telephone lines to transmit viruses and to access, steal, and destroy data. What is this computer fraud technique called?
   a. phishing
   b. phreaking
   c. pharming
   d. vishing

5. Fraud perpetrators threaten to harm a company if it does not pay a specified amount of money. What is this computer fraud technique called?
   a. cyber-terrorism
   b. blackmailing
   c. cyber-extortion
   d. scareware

6. Techniques used to obtain confidential information, often by tricking people, are referred to as what?
   a. pretexting
   b. posing
   c. social engineering
   d. identity theft

7. What type of software secretly collects personal information about users and sends it to someone else without the user's permission?
   a. rootkit
   b. torpedo software
   c. spyware
   d. malware

8. What type of software conceals processes, files, network connections, memory addresses, systems utility programs, and system data from the operating system and other programs?
   a. rootkit
   b. spyware
   c. malware
   d. adware

9. Which type of computer attack takes place between the time a software vulnerability is discovered and the time software developers release a software patch that fixes the problem?
   a. posing
   b. zero-day attack
   c. evil twin
   d. software piracy

10. Someone redirects a Web site's traffic to a bogus Web site, usually to gain access to personal and confidential information. What is this computer fraud technique called?
    a. vishing
    b. phishing
    c. pharming
    d. phreaking

Discussion Questions

1. When U.S. Leasing (USL) computers began acting sluggishly, computer operators were relieved when a software troubleshooter from IBM called. When he offered to correct the problem they were having, he was given a log-on ID and password. The next morning, the computers were worse. A call to IBM confirmed USL's suspicion: Someone had impersonated an IBM repairman to gain unauthorized access to the system and destroy the database. USL was also concerned that the intruder had devised a program that would let him get back into the system even after all the passwords were changed. What techniques might the impostor have employed to breach USL's internal security? What could USL do to avoid these types of incidents in the future?

2. What motives do people have for hacking? Why has hacking become so popular in recent years? Do you regard it as a crime? Explain your position.

3. The UCLA computer lab was filled to capacity when the system slowed and crashed, disrupting the lives of students who could no longer log into the system or access data to prepare for finals. IT initially suspected a cable break or an operating system failure, but diagnostics revealed nothing. After several frustrating hours, a staff member ran a virus detection program and uncovered a virus on the lab's main server. The virus was eventually traced to the computers of unsuspecting UCLA students. Later that evening, the system was brought back online after infected files were replaced with backup copies. What conditions made the UCLA system a potential breeding ground for the virus? What symptoms indicated that a virus was present?

Problems

1. A few years ago, news began circulating about a computer virus named Michelangelo that was set to "ignite" on March 6, the birthday of the famous Italian artist. The virus attached itself to the computer's operating system boot sector. On the magical date, the virus would release itself, destroying all of the computer's data. When March 6 arrived, the virus did minimal damage. Preventive techniques limited the damage to isolated personal and business computers. Though the excitement surrounding the virus was largely illusory, Michelangelo helped the computer-using public realize its systems' vulnerability to outside attack.

   Required
   a. What is a computer virus? Cite at least three reasons why no system is completely safe from a computer virus.
   b. Why do viruses represent a serious threat to information systems? What damage can a virus do to a computer system?
   c. How does a virus resemble a Trojan horse?
   d. What steps can be taken to prevent the spread of a computer virus?

2. The controller of a small business received the following e-mail with an authentic-looking e-mail address and logo:

From:	Big Bank [antifraud@bigbank.com]
To:	Justin Lewis, Controller, Small Business USA
Subject:	Official Notice for all users of Big Bank!

   Due to the increased incidence of fraud and identity theft, we are asking all bank customers to verify their account information on the following Web page: www.antifraudbigbank.com
       Please confirm your account information as soon as possible. Failure to confirm your account information will require us to suspend your account until confirmation is made.

   A week later, the following e-mail was delivered to the controller:

From:	Big Bank [antifraud@bigbank.com]
To:	Justin Lewis, Controller, Small Business USA
Subject:	Official Notice for all users of Big Bank!

   Dear Client of Big Bank,
   Technical services at Big Bank is currently updating our software. Therefore, we kindly ask that you access the website shown below to confirm your data. Otherwise, your access to the system may be blocked.
   web.da-us.bigbank.com/signin/scripts/login2/user_setup.jsp
   We are grateful for your cooperation.

   Required
   a. What should Justin do about these e-mails?
   b. What should Big Bank do about these e-mails?
   c. Identify the computer fraud and abuse technique illustrated.

3. A purchasing department received the following e-mail.

   Dear Accounts Payable Clerk,
   You can purchase everything you need online—including peace of mind—when you shop using Random Account Numbers (RAN). RAN is a free service for Big Credit Card customers that substitutes a random credit card number in place of your normal credit card number when you make online purchases and payments. This random number provides you with additional security. Before every online purchase, simply get a new number from RAN to use at each new vendor. Sign up for an account at www.bigcreditcard.com. Also, take advantage of the following features:

   - *Automatic Form automatically completes a vendor's order form with the RAN, its expiration date, and your shipping and billing addresses.*

- *Set the spending limit and expiration date for each new RAN.*
- *Use RAN once or use it for recurring payments for up to one year.*

Required

Explain which computer fraud and abuse techniques could be prevented using a random account number that links to your corporate credit card.

4. Computer Fraud and Abuse Techniques.

Match the Internet-related computer fraud and abuse technique in the left column with the scenario in the right column. Terms on the left may be used once, more than once, or not at all.

___	**1.** Adware	a.	Software that monitors and reports a user's computing habits
___	**2.** Botnet	b.	A program stored in a Web page that is executed by a Web browser
___	**3.** Bot herder	c.	Sending an e-mail instructing the recipient to do something or else suffer adverse consequences
___	**4.** Click fraud	d.	Using the Internet to pass off the work of another as your own
___	**5.** DoS	e.	E-mailing an unsolicited message to many people at the same time
___	**6.** E-mail threats	f.	Creating Web sites with names similar to real Web sites so users making errors while entering a Web site name are sent to a hacker's site
___	**7.** Hijacking	g.	An e-mail warning regarding a virus that, in reality, does not exist
___	**8.** Internet misinformation	h.	A spam blog that promotes affiliated Web sites to increase their Google PageRank
___	**9.** Internet terrorism	i.	Software that collects consumer surfing and purchasing data
___	**10.** Key logger	j.	E-mails that look like they came from a legitimate source but are actually from a hacker who is trying to get the user to divulge personal information
___	**11.** Pharming	k.	Making an e-mail look like it came from someone else
___	**12.** Phishing	l.	Gaining control of a computer to carry out unauthorized illicit activities
___	**13.** Spamming	m.	Using the Internet to disrupt communications and e-commerce
___	**14.** Splog	n.	Diverting traffic from a legitimate Web site to a hacker's Web site to gain access to personal and confidential information
___	**15.** Spyware	o.	A network of hijacked computers
___	**16.** Spoofing	p.	Using a legion of compromised computers to launch a coordinated attack on an Internet site
___	**17.** Typosquatting	q.	Use of spyware to record a user's keystrokes
		r.	Hackers that control hijacked computers
		s.	Circulating lies or misleading information using the world's largest network
		t.	Overloading an Internet service provider's e-mail server by sending hundreds of e-mail messages per second from randomly generated false addresses
		u.	Inflating advertising revenue by clicking online ads numerous times

5. Computer Fraud and Abuse Techniques.

Match the computer fraud and abuse technique in the left column with the scenario in the right column. Terms on the left may be used once, more than once, or not at all.

____ 1. Bluebugging
____ 2. Bluesnarfing
____ 3. Eavesdropping
____ 4. Evil twin
____ 5. Packet sniffing
____ 6. Phreaking
____ 7. Piggybacking
____ 8. Vishing
____ 9. War dialing
____ 10. War driving

a. Intercepting Internet and other network transmissions

b. E-mails instructing a user to call a phone number where they are asked to divulge personal information

c. Searching for unprotected wireless networks in a vehicle

d. Gaining access to a protected system by latching onto a legitimate user

e. Decoding and organizing captured network data

f. Intercepting and/or listening in on private voice and data transmissions

g. Deep packet filtering

h. Searching for modems on unprotected phone lines in order to access the attached computer and gain access to the network(s) to which it is attached

i. Making phone calls and sending text messages using another user's phone without physically holding that phone

j. Using telephone lines to transmit viruses and to access, steal, and destroy data

k. Capturing data from devices that use Bluetooth technology

l. Devices that hide IP addresses

m. A rogue wireless access point masquerading as a legitimate access point

6. Computer Fraud and Abuse Techniques.

Match the computer fraud and abuse technique in the left column with the scenario in the right column. Terms on the left may be used once, more than once, or not at all.

____ 1. Chipping
____ 2. Data diddling
____ 3. Data leakage
____ 4. Identity theft
____ 5. Round-down
____ 6. Salami technique
____ 7. Scavenging

a. Illegally obtaining confidential information, such as a Social Security number, about another person so that it can be used for financial gain

b. Searching through garbage for confidential data

c. Covertly swiping a credit card in a card reader that records the data for later use

d. Embezzling small fractions of funds over time

e. Inserting a chip that captures financial data in a legitimate credit card reader

f. Copying company data, such as computer files, without permission

g. Concealing data within a large MP3 file

h. Use of spyware to record a user's keystrokes

i. Altering data during the IPO (Input-Process-Output) cycle

j. Placing truncated decimal places in an account controlled by the perpetrator

7. Computer Fraud and Abuse Techniques.

Match the computer fraud and abuse technique in the left column with the scenario in the right column. Terms on the left may be used once, more than once, or not at all.

___	1. Dictionary attack	a. Special software used to bypass system controls
___	2. Hacking	b. A segment of executable code that attaches itself to software
___	3. Logic bomb	c. Capturing and decrypting passwords to gain access to a system
___	4. Malware	d. Malicious computer code that specifically targets a computer's start-up instructions
___	5. Masquerading	e. Using a wireless network without permission
___	6. Password cracking	f. Covertly swiping a credit card in a card reader that records the data for later use
___	7. Piggybacking	g. Concealing data within a large MP3 file
___	8. Posing	h. Attack occurring between the discovery of a software vulnerability and the release of a patch to fix the problem
___	9. Pretexting	i. Entering a system using a back door that bypasses normal system controls
___	10. Rootkit	j. Using software to guess company addresses, send employees blank e-mails, and add unreturned messages to spammer e-mail lists
___	11. Shoulder surfing	k. Unauthorized code in an authorized and properly functioning program
___	12. Skimming	l. Software used to do harm
___	13. Social engineering	m. A program that can replicate itself and travel over networks
___	14. Software piracy	n. Pretending to be a legitimate user, thereby gaining access to a system and all the rights and privileges of the legitimate user
___	15. Steganography	o. Special code or password that bypasses security features
___	16. Superzapping	p. Unauthorized copying or distribution of copyrighted software
___	17. Trap door	q. Software that conceals processes, files, network connections, and system data from the operating system and other programs
___	18. Trojan horse	r. Methods used to trick someone into divulging personal information
___	19. Virus	s. Software that sits idle until a specified circumstance or time triggers it
___	20. Worm	t. The act of duplicating software, music, or movies
___	21. Zero-day attack	u. Acting under false pretenses to gain confidential information
		v. Observing or listening to users as they divulge personal information
		w. Gaining access to a computer system without permission
		x. Creating a seemingly legitimate business, collecting personal information while making a sale, and never delivering the item sold

8. Computer Fraud and Abuse Techniques.

Match the computer fraud and abuse technique in the left column with the scenario in the right column. Terms on the left may be used once, more than once, or not at all.

_____ **1.** Address Resolution Protocol (ARP) spoofing	a.	Inserting a sleeve to trap a card in an ATM, pretending to help the owner and thereby obtaining the PIN, and using the card and PIN to drain the account
_____ **2.** Buffer overflow attack	b.	A segment of executable code that attaches itself to software
_____ **3.** Carding	c.	Using a small storage device to download unauthorized data from a computer
_____ **4.** Caller ID spoofing	d.	Malicious computer code that specifically targets a computer's start-up instructions
_____ **5.** Cyber-extortion	e.	Malicious software that people are frightened into buying
_____ **6.** Cyber-bullying	f.	Covertly swiping a credit card in a card reader that records the data for later use
_____ **7.** Economic espionage	g.	Using the Internet to inflate a stock price so it can be sold for a profit
_____ **8.** E-mail spoofing	h.	Exchanging explicit messages and pictures by telephone
_____ **9.** IP address spoofing	i.	Inserting a malicious database query in input in a way that it can be executed by an application program
_____ **10.** Internet auction fraud	j.	So much input data that storage is exceeded; excess input contains code that takes control of the computer
_____ **11.** Internet pump-and-dump fraud	k.	Making an electronic communication appear as though it originated from a different source
_____ **12.** Lebanese looping	l.	Creating packets with a forged address to impersonate another computing system
_____ **13.** Man-in-the-middle (MITM) attack	m.	Fake computer networking protocol messages sent to an Ethernet LAN to determine a network host's hardware address when only its IP address is known
_____ **14.** Podslurping	n.	Changing the name or number a text message appears to come from
_____ **15.** Ransomware	o.	Special code or password that bypasses security features
_____ **16.** Scareware	p.	A link containing malicious code that takes a victim to a vulnerable Web site. Once there, the victim's browser executes the malicious code embedded in the link.
_____ **17.** Sexting	q.	Using social networking to harass another person
_____ **18.** SQL Injection	r.	Displaying an incorrect phone number to hide the caller's identity
_____ **19.** SMS spoofing	s.	Software that encrypts programs and data until a payment is made to remove it
_____ **20.** XSS attack	t.	A hacker placing himself between a client and a host to intercept network traffic
_____ **21.** Tabnapping	u.	A demand for payment to ensure a hacker does not harm a computer
	v.	Theft of trade secrets and intellectual property
	w.	Using a site that sells to the highest bidder to defraud another person
	x.	Verifying credit card validity
	y.	Secretly changing an already open browser tab

9. Identify the computer fraud and abuse technique used in each the following actual examples of computer wrongdoing.

   a. A teenage gang known as the "414s" broke into the Los Alamos National Laboratory, Sloan-Kettering Cancer Center, and Security Pacific Bank. One gang member appeared in *Newsweek* with the caption "Beware: Hackers at play."

   b. Daniel Baas was the systems administrator for a company that did business with Acxiom, who manages customer information for companies. Baas exceeded his authorized access and downloaded a file with 300 encrypted passwords, decrypted the password file, and downloaded Acxiom customer files containing personal information. The intrusion cost Acxiom over $5.8 million.

   c. Cyber-attacks left high-profile sites such as Amazon.com, eBay, Buy.com, and CNN Interactive staggering under the weight of tens of thousands of bogus messages that tied up the retail sites' computers and slowed the news site's operations for hours.

   d. Susan Gilmour-Latham got a call asking why she was sending the caller multiple adult text messages per day. Her account records proved the calls were not coming from her phone. Neither she nor her mobile company could explain how the messages were sent. After finding no way to block the unsavory messages, she changed her mobile number to avoid further embarrassment by association.

   e. A federal grand jury in Fort Lauderdale claimed that four executives of a rental-car franchise modified a computer-billing program to add five gallons to the actual gas tank capacity of their vehicles. Over three years, 47,000 customers who returned a car without topping it off ended up paying an extra $2 to $15 for gasoline.

   f. A mail-order company programmer truncated odd cents in sales-commission accounts and placed them in the last record in the commission file. Accounts were processed alphabetically, and he created a dummy sales-commission account using the name of Zwana. Three years later, the holders of the first and last sales-commission accounts were honored. Zwana was unmasked and his creator fired.

   g. MicroPatent, an intellectual property firm, was notified that their proprietary information would be broadcast on the Internet if they did not pay a $17 million fee. The hacker was caught by the FBI before any damage was done.

   h. When Estonia removed a Russian World War II war memorial, Estonian government and bank networks were knocked offline in a distributed DoS attack by Russian hackers. A counterfeit letter of apology for removing the memorial statue was placed on the Web site of Estonia's prime minister.

   i. eBay customers were notified by e-mail that their accounts had been compromised and were being restricted unless they re-registered using an accompanying hyperlink to a Web page that had eBay's logo, home page design, and internal links. The form had a place for them to enter their credit card data, ATM PINs, Social Security number, date of birth, and their mother's maiden name. Unfortunately, eBay hadn't sent the e-mail.

   j. A teenager hijacked the eBay.de domain name and several months later the domain name for a large New York ISP. Both hijacked Web sites pointed to a site in Australia.

   k. Travelers who logged into the Alpharetta, Georgia, airport's Internet service had personal information stolen and picked up as many as 45 viruses. A hacker had set up a rogue wireless network with the same name as the airport's wireless access network.

   l. Criminals in Russia used a vulnerability in Microsoft's server software to add a few lines of Java code to users' copies of Internet Explorer. The code recorded the users' keyboard activities, giving the criminals access to usernames and passwords at many banking Web sites. The attacks caused $420 million in damage.

   m. America Online subscribers received a message offering free software. Users who opened the attachments unknowingly unleashed a program hidden inside another program that secretly copied the subscriber's account name and password and forwarded them to the sender.

   n. Rajendrasinh Makwana, an Indian citizen and IT contractor who worked at Fannie Mae's Maryland facility, was terminated at 1:00 P.M. on October 24. Before his network access was revoked, he created a program to wipe out all 4,000 of Fannie Mae's servers on the following January 31.

o. A man accessed millions of ChoicePoint files by claiming in writing and on the phone to be someone he was not.

p. A 31-year-old programmer unleashed a Visual Basic program by deliberately posting an infected document to an alt.sex Usenet newsgroup using a stolen AOL account. The program evaded security software and infected computers using the Windows operating system and Microsoft Word. On March 26, the Melissa program appeared on thousands of e-mail systems disguised as an important message from a colleague or friend. The program sent an infected e-mail to the first 50 e-mail addresses on the users' Outlook address book. Each infected computer would infect 50 additional computers, which in turn would infect another 50 computers. The program spread rapidly and exponentially, causing considerable damage. Many companies had to disconnect from the Internet or shut down their e-mail gateways because of the vast amount of e-mail the program was generating. The program caused more than $400 million in damages.

q. Microsoft filed a lawsuit against two Texas firms that produced software that sent incessant pop-ups resembling system warnings. The messages stated "CRITICAL ERROR MESSAGE! REGISTRY DAMAGED AND CORRUPTED" and instructed users to visit a Web site to download Registry Cleaner XP at a cost of $39.95.

r. As many as 114,000 Web sites were tricked into running database commands that installed malicious HTML code redirecting victims to a malicious Web server that tried to install software to remotely control the Web visitors' computers.

s. Zeus records log-in information when the user of the infected computer logs into a list of target Web sites, mostly banks and other financial institutions. The user's data is sent to a remote server where it is used and sold by cyber-criminals. The new version of Zeus will significantly increase fraud losses, given that 30% of Internet users bank online.

t. It took Facebook 15 hours to kill a Facebook application that infected millions of PCs with software that displays a constant stream of pop-up ads. The program posted a "Sexiest Video Ever" message on Facebook walls that looked like it came from a friend. Clicking the link led to a Facebook installation screen, where users allowed the software to access their profiles and walls. Once approved, the application told users to download an updated, free version of a popular Windows video player. Instead, it inserted a program that displayed pop-up ads and links. A week later a "Distracting Beach Babes" message did the same thing.

u. Robert Thousand, Jr. discovered he lost $400,000 from his Ameritrade retirement account shortly after he began receiving a flood of phone calls with a 30-second recording for a sex hotline. An FBI investigation revealed that the perpetrator obtained his Ameritrade account information, called Ameritrade to change his phone number, created several VoIP accounts, and used automated dialing tools to flood the dentist's phones in case Ameritrade called his real number. The perpetrator requested multiple monetary transfers, but Ameritrade would not process them until they reached Thousand to verify them. When the transfers did not go through, the attacker called Ameritrade, gave information to verify that he was Thousand, claimed he had been having phone troubles, and told Ameritrade he was not happy that the transfers had not gone through. Ameritrade processed the transfers, and Thousand lost $400,000.

v. The Internet Crime Complaint Center reports a "hit man" scam. The scammer claims that he has been ordered to assassinate the victim and an associate has been ordered to kill a family member. The only way to prevent the killings is to send $800 so an Islamic expatriate can leave the United States.

w. In an economic stimulus scam, individuals receive a phone call from President Obama telling them to go to a Web site to apply for the funds. To receive the stimulus money, victims have to enter personal identification information, complete an online application, and pay a $28 fee.

10. On a Sunday afternoon at a hospital in the Pacific Northwest, computers became sluggish, and documents would not print. Monday morning, the situation became worse when employees logged on to their computers. Even stranger things happened—operating-room doors would not open, pagers would not work, and computers in the intensive care

unit shut down. By 10:00 A.M., all 50 IT employees were summoned. They discovered that the hospital was under attack by a botnet that exploited a Microsoft operating system flaw and installed pop-up ads on hospital computers. They got access to the first computer on Sunday and used the hospital's network to spread the infection to other computers. Each infected computer became a zombie that scanned the network looking for new victims. With the network clogged with zombie traffic, hospital communications began to break down. The IT staff tried to halt the attack by shutting off the hospital's Internet connection, but it was too late. The bots were inside the hospital's computer system and infecting other computers faster than they could be cleaned. Monday afternoon IT figured out which malware the bots were installing and wrote a script, which was pushed out hourly, directing computers to remove the bad code. The script helped to slow the bots down a bit.

(*Source:* D. Gage, *Baseline Security* February 6, 2007.)

Required

a. What could the hospital do to stop the attack and contain the damage?
b. Which computer fraud and abuse technique did the hackers use in their attack on the hospital?
c. What steps should the hospital have taken to prevent the damage caused by the attack?

Case 1 Shadowcrew

At 9:00 P.M., Andrew Mantovani, cofounder of the group Shadowcrew, received a knock at his door while chatting on his computer. For Mantovani and 27 others, that knock marked the end of Shadowcrew, which provided online marketplaces and discussion forums for identity thieves. Shadowcrew members used the organization's Web site to traffic in stolen Social Security numbers, names, e-mail addresses, counterfeit driver's licenses, birth certificates, and foreign and domestic passports. It also shared best practices for carrying out fraudulent activity. By the time it was shut down, Shadowcrew had trafficked in at least 1.7 million credit cards and it was responsible for more than $4.3 million in fraud losses.

Considered the online equivalent of the Russian Mafia, Shadowcrew operated as a highly sophisticated and hierarchical organization. All users operated under aliases, never revealing their true names or other personal information. Operations and communications were conducted using proxy servers that hid the location and identity of the users. Shadowcrew users were divided into five different roles: administrators, moderators, reviewers, vendors, and members.

Administrators Shadowcrew administrators were the heads of the organization.

Moderators A dozen moderators, chosen from the general membership based on proven skill in fraudulent activity, controlled the flow of information.

Reviewers Reviewers tested the quality of illicit goods (credit cards, passports, etc.) trafficked on the Shadowcrew site. For example, reviewers would run a test called a "dump check" on credit card numbers by hacking into a retailer's cash register system. The fraudster accessed the system through back doors used by technical support personnel to remotely perform maintenance or repairs. The reviewer would then enter a trivial charge of $1 or $2 to see whether the charge was approved. Reviewers would then write up and post detailed descriptions of the credit cards or other merchandise tested.

Vendors Vendors managed the sale of stolen data. Prices were posted and products were sold using an auction forum much like eBay. Payments were processed via Western Union money transfers or an electronic currency and were made using a fraud victim's stolen data.

Members Thousands of people used the Shadowcrew Web site to gather and share information on committing identity fraud. Shadowcrew practiced open registration, but more sensitive discussion areas were password protected, and members needed another trusted member to vouch for them in order to join the forum.

Members could be promoted up the organization by providing quality products or by sharing new or unique tips or techniques for committing fraud. Shadowcrew punished acts of disloyalty. For instance, one disloyal group member had his actual name, address, and phone number posted on the Web site for all to see.

Shadowcrew's demise began when MasterCard informed the United States government that a hundred Web sites promoted and supported identity fraud. The United States Secret Service covertly infiltrated Shadowcrew. Acting as trusted members, agents set up a Virtual Private Network (VPN) over which Shadowcrew leaders could conduct illicit business. The VPN allowed the Secret Service to track the organization's doings and discover the real identities and locations of Shadowcrew users.

It was vital that all arrests occur simultaneously, because any one of the targets could instantly warn the others via Shadowcrew's discussion forum. With the help of the Justice Department, the Homeland Security Department, the Royal Canadian Mounted Police, Europol, and local police departments, authorities simultaneously knocked on the suspects' doors at precisely 9:00 P.M. The operation led to 28 arrests, 21 in the United States. Rather than immediately deactivating the Web site, investigators replaced the home page with the following warning: "Activities by Shadowcrew members are being investigated by the United States Secret Service." Under a picture of hands clutching bars of a jail cell, agents listed the criminal charges that Shadowcrew members faced and called on visitors to turn themselves in: "Contact your local United States Secret Service field office before we contact you!"

(*Source:* J. McCormick and D. Gage, *Baseline Security*, March 7, 2005.)

1. How did Shadowcrew members conceal their identities? How can average citizens protect their identities while interacting online?
2. How has the Internet made detecting and identifying identity fraudsters difficult?
3. What are some of the most common electronic means of stealing personal information?
4. What is the most common way that fraudsters use personal data?
5. What measures can consumers take to protect against the online brokering of their personal data?
6. What are the most effective means of detecting identity theft?
7. What pieces of personal information are most valuable to identity fraudsters?

AIS IN ACTION SOLUTIONS

Quiz Key

1. A set of instructions to increase a programmer's pay rate by 10% is hidden inside an authorized program. It changes and updates the payroll file. What is this computer fraud technique called?
   a. virus (Incorrect. A virus damages a system using a segment of executable code that attaches itself to software, replicates itself, and spreads to other systems or files.)
   b. worm (Incorrect. A worm is a program that hides in a host program and copies and actively transmits itself directly to other systems.)
   c. trap door (Incorrect. A trap door is entering a system using a back door that bypasses normal system controls.)
   ▶ d. Trojan horse (Correct. Placing unauthorized computer instructions, such as fraudulently increasing an employee's pay, in an authorized and properly functioning program is an example of a Trojan horse.)

2. Which computer fraud technique involves a set of instructions hidden inside a calendar utility that copies itself each time the utility is enabled until memory is filled and the system crashes?
   a. logic bomb (Incorrect. A logic bomb sabotages a system using a program that lies idle until some specified circumstance or a particular time triggers it.)
   b. trap door (Incorrect. A trap door is a means of bypassing normal system controls to enter a system.)
   ▶ c. virus (Correct. A virus damages a system using a segment of executable code that attaches itself to software, replicates itself, and spreads to other systems or files.)
   d. Trojan horse (Incorrect. Placing unauthorized computer instructions, such as fraudulently increasing an employee's pay, in an authorized and properly functioning program is an example of a Trojan horse.)

3. Interest calculations are truncated at two decimal places, and the excess decimals are put into an account the perpetrator controls. What is this fraud called?
   a. typosquatting (Incorrect. Typosquatting is the practice of setting up Web sites with names similar to real Web sites so that users who make typographical errors when typing Web site names are sent to a site filled with malware.)

    b. URL hijacking (Incorrect. URL hijacking is another name for typosquatting, which is explained above.)

    c. chipping (Incorrect. Chipping is planting a chip that records transaction data in a legitimate credit card reader.)

▶ **d.** round-down fraud (Correct.)

4. A perpetrator attacks phone systems to obtain free phone line access or uses telephone lines to transmit viruses and to access, steal, and destroy data. What is this computer fraud technique called?

    a. phishing (Incorrect. Phishing is the practice of sending e-mails requesting recipients to visit a Web page and verify data or fill in missing data. The e-mails and Web sites look like legitimate companies, primarily financial institutions.)

▶ **b.** phreaking (Correct.)

    c. pharming (Incorrect. Pharming is redirecting traffic to a spoofed Web site to gain access to personal and confidential information.)

    d. vishing (Incorrect. Vishing is voice phishing, in which e-mail recipients are asked to call a phone number where they are asked to divulge confidential data.)

5. Fraud perpetrators threaten to harm a company if it does not pay a specified amount of money. What is this fraud technique called?

    a. cyber-terrorism (Incorrect. Cyber-terrorism, or Internet terrorism, is using the Internet to disrupt communications and e-commerce.)

    b. blackmailing (Incorrect. Blackmailing is the extortion of money or something else of value from a person by the threat of exposing a criminal act or discreditable information.)

▶ **c.** cyber-extortion (Correct.)

    d. scareware (Incorrect. Scareware is software of limited or no benefit, often malicious in nature, that is sold using scare tactics. The most common scare tactic is a dire warning that the person's computer is infected with viruses, spyware, or some other catastrophic problem.)

6. Techniques used to obtain confidential information, often by tricking people, are referred to as what?

    a. pretexting (Incorrect. Pretexting is one specific type of social engineering. It involves acting under false pretenses to gain confidential information.)

    b. posing (Incorrect. Posing is one specific type of social engineering in which someone creates a seemingly legitimate business, collects personal information while making a sale, and never delivers the item sold.)

▶ **c.** social engineering (Correct.)

    d. identity theft (Incorrect. Identity theft is a type of social engineering in which one person assumes another's identity, usually for economic gain, by illegally obtaining confidential information, such as a Social Security number.)

7. What type of software secretly collects personal information about users and sends it to someone else without the user's permission?

    a. rootkit (Incorrect. A rootkit is software that conceals processes, files, network connections, and system data from the operating system and other programs.)

    b. torpedo software (Incorrect. Torpedo software is software that destroys competing malware, resulting in "malware warfare" between competing developers.)

▶ **c.** spyware (Correct.)

    d. malware (Incorrect. *Malware* is a general term that applies to any software used to do harm. There is a more specific correct answer to this question.)

8. What type of software conceals processes, files, network connections, memory addresses, systems utility programs, and system data from the operating system and other programs?

▶ **a.** rootkit (Correct.)

    b. spyware (Incorrect. Spyware is software that is used to monitor computing habits and send that data to someone else, often without the computer user's permission.)

    c. malware (Incorrect. Malware is any software that is used to do harm.)

    d. adware (Incorrect. Adware is software used to collect Web-surfing and spending data and forward it to advertising or media organizations. It also causes banner ads to pop up on computer monitors as the Internet is surfed.)

9. Which type of computer attack takes place between the time a software vulnerability is discovered and the time software developers release a software patch that fixes the problem?
    a. posing (Incorrect. Posing is creating a seemingly legitimate business, collecting personal information while making a sale, and never delivering the item sold.)
▶ **b.** zero-day attack (Correct.)
    c. evil twin (Incorrect. An evil twin is a wireless network with the same name as a local wireless access point that unsuspecting people use, allowing hackers to monitor the network's traffic looking for useful information.)
    d. software piracy (Incorrect. Software piracy is the illegal copying of computer software.)

10. Someone redirects a Web site's traffic to a bogus Web site, usually to gain access to personal and confidential information. What is this computer fraud technique called?
    a. vishing (Incorrect. Vishing is voice phishing, in which e-mail recipients are asked to call a phone number where they are asked to divulge confidential data.)
    b. phishing (Incorrect. Phishing is sending e-mails requesting recipients to visit a Web page and verify data or fill in missing data. The e-mails and Web sites look like legitimate companies, primarily financial institutions.)
▶ **c.** pharming (Correct.)
    d. phreaking (Incorrect. Phreaking is attacking phone systems and using telephone lines to transmit viruses and to access, steal, and destroy data.)

Chapter 7

Control and Accounting Information Systems

From Chapter 7 of *Accounting Information Systems*, 12/e. Marshall B. Romney. Paul John Steinbart. Copyright © 2012 by Pearson Education. Published by Prentice Hall. All rights reserved.

Control and Accounting Information Systems

INTEGRATIVE CASE SPRINGER'S LUMBER & SUPPLY

Jason Scott, an internal auditor for Northwest Industries, is auditing Springer's Lumber & Supply, Northwest's building materials outlet in Bozeman, Montana. His supervisor, Maria Pilier, asked him to trace a sample of purchase transactions from purchase requisition to cash disbursement to verify that proper control procedures were followed. Jason is frustrated with this task, and for good reasons:

- The purchasing system is poorly documented.
- He keeps finding transactions that have not been processed as Ed Yates, the accounts payable manager, said they should be.

192

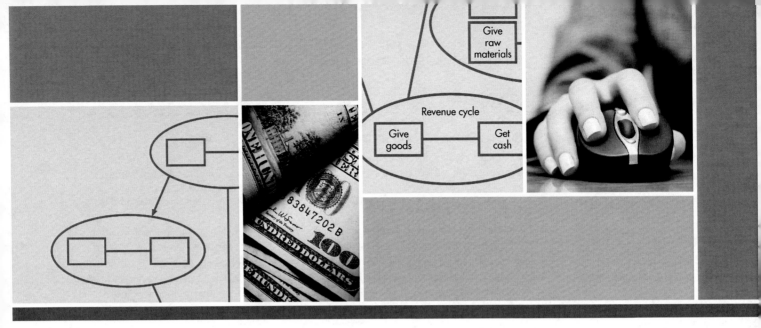

- Purchase requisitions are missing for several items personally authorized by Bill Springer, the purchasing vice president.
- Some vendor invoices have been paid without supporting documents, such as purchase orders and receiving reports.
- Prices for some items seem unusually high, and there are a few discrepancies in item prices between the vendor invoice and the corresponding purchase order.

Yates had a logical answer for every question Jason raised and advised Jason that the real world is not as tidy as the world portrayed in college textbooks. Maria also has some concerns:

- Springer's is the largest supplier in the area and has a near monopoly.
- Management authority is held by the company president, Joe Springer, and his two sons, Bill (the purchasing vice president) and Ted (the controller). Several relatives and friends are on the payroll. Together, the Springers own 10% of the company.
- Lines of authority and responsibility within the company are loosely defined and confusing.
- Maria believes that Ted Springer may have engaged in "creative accounting" to make Springer's one of Northwest's best-performing retail outlets.

After talking to Maria, Jason ponders the following issues:

1. Because Ed Yates had a logical explanation for every unusual transaction, should Jason describe these transactions in his report?
2. Is a violation of control procedures acceptable if management has authorized it?
3. Maria's concerns about Springer's loosely defined lines of authority and possible use of "creative accounting" are matters of management policy. With respect to Jason's control procedures assignment, does he have a professional or an ethical responsibility to get involved?

193

Introduction

Why Threats to Accounting Information Systems Are Increasing

In most years, more than 60% of organizations experience a major failure in controlling the security and integrity of their computer systems. Reasons for the failures include the following:

- Information is available to an unprecedented number of workers. Chevron, for example, has over 35,000 PCs.
- Information on distributed computer networks is hard to control. At Chevron, information is distributed among many systems and thousands of employees worldwide. Each system and each employee represent a potential control vulnerability point.
- Customers and suppliers have access to each others' systems and data. For example, WalMart allows vendors to access their databases. Imagine the confidentiality problems as these vendors form alliances with WalMart competitors.

Organizations have not adequately protected data for several reasons:

- Some companies view the loss of crucial information as a distant, unlikely threat.
- The control implications of moving from centralized computer systems to Internet-based systems are not fully understood.
- Many companies do not realize that information is a strategic resource and that protecting it must be a strategic requirement. For example, one company lost millions of dollars because it did not protect data transmissions. A competitor tapped into its phone lines and obtained faxes of new product designs.
- Productivity and cost pressures motivate management to forgo time-consuming control measures.

Any potential adverse occurrence is called a *threat* or an event. The potential dollar loss from a threat is called the *exposure* or *impact*. The probability that it will happen is called the *likelihood* of the threat.

Overview of Control Concepts

Internal control is the process implemented to provide reasonable assurance that the following control objectives are achieved:

- Safeguard assets: prevent or detect their unauthorized acquisition, use, or disposition.
- Maintain records in sufficient detail to report company assets accurately and fairly.
- Provide accurate and reliable information.
- Prepare financial reports in accordance with established criteria.
- Promote and improve operational efficiency.
- Encourage adherence to prescribed managerial policies.
- Comply with applicable laws and regulations.

Internal control is a process because it permeates an organization's operating activities and is an integral part of management activities. Internal control provides reasonable assurance—complete assurance is difficult to achieve and prohibitively expensive. In addition, internal control systems have inherent limitations, such as susceptibility to simple errors and mistakes, faulty judgments and decision making, management overrides, and collusion.

Developing an internal control system requires a thorough understanding of information technology (IT) capabilities and risks, as well as how to use IT to achieve an organization's control objectives. Accountants and systems developers help management achieve their control objectives by (1) designing effective control systems that take a proactive approach to eliminating system threats and that detect, correct, and recover from threats when they occur; and (2) making it easier to build controls into a system at the initial design stage than to add them after the fact.

Internal controls perform three important functions:

1. *Preventive controls* deter problems before they arise. Examples include hiring qualified personnel, segregating employee duties, and controlling physical access to assets and information.
2. *Detective controls* discover problems that are not prevented. Examples include duplicate checking of calculations and preparing bank reconciliations and monthly trial balances.
3. *Corrective controls* identify and correct problems as well as correct and recover from the resulting errors. Examples include maintaining backup copies of files, correcting data entry errors, and resubmitting transactions for subsequent processing.

Internal controls are often segregated into two categories:

1. *General controls* make sure an organization's control environment is stable and well managed. Examples include security; IT infrastructure; and software acquisition, development, and maintenance controls.
2. *Application controls* make sure transactions are processed correctly. They are concerned with the accuracy, completeness, validity, and authorization of the data captured, entered, processed, stored, transmitted to other systems, and reported.

Robert Simons, a Harvard business professor, has espoused four levels of control to help management reconcile the conflict between creativity and controls.

1. A *belief system* describes how the company creates value, helps employees understand management's vision, communicates company core values, and inspires employees to live by those values.
2. A *boundary system* helps employees act ethically by setting boundaries on employee behavior. Employees are not told exactly what to do. Instead, they are encouraged to creatively solve problems and meet customer needs while meeting minimum performance standards, shunning off-limit activities, and avoiding actions that might damage their reputation.
3. A *diagnostic control system* measures, monitors, and compares actual company progress to budgets and performance goals. Feedback helps management adjust and fine-tune inputs and processes so future outputs more closely match goals.
4. An *interactive control system* helps managers to focus subordinates' attention on key strategic issues and to be more involved in their decisions. Interactive system data are interpreted and discussed in face-to-face meetings of superiors, subordinates, and peers.

Regrettably, not all organizations have an effective internal control system. For instance, one report indicated that the FBI is plagued by IT infrastructure vulnerabilities and security problems, some of which were identified in an audit 13 years previously. Specific areas of concern were security standards, guidelines, and procedures; segregation of duties; access controls, including password management and usage; backup and recovery controls; and software development and change controls.

The Foreign Corrupt Practices and Sarbanes–Oxley Acts

In 1977, the *Foreign Corrupt Practices Act (FCPA)* was passed to prevent companies from bribing foreign officials to obtain business. Congress incorporated language from an American Institute of Certified Public Accountants (AICPA) pronouncement into the FCPA that required corporations to maintain good systems of internal control. Unfortunately, these requirements were not sufficient to prevent further problems.

In the late 1990s and early 2000s, news stories were reporting accounting frauds at Enron, WorldCom, Xerox, Tyco, Global Crossing, Adelphia, and other companies. When Enron, with $62 billion in assets, declared bankruptcy in December 2001, it was the largest bankruptcy in U.S. history. In June 2002, Arthur Andersen, once the largest CPA firm, collapsed. The Enron bankruptcy was dwarfed when WorldCom, with over $100 billion in assets, filed for bankruptcy in July 2002. In response to these frauds, Congress passed the *Sarbanes–Oxley Act (SOX)* of 2002. SOX applies to publicly held companies and their auditors and was designed to prevent financial statement fraud, make financial reports more transparent, protect investors, strengthen internal controls, and punish executives who perpetrate fraud.

SOX is the most important business-oriented legislation in the last 75 years. It changed the way boards of directors and management operate and had a dramatic impact on CPAs who audit them. The following are some of the most important aspects of SOX:

- *Public Company Accounting Oversight Board (PCAOB).* SOX created the *Public Company Accounting Oversight Board (PCAOB)* to control the auditing profession. The PCAOB sets and enforces auditing, quality control, ethics, independence, and other auditing standards.
- *New rules for auditors.* Auditors must report specific information to the company's audit committee, such as critical accounting policies and practices. Audit partners must be rotated periodically. SOX prohibits auditors from performing certain nonaudit services, such as information systems design and implementation. Audit firms cannot provide services to companies if top management was employed by the auditing firm and worked on the company's audit in the preceding 12 months.
- *New roles for audit committees.* Audit committee members must be on the company's board of directors and be independent of the company. One member of the audit committee must be a financial expert. The audit committee hires, compensates, and oversees the auditors, who report directly to them.
- *New rules for management.* SOX requires the CEO and CFO to certify that (1) financial statements and disclosures are fairly presented, were reviewed by management, and are not misleading; and that (2) the auditors were told about all material internal control weaknesses and fraud. If management knowingly violates these rules, they can be prosecuted and fined. Companies must disclose, in plain English, material changes to their financial condition on a timely basis.
- *New internal control requirements.* Section 404 requires companies to issue a report accompanying the financial statements stating that management is responsible for establishing and maintaining an adequate internal control system. The report must contain management's assessment of the company's internal controls, attest to their accuracy, and report significant weaknesses or material noncompliance.

After SOX was passed, the SEC mandated that management must:

- Base its evaluation on a recognized control framework. The most likely frameworks, formulated by COSO, are discussed in this chapter.
- Disclose all material internal control weaknesses.
- Conclude that a company does not have effective financial reporting internal controls if there are material weaknesses.

Control Frameworks

This section discusses three frameworks used to develop internal control systems.

COBIT Framework

The Information Systems Audit and Control Association (ISACA) developed the *Control Objectives for Information and Related Technology (COBIT)* framework. COBIT consolidates control standards from 36 different sources into a single framework that allows (1) management to benchmark security and control practices of IT environments, (2) users to be assured that adequate IT security and control exist, and (3) auditors to substantiate their internal control opinions and to advise on IT security and control matters.

The framework addresses control from three vantage points:

1. *Business objectives.* To satisfy business objectives, information must conform to seven categories of criteria that map into the objectives established by the Committee of Sponsoring Organizations (COSO; see next section).
2. *IT resources.* These include people, application systems, technology, facilities, and data.
3. *IT processes.* These are broken into four domains: planning and organization, acquisition and implementation, delivery and support, and monitoring and evaluation.

COSO's Internal Control Framework

The *Committee of Sponsoring Organizations (COSO)* consists of the American Accounting Association, the American Institute of Certified Public Accountants, the Institute of Internal Auditors, the Institute of Management Accountants, and the Financial Executives Institute. In 1992, COSO issued *Internal Control—Integrated Framework (IC)*, which is widely accepted as the authority on internal controls and is incorporated into policies, rules, and regulations used to control business activities.

The five components of the IC framework, summarized in Table 1, are part of COSO's newer Enterprise Risk Management framework.

COSO's Enterprise Risk Management Framework

To improve the risk management process, COSO developed a second control framework called *Enterprise Risk Management—Integrated Framework (ERM)*. ERM is the process the board of directors and management use to set strategy, identify events that may affect the entity, assess and manage risk, and provide reasonable assurance that the company achieves its objectives and goals. The basic principles behind ERM are as follows:

- Companies are formed to create value for their owners.
- Management must decide how much uncertainty it will accept as it creates value.
- Uncertainty results in risk, which is the possibility that something negatively affects the company's ability to create or preserve value.
- Uncertainty results in opportunity, which is the possibility that something positively affects the company's ability to create or preserve value.
- The ERM framework can manage uncertainty as well as create and preserve value.

COSO developed Figure 1 to illustrate the elements of ERM. The four columns at the top represent the objectives management must meet to achieve company goals. The columns on the right represent the company's units. The horizontal rows are the eight interrelated risk and control components of ERM. The ERM model is three-dimensional. Each of the eight risk and control elements applies to each of the four objectives and to the company and/or one of its subunits. For example, XYZ Company could look at the control activities for the operations objectives in its Pacific Division.

The Enterprise Risk Management Framework versus the Internal Control Framework

The IC framework has been widely adopted as the way to evaluate internal controls, as required by Sarbanes–Oxley. However, it examines controls without looking at the purposes and risks of business processes and provides little context for evaluating the results. Under the IC framework,

TABLE 1 Five Interrelated Components of COSO's Internal Control Model

Component	Description
Control environment	The core of any business is its people—their individual attributes, including integrity, ethical values, and competence—and the environment in which they operate. They are the engine that drives the organization and the foundation on which everything rests.
Control activities	Control policies and procedures help ensure that the actions identified by management as necessary to address risks and achieve the organization's objectives are effectively carried out.
Risk assessment	The organization must identify, analyze, and manage its risks. It must set objectives so that the organization is operating in concert.
Information and communication	Information and communication systems capture and exchange the information needed to conduct, manage, and control the organization's operations.
Monitoring	The entire process must be monitored, and modifications made as necessary so the system can change as conditions warrant.

FIGURE 1
COSO's Enterprise Risk
Management Model

it is hard to know which control systems are most important, whether they adequately deal with risk, and whether important controls are missing.

The more comprehensive ERM framework takes a risk-based rather than a controls-based approach. ERM adds three additional elements to COSO's IC framework: setting objectives, identifying events that may affect the company, and developing a response to assessed risk. As a result, controls are flexible and relevant because they are linked to current organizational objectives. The ERM model also recognizes that risk, in addition to being controlled, can be accepted, avoided, diversified, shared, or transferred.

Because it is more comprehensive, the ERM model will likely become the more widely adopted model. The eight ERM components shown in Figure 1 are the topic of the remainder of the chapter.

The Internal Environment

The *internal environment*, or company culture, influences how organizations establish strategies and objectives; structure business activities; and identify, assess, and respond to risk. It is the foundation for all other ERM components. A weak or deficient internal environment often results in breakdowns in risk management and control. It is essentially the same thing as the control environment in the IC framework.

An internal environment consists of the following:

1. Management's philosophy, operating style, and risk appetite
2. The board of directors
3. Commitment to integrity, ethical values, and competence
4. Organizational structure
5. Methods of assigning authority and responsibility
6. Human resource standards
7. External influences

Enron is an example of an ineffective internal environment that resulted in financial failure. Although Enron appeared to have an effective ERM system, its internal environment was defective. Management engaged in risky and dubious business practices, which the board of directors never questioned. Management misrepresented the company's financial condition, lost the confidence of shareholders, and finally filed for bankruptcy.

Management's Philosophy, Operating Style, and Risk Appetite

Collectively, an organization has a philosophy, or shared beliefs and attitudes, about risk that affects policies, procedures, oral and written communications, and decisions. Companies also have a *risk appetite*, which is the amount of risk they are willing to accept to achieve their goals. To avoid undue risk, risk appetite must be in alignment with company strategy.

The more responsible management's philosophy and operating style, and the more clearly they are communicated, the more likely employees will behave responsibly. If management has little concern for internal controls and risk management, then employees are less diligent in achieving control objectives. The culture at Springer's Lumber & Supply provides an example. Maria Pilier found that lines of authority and responsibility were loosely defined and suspected management might have used "creative accounting" to improve company performance. Jason Scott found evidence of poor internal control practices in the purchasing and accounts payable functions. These two conditions may be related; management's loose attitude may have contributed to the purchasing department's inattentiveness to good internal control practices.

Management's philosophy, operating style, and risk appetite can be assessed by answering questions such as these:

- Does management take undue business risks to achieve its objectives, or does it assess potential risks and rewards prior to acting?
- Does management manipulate performance measures, such as net income, so they are seen in a more favorable light?
- Does management pressure employees to achieve results regardless of the methods, or does it demand ethical behavior? In other words, do the ends justify the means?

The Board of Directors

An involved board of directors represents shareholders and provides an independent review of management that acts as a check and balance on its actions. Sarbanes–Oxley requires public companies to have an *audit committee* of outside, independent directors. The audit committee is responsible for financial reporting, regulatory compliance, internal control, and hiring and overseeing internal and external auditors, who report all critical accounting policies and practices to them. Directors should also approve company strategy and review security policies.

Commitment to Integrity, Ethical Values, and Competence

Organizations need a culture that stresses integrity and commitment to ethical values and competence. Ethics pays—ethical standards are good business. Integrity starts at the top, as company employees adopt top management attitudes about risks and controls. A powerful message is sent when the CEO, confronted with a difficult decision, makes the ethically correct choice.

Companies endorse integrity by:

- Actively teaching and requiring it—for example, making it clear that honest reports are more important than favorable ones.
- Avoiding unrealistic expectations or incentives that motivate dishonest or illegal acts, such as overly aggressive sales practices, unfair or unethical negotiation tactics, and bonuses excessively based on reported financial results.
- Consistently rewarding honesty and giving verbal labels to honest and dishonest behavior. If companies punish or reward honesty without labeling it as such, or if the standard of honesty is inconsistent, then employees will display inconsistent moral behavior.
- Developing a written code of conduct that explicitly describes honest and dishonest behaviors. For example, most purchasing agents agree that accepting $5,000 from a supplier is dishonest, but a weekend vacation is not as clear-cut. A major cause of dishonesty comes from rationalizing unclear situations and allowing the criterion of expediency to replace the criterion of right versus wrong. Companies should document that employees have read and understand the code of conduct.
- Requiring employees to report dishonest or illegal acts and disciplining employees who knowingly fail to report them. All dishonest acts should be investigated, and dishonest employees should be dismissed and prosecuted to show that such behavior is not allowed.
- Making a commitment to competence. Companies should hire competent employees with the necessary knowledge, experience, training, and skills.

199

Organizational Structure

A company's organizational structure provides a framework for planning, executing, controlling, and monitoring operations. Important aspects of the organizational structure include the following:

- Centralization or decentralization of authority
- A direct or matrix reporting relationship
- Organization by industry, product line, location, or marketing network
- How allocation of responsibility affects information requirements
- Organization of and lines of authority for accounting, auditing, and information system functions
- Size and nature of company activities

A complex or unclear organizational structure may indicate serious problems. For example, ESM, a brokerage company, used a multilayered organizational structure to hide a $300 million fraud. Management hid stolen cash in their financial statements using a fictitious receivable from a related company.

In today's business world, hierarchical structures, with layers of management who supervise others, are being replaced with flat organizations of self-directed work teams that make decisions without needing multiple layers of approval. The emphasis is on continuous improvement rather than periodic reviews and appraisals. These organizational structure changes impact the nature and type of controls used.

Methods of Assigning Authority and Responsibility

Management should make sure employees understand entity goals and objectives, assign authority and responsibility for them to departments and individuals, hold them accountable for achieving them, and encourage the use of initiative to solve problems. It is especially important to identify who is responsible for the company's information security policy.

Authority and responsibility are assigned and communicated using formal job descriptions, employee training, operating schedules, budgets, a code of conduct, and written policies and procedures. The *policy and procedures manual* explains proper business practices, describes needed knowledge and experience, explains document procedures, explains how to handle transactions, and lists the resources provided to carry out specific duties. The manual includes the chart of accounts and copies of forms and documents. It is a helpful on-the-job reference for current employees and a useful tool for training new employees.

Human Resources Standards

One of the greatest control strengths is the honesty of employees; one of the greatest control weaknesses is the dishonesty of employees. Human resource policies and practices governing working conditions, job incentives, and career advancement can be a powerful force in encouraging honesty, efficiency, and loyal service. Policies should convey the required level of expertise, competence, ethical behavior, and integrity required. The following policies and procedures are important.

HIRING   Employees should be hired based on educational background, experience, achievements, honesty and integrity, and meeting written job requirements. All company personnel, including cleaning crews and temporary employees, should be subject to hiring policies. Some fraudsters pose as janitors or temporary employees to gain physical access to company computers.

Applicant qualifications can be evaluated using resumes, reference letters, interviews, and background checks. A thorough *background check* includes talking to references, checking for a criminal record, examining credit records, and verifying education and work experience. Many applicants include false information in their applications or resumes. Philip Crosby Associates (PCA) hired John Nelson, MBA, CPA, without conducting a background check. In reality, the CPA designation and his glowing references were phony. Nelson was actually Robert W. Liszewski, who had served an 18-month jail sentence for embezzling $400,000. By the time PCA discovered this, Liszewski had embezzled $960,000 using wire transfers to a dummy corporation, supported by forged signatures on contracts and authorization documents.

Many firms hire companies that specialize in background checks because some applicants buy phony degrees from Web site operators who "validate" the bogus education when employers call. Some applicants even pay hackers to break into university databases and enter fake graduation or grade data.

Compensating, Evaluating and Promoting   Poorly compensated employees are more likely to feel resentment and financial pressures that can motivate fraud. Fair pay and appropriate bonus incentives help motivate and reinforce outstanding employee performance. Employees should be given periodic performance appraisals to help them understand their strengths and weaknesses. Promotions should be based on performance and qualifications.

TRAINING   Training programs should teach new employees their responsibilities; expected levels of performance and behavior; and the company's policies and procedures, culture, and operating style. Employees can be trained by conducting informal discussions and formal meetings, issuing periodic memos, distributing written guidelines and codes of professional ethics, circulating reports of unethical behavior and its consequences, and promoting security and fraud training programs. Ongoing training helps employees tackle new challenges, stay ahead of the competition, adapt to changing technologies, and deal effectively with the evolving environment.

Fraud is less likely to occur when employees believe security is everyone's business, are proud of their company and protective of its assets, and recognize the need to report fraud. Such a culture has to be created, taught, and practiced. Acceptable and unacceptable behavior should be defined. Many computer professionals see nothing wrong with using corporate computer resources to gain unauthorized access to databases and browse them. The consequences of unethical behavior (reprimands, dismissal, and prosecution) should also be taught and reinforced.

MANAGING DISGRUNTLED EMPLOYEES   Some disgruntled employees, seeking revenge for a perceived wrong, perpetrate fraud or sabotage systems. Companies need procedures to identify disgruntled employees and either help them resolve their feelings or remove them from sensitive jobs. For example, a company may choose to establish grievance channels and provide employee counseling. Helping employees resolve their problems is not easy to do, however, because most employees fear that airing their feelings could have negative consequences.

DISCHARGING   Dismissed employees should be removed from sensitive jobs immediately and denied access to the information system. One terminated employee lit a butane lighter under a smoke detector located just outside the computer room. It set off a sprinkler system that ruined most of the computer hardware.

VACATIONS AND ROTATION OF DUTIES   Fraud schemes that require ongoing perpetrator attention are uncovered when the perpetrator takes time off. Periodically rotating employee duties and making employees take vacations can achieve the same results. For example, the FBI raided a gambling establishment and discovered that Roswell Steffen, who earned $11,000 a year, was betting $30,000 a day at the racetrack. The bank where he worked discovered that he embezzled and gambled away $1.5 million over a three-year period. A compulsive gambler, Steffen borrowed $5,000 to bet on a "sure thing" that did not pan out. He embezzled ever-increasing amounts in an effort to win back the money he had "borrowed." Steffen's scheme was simple; he transferred money from inactive accounts to his own account. If anyone complained, Steffen, the chief teller with the power to resolve these types of problems, replaced the money by taking it from another inactive account. When asked, after his arrest, how the fraud could have been prevented, Steffen said the bank could have coupled a two-week vacation with several weeks of rotation to another job function. Had the bank taken these measures, Steffen's embezzlement, which required his physical presence at the bank, would have been almost impossible to cover up.

CONFIDENTIALITY AGREEMENTS AND FIDELITY BOND INSURANCE   All employees, suppliers, and contractors should sign and abide by a confidentiality agreement. Fidelity bond insurance coverage of key employees protects companies against losses arising from deliberate acts of fraud.

PROSECUTE AND INCARCERATE PERPETRATORS   Most fraud is not reported or prosecuted for several reasons:

1. Companies are reluctant to report fraud because it can be a public relations disaster. The disclosure can also reveal system vulnerabilities and attract more fraud or hacker attacks.
2. Law enforcement and the courts are busy with violent crimes and have less time and interest for computer crimes in which no physical harm occurs.

201

3. Fraud is difficult, costly, and time-consuming to investigate and prosecute.
4. Many law enforcement officials, lawyers, and judges lack the computer skills needed to investigate and prosecute computer crimes.
5. Fraud sentences are often light. A famous example involved C. Arnold Smith, former owner of the San Diego Padres, who was named Mr. San Diego of the Century. Smith was involved in the community and made large political contributions. When investigators discovered he had stolen $200 million from his bank, he pleaded no contest. His sentence was four years of probation. He was fined $30,000, to be paid at the rate of $100 a month for 25 years with no interest. Mr. Smith was 71 at the time. The embezzled money was never recovered.

External Influences

External influences include requirements imposed by stock exchanges, the Financial Accounting Standards Board (FASB), the Public Company Accounting Oversight Board (PCAOB), and the Securities and Exchange Commission (SEC). They also include requirements imposed by regulatory agencies, such as those for banks, utilities, and insurance companies.

Objective Setting

Objective setting is the second ERM component. Management determines what the company hopes to achieve, often referred to as the *corporate* vision or mission. Management sets objectives at the corporate level and then subdivides them into more specific objectives for company subunits. The company determines what must go right to achieve the objectives and establishes performance measures to determine whether they are met.

Strategic objectives, which are high-level goals that are aligned with the company's mission, support it, and create shareholder value, are set first. Management should identify alternative ways of accomplishing the strategic objectives; identify and assess the risks and implications of each alternative; formulate a corporate strategy; and set operations, compliance, and reporting objectives.

Operations objectives, which deal with the effectiveness and efficiency of company operations, determine how to allocate resources. They reflect management preferences, judgments, and style and are a key factor in corporate success. They vary significantly—one company may decide to be an early adopter of technology, another may adopt technology when it is proven, and a third may adopt it only after it is generally accepted.

Reporting objectives help ensure the accuracy, completeness, and reliability of company reports; improve decision making; and monitor company activities and performance. *Compliance objectives* help the company comply with all applicable laws and regulations. Most compliance objectives, and many reporting objectives, are imposed by external entities in response to laws or regulations. How well a company meets its compliance and reporting objectives can significantly impact a company's reputation.

ERM provides reasonable assurance that reporting and compliance objectives are achieved because companies have control over them. However, the only reasonable assurance ERM can provide about strategic and operations objectives, which are sometimes at the mercy of uncontrollable external events, is that management and directors are informed on a timely basis of the progress the company is making in achieving them.

Event Identification

COSO defines an *event* as "an incident or occurrence emanating from internal or external sources that affects implementation of strategy or achievement of objectives. Events may have positive or negative impacts or both." An event represents uncertainty; it may or may not occur. If it does occur, it is hard to know when. Until it occurs, it may be difficult to determine its impact. When it occurs, it may trigger another event. Events may occur individually or concurrently. Management must try to anticipate all possible positive or negative events, determine which are most and least likely to occur, and understand the interrelationship of events.

As an example, consider the implementation of an electronic data interchange (EDI) system that creates electronic documents, transmits them to customers and suppliers, and receives electronic responses in return. A few of the events a company could face are choosing an inappropriate technology, unauthorized access, loss of data integrity, incomplete transactions, system failures, and incompatible systems.

Some techniques companies use to identify events include using a comprehensive list of potential events, performing an internal analysis, monitoring leading events and trigger points, conducting workshops and interviews, using data mining, and analyzing business processes.

Risk Assessment and Risk Response

The risks of an identified event are assessed in several different ways: likelihood, positive and negative impacts, individually and by category, their effect on other organizational units, and on an inherent and a residual basis. *Inherent risk* exists before management takes any steps to control the likelihood or impact of an event. *Residual risk* is what remains after management implements internal controls or some other response to risk. Companies should assess inherent risk, develop a response, and then assess residual risk.

To align identified risks with the company's tolerance for risk, management must take an entity-wide view of risk. They assess a risk's likelihood and impact, as well as the costs and benefits of the alternative responses. Management can respond to risk in one of four ways:

- *Reduce.* Reduce the likelihood and impact of risk by implementing an effective system of internal controls.
- *Accept.* Accept the likelihood and impact of the risk.
- *Share.* Share risk or transfer it to someone else by buying insurance, outsourcing an activity, or entering into hedging transactions.
- *Avoid.* Avoid risk by not engaging in the activity that produces the risk. This may require the company to sell a division, exit a product line, or not expand as anticipated.

Accountants and systems designers help management design effective control systems to reduce inherent risk. They also evaluate internal control systems to ensure that they are operating effectively. They assess and reduce inherent risk using the risk assessment and response strategy shown in Figure 2. The first step, event identification, has already been discussed.

Estimate Likelihood and Impact

Some events pose a greater risk because they are more likely to occur. Employees are more likely to make a mistake than to commit fraud, and a company is more likely to be the victim of a fraud than an earthquake. The likelihood of an earthquake may be small, but its impact could destroy a company. The impact of fraud is usually not as great, because most instances of fraud do not threaten a company's existence. Likelihood and impact must be considered together. As either increases, both the materiality of the event and the need to protect against it rise.

Software tools help automate risk assessment and response. Blue Cross Blue Shield of Florida uses ERM software that lets managers enter perceived risks; assess their nature, likelihood, and impact; and assign them a numerical rating. An overall corporate assessment of risk is developed by aggregating all the rankings.

Identify Controls

Management should identify controls that protect the company from each event. Preventive controls are usually superior to detective controls. When preventive controls fail, detective controls are essential for discovering the problem. Corrective controls help recover from any problems. A good internal control system should employ all three.

FIGURE 2

Risk Assessment Approach to Designing Internal Controls

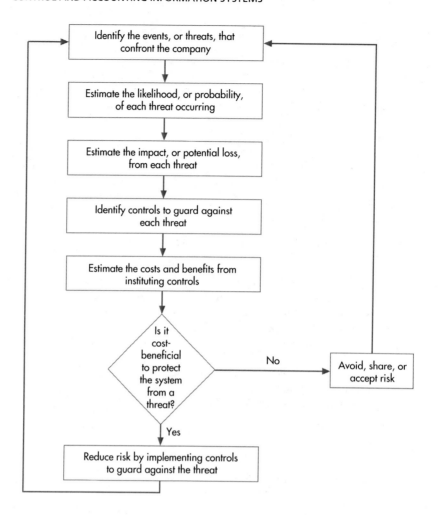

FIGURE 2

Risk Assessment Approach to Designing Internal Controls

Estimate Costs and Benefits

The objective in designing an internal control system is to provide reasonable assurance that events do not take place. No internal control system provides foolproof protection against all events, because having too many controls is cost-prohibitive and negatively affects operational efficiency. Conversely, having too few controls will not provide the needed reasonable assurance.

The benefits of an internal control procedure must exceed its costs. Benefits, which can be hard to quantify accurately, include increased sales and productivity, reduced losses, better integration with customers and suppliers, increased customer loyalty, competitive advantages, and lower insurance premiums. Costs are usually easier to measure than benefits. A primary cost element is personnel, including the time to perform control procedures, the costs of hiring additional employees to achieve effective segregation of duties, and the costs of programming controls into a computer system.

One way to estimate the value of internal controls involves *expected loss*, the mathematical product of impact and likelihood:

$$\text{Expected loss} = \text{Impact} \times \text{Likelihood}$$

The value of a control procedure is the difference between the expected loss with the control procedure(s) and the expected loss without it.

Determine Cost/Benefit Effectiveness

Management should determine whether a control is cost beneficial. For example, at Atlantic Richfield data errors occasionally required an entire payroll to be reprocessed, at a cost of $10,000. A data validation step would reduce the event likelihood from 15% to 1%, at a cost of $600 per pay period. The cost/benefit analysis that determined that the validation step should be employed is shown in Table 2.

TABLE 2 Cost/Benefit Analysis of Payroll Validation Procedure

	Without Validation Procedure	With Validation Procedure	Net Expected Difference
Cost to reprocess entire payroll	$10,000	$10,000	
Likelihood of payroll data errors	15%	1%	
Expected reprocessing cost ($10,000 ×likelihood)	$1,500	$100	$1,400
Cost of validation procedure	$0	$600	$(600)
Net expected benefit of validation procedure			$800

In evaluating internal controls, management must consider factors other than those in the expected benefit calculation. For example, if an event threatens an organization's existence, its extra cost can be viewed as a catastrophic loss insurance premium.

Implement Control or Accept, Share, or Avoid the Risk

Cost-effective controls should be implemented to reduce risk. Risks not reduced must be accepted, shared, or avoided. Risk can be accepted if it is within the company's risk tolerance range. An example is a risk with a small likelihood and a small impact. A response to reduce or share risk helps bring residual risk into an acceptable risk tolerance range. A company may choose to avoid the risk when there is no cost-effective way to bring risk into an acceptable risk tolerance range.

Control Activities

Control activities are policies and procedures that provide reasonable assurance that control objectives are met and risk responses are carried out. It is management's responsibility to develop a secure and adequately controlled system. Management establishes a set of procedures to ensure control compliance and enforcement. The information security officer and the operations staff are responsible for ensuring that control procedures are followed.

Controls are much more effective when placed in the system as it is built, rather than as an afterthought. As a result, managers need to involve systems analysts, designers, and end users when designing computer-based control systems. It is important that control activities be in place during the end-of-the-year holiday season, because a disproportionate amount of computer fraud and security break-ins takes place during this time. Some reasons for this are (1) extended employee vacations mean that there fewer people to "mind the store"; (2) students are out of school and have more time on their hands; and (3) lonely counterculture hackers increase their attacks.

Control procedures fall into the following categories:

1. Proper authorization of transactions and activities
2. Segregation of duties
3. Project development and acquisition controls
4. Change management controls
5. Design and use of documents and records
6. Safeguarding assets, records, and data
7. Independent checks on performance

Focus 1 discusses how a violation of specific control activities, combined with internal environment factors, resulted in a fraud.

Proper Authorization of Transactions and Activities

Because management lacks the time and resources to supervise each company activity and decision, it establishes policies for employees to follow and then empowers them. This empowerment, called *authorization*, is an important control procedure. Authorizations are often documented by signing, initializing, or entering an authorization code on a document or

Control Problems in a School District

The audit report for a school district disclosed serious internal control deficiencies. To improve controls, the district (1) selected a new software package, (2) standardized accounting procedures, (3) instituted purchase order procedures, (4) implemented a separation of duties, and (5) created a control system for vending machine cash and inventory.

After the changes, the director noted that middle school fee balances were low and asked the auditors to investigate. The secretary, responsible for depositing student fees daily and sending them to the central office, said the low amount was due to the principal's waiver of fees for students who qualified for free or reduced-cost lunches. The principal denied having waived the fees.

The auditor examined fee cards for each child and found that the daily deposits did not agree with the dates on student fee cards. They also discovered that the secretary was in charge of a faculty welfare fund that was never

audited or examined, nor was it subject to the newly implemented internal controls. Deposits to the fund were checks from the faculty and cash from the vending machines. To perpetrate her $20,000 fraud, the secretary had stolen all the cash from the vending machines, replaced the payee name on vendor checks with her name, and deposited student fees into the faculty welfare fund to cover up the stolen money.

The secretary was immediately discharged. Because the secretary was bonded, the district was able to recover all of its missing funds.

The school district strengthened controls. Internal auditors examine all funds at the schools. Control of faculty welfare funds was transferred to a faculty member. Because the investigation had revealed the secretary's prior criminal record, a background check was required for all future hires.

record. Computer systems can record a *digital signature*, a means of signing a document with data that cannot be forged.

Employees who process transactions should verify the presence of appropriate authorizations. Auditors review transactions to verify proper authorization, as their absence indicates a possible control problem. For example, Jason Scott discovered that some purchases did not have a purchase requisition. Instead, they had been "personally authorized" by Bill Springer, the purchasing vice president. Jason also found that some payments had been authorized without proper supporting documents, such as purchase orders and receiving reports. These findings raise questions about the adequacy of Springer's internal control procedures.

Certain activities or transactions may be of such consequence that management grants *specific authorization* for them to occur. For example, management review and approval may be required for sales in excess of $50,000. In contrast, management can authorize employees to handle routine transactions without special approval, a procedure known as *general authorization*. Management should have written policies on both specific and general authorization for all types of transactions.

Segregation of Duties

Good internal control requires that no single employee be given too much responsibility over business transactions or processes. An employee should not be in a position to commit *and* conceal fraud. Segregation of duties is discussed in two separate sections: segregation of accounting duties and segregation of systems duties.

SEGREGATION OF ACCOUNTING DUTIES   As shown in Figure 3, effective *segregation of accounting duties* is achieved when the following functions are separated:

- *Authorization*—approving transactions and decisions
- *Recording*—preparing source documents; entering data into online systems; maintaining journals, ledgers, files or databases; and preparing reconciliations and performance reports
- *Custody*—handling cash, tools, inventory, or fixed assets; receiving incoming customer checks; writing checks

If one person performs two of these functions, problems can arise. For example, the city treasurer of Fairfax, Virginia, embezzled $600,000. When residents used cash to pay their taxes, she kept the currency and entered the payments on property tax records, but did not report them

Prevents employees from falsifying records in
order to conceal theft of assets entrusted to them

FIGURE 3

Separation of Duties

CUSTODIAL FUNCTIONS

• Handling cash
• Handling inventories,
  tools, or fixed assets
• Writing checks
• Receiving checks in the mail

RECORDING FUNCTIONS

• Preparing source documents
  or entering data online
• Maintaining journals,
  ledgers, files, databases
• Preparing reconciliations
• Preparing performance reports

AUTHORIZATION FUNCTIONS

• Authorization of transactions
  or decisions

Prevents authorization of a fictitious
or inaccurate transaction as a means
of concealing asset thefts

Prevents an employee from falsifying
records to cover up an inaccurate
or false transaction that was
inappropriately authorized

to the controller. Periodically, she made an adjusting journal entry to bring her records into agreement with those of the controller. When she received checks in the mail that would not be missed if not recorded, she put them in the cash register and stole that amount of cash. Because the treasurer was responsible for both the *custody* of cash receipts and the *recording* of those receipts, she was able to steal cash receipts and falsify the accounts to conceal the theft.

In another example, the utilities director of Newport Beach, California, embezzled $1.2 million. Responsible for authorizing transactions, he forged invoices or easement documents authorizing payments to real or fictitious property owners. Finance department officials gave him the checks to deliver to the property owners. He forged signatures and deposited the checks in his own account. Because he was given *custody* of the checks he authorized, he could *authorize* fictitious transactions and steal the payments.

The payroll director of the Los Angeles Dodgers embezzled $330,000. He credited employees for hours not worked and received a kickback of 50% of the extra compensation. He added fictitious names to the Dodgers payroll and cashed the paychecks. The fraud was discovered while he was ill and another employee performed his duties. Because the perpetrator was responsible for *authorizing* the hiring of employees and for *recording* employee hours, he did not need to prepare or handle the paychecks. The company mailed the checks to the address he specified.

Computers can be programmed to perform one or more of the authorization, custody, and recording functions. Segregation of duties is maintained, except that the computer performs the function. For example, people can pay for gas using a credit or debit card. The computer performs both the custody and the recording function. In addition to better internal control, this better serves the customer by increasing convenience and eliminating lines to pay for the gas.

In a system with effective separation of duties, it is difficult for any single employee to embezzle successfully. Detecting fraud where two or more people are in **collusion** to override controls is more difficult because it is much easier to commit and conceal the fraud. For example, two women at a credit card company colluded. One woman authorized new credit card accounts, and the other wrote off unpaid accounts of less than $1,000. The first woman created a new account for each of them using fictitious data. When the amounts outstanding neared the $1,000 limit, the woman in collections wrote them off. The process would then be repeated. They were caught when a jilted boyfriend seeking revenge reported the scheme to the credit card company.

Employees can collude with other employees, customers, or vendors. The most frequent employee/vendor collusion includes billing at inflated prices, performing substandard work and receiving full payment, payment for nonperformance, duplicate billings, and improperly purchasing more goods from a colluding company. The most frequent employee/customer collusion includes unauthorized loans or insurance payments, receipt of assets or services at unauthorized discount prices, forgiveness of amounts owed, and unauthorized extension of due dates.

SEGREGATION OF SYSTEMS DUTIES In an information system, procedures once performed by separate individuals are combined. Therefore, any person who has unrestricted access to the computer, its programs, and live data could perpetrate and conceal fraud. To combat this threat, organizations implement *segregation of systems duties*. Authority and responsibility should be divided clearly among the following functions:

1. *Systems administration.* *Systems administrators* make sure all information system components operate smoothly and efficiently.
2. *Network management.* *Network managers* ensure that devices are linked to the organization's internal and external networks and that those networks operate properly.
3. *Security management.* *Security management* makes sure that systems are secure and protected from internal and external threats.
4. *Change management.* *Change management* is the process of making sure that changes are made smoothly and efficiently and that they do not negatively affect systems reliability, security, confidentiality, integrity, and availability.
5. *Users.* Users record transactions, authorize data to be processed, and use system output.
6. *Systems analysis.* *Systems analysts* help users determine their information needs and design systems to meet those needs.
7. *Programming.* *Programmers* take the analysts' design and create a system by writing the computer programs.
8. *Computer operations.* *Computer operators* run the software on the company's computers. They ensure that data are input properly, that they are processed correctly, and that output is produced when needed.
9. *Information system library.* The information system librarian maintains custody of corporate databases, files, and programs in a separate storage area called the *information system library*.
10. *Data control.* The *data control group* ensures that source data have been properly approved, monitors the flow of work through the computer, reconciles input and output, maintains a record of input errors to ensure their correction and resubmission, and distributes systems output.

Allowing a person to do two or more of these jobs exposes the company to fraud. For example, if a credit union programmer uses actual data to test her program, she could erase her car loan balance during the test. Likewise, if a computer operator has access to programming logic and documentation, he might be able to increase his salary while processing payroll.

Project Development and Acquisition Controls

It is important to have a proven methodology to govern the development, acquisition, implementation, and maintenance of information systems. It should contain appropriate controls for management approval, user involvement, analysis, design, testing, implementation, and conversion.
Important systems development controls include the following:

1. A *steering committee* guides and oversees systems development and acquisition.
2. A *strategic master plan* is developed and updated yearly to align an organization's information system with its business strategies. It shows the projects that must be completed, and it addresses the company's hardware, software, personnel, and infrastructure requirements.
3. A *project development plan* shows the tasks to be performed, who will perform them, project costs, completion dates, and *project milestones*—significant points when progress is reviewed and actual and estimated completion times are compared. Each project is assigned to a manager and team who are responsible for its success or failure.
4. A *data processing schedule* shows when each task should be performed.

5. *System performance measurements* are established to evaluate the system. Common measurements include *throughput* (output per unit of time), *utilization* (percentage of time the system is used), and *response time* (how long it takes the system to respond).
6. A *post-implementation review* is performed after a development project is completed to determine whether the anticipated benefits were achieved.

Some companies hire a **systems integrator** to manage a systems development effort involving its own personnel, its client, and other vendors. These development projects are subject to the same cost overruns and missed deadlines as systems developed internally. For example, Westpac Banking began a five-year, $85 million systems development project to decentralize its systems, create new financial products, and downsize its systems department. Three years and $150 million later, no usable results had been attained, and it was clear the scheduled completion date would not be met. With a runaway on its hands, Westpac fired IBM, the primary software developer, and brought in Accenture to review the project and develop recommendations for salvaging it.

Companies using systems integrators should use the same project management processes and controls as internal projects. In addition, they should:

- *Develop clear specifications.* This includes exact descriptions and system definitions, explicit deadlines, and precise acceptance criteria. Suffolk County, New York, spent 12 months and $500,000 preparing detailed specifications for a $16 million criminal justice system before accepting bids. Only 6 of 22 invited integrators bid on the project because of the county's rigorous cost and quality standards. County officials believe their diligent up-front efforts helped ensure their new system's success and saved the county $3 million.
- *Monitor the project.* Companies should establish formal procedures for measuring and reporting a project's status. The best approach is to divide the project into manageable tasks, assign responsibility for each task, and meet at least monthly to review progress and assess quality.

Change Management Controls

Organizations modify existing systems to reflect new business practices and to take advantage of IT advancements. Those in charge of changes should make sure they do not introduce errors and facilitate fraud.

Design and Use of Documents and Records

The proper design and use of electronic and paper documents and records help ensure the accurate and complete recording of all relevant transaction data. Their form and content should be as simple as possible, minimize errors, and facilitate review and verification. Documents that initiate a transaction should contain a space for authorizations. Those that transfer assets need a space for the receiving party's signature. Documents should be sequentially prenumbered so each can be accounted for. An audit trail facilitates tracing individual transactions through the system, correcting errors, and verifying system output.

Safeguard Assets, Records, and Data

A company must protect its cash and physical assets as well as its information. A reporter for Reuters noticed that Intentia, a Swedish software developer, released its first- and second-quarter earnings reports on Web sites with nearly identical Web addresses. He guessed the third-quarter Web address, found their unreleased numbers, and ran a story on the disappointing results. Intentia filed criminal hacking charges, but they were dismissed. The Swedish Stock Exchange censored Intentia for not protecting its financial information.

Employees are a much greater security risk than outsiders are. They are better able to hide their illegal acts, because they know system weakness better. Almost 50% of companies report that insiders access data without the proper authorization. A software engineer at America Online was charged with selling 92 million e-mail addresses he illegally obtained using another employee's ID and password. An Internet gambling business bought the names and used them to increase company earnings by $10,000 to $20,000 a day. The data theft was not uncovered for a year, until an anonymous tipster informed authorities that the gambling business was reselling the names to spammers selling herbal male enhancement products.

Employees also cause unintentional threats, such as accidentally deleting company data, opening virus-laden e-mail attachments, or trying to fix hardware or software without the appropriate expertise. These can result in crashed networks, corrupt data, and hardware and software malfunctions.

It is important to:

- *Create and enforce appropriate policies and procedures.* All too often, policies and procedures are created but not enforced. A laptop with the names, Social Security numbers, and birthdates of 26.5 million people was stolen from the home of a Veteran Affairs (VA) Department analyst. The VA did not enforce its policies that sensitive data be encrypted and not leave VA offices. The cost to taxpayers of notifying all 26.5 million people and buying them a credit-checking service was $100 million. Two years prior to the theft, an inspector general report identified the inadequate control of sensitive data as a weakness, but it had never been addressed.
- *Maintain accurate records of all assets.* Periodically reconcile the recorded amounts of company assets to physical counts of those assets.
- *Restrict access to assets.* Restricting access to storage areas protects inventories and equipment. Cash registers, safes, lockboxes, and safety deposit boxes limit access to cash and paper assets. Over $1 million was embezzled from Perini Corp. because blank checks were kept in an unlocked storeroom. An employee made out checks to fictitious vendors, ran them through an unlocked check-signing machine, and cashed the checks.
- *Protect records and documents.* Fireproof storage areas, locked filing cabinets, backup files, and off-site storage protect records and documents. Access to blank checks and documents should be limited to authorized personnel. In Inglewood, California, a janitor stole 34 blank checks, wrote checks from $50,000 to $470,000, forged the names of city officials, and cashed them.

Independent Checks on Performance

Independent checks on performance, done by someone other than the person who performs the original operation, help ensure that transactions are processed accurately. They include the following:

- *Top-level reviews.* Management should monitor company results and periodically compare actual company performance to (a) planned performance, as shown in budgets, targets, and forecasts; (b) prior period performance; and (c) competitors' performance.
- *Analytical reviews.* An *analytical review* is an examination of the relationships between different sets of data. For example, as credit sales increase, so should accounts receivable. In addition, there are relationships between sales and accounts such as cost of goods sold, inventory, and freight out.
- *Reconciliation of independently maintained records.* Records should be reconciled to documents or records with the same balance. For example, a bank reconciliation verifies that company checking account balances agree with bank statement balances. Another example is comparing subsidiary ledger totals with general ledger totals.
- *Comparison of actual quantities with recorded amounts.* Significant assets are periodically counted and reconciled to company records. At the end of each clerk's shift, cash in a cash register drawer should match the amount on the cash register tape. Inventory should be periodically counted and reconciled to inventory records.
- *Double-entry accounting.* The maxim that debits equal credits provides numerous opportunities for independent checks. Debits in a payroll entry may be allocated to numerous inventory and/or expense accounts; credits are allocated to liability accounts for wages payable, taxes withheld, employee insurance, and union dues. After the payroll entries, comparing total debits and credits is a powerful check on the accuracy of both processes. Any discrepancy indicates the presence of an error.
- *Independent review.* After a transaction is processed, a second person reviews the work of the first, checking for proper authorization, reviewing supporting documents, and checking the accuracy of prices, quantities, and extensions.

Information and Communication

Information and communication constitute the seventh component of the ERM model. This relates directly to the primary purpose of an AIS, which is to gather, record, process, store, summarize, and communicate information about an organization. This includes understanding how transactions are initiated, data are captured, files are accessed and updated, data are processed, and information is reported. It includes understanding accounting records and procedures, supporting documents, and financial statements. These items provide an *audit trail*, which allows transactions to be traced back and forth between their origination and the financial statements.

According to the AICPA, an AIS has five primary objectives: to identify and record all valid transactions, properly classify transactions, record transactions at their proper monetary value, record transactions in the proper accounting period, and properly present transactions and related disclosures in the financial statements.

Accounting systems generally consist of several subsystems, each designed to process a particular type of transaction using the same sequence of procedures, called accounting cycles.

Monitoring

ERM processes must be continuously monitored and modified as needed, and deficiencies must be reported to management. Key methods of monitoring performance include the following:

Perform ERM Evaluations

ERM effectiveness is measured using a formal or a self-assessment ERM evaluation. A team can be formed to conduct the evaluation, or it can be done by internal auditing.

Implement Effective Supervision

Effective supervision involves training and assisting employees, monitoring their performance, correcting errors, and overseeing employees who have access to assets. Supervision is especially important in organizations without responsibility reporting or an adequate segregation of duties.

Use Responsibility Accounting Systems

Responsibility accounting systems include budgets, quotas, schedules, standard costs, and quality standards; reports comparing actual and planned performance; and procedures for investigating and correcting significant variances.

Monitor System Activities

Risk analysis and management software packages review computer and network security measures, detect illegal access, test for weaknesses and vulnerabilities, report weaknesses found, and suggest improvements. Cost parameters can be entered to balance acceptable levels of risk tolerance and cost-effectiveness. Software also monitors and combats viruses, spyware, adware, spam, phishing, and inappropriate e-mails. It blocks pop-up ads, prevents browsers from being hijacked, and validates a phone caller's identity by comparing the caller's voice to a previously recorded voiceprint. Software can help companies recover from malicious actions. One package helped a company recover from a disgruntled employee's rampage. After a negative performance evaluation, the perpetrator ripped cables out of PCs, changed the inventory control files, and edited the password file to stop people from logging on to the network. The software quickly identified the corrupted files and alerted company headquarters. The damage was undone by utility software, which restored the corrupted file to its original status.

All system transactions and activities should be recorded in a log that indicates who accessed what data, when, and from which online device. These logs should be reviewed frequently and used to monitor system activity, trace problems to their source, evaluate employee productivity, control company costs, fight espionage and hacking attacks, and comply with legal requirements. One company used these logs to analyze why an employee had almost zero productivity and found that he spent six hours a day visiting Internet pornography sites.

The Privacy Foundation estimated that one-third of all American workers with computers are monitored, and that number is expected to increase. Companies who monitor system activities should not violate employee privacy. One way to do that is to have employees agree in writing to written policies that include the following:

- The technology an employee uses on the job belongs to the company.
- E-mails received on company computers are not private and can be read by supervisory personnel. This policy allowed a large pharmaceutical company to identify and terminate an employee who was e-mailing confidential drug-manufacturing data to an external party.
- Employees should not use technology to contribute to a hostile work environment.

Track Purchased Software and Mobile Devices

The Business Software Alliance (BSA) tracks down and fines companies that violate software license agreements. To comply with copyrights and protect themselves from software piracy lawsuits, companies should periodically conduct software audits. There should be enough licenses for all users, and the company should not pay for more licenses than needed. Employees should be informed of the consequences of using unlicensed software.

The increasing number of mobile devices should be tracked and monitored, because their loss could represent a substantial exposure. Items to track are the devices, who has them, what tasks they perform, the security features installed, and what software the company needs to maintain adequate system and network security.

Conduct Periodic Audits

External, internal, and network security audits can assess and monitor risk as well as detect fraud and errors. Informing employees of audits helps resolve privacy issues, deters fraud, and reduces errors. Auditors should regularly test system controls and periodically browse system usage files looking for suspicious activities. During the security audit of a health care company, auditors pretending to be computer support staff persuaded 16 of 22 employees to reveal their user IDs and passwords. They also found that employees testing a new system left the company's network exposed to outside attacks.

Internal audits assess the reliability and integrity of financial and operating information, evaluate internal control effectiveness, and assess employee compliance with management policies and procedures as well as applicable laws and regulations. The internal audit function should be organizationally independent of accounting and operating functions. Internal audit should report to the audit committee, not the controller or chief financial officer.

One internal auditor noted that a department supervisor took the office staff to lunch in a limousine on her birthday. Wondering whether her salary could support her lifestyle, he investigated and found she set up several fictitious vendors, sent the company invoices from these vendors, and cashed the checks mailed to her. Over a period of several years, she embezzled over $12 million.

Employ a Computer Security Officer and a Chief Compliance Officer

A *computer security officer (CSO)* is in charge of system security, independent of the information system function, and reports to the chief operating officer (COO) or the CEO. The overwhelming tasks related to SOX and other forms of compliance have led many companies to delegate all compliance issues to a *chief compliance officer (CCO)*. Many companies use outside computer consultants or in-house teams to test and evaluate security procedures and computer systems.

Engage Forensic Specialists

Forensic investigators who specialize in fraud are a fast-growing group in the accounting profession. Their increasing presence is due to several factors, most notably SOX, new accounting rules, and demands by boards of directors that forensic investigations be an ongoing part of the financial reporting and corporate governance process. Most forensic investigators received specialized training with the FBI, IRS, or other law enforcement agencies. Investigators with the computer skills to ferret out fraud perpetrators are in great demand. The Association of Certified Fraud Examiners sponsors a Certified Fraud Examiner (CFE) professional certification program. To become a CFE, candidates must pass a two-day exam. Currently there are about 30,000 CFEs worldwide.

Computer forensics specialists discover, extract, safeguard, and document computer evidence such that its authenticity, accuracy, and integrity will not succumb to legal challenges. Computer forensics can be compared to performing an "autopsy" on a computer system to determine whether a crime was committed as well as who committed it, and then marshalling the evidence lawyers need to prove the charges in court. Some of the more common matters investigated are improper Internet usage; fraud; sabotage; the loss, theft, or corruption of data; retrieving "erased" information from e-mails and databases; and figuring out who performed certain computer activities. A Deloitte & Touche forensics team uncovered evidence that helped convict a Giant Supermarket purchasing manager who had accepted over $600,000 in supplier kickbacks.

Install Fraud Detection Software

Fraudsters follow distinct patterns and leave clues behind that can be discovered by fraud detection software. ReliaStar Financial used software from IBM to detect the following:

- A Los Angeles chiropractor submitted hundreds of thousands of dollars in fraudulent claims. The software identified an unusual number of patients who lived more than 50 miles away from the doctor's office and flagged these bills for investigation.
- A Long Island doctor submitted weekly bills for a rare and expensive procedure normally done only once or twice in a lifetime.
- A podiatrist saw four patients and billed for 500 separate procedures.

Neural networks (programs with learning capabilities) can accurately identify fraud. The Visa and MasterCard operation at Mellon Bank uses a neural network to track 1.2 million accounts. It can spot illegal credit card use and notify the owner shortly after the card is stolen. It can also spot trends before bank investigators do. For example, an investigator learned about a new fraud from another bank. When he went to check for the fraud, the neural network had already identified it and had printed out transactions that fit its pattern. The software cost the bank less than $1 million and paid for itself in six months.

Implement a Fraud Hotline

People witnessing fraudulent behavior are often torn between two conflicting feelings. Although they want to protect company assets and report fraud perpetrators, they are uncomfortable blowing the whistle, so all too often they remain silent. This reluctance is stronger if they are aware of whistle-blowers who have been ostracized, been persecuted, or suffered damage to their careers.

SOX mandates a mechanism for employees to report fraud and abuse. A *fraud hotline* is an effective way to comply with the law and resolve whistle-blower conflict. In one study, researchers found that 33% of 212 frauds were detected through anonymous tips. The insurance industry set up a hotline to control $17 billion a year in fraudulent claims. In the first month, more than 2,250 calls were received; 15% resulted in investigative action. The downside of hotlines is that many calls are not worthy of investigation; some are motivated by a desire for revenge, some are vague reports of wrongdoing, and others have no merit.

Summary and Case Conclusion

One week after Jason and Maria filed their audit report, they were summoned to the office of Northwest's director of internal auditing to explain their findings. Shortly thereafter, a fraud investigation team was dispatched to Bozeman to take a closer look at the situation. Six months later, a company newsletter indicated that the Springer family sold its 10% interest in the business and resigned from all management positions. Two Northwest executives were transferred in to replace them. There was no other word on the audit findings.

Two years later, Jason and Maria worked with Frank Ratliff, a member of the high-level audit team. After hours, Frank told them the investigation team examined a large sample of purchasing transactions and all employee timekeeping and payroll records for a 12-month period. The team also took a detailed physical inventory. They discovered that the problems Jason identified—including missing purchase requisitions, purchase orders, and receiving reports, as well as excessive prices—were widespread. These problems occurred in transactions with three large vendors from whom Springer's had purchased several million dollars of inventory. The investigators discussed the unusually high prices with the vendors but did not receive a satisfactory explanation. The county business-licensing bureau revealed that Bill Springer held a majority ownership interest in each of these companies. By authorizing excessive prices to companies he owned, Springer earned a significant share of several hundred thousand dollars of excessive profits, all at the expense of Northwest Industries.

Several Springer employees were paid for more hours than they worked. Inventory was materially overstated; a physical inventory revealed that a significant portion of recorded inventory did not exist and that some items were obsolete. The adjusting journal entry reflecting Springer's real inventory wiped out much of their profits over the past three years.

When confronted, the Springers vehemently denied breaking any laws. Northwest considered going to the authorities but was concerned that the case was not strong enough to prove in court. Northwest also worried that adverse publicity might damage the company's position in Bozeman. After months of negotiation, the Springers agreed to the settlement reported in the newsletter. Part of the settlement was that no public statement would be made about any alleged fraud or embezzlement involving the Springers. According to Frank, this policy was normal. In many fraud cases, settlements are reached quietly, with no legal action taken, so that the company can avoid adverse publicity.

Key Terms

threat
exposure
impact
likelihood
internal control
preventive control
detective control
corrective control
general control
application control
belief system
boundary system
diagnostic control system
interactive control system
Foreign Corrupt Practices Act
Sarbanes–Oxley Act (SOX)
Public Company Accounting Oversight Board (PCAOB)
Control Objectives for Information and Related Technology (COBIT)

Committee of Sponsoring Organizations (COSO)
Internal Control—Integrated Framework (IC)
Enterprise Risk Management—Integrated Framework (ERM)
internal environment
risk appetite
audit committee
policy and procedures manual
background check
strategic objective
operations objective
reporting objective
compliance objective
event
inherent risk
residual risk
expected loss
control activities
authorization
digital signature
specific authorization

general authorization
segregation of accounting duties
collusion
segregation of systems duties
systems administrator
network manager
security management
change management
systems analyst
programmer
computer operator
information system library
data control group
steering committee
strategic master plan
project development plan
project milestone
data processing schedule
system performance measurements
throughput
utilization

response time
post-implementation
review
systems integrator
analytical review

audit trail
computer security officer
(CSO)
chief compliance officer
(CCO)

forensic investigators
computer forensics
specialist
neural network
fraud hot line

AIS IN ACTION

Chapter Quiz

1. COSO identified five interrelated components of internal control. Which of the following is NOT one of those five?
   a. risk assessment
   b. internal control policies
   c. monitoring
   d. information and communication

2. In the ERM model, COSO specified four types of objectives that management must meet to achieve company goals. Which of the following is NOT one of those types?
   a. responsibility objectives
   b. strategic objectives
   c. compliance objectives
   d. reporting objectives
   e. operations objectives

3. Which of the following statements is true?
   a. COSO's enterprise risk management framework is narrow in scope and is limited to financial controls.
   b. COSO's internal control integrated framework has been widely accepted as the authority on internal controls.
   c. The Foreign Corrupt Practices Act had no impact on internal accounting control systems.
   d. It is easier to add controls to an already designed system than to include them during the initial design stage.

4. All other things being equal, which of the following is true?
   a. Detective controls are superior to preventive controls.
   b. Corrective controls are superior to preventive controls.
   c. Preventive controls are equivalent to detective controls.
   d. Preventive controls are superior to detective controls.

5. Which of the following statements about the control environment is FALSE?
   a. Management's attitudes toward internal control and ethical behavior have little impact on employee beliefs or actions.
   b. An overly complex or unclear organizational structure may be indicative of problems that are more serious.
   c. A written policy and procedures manual is an important tool for assigning authority and responsibility.
   d. Supervision is especially important in organizations that cannot afford elaborate responsibility reporting or are too small to have an adequate separation of duties.

6. To achieve effective segregation of duties, certain functions must be separated. Which of the following is the correct listing of the accounting-related functions that must be segregated?
   a. control, recording, and monitoring
   b. authorization, recording, and custody
   c. control, custody, and authorization
   d. monitoring, recording, and planning

7. Which of the following is NOT an independent check?
   a. bank reconciliation
   b. periodic comparison of subsidiary ledger totals to control accounts
   c. trial balance
   d. re-adding the total of a batch of invoices and comparing it with your first total

8. Which of the following is a control procedure relating to both the design and use of documents and records?
   a. locking blank checks in a drawer
   b. reconciling the bank account
   c. sequentially prenumbering sales invoices
   d. comparing actual physical quantities with recorded amounts

9. Which of the following is the correct order of the risk assessment steps discussed in this chapter?
   a. Identify threats, estimate risk and exposure, identify controls, and estimate costs and benefits.
   b. Identify controls, estimate risk and exposure, identify threats, and estimate costs and benefits.
   c. Estimate risk and exposure, identify controls, identify threats, and estimate costs and benefits.
   d. Estimate costs and benefits, identify threats, identify controls, and estimate risk and exposure.

10. Your current system is deemed to be 90% reliable. A major threat has been identified with an impact of $3,000,000. Two control procedures exist to deal with the threat. Implementation of control A would cost $100,000 and reduce the likelihood to 6%. Implementation of control B would cost $140,000 and reduce the likelihood to 4%. Implementation of both controls would cost $220,000 and reduce the likelihood to 2%. Given the data, and based solely on an economic analysis of costs and benefits, what should you do?
    a. Implement control A only.
    b. Implement control B only.
    c. Implement both controls A and B.
    d. Implement neither control.

Discussion Questions

1. Answer the following questions about the audit of Springer's Lumber & Supply.
   a. What deficiencies existed in the internal environment at Springer's?
   b. Do you agree with the decision to settle with the Springers rather than to prosecute them for fraud and embezzlement? Why or why not?
   c. Should the company have told Jason and Maria the results of the high-level audit? Why or why not?

2. Effective segregation of duties is sometimes not economically feasible in a small business. What internal control elements do you think can help compensate for this threat?

3. One function of the AIS is to provide adequate controls to ensure the safety of organizational assets, including data. However, many people view control procedures as "red tape." They also believe that instead of producing tangible benefits, business controls create resentment and loss of company morale. Discuss this position.

4. In recent years, Supersmurf's external auditors have given clean opinions on its financial statements and favorable evaluations of its internal control systems. Discuss whether it is necessary for this corporation to take any further action to comply with the Sarbanes–Oxley Act.

5. When you go to a movie theater, you buy a prenumbered ticket from the cashier. This ticket is handed to another person at the entrance to the movie. What kinds of irregularities is the theater trying to prevent? What controls is it using to prevent these irregularities? What remaining risks or exposures can you identify?

6. Some restaurants use customer checks with prenumbered sequence codes. Each food server uses these checks to write up customer orders. Food servers are told not to destroy any customer checks; if a mistake is made, they are to void that check and write a new one. All voided checks are to be turned in to the manager daily. How does this policy help the restaurant control cash receipts?

7. Compare and contrast the following three frameworks: COBIT, COSO Integrated Control, and ERM.

8. Explain what an event is. Using the Internet as a resource, create a list of some of the many internal and external factors that COSO indicated could influence events and affect a company's ability to implement its strategy and achieve its objectives.

9. Explain what is meant by objective setting, and describe the four types of objectives used in ERM.

10. Discuss several ways that ERM processes can be continuously monitored and modified so that deficiencies are reported to management.

Problems

1. You are an audit supervisor assigned to a new client, Go-Go Corporation, which is listed on the New York Stock Exchange. You visited Go-Go's corporate headquarters to become acquainted with key personnel and to conduct a preliminary review of the company's accounting policies, controls, and systems. During this visit, the following events occurred:
   a. You met with Go-Go's audit committee, which consists of the corporate controller, treasurer, financial vice president, and budget director.
   b. You recognized the treasurer as a former aide to Ernie Eggers, who was convicted of fraud several years ago.
   c. Management explained its plans to change accounting methods for depreciation from the accelerated to the straight-line method. Management implied that if your firm does not concur with this change, Go-Go will employ other auditors.
   d. You learned that the financial vice president manages a staff of five internal auditors.
   e. You noted that all management authority seems to reside with three brothers, who serve as chief executive officer, president, and financial vice president.
   f. You were told that the performance of division and department managers is evaluated on a subjective basis, because Go-Go's management believes that formal performance evaluation procedures are counterproductive.
   g. You learned that the company has reported increases in earnings per share for each of the past 25 quarters; however, earnings during the current quarter have leveled off and may decline.
   h. You reviewed the company's policy and procedures manual, which listed policies for dealing with customers, vendors, and employees.
   i. Your preliminary assessment is that the accounting systems are well designed and that they employ effective internal control procedures.
   j. Some employees complained that some managers occasionally contradict the instructions of other managers regarding proper data security procedures.
   k. After a careful review of the budget for data security enhancement projects, you feel the budget appears to be adequate.
   l. The enhanced network firewall project appeared to be on a very aggressive implementation schedule. The IT manager mentioned that even if he put all of his personnel on the project for the next five weeks, he still would not complete the project in time. The

manager has mentioned this to company management, which seems unwilling to modify the schedule.

m. Several new employees have had trouble completing some of their duties, and they do not appear to know who to ask for help.

n. Go-Go's strategy is to achieve consistent growth for its shareholders. However, its policy is not to invest in any project unless its payback period is no more than 48 months and yields an internal rate of return that exceeds its cost of capital by 3%.

o. You observe that company purchasing agents wear clothing and exhibit other paraphernalia from major vendors. The purchasing department manager proudly displays a picture of himself holding a big fish on the deck of a luxury fishing boat that has the logo of a major Go-Go vendor painted on its wheelhouse.

Required

The information you have obtained suggests potential problems relating to Go-Go's internal environment. Identify the problems, and explain them in relation to the internal environment concepts discussed in this chapter.

2. Explain how the principle of separation of duties is violated in each of the following situations. Also, suggest one or more procedures to reduce the risk and exposure highlighted in each example.

a. A payroll clerk recorded a 40-hour workweek for an employee who had quit the previous week. He then prepared a paycheck for this employee, forged her signature, and cashed the check.

b. While opening the mail, a cashier set aside, and subsequently cashed, two checks payable to the company on account.

c. A cashier prepared a fictitious invoice from a company using his brother-in-law's name. He wrote a check in payment of the invoice, which the brother-in-law later cashed.

d. An employee of the finishing department walked off with several parts from the storeroom and recorded the items in the inventory ledger as having been issued to the assembly department.

e. A cashier cashed a check from a customer in payment of an account receivable, pocketed the cash, and concealed the theft by properly posting the receipt to the customer's account in the accounts receivable ledger.

f. Several customers returned clothing purchases. Instead of putting the clothes into a return bin to be put back on the rack, a clerk put the clothing in a separate bin under some cleaning rags. After her shift, she transferred the clothes to a gym bag and took them home.

g. A receiving clerk noticed that four cases of MP3 players were included in a shipment when only three were ordered. The clerk put the extra case aside and took it home after his shift ended.

h. An insurance claims adjuster had check-signing authority of up to $6,000. The adjuster created three businesses that billed the insurance company for work not performed on valid claims. The adjuster wrote and signed checks to pay for the invoices, none of which exceeded $6,000.

i. An accounts payable clerk recorded invoices received from a company that he and his wife owned and authorized their payment.

j. A cashier created false purchase return vouchers to hide his theft of several thousand dollars from his cash register.

k. A purchasing agent received a 10% kickback of the invoice amount for all purchases made from a specific vendor.

3. The following description represents the policies and procedures for agent expense reimbursements at Excel Insurance Company.

Agents submit a completed expense reimbursement form to their branch manager at the end of each week. The branch manager reviews the expense report to determine whether the claimed expenses are reimbursable based on the company's expense reimbursement policy and reasonableness of amount. The company's policy manual states that agents are to document any questionable expense item and that the branch manager must approve in advance expenditures exceeding $500.

After the expenses are approved, the branch manager sends the expense report to the home office. There, accounting records the transaction, and cash disbursements prepares the expense reimbursement check. Cash disbursements sends the expense reimbursement checks to the branch manager, who distributes them to the agents.

To receive cash advances for anticipated expenses, agents must complete a Cash Advance Approval form. The branch manager reviews and approves the Cash Advance Approval form and sends a copy to accounting and another to the agent. The agent submits the copy of the Cash Advance Approval form to the branch office cashier to obtain the cash advance.

At the end of each month, internal audit at the home office reconciles the expense reimbursements. It adds the total dollar amounts on the expense reports from each branch, subtracts the sum of the dollar totals on each branch's Cash Advance Approval form, and compares the net amount to the sum of the expense reimbursement checks issued to agents. Internal audit investigates any differences.

Required

Identify the internal control strengths and weaknesses in Excel's expense reimbursement process. Look for authorization, recording, safeguarding, and reconciliation strengths and weaknesses. (*CMA Examination, adapted*)

4. The Gardner Company, a client of your firm, has come to you with the following problem. It has three clerical employees who must perform the following functions:
   a. Maintain the general ledger
   b. Maintain the accounts payable ledger
   c. Maintain the accounts receivable ledger
   d. Prepare checks for signature
   e. Maintain the cash disbursements journal
   f. Issue credits on returns and allowances
   g. Reconcile the bank account
   h. Handle and deposit cash receipts

   Assuming equal abilities among the three employees, the company asks you to assign the eight functions to them to maximize internal control. Assume that these employees will perform no accounting functions other than the ones listed.

Required

   a. List four possible unsatisfactory pairings of the functions.
   b. State how you would distribute the functions among the three employees. Assume that with the exception of the nominal jobs of the bank reconciliation and the issuance of credits on returns and allowances, all functions require an equal amount of time. (*CPA Examination, adapted*)

5. During a recent review, ABC Corporation discovered that it has a serious internal control problem. It is estimated that the impact associated with this problem is $1 million and that the likelihood is currently 5%. Two internal control procedures have been proposed to deal with this problem. Procedure A would cost $25,000 and reduce likelihood to 2%; procedure B would cost $30,000 and reduce likelihood to 1%. If both procedures were implemented, likelihood would be reduced to 0.1%.

Required

   a. What is the estimated expected loss associated with ABC Corporation's internal control problem before any new internal control procedures are implemented?
   b. Compute the revised estimate of expected loss if procedure A were implemented, if procedure B were implemented, and if both procedures were implemented.
   c. Compare the estimated costs and benefits of procedure A, procedure B, and both procedures combined. If you consider only the estimates of cost and benefit, which procedure(s) should be implemented?

CONTROL AND ACCOUNTING INFORMATION SYSTEMS

d. What other factors might be relevant to the decision?
e. Use the Goal Seek function in Microsoft Excel to determine the likelihood of occurrence without the control and the reduction in expected loss if the net benefit/cost is 0. Do this for procedure A, procedure B, and both procedures together.

6. The management at Covington, Inc., recognizes that a well-designed internal control system provides many benefits. Among the benefits are reliable financial records that facilitate decision making and a greater probability of preventing or detecting errors and fraud. Covington's internal auditing department periodically reviews the company's accounting records to determine the effectiveness of internal controls. In its latest review, the internal audit staff found the following eight conditions:
    1. Daily bank deposits do not always correspond with cash receipts.
    2. Bad debt write-offs are prepared and approved by the same employee.
    3. There are occasional discrepancies between physical inventory counts and perpetual inventory records.
    4. Alterations have been made to physical inventory counts and to perpetual inventory records.
    5. There are many customer refunds and credits.
    6. Many original documents are missing or lost. However, there are substitute copies of all missing originals.
    7. An unexplained decrease in the gross profit percentage has occurred.
    8. Many documents are not approved.

Required

For each of the eight conditions detected by the Covington internal audit staff:
a. Describe a possible cause of the condition.
b. Recommend actions to be taken and/or controls to be implemented that would correct the condition. (*CMA, adapted*)

7. Consider the following two situations:
    1. Many employees of a firm that manufactures small tools pocket some of the tools for their personal use. Because the quantities taken by any one employee are immaterial, the individual employees do not consider the act as fraudulent or detrimental to the company. The company is now large enough to hire an internal auditor. One of the first things she did was to compare the gross profit rates for industrial tools to the gross profit for personal tools. Noting a significant difference, she investigated and uncovered the employee theft.
    2. A manufacturing firm's controller created a fake subsidiary. He then ordered goods from the firm's suppliers, told them to ship the goods to a warehouse he rented, and approved the vendor invoices for payment when they arrived. The controller later sold the diverted inventory items, and the proceeds were deposited to the controller's personal bank account. Auditors suspected something was wrong when they could not find any entries regarding this fake subsidiary office in the property, plant, and equipment ledgers or a title or lease for the office in the real-estate records.

Required

For the situations presented, describe the recommendations the internal auditors should make to prevent similar problems in the future. (*CMA, adapted*)

8. Tralor Corporation manufactures and sells several different lines of small electric components. Its internal audit department completed an audit of its expenditure processes. Part of the audit involved a review of the internal accounting controls for payables, including the controls over the authorization of transactions, accounting for transactions, and the protection of assets. The auditors noted the following items:
    1. Routine purchases are initiated by inventory control notifying the purchasing department of the need to buy goods. The purchasing department fills out a prenumbered purchase order and gets it approved by the purchasing manager. The original of the five-part purchase order goes to the vendor. The other four copies are for purchasing, the user department, receiving for use as a receiving report, and accounts payable.

220

2. For efficiency and effectiveness, purchases of specialized goods and services are negotiated directly between the user department and the vendor. Company procedures require that the user department and the purchasing department approve invoices for any specialized goods and services before making payment.

3. Accounts payable maintains a list of employees who have purchase order approval authority. The list was updated two years ago and is seldom used by accounts payable clerks.

4. Prenumbered vendor invoices are recorded in an invoice register that indicates the receipt date, whether it is a special order, when a special order is sent to the requesting department for approval, and when it is returned. A review of the register indicated that there were seven open invoices for special purchases, which had been forwarded to operating departments for approval over 30 days previously and had not yet been returned.

5. Prior to making entries in accounting records, the accounts payable clerk checks the mathematical accuracy of the transaction, makes sure that all transactions are properly documented (the purchase order matches the signed receiving report and the vendor's invoice), and obtains departmental approval for special purchase invoices.

6. All approved invoices are filed alphabetically. Invoices are paid on the 5th and 20th of each month, and all cash discounts are taken regardless of the terms.

7. The treasurer signs the checks and cancels the supporting documents. An original document is required for a payment to be processed.

8. Prenumbered blank checks are kept in a locked safe accessible only to the cash disbursements department. Other documents and records maintained by the accounts payable section are readily accessible to all persons assigned to the section and to others in the accounting function.

Required

Review the eight items listed, and decide whether they represent an internal control strength or weakness.

a. For each internal control strength you identified, explain how the procedure helps achieve good authorization, accounting, or asset protection control.

b. For each internal control weakness you identified, explain why it is a weakness and recommend a way to correct the weakness. (*CMA, adapted*)

9. Lancaster Company makes electrical parts for contractors and home improvement retail stores. After their annual audit, Lancaster's auditors commented on the following items regarding internal controls over equipment:

1. The operations department that needs the equipment normally initiates a purchase requisition for equipment. The operations department supervisor discusses the proposed purchase with the plant manager. If there are sufficient funds in the requesting department's equipment budget, a purchase requisition is submitted to the purchasing department once the plant manager is satisfied that the request is reasonable.

2. When the purchasing department receives either an inventory or an equipment purchase requisition, the purchasing agent selects an appropriate supplier and sends them a purchase order.

3. When equipment arrives, the user department installs it. The property, plant, and equipment control accounts are supported by schedules organized by year of acquisition. The schedules are used to record depreciation using standard rates, depreciation methods, and salvage values for each type of fixed asset. These rates, methods, and salvage values were set 10 years ago during the company's initial year of operation.

4. When equipment is retired, the plant manager notifies the accounting department so the appropriate accounting entries can be made.

5. There has been no reconciliation since the company began operations between the accounting records and the equipment on hand.

Required

Identify the internal control weaknesses in Lancaster's system, and recommend ways to correct them. (*CMA, adapted*)

10. The Langston Recreational Company (LRC) manufactures ice skates for racing, figure skating, and hockey. The company is located in Kearns, Utah, so it can be close to the Olympic Ice Shield, where many Olympic speed skaters train.

    Given the precision required to make skates, tracking manufacturing costs is very important to management so it can price the skates appropriately. To capture and collect manufacturing costs, the company acquired an automated cost accounting system from a national vendor. The vendor provides support, maintenance, and data and program backup service for LRC's system.

    LRC operates one shift, five days a week. All manufacturing data are collected and recorded by Saturday evening so that the prior week's production data can be processed. One of management's primary concerns is how the actual manufacturing process costs compare with planned or standard manufacturing process costs. As a result, the cost accounting system produces a report that compares actual costs with standards costs and provides the difference, or variance. Management focuses on significant variances as one means of controlling the manufacturing processes and calculating bonuses.

    Occasionally, errors occur in processing a week's production cost data, which requires the entire week's cost data to be reprocessed at a cost of $34,500. The current risk of error without any control procedures is 8%. LRC's management is currently considering a set of cost accounting control procedures that is estimated to reduce the risk of the data errors from 8% to 3%. This data validation control procedure is projected to cost $1,000 per week.

    Required

    a. Perform a cost/benefit analysis of the data validation control procedures.
    b. Based on your analysis, make a recommendation to management regarding the control procedure.
    c. The current risk of data errors without any control procedures is estimated to be 8%. The data control validation procedure costs $1,000 and reduces the risk to 3%. At some point between 8% and 3% is a point of indifference—that is, Cost of reprocessing the data without controls = Cost of processing the data with the controls + Cost of controls. Use a spreadsheet application such as Excel Goal Seek to find the solution.

11. Spring Water Spa Company is a 15-store chain in the Midwest that sells hot tubs, supplies, and accessories. Each store has a full-time, salaried manager and an assistant manager. The sales personnel are paid an hourly wage and a commission based on sales volume.

    The company uses electronic cash registers to record each transaction. The salesperson enters his or her employee number at the beginning of his/her shift. For each sale, the salesperson rings up the order by scanning the item's bar code, which then displays the item's description, unit price, and quantity (each item must be scanned). The cash register automatically assigns a consecutive number to each transaction. The cash register prints a sales receipt that shows the total, any discounts, the sales tax, and the grand total.

    The salesperson collects payment from the customer, gives the receipt to the customer, and either directs the customer to the warehouse to obtain the items purchased or makes arrangements with the shipping department for delivery. The salesperson is responsible for using the system to determine whether credit card sales are approved and for approving both credit sales and sales paid by check. Sales returns are handled in exactly the reverse manner, with the salesperson issuing a return slip when necessary.

    At the end of each day, the cash registers print a sequentially ordered list of sales receipts and provide totals for cash, credit card, and check sales, as well as cash and credit card returns. The assistant manager reconciles these totals to the cash register tapes, cash in the cash register, the total of the consecutively numbered sales invoices, and the return slips. The assistant manager prepares a daily reconciled report for the store manager's review.

    Cash sales, check sales, and credit card sales are reviewed by the manager, who prepares the daily bank deposit. The manager physically makes the deposit at the bank and files the validated deposit slip. At the end of the month, the manager performs the bank reconciliation. The cash register tapes, sales invoices, return slips, and reconciled report are mailed daily to corporate headquarters to be processed with files from all the other stores. Corporate headquarters returns a weekly Sales and Commission Activity Report to each store manager for review.

Required

Please respond to the following questions about Spring Water Spa Company's operations:

a. The fourth component of the COSO ERM framework is risk assessment. What risk(s) does Spring Water face?

b. Identify control strengths in Spring Water's sales/cash receipts system.

c. The sixth component of the COSO ERM framework deals with control activities. What control activities do these strengths fall under?

d. What problems were avoided or risks mitigated by the controls identified in question b?

e. How might Spring Water improve its system of controls?

12. PriceRight Electronics (PEI) is a small wholesale discount supplier of electronic instruments and parts. PEI's competitive advantage is its deep-discount, three-day delivery guarantee, which allows retailers to order materials often to minimize in-store inventories. PEI processes its records with stand-alone, incompatible computer systems except for integrated enterprise resource planning (ERP) inventory and accounts receivable modules. PEI decided to finish integrating its operations with more ERP modules, but because of cash flow considerations, this needs to be accomplished on a step-by-step basis.

It was decided that the next function to be integrated should be sales order processing to enhance quick response to customer needs. PEI implemented and modified a commercially available software package to meet PEI's operations. In an effort to reduce the number of slow-paying or delinquent customers, PEI installed Web-based software that links to the Web site of a commercial credit rating agency to check customer credit at the time of purchase. The following are the new sales order processing system modules:

- **Sales.** Sales orders are received by telephone, fax, e-mail, Web site entry, or standard mail. They are entered into the sales order system by the Sales department. If the order does not cause a customer to exceed his credit limit, the system generates multiple copies of the sales order.

- **Credit.** When orders are received from new customers, the system automatically accesses the credit rating Web site and suggests an initial credit limit. On a daily basis, the credit manager reviews new customer applications for creditworthiness, reviews the suggested credit limits, and accepts or changes the credit limits in the customer database. On a monthly basis, the credit manager reviews the accounts receivable aging report to identify slow-paying or delinquent accounts for potential revisions to or discontinuance of credit. As needed, the credit manager issues credit memos for merchandise returns based on requests from customers and forwards copies of the credit memos to Accounting for appropriate account receivable handling.

- **Warehousing.** Warehouse personnel update the inventory master file for inventory purchases and sales, confirm availability of materials to fill sales orders, and establish back orders for sales orders that cannot be completed from stock on hand. Warehouse personnel gather and forward inventory to Shipping and Receiving along with the corresponding sales orders. They also update the inventory master file for merchandise returned to Receiving.

- **Shipping and receiving.** Shipping and Receiving accepts inventory and sales orders from Warehousing, packs and ships the orders with a copy of the sales order as a packing slip, and forwards a copy of the sales order to Billing. Customer inventory returns are unpacked, sorted, inspected, and sent to Warehousing.

- **Accounting.** Billing prices all sales orders received, which is done approximately 5 days after the order ships. To spread the work effort throughout the month, customers are placed in one of six 30-day billing cycles. Monthly statements, prepared by Billing, are sent to customers during the cycle billing period. Outstanding carry-forward balances reported by Accounts Receivable and credit memos prepared by the credit manager are included on the monthly statement. Billing also prepares electronic sales and credit memos for each cycle. Electronic copies of invoices and credit memos are forwarded to Accounts Receivable for entry into the accounts receivable master file by customer account. An aging report is prepared at the end of each month and forwarded to the credit manager. The general accounting office staff access the accounts receivable master file that reflects total charges and credits processed through the accounts receivable system for each cycle. General accounting runs a query to compare this information to the electronic sales and credit memo and posts the changes to the general ledger master file.

Required

a. Identify the internal control strengths in PEI's system.
b. Identify the internal control weaknesses in PEI's system, and suggest ways to correct them.

Case 1 The Greater Providence Deposit & Trust Embezzlement

Nino Moscardi, president of Greater Providence Deposit & Trust (GPD&T), received an anonymous note in his mail stating that a bank employee was making bogus loans. Moscardi asked the bank's internal auditors to investigate the transactions detailed in the note. The investigation led to James Guisti, manager of a North Providence branch office and a trusted 14-year employee who had once worked as one of the bank's internal auditors. Guisti was charged with embezzling $1.83 million from the bank using 67 phony loans taken out over a three-year period.

Court documents revealed that the bogus loans were 90-day notes requiring no collateral and ranging in amount from $10,000 to $63,500. Guisti originated the loans; when each one matured, he would take out a new loan, or rewrite the old one, to pay the principal and interest due. Some loans had been rewritten five or six times.

The 67 loans were taken out by Guisti in five names, including his wife's maiden name, his father's name, and the names of two friends. These people denied receiving stolen funds or knowing anything about the embezzlement. The fifth name was James Vanesse, who police said did not exist. The Social Security number on Vanesse's loan application was issued to a female, and the phone number belonged to a North Providence auto dealer.

Lucy Fraioli, a customer service representative who cosigned the checks, said Guisti was her supervisor and she thought nothing was wrong with the checks, though she did not know any of the people. Marcia Perfetto, head teller, told police she cashed checks for Guisti made out to four of the five persons. Asked whether she gave the money to Guisti when he gave her checks to cash, she answered, "Not all of the time," though she could not recall ever having given the money directly to any of the four, whom she did not know.

Guisti was authorized to make consumer loans up to a certain dollar limit without loan committee approvals, which is a standard industry practice. Guisti's original lending limit was $10,000, the amount of his first fraudulent loan. The dollar limit was later increased to $15,000 and then increased again to $25,000. Some of the loans, including the one for $63,500, far exceeded his lending limit. In addition, all loan applications should have been accompanied by the applicant's credit history report, purchased from an independent credit rating

firm. The loan taken out in the fictitious name would not have had a credit report and should have been flagged by a loan review clerk at the bank's headquarters.

News reports raised questions about why the fraud was not detected earlier. State regulators and the bank's internal auditors failed to detect the fraud. Several reasons were given for the failure to find the fraud earlier. First, in checking for bad loans, bank auditors do not examine all loans and generally focus on loans much larger than the ones in question. Second, Greater Providence had recently dropped its computer services arrangement with a local bank in favor of an out-of-state bank. This changeover may have reduced the effectiveness of the bank's control procedures. Third, the bank's loan review clerks were rotated frequently, making follow-up on questionable loans more difficult.

Guisti was a frequent gambler and used the embezzled money to pay gambling debts. The bank's losses totaled $624,000, which was less than the $1.83 million in bogus loans, because Guisti used a portion of the borrowed money to repay loans as they came due. The bank's bonding company covered the loss.

The bank experienced other adverse publicity prior to the fraud's discovery. First, the bank was fined $50,000 after pleading guilty to failure to report cash transactions exceeding $10,000, which is a felony. Second, bank owners took the bank private after a lengthy public battle with the State Attorney General, who alleged that the bank inflated its assets and overestimated its capital surplus to make its balance sheet look stronger. The bank denied this charge.

1. How did Guisti commit the fraud, conceal it, and convert the fraudulent actions to personal gain?
2. Good internal controls require that the custody, recording, and authorization functions be separated. Explain which of those functions Guisti had and how the failure to segregate them facilitated the fraud.
3. Identify the preventive, detective, and corrective controls at GPD&T, and discuss whether they were effective.
4. Explain the pressures, opportunities, and rationalizations that were present in the Guisti fraud.

5. Discuss how Greater Providence Deposit & Trust might improve its control procedures over the disbursement of loan funds to minimize the risk of this type of fraud. In what way does this case indicate a lack of proper segregation of duties?

6. Discuss how Greater Providence might improve its loan review procedures at bank headquarters to minimize its fraud risk. Was it a good idea to rotate the assignments of loan review clerks? Why or why not?

7. Discuss whether Greater Providence's auditors should have been able to detect this fraud.

8. Are there any indications that the internal environment at Greater Providence may have been deficient? If so, how could it have contributed to this embezzlement?

Source: John Kostrezewa, "Charge: Embezzlement," *Providence Journal-Bulletin* (July 31, 1988): F-1.

AIS IN ACTION SOLUTIONS

Quiz Key

1. COSO identified five interrelated components of internal control. Which of the following is NOT one of those five?
   a. risk assessment (Incorrect. The organization must be aware of and deal with the risks it faces.)
   ▶ b. internal control policies (Correct. Internal control policies are NOT one of COSO's five components of internal control. However, control environment and control activities are two of the five internal control framework components.)
   c. monitoring (Incorrect. The entire internal control process must be monitored, and modifications made as necessary.)
   d. information and communication (Incorrect. The primary purpose of an AIS is to process and communicate information about an organization, and these activities are an essential part of an internal control system.)

2. In the ERM model, COSO specified four types of objectives that management must meet to achieve company goals. Which of the following is NOT one of those types?
   ▶ a. responsibility objectives (Correct. Responsibility objectives are NOT one of the objectives in COSO's ERM model.)
   b. strategic objectives (Incorrect. Strategic objectives are high-level goals aligned with the company's mission and are one of the objectives in COSO's ERM model.)
   c. compliance objectives (Incorrect. Compliance objectives help the company comply with all applicable laws and regulations and are one of the objectives in COSO's ERM model.)
   d. reporting objectives (Incorrect. Reporting objectives help ensure the accuracy, completeness, and reliability of internal and external reports and are one of the objectives in COSO's ERM model.)
   e. operations objectives (Incorrect. Operations objectives deal with the effectiveness and efficiency of operations and are one of the objectives in COSO's ERM model.)

3. Which of the following statements is true?
   a. COSO's enterprise risk management framework is narrow in scope and is limited to financial controls. (Incorrect. The ERM framework incorporates all kinds of internal controls, not just financial controls, and provides an all-encompassing focus on the broader subject of enterprise risk management.)
   ▶ b. COSO's internal control integrated framework has been widely accepted as the authority on internal controls. (Correct. The internal control integrated framework is the accepted authority on internal controls and is incorporated into policies, rules, and regulations that are used to control business activities.)

    c. The Foreign Corrupt Practices Act had no impact on internal accounting control systems. (Incorrect. The Foreign Corrupt Practices Act specifically requires corporations to maintain good systems of internal accounting control.)

    d. It is easier to add controls to an already designed system than to include them during the initial design stage. (Incorrect. The opposite is true: It is easier to include internal controls at the initial design stage than after the system is already designed.)

4. All other things being equal, which of the following is true?

    a. Detective controls are superior to preventive controls. (Incorrect. The reverse is true—preventive controls are superior to detective controls. Preventive controls keep an error or irregularity from occurring. Detective controls uncover an error or irregularity after the fact.)

    b. Corrective controls are superior to preventive controls. (Incorrect. The reverse is true—preventive controls are superior to corrective controls. Preventive controls keep an error or irregularity from occurring. Corrective controls fix an error after the fact.)

    c. Preventive controls are equivalent to detective controls. (Incorrect. Preventive controls keep an error or irregularity from occurring. Detective controls uncover an error or irregularity after the fact.)

▶ d. Preventive controls are superior to detective controls. (Correct. With respect to controls, it is always of utmost importance to prevent errors from occurring.)

5. Which of the following statements about the control environment is FALSE?

▶ a. Management's attitudes toward internal control and ethical behavior have little impact on employee beliefs or actions. (Correct. This statement is false. Management's attitude toward internal control is critical to the organization's effectiveness and success. They set the "tone at the top" that other employees follow.)

    b. An overly complex or unclear organizational structure may be indicative of problems that are more serious. (Incorrect. This is a true statement. Management may intentionally build overly complex or unclear organizational structures to hide fraud or errors.)

    c. A written policy and procedures manual is an important tool for assigning authority and responsibility. (Incorrect. This is a true statement. A written policy and procedures manual explains proper business practices, describes the knowledge and experience needed by key personnel, and lists the resources provided to carry out specific duties.)

    d. Supervision is especially important in organizations that cannot afford elaborate responsibility reporting or are too small to have an adequate separation of duties. (Incorrect. This is a true statement. In many organizations, effective supervision takes the place of more expensive controls. Effective supervision involves training and assisting employees, monitoring their performance, correcting errors, and safeguarding assets by overseeing employees who have access to them.)

6. To achieve effective segregation of duties, certain functions must be separated. Which of the following is the correct listing of the accounting-related functions that must be segregated?

    a. control, recording, and monitoring (Incorrect. See Figure 3.)

▶ b. authorization, recording, and custody (Correct. See Figure 3.)

    c. control, custody, and authorization (Incorrect. See Figure 3.)

    d. monitoring, recording, and planning (Incorrect. See Figure 3.)

7. Which of the following is NOT an independent check?

    a. bank reconciliation (Incorrect. A bank reconciliation is an independent check, as are top-level reviews, analytical reviews, reconciling two independently maintained sets of records, comparisons of actual quantities with recorded amounts, double-entry accounting, and independent reviews.)

    b. periodic comparison of subsidiary ledger totals to control accounts (Incorrect. A periodic comparison of subsidiary ledger totals to control accounts is an independent check, as are top-level reviews, analytical reviews, reconciling two independently maintained sets of records, comparisons of actual quantities with recorded amounts, double-entry accounting, and independent reviews.)

    c. trial balance (Incorrect. A trial balance is an independent check, as are top-level reviews, analytical reviews, reconciling two independently maintained sets of records,

comparisons of actual quantities with recorded amounts, double-entry accounting, and independent reviews.)
▶ d. re-adding the total of a batch of invoices and comparing it with your first total (Correct. One person performing the same procedure twice using the same documents, such as re-adding invoice batch totals, is not an independent check because it does not involve a second person, a second set of documents or records, or a second process.)

8. Which of the following is a control procedure relating to both the design and use of documents and records?
   a. locking blank checks in a drawer (Incorrect. Locking blank checks in a drawer is not a control procedure related to the design of documents.)
   b. reconciling the bank account (Incorrect. Reconciling the bank account is not a control procedure related to the design of documents.)
▶ c. sequentially prenumbering sales invoices (Correct. Designing documents so that they are sequentially prenumbered and then using them in order is a control procedure relating to both the design and use of documents.)
   d. comparing actual physical quantities with recorded amounts (Incorrect. Comparing actual quantities to recorded amounts is not a control procedure related to the design of documents.)

9. Which of the following is the correct order of the risk assessment steps discussed in this chapter?
▶ a. Identify threats, estimate risk and exposure, identify controls, and estimate costs and benefits. (Correct. See Figure 2.)
   b. Identify controls, estimate risk and exposure, identify threats, and estimate costs and benefits. (Incorrect. See Figure 2.)
   c. Estimate risk and exposure, identify controls, identify threats, and estimate costs and benefits. (Incorrect. See Figure 2.)
   d. Estimate costs and benefits, identify threats, identify controls, and estimate risk and exposure. (Incorrect. See Figure 2.)

10. Your current system is deemed to be 90% reliable. A major threat has been identified with an impact of $3,000,000. Two control procedures exist to deal with the threat. Implementation of control A would cost $100,000 and reduce the likelihood to 6%. Implementation of control B would cost $140,000 and reduce the likelihood to 4%. Implementation of both controls would cost $220,000 and reduce the likelihood to 2%. Given the data, and based solely on an economic analysis of costs and benefits, what should you do?
   a. Implement control A only. (Incorrect. Control procedure A provides a net benefit of only $20,000, whereas control procedure B provides a net benefit of $40,000.)
▶ b. Implement control B only. (Correct. Control procedure B provides a net benefit of $40,000. Procedure A and the combination of A and B provide a benefit of only $20,000.)
   c. Implement both controls A and B. (Incorrect. The combination of procedures A and B provides a net benefit of only $20,000, whereas control procedure B provides a net benefit of $40,000.)
   d. Implement neither control. (Incorrect. Both controls provide a net benefit. Control procedure B provides a net benefit of $40,000. Procedure A and the combination of A and B each provide a net benefit of $20,000.)

Expected loss = Impact × Likelihood ($300,000 = $3,000,000 × 10%)

Control Procedure	Likelihood	Impact	Revised Expected Loss	Reduction in Expected Loss	Cost of Control(s)	Net Benefit (Cost)
A	0.06	$3,000,000	$180,000	$120,000	$100,000	$20,000
B	0.04	$3,000,000	$120,000	$180,000	$140,000	$40,000
Both	0.02	$3,000,000	$60,000	$240,000	$220,000	$20,000

Chapter 8

Information Systems Controls for System Reliability— Part 1: Information Security

From Chapter 8 of *Accounting Information Systems*, 12/e. Marshall B. Romney. Paul John Steinbart. Copyright © 2012 by Pearson Education. Published by Prentice Hall. All rights reserved.

Information Systems Controls for System Reliability— Part 1: Information Security

Learning Objectives

After studying this chapter, you should be able to:

1. Discuss how the COBIT framework can be used to develop sound internal control over an organization's information systems.

2. Explain the factors that influence information systems reliability.

3. Describe how a combination of preventive, detective, and corrective controls can be employed to provide reasonable assurance about information security.

INTEGRATIVE CASE NORTHWEST INDUSTRIES

Jason Scott's next assignment is to review the internal controls over Northwest Industries' information systems. Jason realizes that the Committee of Sponsoring Organizations (COSO) Enterprise Risk Management (ERM) framework does not specifically address information technology. A friend who is an information systems auditor for a major international audit firm tells him that the Control Objectives for Information and Related Technology (COBIT) framework developed by ISACA (formerly the Information Systems Audit and Control Association, but now goes by its acronym only) discusses internal controls and governance issues related to information systems. It also provides specific suggestions for how to audit information systems controls and identifies those information systems controls most directly relevant to achieving compliance with the requirements of the Sarbanes-Oxley Act.

Jason obtains a copy of the COBIT framework and is impressed by its thoroughness. He finds particularly helpful the report that explains how specific information technology (IT) controls relate to Sarbanes-Oxley, and he decides that he will begin his review of Northwest Industries' accounting system by focusing on the controls designed

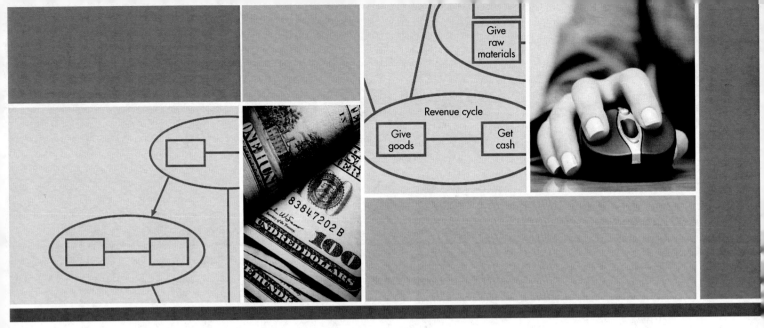

to provide reasonable assurance about information security. He writes down the following questions that will guide his investigation:

1. What controls does Northwest Industries employ to prevent unauthorized access to its accounting system?
2. How can successful and unsuccessful attempts to compromise the company's accounting system be detected in a timely manner?
3. What procedures are in place to respond to security incidents?

Introduction

Today, every organization relies on information technology. Management wants assurance that the information produced by its accounting system is reliable. It also wants to know that its investment in information technology is cost-effective. Although the COSO and COSO-ERM frameworks provide broad coverage of internal controls, neither specifically addresses controls over information technology. The COBIT framework developed by ISACA fills that void. COBIT presents a comprehensive view of the controls necessary for systems reliability.

Figure 1 summarizes the COBIT framework. It shows that achieving the organization's business and governance objectives requires adequate controls over IT resources to ensure that information provided to management satisfies seven key criteria:

1. *Effectiveness*—the information must be relevant and timely.
2. *Efficiency*—the information must be produced in a cost-effective manner.
3. *Confidentiality*—sensitive information must be protected from unauthorized disclosure.
4. *Integrity*—the information must be accurate, complete, and valid.
5. *Availability*—the information must be available whenever needed.
6. *Compliance*—controls must ensure compliance with internal policies and with external legal and regulatory requirements.
7. *Reliability*—management must have access to appropriate information needed to conduct daily activities and to exercise its fiduciary and governance responsibilities.

Figure 1 shows 34 generic IT processes that must be properly managed and controlled in order to produce information that satisfies the seven criteria listed above. Those processes are grouped into four basic management activities, which COBIT refers to as *domains*:

1. *Plan and Organize (PO).*   Figure 1 lists 10 important processes for properly designing and managing an organization's information systems.

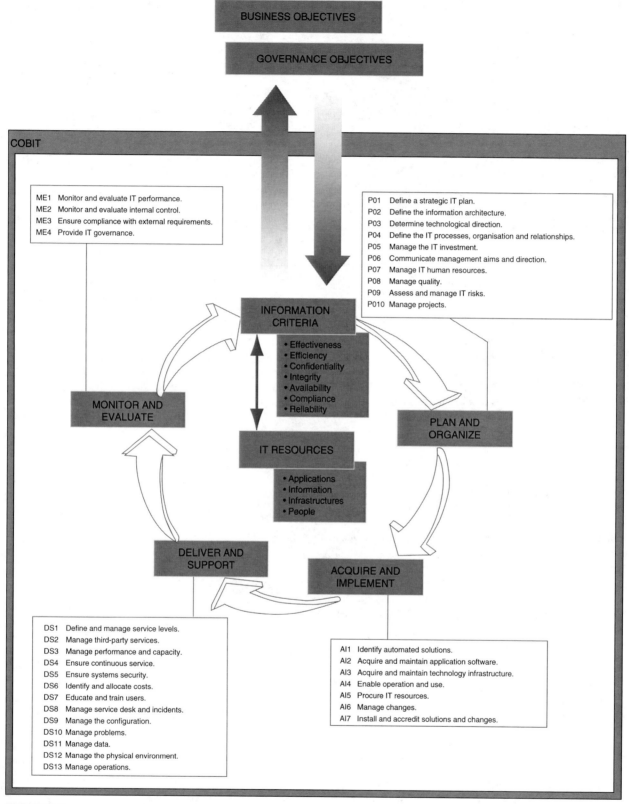

FIGURE 1

Overview of the COBIT Framework

(*Source:* Figure 23 in COBIT 4.1, IT Governance Institute, p. 26; note: adapted to use American spelling)

2. *Acquire and Implement (AI).*   Figure 1 lists seven fundamental processes for obtaining and installing technology solutions.

3. *Deliver and Support (DS).*   Figure 1 lists 13 critical processes for effectively and efficiently operating information systems and providing the information management needs to run the organization.

4. *Monitor and Evaluate (ME).*   Figure 1 lists four essential processes for assessing the operation of an organization's information systems.

Note the circle of arrows in Figure 1, which indicates that effective operation, control, and governance of an information system is an ongoing process. Management develops plans to organize information resources to provide the information it needs. It then authorizes and oversees efforts to acquire (or build internally) the desired functionality. Management then performs a number of activities to ensure that the resulting system actually delivers the desired information. Finally, there is a need for constant monitoring and evaluation of performance against the established criteria. The entire cycle constantly repeats, as management modifies existing plans and procedures or develops new ones to respond to changes in business objectives and new developments in information technology.

COBIT specifies 210 detailed control objectives for these 34 processes to enable effective management of an organization's information resources. It also describes specific audit procedures for assessing the effectiveness of those controls and suggests metrics that management can use to evaluate performance. This comprehensiveness is one of the strengths of COBIT and underlies its growing international acceptance as a framework for managing and controlling information systems. External auditors, however, may be concerned only with a subset of the issues covered by COBIT, specifically those that most directly pertain to the accuracy of an organization's financial statements and compliance with the Sarbanes-Oxley (SOX) Act. Consequently, ISACA issued a document entitled "IT Control Objectives for Sarbanes-Oxley, 2nd Edition" that discusses the portions of COBIT most directly relevant for compliance with SOX and provides guidance for assessing the adequacy of those controls. In addition, the Trust Services Framework developed jointly by the American Institute of Certified Public Accountants and the Canadian Institute of Chartered Accountants classifies information systems controls into five categories that most directly pertain to systems reliability (and the reliability of an organization's financial statements):

1. *Security*—access to the system and its data is controlled and restricted to legitimate users.

2. *Confidentiality*—sensitive organizational information (e.g., marketing plans, trade secrets) is protected from unauthorized disclosure.

3. *Privacy*—personal information about customers is collected, used, disclosed, and maintained only in compliance with internal policies and external regulatory requirements and is protected from unauthorized disclosure.

4. *Processing Integrity*—data are processed accurately, completely, in a timely manner, and only with proper authorization.

5. *Availability*—the system and its information are available to meet operational and contractual obligations.

The Trust Services framework is not a substitute for COBIT, because it addresses only a subset of the issues covered by COBIT. We adopt it to guide our discussion of IT controls in this text, however, because it provides a useful means for consolidating COBIT's control objectives to focus on a specific aspect of IT governance that has become especially relevant because of SOX: systems reliability. For example, the various audit issues and control objectives pertaining to information security occur in all four COBIT domains (PO, AI, DS, and ME), and the same holds true for confidentiality, privacy, processing integrity, and availability. We will identify the specific subsections of COBIT that pertain to the topics discussed in the text by using COBIT two-letter domain abbreviations followed by the number of a specific control objective. For example, COBIT control objective DS 5.5 discusses the need to regularly test and evaluate the effectiveness of information security controls.

Figure 2 shows how the five fundamental Trust Services principles contribute to the overall objective of systems reliability. Note the importance of information security. Security procedures restrict system access to authorized users only, thereby protecting the confidentiality of

FIGURE 2

Relationships Among the Five Trust Services Principles for Systems Reliability

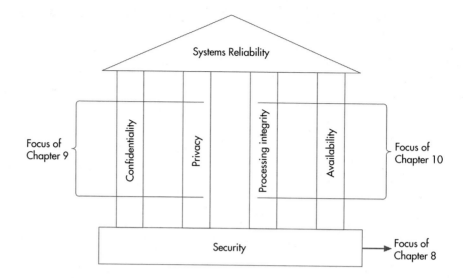

sensitive organizational data and the privacy of personal information collected from customers. Security procedures protect information integrity by preventing submission of unauthorized or fictitious transactions and preventing unauthorized changes to stored data or programs. Finally, security procedures provide protection against a variety of attacks, including viruses and worms, thereby ensuring that the system is available when needed. Thus, as Figure 2 shows, information security is the foundation of systems reliability. Consequently, this chapter focuses on the Trust Services principle of information security.

Two Fundamental Information Security Concepts

1 Security Is a Management Issue, Not a Technology Issue

Section 302 of SOX requires the CEO and the CFO to certify that the financial statements fairly present the results of the company's activities. The accuracy of an organization's financial statements depends upon the reliability of its information systems. As Figure 2 shows, information security is the foundation for systems reliability. Consequently, information security is management's responsibility. Therefore, although information security is a complex technical subject, it is first and foremost a management issue, not an information technology issue.

The importance of management's role in information security is reflected in the fact that COBIT's first detailed security control objective (DS 5.1) calls for information security to be managed at the highest appropriate level. Indeed, as Table 1 shows, the active involvement and support of senior management is necessary in every facet of information security. Management involvement is especially important in the planning stage (steps 1–4 in Table 1). Recall that COSO stresses the importance of the "tone at the top" for creating a good internal environment; in the same manner, senior management's attitudes and behaviors are critical to shaping the organization's security culture. The identification and valuation of information resources also requires management's input; just as senior management does not have the necessary knowledge to select which firewall or encryption software to purchase, information security professionals cannot accurately assess the value of the organization's information. Although information security professionals can identify and estimate the risk of various threats, only senior management can properly assess their impact and select the appropriate risk response. Finally, employees are more likely to comply with policies and procedures when they know that senior management fully supports them.

TABLE 1 Management's Role in Information Security

Activity	Management's Role
1. Create and foster a pro-active "security-aware" culture.	COSO stresses the importance of management's operating philosophy and ethics in creating a "tone at the top" conducive to building a sound internal environment. The same principle applies to information security. Every employee must practice "safe" computing. This will only occur if senior management demonstrates, by example, that information security is important. Management must also provide the time and resources for security awareness training for all employees. The COBIT framework recognizes the importance of senior management involvement in and support for creating a "security-aware" culture by devoting several sections (PO 4, PO 7, and DS 7) to the various aspects of hiring, training, and properly managing the employees who work in the IT function.
2. Inventory and value the organization's information resources.	COBIT control objective PO 2.3 indicates that organizations need to identify and place a value on all their information resources (hardware, software, and information). Management must provide the time and funding necessary to perform this task. Moreover, only management possesses the breadth of understanding needed to accurately determine the value of specific information resources.
3. Assess risks and select a risk response.	It is generally not possible to totally eliminate all risk. Therefore, COBIT section PO 9 discusses the importance of developing a risk management program involving risk mitigation strategies that reduce residual risk to an acceptable level. The previous chapter explained the four possible responses to risk (reduce, accept, share, or avoid) and the process for choosing a specific response. Although systems professionals possess knowledge about the technical merits of each potential security investment and the risks of various threats, senior managers must also participate in this process to ensure that all relevant organizational factors are considered so that the funds invested in information security reflect the organization's risk appetite.
4. Develop and communicate security plans, policies, and procedures.	COBIT section PO 6 stresses the need for management to develop and communicate an enterprise-wide IT control framework. A key component of that framework is an enterprise-wide security plan. Without such a plan, the organization will most likely end up purchasing a mish-mash of security products that do not protect every information system resource.

COBIT control objective DS 5.2 notes that management must then translate the organization's information security plan into a set of policies and procedures and communicate those policies and procedures to all employees. To be effective, this communication must involve more than just handing people a written document and asking them to sign an acknowledgment that they received and read it. Instead, employees must receive regular, periodic reminders about security policies and training on how to comply with them. Only the active support and involvement of top management can ensure that information security training and communication is taken seriously. |
| 5. Acquire and deploy information security technologies and products. | COBIT sections DS 5, DS 11, DS 12, and DS 13 identify a number of specific actions that are necessary to protect an organization's information resources. Management must provide the resources to implement those control activities. |
| 6. Monitor and evaluate the effectiveness of the organization's information security program. | Information security is a moving target. Advances in information technology create new threats and alter the risks associated with existing threats. Therefore, COBIT section ME 2 indicates that effective control over information systems involves a continuous cycle of developing policies to address identified threats, communicating those policies to all employees, implementing specific control procedures to mitigate risk, monitoring performance, and taking corrective actions in response to identified problems. Often, the necessary corrective actions involve the modification of existing policies and the development of new ones, thereby beginning the entire cycle anew (refer to Figure 1). Senior management needs to be involved in this process to ensure that security policies remain consistent with and support the organization's business strategy. Finally, for security policies to be effective, there need to be sanctions associated with their violation. Therefore, senior management must support enforcing sanctions against employees who violate security policies. |

2 Defense-in-Depth and the Time-Based Model of Information Security

The idea of *defense-in-depth* is to employ multiple layers of controls in order to avoid having a single point of failure. For example, many organizations use not only firewalls but also multiple authentication methods (passwords, tokens, and biometrics) to restrict access. The use of over-lapping, complementary, and redundant controls increases overall effectiveness because if one control fails or gets circumvented, another may function as planned.

Defense-in-depth typically involves the use of a combination of preventive, detective, and corrective controls. The role of preventive controls is to limit actions to specified individuals in accordance with the organization's security policy. However, auditors have long recognized that preventive controls can never provide 100% protection. Given enough time and resources, any preventive control can be circumvented. Consequently, it is necessary to supplement preventive controls with methods for detecting incidents and procedures for taking corrective remedial action.

Detecting a security breach and initiating corrective remedial action must be timely, because once preventive controls have been breached, it takes little time to destroy, compromise, or steal the organization's economic and information resources. Therefore, the goal of the *time-based model of security* is to employ a combination of detective and corrective controls that identify an information security incident early enough to prevent the loss or compromise of information. This objective can be expressed in a formula that uses the following three variables:

P = the time it takes an attacker to break through the organization's preventive controls

D = the time it takes to detect that an attack is in progress

C = the time it takes to respond to the attack

Those three variables are then evaluated as follows: If $P > D + C$, then the organization's security procedures are effective. Otherwise, security is ineffective.

The time-based model of security provides a means for management to identify the most cost-effective approach to improving security by comparing the effects of additional investments in preventive, detective, or corrective controls. For example, management may be considering the investment of an additional $100,000 to enhance security. One option might be the purchase of a new firewall that would increase the value of P by 10 minutes. A second option might be to upgrade the organization's intrusion detection system in a manner that would decrease the value of D by 12 minutes. A third option might be to invest in new methods for responding to information security incidents so as to decrease the value of C by 30 minutes. In this example, the most cost-effective choice would be to invest in additional corrective controls that enable the organization to respond to attacks more quickly.

Although the time-based model of security provides a sound theoretical basis for evaluating and managing an organization's information security practices, it should be viewed as a strategic tool and not as a precise mathematical formula. One problem is that it is hard, if not impossible, to derive accurate, reliable measures of the parameters P, D, and C. In addition, even when those parameter values can be reliably calculated, new IT developments can quickly diminish their validity. For example, discovery of a major new vulnerability can effectively reduce the value of P to zero. Consequently, the time-based model of security is best used as a high-level framework for strategic analysis. For tactical and daily management of security, most organizations follow the principle of defense-in-depth and employ multiple preventive, detective, and corrective controls.

Understanding Targeted Attacks

Before we discuss the preventive, detective, and corrective controls that can be used to mitigate the risk of systems intrusions, it is helpful to understand the basic steps criminals use to attack an organization's information system:

1. *Conduct reconnaissance.*   Bank robbers usually do not just drive up to a bank and attempt to rob it. Instead, they first study their target's physical layout to learn about the controls it has in place (alarms, number of guards, placement of cameras, etc.). Similarly, computer attackers begin by collecting information about their target. Perusing an organization's financial statements, SEC filings, Web site, and press releases can yield much valuable information. The objective of this initial reconnaissance is to learn as much as possible about the target and to identify potential vulnerabilities.

2. *Attempt social engineering.*   Why go through all the trouble of trying to break into a system if you can get someone to let you in? Attackers will often try to use the information

obtained during their initial reconnaissance to "trick" an unsuspecting employee into granting them access, a process referred to as *social engineering*. Social engineering can take place in countless ways, limited only by the creativity and imagination of the attacker. Social engineering attacks often take place over the telephone. One common technique is for the attacker to impersonate an executive who cannot obtain remote access to important files. The attacker calls a newly hired administrative assistant and asks that person to help obtain the critical files. Another common ruse is for the attacker to pose as a clueless temporary worker who cannot log onto the system and calls the help desk for assistance. Social engineering attacks can also take place via e-mail. An attack known as *spear phishing* involves sending e-mails purportedly from someone that the victim knows, or should know. The spear phishing e-mail asks the victim to click on an embedded link, which contains a Trojan horse program that enables the attacker to obtain access to the system. Yet another social engineering tactic is to spread USB drives in the targeted organization's parking lot. An unsuspecting or curious employee who picks up the drive and plugs it into their computer will load a Trojan horse program that enables the attacker to gain access to the system.

3. *Scan and map the target*.   If an attacker cannot successfully penetrate the target system via social engineering, the next step is to conduct more detailed reconnaissance to identify potential points of remote entry. The attacker uses a variety of automated tools to identify computers that can be remotely accessed and the types of software they are running.

4. *Research*.   Once the attacker has identified specific targets and knows what versions of software are running on them, the next step is to conduct research to find known vulnerabilities for those programs and learn how to take advantage of those vulnerabilities.

5. *Execute the attack*   and obtain unauthorized access to the system.

6. *Cover tracks*.   After penetrating the victim's information system, most attackers will try to cover their tracks and create "back doors" that they can use to obtain access if their initial attack is discovered and controls are implemented to block that method of entry.

Now that we have a basic understanding of how criminals attack an organization's information system, we can proceed to methods for mitigating the risk that such attacks will be successful. The following sections discuss the major types of preventive, detective, and corrective controls listed in Table 2 that can be used to provide information security through defense-in-depth.

Preventive Controls

This section discusses the preventive controls listed in Table 2 that organizations commonly use to restrict access to information resources.

TABLE 2 Commonly Used Information Security Controls

Type of Control	Examples
Preventive	• Training
	• User access controls (authentication and authorization)
	• Physical access controls (locks, guards, etc.)
	• Network access controls (firewalls, intrusion prevention systems, etc.)
	• Device and software hardening controls (configuration options)
Detective	• Log analysis
	• Intrusion detection systems
	• Security testing and audits
	• Managerial reports
Corrective	• Computer incident response teams (CIRT)
	• Chief information security officer (CISO)
	• Patch management

Training

People play a critical role in information security. Employees must understand and follow the organization's security policies. Thus, training is a critical preventive control. Indeed, its importance is reflected in the fact that one of the 34 top-level control processes in the COBIT framework, DS 7, focuses exclusively on the need to train both users and systems professionals.

All employees should be taught why security measures are important to the organization's long-run survival. They also need to be trained to follow safe computing practices, such as never opening unsolicited e-mail attachments, using only approved software, not sharing passwords, and taking steps to physically protect laptops. Training is especially needed to educate employees about social engineering attacks. For example, employees should be taught never to divulge passwords or other information about their accounts or their workstation configurations to anyone who contacts them by telephone, e-mail, or instant messaging and claims to be part of the organization's information systems security function. Employees also need to be trained not to allow other people to follow them through restricted access entrances. This social engineering attack, called *piggybacking*, can take place not only at the main entrance to the building but also at any internal locked doors, especially to rooms that contain computer equipment. Piggybacking may be attempted not only by outsiders but also by other employees who are not authorized to enter a particular area. Piggybacking often succeeds because many people feel it is rude to not let another person come through the door with them or because they want to avoid confrontations. Role-playing exercises are particularly effective for increasing sensitivity to and skills for dealing with social engineering attacks.

Security awareness training is important for senior management, too, because in recent years many social engineering attacks, such as spear phishing, have been targeted at them. Training of information security professionals is also important. New developments in technology continuously create new security threats and make old solutions obsolete. Therefore, it is important for organizations to support continuing professional education for their security specialists.

However, an organization's investment in security training will be effective only if management clearly demonstrates that it supports employees who follow prescribed security policies. This is especially important for combating social engineering attacks, because countermeasures may sometimes create embarrassing confrontations with other employees. For example, one of the authors heard an anecdote about a systems professional at a major bank who refused to allow a person who was not on the list of authorized employees to enter the room housing the servers that contained the bank's key financial information. The person denied entry happened to be a new executive who was just hired. Instead of reprimanding the employee, the executive demonstrated the bank's commitment to and support for strong security by writing a formal letter of commendation for meritorious performance to be placed in the employee's performance file. It is this type of visible top management support for security that enhances the effectiveness of all security policies. Top management also needs to support the enforcement of sanctions, up to and including termination, against employees who willfully violate security policies. Doing so not only sends a strong message to other employees but also may sometimes lessen the consequences to the organization if the employee had engaged in illegal behavior.

User Access Controls

COBIT control objective DS 5.3 stresses the importance of being able to uniquely identify everyone who accesses the organization's information system and track the actions that they perform. There are two related but distinct types of user access controls that accomplish that objective. Authentication controls restrict who can access the organization's information system. Authorization controls limit what those individuals can do once they have been granted access.

AUTHENTICATION CONTROLS   *Authentication* is the process of verifying the identity of the person or device attempting to access the system. The objective is to ensure that only legitimate users can access the system.

Three types of credentials can be used to verify a person's identity:

1. Something they know, such as passwords or personal identification numbers (PINs)
2. Something they have, such as smart cards or ID badges

FOCUS 1   The Debate Over Passwords

To be effective, passwords must satisfy a number of requirements:

- **Length.** The strength of a password is directly related to its length. Most security experts recommend that strong passwords include at least eight characters.
- **Multiple character types.** Using a mixture of upper- and lowercase alphabetic, numeric, and special characters greatly increases the strength of the password.
- **Randomness.** Passwords should not be words found in dictionaries. Nor should they be words with either a preceding or following numeric character (such as 3Diamond or Diamond3). They must also not be related to the employee's personal interests or hobbies; special-purpose password-cracking dictionaries that contain the most common passwords related to various topics are available on the Internet. For example, the password Ncc1701 appears, at first glance, to fit the requirements of a strong password because it contains a mixture of upper- and lowercase characters and numbers. But *Star Trek* fans will instantly recognize it as the designation of the starship *Enterprise*. Consequently, Ncc1701 and many variations on it (changing which letters are capitalized, replacing the number 1 with the ! symbol, etc.) are included in most password-cracking dictionaries and, therefore, are quickly compromised.
- **Changed frequently.** Passwords should be changed at regular intervals. Most users should change their passwords at least every 90 days; users with access to sensitive information should change their passwords more often, possibly every 30 days.

Most important, passwords must be kept secret to be effective. However, a problem with strong passwords, such as dX%m8K#2, is that they are not easy to remember.

Consequently, when following the requirements for creating strong passwords, people tend to write those passwords down. This weakens the value of the password by changing it from something they know to something they have—which can then be stolen and used by anyone.

These problems have led some information security experts to conclude that the attempt to enforce the use of strong passwords is counterproductive. They note that a major component of help desk costs is associated with resetting passwords that users forgot. Consequently, they argue for abandoning the quest to develop and use strong passwords and to rely on the use of dual-factor authentication methods, such as a combination of a smart card and a simple PIN, instead.

Other information security experts disagree. They note that operating systems can now accommodate passwords that are longer than 15 characters. This means that users can create strong, yet easy-to-remember, passphrases, such as Ilove2gosnorkelinginHawaiidoU?. Such long passphrases dramatically increase the effort required to crack them by brute-force guessing of every combination. For example, an eight-character password consisting solely of lower- and uppercase letters and numerals has 62^8 possible combinations, but a 20-character passphrase has 62^{20} possible combinations. This means that passphrases do not need to be changed as frequently as passwords. Therefore, some information security experts argue that the ability to use the same passphrase for long periods of time, coupled with the fact that it is easier to remember a long passphrase than a strong password, should dramatically cut help desk costs while improving security. However, it remains to be seen whether users will balk at having to enter long passphrases, especially if they need to do so frequently because they are required to use passphrase-protected screen savers.

3. Some physical characteristic (referred to as a *biometric identifier*), such as their fingerprints or voice

Passwords are probably the most commonly used authentication method, and also the most controversial. Focus 1 discusses some of the requirements for creating strong passwords as well as the ongoing debate about their continued use in the future.

Individually, each authentication method has its limitations. Passwords can be guessed, lost, written down, or given away. Physical identification techniques (cards, badges, USB devices, etc.) can be lost, stolen, or duplicated. Even biometric techniques are not yet 100% accurate, sometimes rejecting legitimate users (for example, voice recognition systems may not recognize an employee who has a cold) and sometimes allowing access to unauthorized people. Moreover, some biometric techniques, such as fingerprints, carry negative connotations that may hinder their acceptance. There are also security concerns about storage of the biometric information itself. Biometric templates, such as the digital representation of an individual's fingerprints or voice, must be stored somewhere. The compromising of those templates would create serious, lifelong problems for the donor because biometric characteristics, unlike passwords or physical tokens, cannot be replaced or changed.

Although none of the three basic authentication credentials, by itself, is foolproof, the use of two or all three types in conjunction, a process referred to as *multifactor authentication*, is quite effective. For example, requiring a user both to insert a smart card in a card reader and enter a password provides much stronger authentication than using either method alone. In some situations, using multiple credentials of the same type, a process referred to as *multimodal authentication*, can also improve security. For example, many online banking sites use several things that a person knows (password, user ID, and recognition of a graphic image) for authentication. Similarly, because most laptops now are equipped with a camera and a microphone, plus a fingerprint reader, it is possible to employ multimodal biometric authentication involving a combination of face, voice, and fingerprint recognition to verify identity. Both multifactor authentication and multimodal authentication are examples of applying the principle of defense-in-depth.

It is important to authenticate not only people, but also every device attempting to connect to the network. Every workstation, printer, or other computing device needs a network interface card (NIC) to connect to the organization's internal network. Each NIC has a unique identifier, referred to as its media access control (MAC) address. Therefore, an organization can restrict network access to only corporate-owned devices by comparing the device's MAC to a list of recognized MAC addresses. There exists software, however, that can be used to change a device's MAC address, thereby enabling malicious users to "spoof" their device's identity. Therefore, a stronger way to authenticate devices involves the use of digital certificates that employ encryption techniques to assign unique identifiers to each device.

AUTHORIZATION CONTROLS   *Authorization* is the process of restricting access of authenticated users to specific portions of the system and limiting what actions they are permitted to perform. For example, a customer service representative should not be authorized to access the payroll system. In addition, that employee should be permitted only to read, but not to change, the prices of inventory items.

Authorization controls are often implemented by creating an *access control matrix* (Figure 3). Then, when an employee attempts to access a particular information systems resource, the system performs a *compatibility test* that matches the user's authentication credentials against the access control matrix to determine whether that employee should be allowed to access that resource and perform the requested action. It is important to regularly update the access control matrix to reflect changes in job duties due to promotions or transfers. Otherwise, over time an employee may accumulate a set of rights and privileges that is incompatible with proper segregation of duties.

It is possible to achieve even greater control and segregation of duties by using business process management systems to embed authorization into automated business processes, rather than relying on a static access control matrix. For example, authorization can be granted only to perform a specific task for a specific transaction. Thus, a particular employee may be permitted to access credit information about the customer who is currently requesting service, but simultaneously prevented from "browsing" through the rest of the customer file. In addition, business process management systems enforce segregation of duties because employees can perform only the specific tasks that the system has assigned them. Employees cannot delete tasks from their

FIGURE 3

Example of an Access Control Matrix

User	Files			Programs			
User ID	A	B	C	1	2	3	4
NHale	0	0	1	0	0	0	0
JPJones	0	2	0	0	0	0	1
BArnold	1	1	0	1	1	0	0
....	....	....	....	....	....	....	....

Codes for File Access:
0 = No Access
1 = Read/display only
2 = Read/display and update
3 = Read/display, update, create, and delete

Codes for Program Access:
0 = No Access
1 = Execute

assigned task list, and the system sends reminder messages until the task is completed—two more measures that further enhance control. Business process management software also can instantly route transactions that require specific authorization (such as a credit sale above a certain amount) electronically to a manager for approval. The transaction cannot continue until authorization is granted, but because the need for such approval is indicated and granted or denied electronically, this important control is enforced without sacrificing efficiency.

Like authentication controls, authorization controls can and should be applied not only to people but also to devices. For example, including MAC addresses or digital certificates in the access control matrix makes it possible to restrict access to the payroll system and payroll master files to only payroll department employees and only when they log in from their desktop or assigned laptop computer. After all, why would a payroll clerk need to log in from a workstation located in the warehouse or attempt to establish dial-in access from another country? Applying authentication and authorization controls to both humans and devices is another way in which defense-in-depth increases security.

Physical Access Controls

It is absolutely essential to control physical access to information resources. A skilled attacker needs only a few minutes of unsupervised direct physical access in order to bypass existing information security controls. For example, an attacker with unsupervised direct physical access can install a keystroke logging device that captures a user's authentication credentials, thereby enabling the attacker to subsequently obtain unauthorized access to the system by impersonating a legitimate user. Someone with unsupervised physical access could also insert special "boot" disks that provide direct access to every file on the computer and then copy sensitive files to a portable device such as a USB drive or an iPod. Alternatively, an attacker with unsupervised physical access could simply remove the hard drive or even steal the entire computer. Given this wide range of potential threats associated with unsupervised physical access, it should not be surprising that another of COBIT's 34 top-level control objectives, DS 12, focuses specifically on physical access controls.

Physical access control begins with entry points to the building itself. Ideally, there should only be one regular entry point that remains unlocked during normal office hours. Fire codes usually require additional emergency exits, but these should not permit entry from the outside and should be connected to an alarm system that is automatically triggered whenever the fire exit is opened. In addition, either a receptionist or a security guard should be stationed at the main entrance to verify the identity of employees. Visitors should be required to sign in and be escorted by an employee wherever they go in the building.

Once inside the building, physical access to rooms housing computer equipment must also be restricted. These rooms should be securely locked and all entry/exit monitored by closed-circuit television systems. Multiple failed access attempts should trigger an alarm. Rooms housing servers that contain especially sensitive data should supplement regular locks with stronger technologies—card readers, numeric keypads, or various biometric devices, such as iris or retina scanners, fingerprint readers, or voice recognition. Focus 2 describes an especially elaborate set of physical access controls referred to as a *man-trap*.

Access to the wiring used in the organization's LANs also needs to be restricted in order to prevent wiretapping. That means that cables and wiring should not be exposed in areas accessible to casual visitors. Wiring closets containing telecommunications equipment need to be securely locked. If wiring closets are shared with other tenants of an office building, the organization should place its telecommunications equipment inside locked steel cages to prevent unauthorized physical access by anyone else with access to that wiring closet. Wall jacks not in current use should be physically disconnected from the network to prevent someone from just plugging in their laptop and attempting to access the network.

Physical access controls must be cost-effective. This requires the involvement of top management in planning physical access security controls to ensure that all information system resources are properly valued and that the nature and combination of access controls reflect the value of the assets being protected.

Laptops, cell phones, and PDA devices require special attention. Laptop theft is a large problem. The major cost is not the price of replacing the laptop, but rather the loss of the confidential information it contains and the costs of notifying those affected. Often, companies also

F(O)CUS 2 — Controlling Physical Access with Man-Traps

Financial institutions, defense contractors, and various intelligence agencies store especially valuable data. Therefore, they often need to employ much more elaborate physical access control measures to their data centers than those used by most other organizations. One such technique involves the use of specially designed rooms called man-traps. These rooms typically contain two doors, each of which uses multiple authentication methods to control access. For example, entry to the first door may require that the person both insert an ID card or smart card into a reader and enter an identification code into a keypad. Successful authentication opens the first door and provides access to the entrance room. Once inside the room, the first door automatically closes behind the person, locks, and cannot be opened from inside the room. The other door, which opens into the data center, is also locked. Thus, the person is now trapped in this small room (hence the name *man-trap*). The only way out is to successfully pass a second set of authentication controls that restrict access through the door leading to the data center. Typically, this involves multifactor authentication that includes a biometric credential. Failure to pass this second set of tests leaves the person in the room until members of the security staff arrive.

have to pay for credit-monitoring services for customers whose personal information was lost or stolen. There may even be class action lawsuits and fines by regulatory agencies.

To deal with the threat of laptop theft, employees should be trained to always lock their laptops to an immovable object. This is necessary even when in the office, as there have been cases where thieves disguised as cleaning crews have stolen laptops and other equipment during working hours. Ideally, sensitive information should not be stored on laptops. If it is, security experts suggest that it be encrypted during storage to minimize the likelihood that a thief will be able to access it. Some organizations are also installing special software on laptops that sends a message to a security server whenever the laptop connects to the Internet. Then, if the laptop is lost or stolen, its location can be identified the next time it is connected to the Internet. The security server can also send a reply message that permanently erases all information stored on the laptop.

Cell phones and PDAs also increasingly store confidential information and therefore need the same types of controls that are used for laptops. It is also important to restrict access to network printers, because they often store document images on their hard drives. There have been cases where intruders have stolen the hard drives in those printers, thereby gaining access to sensitive information.

Network Access Controls

Most organizations provide employees, customers, and suppliers with remote access to their information systems. Usually this access occurs via the Internet, but some organizations still maintain their own proprietary networks or provide direct dial-up access by modem. Many organizations also provide wireless access to their systems. We now discuss the various methods that can be used to satisfy COBIT control objective DS 5.10 to control remote access to information resources.

PERIMETER DEFENSE: ROUTERS, FIREWALLS, AND INTRUSION PREVENTION SYSTEMS   Figure 4 shows the relationship between an organization's information system and the Internet. A device called a **border router** connects an organization's information system to the Internet. Behind the border router is the main *firewall*, which is either a special-purpose hardware device or software running on a general-purpose computer. The **demilitarized zone (DMZ)** is a separate network that permits controlled access from the Internet to selected resources, such as the organization's e-commerce Web server. Together, the border router and firewall act as filters to control which information is allowed to enter and leave the organization's information system. To understand how they function, it is first necessary to briefly discuss how information is transmitted on the Internet.

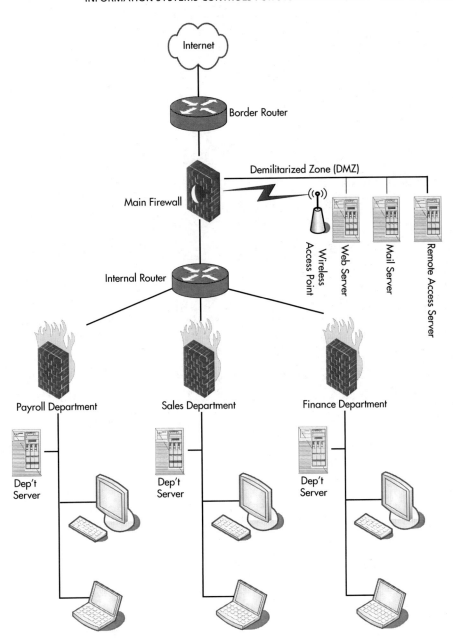

FIGURE 4
Example Organizational Network Architecture

Overview of TCP/IP and Routers.   Information traverses the Internet and internal local area networks in the form of packets. Thus, the documents and files on your computer are not sent intact to a printer or a colleague. Instead, they are first divided into packets, and those packets are then sent over the local area network, and perhaps the Internet, to their destination. The device receiving those packets must then reassemble them to recreate the original document or file. Well-defined rules and procedures called protocols dictate how to perform all these activities. Figure 5 shows how two important protocols, referred to as TCP/IP, govern the process for transmitting information over the Internet. The *Transmission Control Protocol (TCP)* specifies the procedures for dividing files and documents into packets to be sent over the Internet and the methods for reassembly of the original document or file at the destination. The *Internet Protocol (IP)* specifies the structure of those packets and how to route them to the proper destination.

The structure of IP packets facilitates their efficient transmission over the Internet. Every IP packet consists of two parts: a header and a body. The header contains the packet's origin and destination addresses, as well as information about the type of data contained in the body of the packet. The IP protocol prescribes the size of the header and the sequence of information fields

FIGURE 5
Functions of TCP/IP Protocols

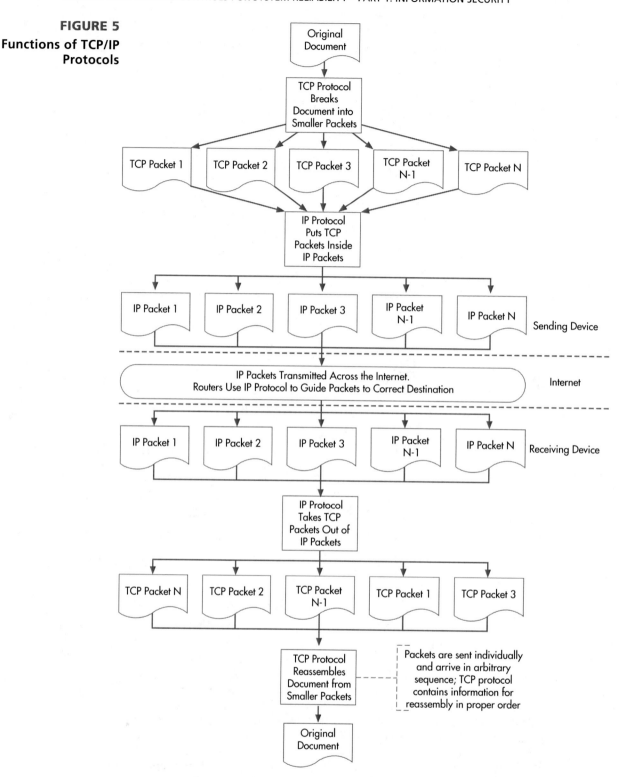

in it. For example, in IP version 4, which is still commonly used in North America, the 13th through 16th bytes in the header *always* contain the IP address of the source of the packet, and the 17th through 20th bytes *always* contain the destination address. This well-defined structure makes it easy for computers to decide where to send each packet that arrives.

Special-purpose devices called **routers** are designed to read the destination address fields in IP packet headers to decide where to send (route) the packet next. The current version of the IP protocol, IPv4, uses 32-bit-long addresses. Those addresses consist of four 8-bit numbers separated by periods. When users type a URL in their browser, that name is translated into the appropriate address. For example, the Acme Manufacturing Company's publicly accessible Web server might have an IP address of 135.22.74.10, but anyone wishing to visit the site can enter the URL of www.acme.com in their browser instead of that IP address. An organization's border router checks the contents of the destination address field of every packet it receives. If the address is not that of the organization, the packet is forwarded on to another router on the Internet. If the destination address matches that of the organization, the packet undergoes one or more tests before being allowed in.

Controlling Access by Filtering Packets. A set of rules, called an *access control list (ACL)*, determines which packets are allowed entry and which are dropped. Border routers typically perform *static packet filtering*, which screens individual IP packets based solely on the contents of the source and/or destination fields in the IP packet header. Typically, the border router's ACL identifies source and destination addresses that should not be permitted to enter the organization's internal network. The function of the border router is to quickly identify and drop certain types of packets and to pass all other packets to the firewall, where they will be subjected to more detailed testing before being allowed to enter the organization's internal network. Thus, most rules in the border router's ACL focus on dropping packets. The last rule in the ACL, however, usually specifies that any packet not dropped because of the preceding rules should be passed on to the firewall.

Like the border router, firewalls use ACLs to determine what to do with each packet that arrives. A major difference, however, is that firewalls are designed to permit entry only to those packets that meet specific conditions. Thus, unlike border routers, the final rule in a firewall ACL usually specifies that any packet not allowed entry by any of the previous rules in the ACL should be dropped. Note, however, that firewalls do not block *all* traffic, but only filter it. That is why all the firewalls in Figure 4 have holes in them—to show that certain kinds of traffic can pass through.

To filter packets, firewalls use more sophisticated techniques than border routers do. For example, most firewalls employ stateful packet filtering. Whereas static packet filtering examines each IP packet in isolation, *stateful packet filtering* creates and maintains a table in memory that lists all established connections between the organization's computers and the Internet. The firewall consults this table to determine whether an incoming packet is part of an ongoing communication initiated by an internal computer. Stateful packet filtering enables the firewall to reject specially crafted attack packets that would have passed a simple static packet filter by pretending to be a response to an internally initiated request, when in fact no such preceding request occurred.

Deep Packet Inspection. Stateful packet filtering is still limited to examining only information in the IP packet header, however. Essentially, this is the same thing as trying to screen mail simply by looking at the destination and return addresses on the envelope. Such a process is fast and can catch patently undesirable packages (e.g., businesses may not want to accept mail from casinos or pornographic magazines), but its effectiveness is limited. Undesirable mail can get through if the IP address is not on the list of unacceptable sources or if the sender purposely disguises the true source address. Clearly, control over incoming mail would be more effective if each envelope or package were opened and inspected.

Similarly, firewalls that examine the data in the body of an IP packet can provide more effective access control than those that look only at information in the IP header. Thus, a Web application firewall can better protect an organization's e-commerce Web server by examining the contents of incoming packets to ensure that they contain only HTML code. The firewall can even restrict the types of commands permitted. For example, requests for data using the HTML "get" command would be allowed, but requests to upload data to the Web server using the HTML "put" command would be blocked to prevent an attacker from defacing the Web site.

This process of examining the data contents of a packet is called *deep packet inspection*. The added control provided by deep packet inspection, however, comes at the cost of speed: It takes more time to examine the body of an IP packet, which could contain more than a thousand bytes of data, than to examine only the 20 bytes in the header of an IPv4 packet.

Deep packet inspection is the heart of a new type of security technology called ***intrusion prevention systems (IPS)*** that monitors *patterns* in the traffic flow, rather than only inspecting individual packets, to identify and automatically block attacks. This is important because examining a pattern of traffic is often the only way to identify undesirable activity. For example, a firewall performing deep packet inspection would permit incoming packets that contained allowable HTML commands to connect to TCP port 80 on the organization's e-commerce Web server and block all other incoming packets. Such a firewall would dutifully pass or block packets, and perhaps record its decisions in a log. An IPS, in contrast, could identify a sequence of packets attempting to connect to various TCP ports on the e-commerce Web server as being an indicator of an attempt to scan and map the Web server (step 3 in a targeted attack). The IPS would not only block the offending packets, but also notify a security administrator that an attempted scan was in progress. Thus, IPSs provide the opportunity for real-time response to attacks.

An IPS consists of a set of sensors and a central monitor unit that analyzes the data collected. Sensors must be installed in several places to effectively monitor network traffic. A sensor located just inside the main firewall can monitor all incoming traffic. Placing another sensor outside the main firewall provides a means to monitor the number of attempted intrusions that were successfully blocked by the firewall, which may provide early warning that the organization is being targeted. Additional sensors inside each internal firewall can be used to monitor the effectiveness of policies concerning employee access to information resources.

IPSs use several different techniques to identify undesirable traffic patterns. The simplest approach is to compare traffic patterns to a database of signatures of known attacks. Another approach involves developing a profile of "normal" traffic and using statistical analysis to identify packets that do not fit that profile. Most promising is the use of rule bases that specify acceptable standards for specific types of traffic and that drop all packets that do not conform to those standards. The beauty of this approach is that it blocks not only known attacks, for which signatures already exist, but also any new attacks that violate the standards.

Although IPSs are a promising addition to the arsenal of security products, they are relatively new and, therefore, not without problems. As mentioned earlier, deep packet inspection slows overall throughput. In addition, there is the danger of false alarms, which results in blocking legitimate traffic. Nevertheless, a great deal of research is being undertaken to improve the intelligence of IPSs, and they are likely to become an important part of an organization's security toolkit. IPSs will not, however, replace the need for firewalls. Instead, they are a complementary tool and provide yet another layer of perimeter defense.

Using Defense-in-Depth to Restrict Network Access. The use of multiple perimeter filtering devices is more efficient and effective than relying on only one device. Thus, most organizations use border routers to quickly filter out obviously bad packets and pass the rest to the main firewall. The main firewall does more detailed checking, using either stateful packet filtering or deep packet inspection. The IPS then monitors the traffic passed by the firewall to identify and block suspicious network traffic patterns that may indicate that an attack is in progress.

Figure 4 illustrates one other dimension of the concept of defense-in-depth: the use of multiple internal firewalls to segment different departments within the organization. Recall that many security incidents involve employees, not outsiders. Internal firewalls help to restrict what data and portions of the organization's information system particular employees can access. This not only increases security but also strengthens internal control by providing a means for enforcing segregation of duties.

Finally, an especially effective way to achieve defense-in-depth is to integrate physical and remote access control systems. For example, if an organization uses keypads, card or badge readers, or biometric identifiers to control and log physical access to the office, that data should be considered when applying remote access controls. This would identify situations likely to represent security breaches, such as when an employee who supposedly is inside the office is simultaneously trying to log into the system remotely from another geographically distant location.

SECURING DIAL-UP CONNECTIONS Many organizations still permit employees to remotely access the organizational network by dialing in with a modem. It is important to verify the identity of users attempting to obtain dial-in access. The ***Remote Authentication Dial-In User Service (RADIUS)*** is a standard method for doing that. Dial-in users connect to a remote access server and submit their log-in credentials. The remote access server passes those credentials to the RADIUS server, which performs compatibility tests to authenticate the identity of that user. Note that Figure 4 shows the remote access server located in the DMZ. Thus, only *after* the user has been authenticated is access to the internal corporate network granted. This subjects dial-in users to the same controls applied to traffic coming in from the untrusted Internet.

Modems, however, are cheap and easy to install, so employees are often tempted to install them on their desktop workstations without seeking permission or notifying anyone that they have done so. This creates a huge hole in perimeter security, because the incoming connection is not filtered by the main firewall. Moreover, when employees install modems, they seldom configure any strong authentication controls. Consequently, a single unauthorized ("rogue") modem connected to an employee's desktop workstation creates a "back door" through which attackers can often easily compromise an otherwise well-protected system. Therefore, either information security or internal audit staff must periodically check for the existence of rogue modems. The most efficient and effective way to do this is to use *war dialing* software, which calls every telephone number assigned to the organization to identify those which are connected to modems. (Hackers do this also, to identify targets). Any rogue modems discovered by war dialing should be disconnected, with sanctions applied to the employees responsible for installing them.

SECURING WIRELESS ACCESS   Many organizations also provide wireless access to their information systems. Wireless access is convenient and easy, but it also provides another venue for attack and extends the perimeter that must be protected. For example, a number of companies have experienced security incidents in which intruders obtained unauthorized wireless access to the organization's corporate network from a laptop while sitting in a car parked outside the building.

It is not enough to monitor the parking lot, because wireless signals can often be picked up miles away. Figure 4 shows that to secure wireless access, all wireless access points (the devices that accept incoming wireless communications and permit the sending device to connect to the organization's network) should be located in the DMZ. This treats all wireless access as though it were coming in from the Internet and forces all wireless traffic to go through the main firewall and any intrusion prevention systems that are used to protect the perimeter of the internal network. In addition, the following procedures need to be followed to adequately secure wireless access:

- Turn on available security features. Most wireless equipment is sold and installed with these features disabled. For example, the default installation configuration for most wireless routers does not turn on encryption.
- Authenticate all devices attempting to establish wireless access to the network *before* assigning them an IP address. This can be done by treating incoming wireless connections as attempts to access the network from the Internet and routing them first through a RADIUS server or other authentication device.
- Configure all authorized wireless devices to operate only in infrastructure mode, which forces the device to connect only to wireless access points. (Wireless devices can also be set to operate in ad hoc mode, which enables them to communicate directly with any other wireless device. This is a security threat because it creates peer-to-peer networks with little or no authentication controls.) In addition, predefine a list of authorized MAC addresses, and configure wireless access points to accept connections only if the device's MAC address is on the authorized list.
- Use noninformative names for the access point's address, which is called a service set identifier (SSID). SSIDs such as "payroll," "finance," or "R&D" are more obvious targets to attack than devices with generic SSIDs such as "A1" or "X2."
- Reduce the broadcast strength of wireless access points, locate them in the interior of the building, and use directional antennas to make unauthorized reception off-premises more difficult. Special paint and window films can also be used to contain wireless signals within a building.
- Encrypt all wireless traffic.

However, as is the case with modems, it is easy and inexpensive for employees to set up unauthorized wireless access points in their offices. Therefore, information security or internal audit staff must periodically test for the existence of such rogue access points, disable any that are discovered, and appropriately discipline the employees responsible for installing them.

Device and Software Hardening Controls

Routers, firewalls, and intrusion prevention systems are designed to protect the network perimeter. However, just as many homes and businesses supplement exterior door locks and alarm systems with locked cabinets and safes to store valuables, an organization can enhance information system security by supplementing preventive controls on the network perimeter with additional preventive controls on the workstations, servers, printers, and other devices (collectively referred to as *endpoints*) that comprise the organization's network. Three areas deserve special attention: (1) endpoint configuration, (2) user account management, and (3) software design.

1 ENDPOINT CONFIGURATION Endpoints can be made more secure by modifying their configurations. Default configurations of most devices typically turn on a large number of optional settings that are seldom, if ever, used. Similarly, default installations of many operating systems turn on many special-purpose programs, called *services*, that are not essential. Turning on unnecessary features and extra services makes it more likely that installation will be successful without the need for customer support. This convenience, however, comes at the cost of creating security weaknesses. Every program that is running represents a potential point of attack because it probably contains flaws, called *vulnerabilities*, that can be exploited to either crash the system or take control of it. Therefore, any optional programs and features that are not used should be disabled. Tools called *vulnerability scanners* can be used to identify unused and, therefore, unnecessary programs that represent potential security threats. This process of modifying the default configuration of endpoints to eliminate unnecessary settings and services is called *hardening*.

In addition to hardening, every endpoint needs to be running antivirus and firewall software that is regularly updated. IPS may also be installed to prevent unauthorized attempts to change the configuration of a specific device. COBIT control objective DS 5.7 recognizes that it is especially important to harden and properly configure every device used to protect the network (firewalls, IPS, routers, etc.), to make them resistant to tampering.

2 USER ACCOUNT MANAGEMENT COBIT control objective DS 5.4 stresses the need to carefully manage all user accounts, especially those accounts that have unlimited (administrative) rights on that computer. Administrative rights are needed in order to install software and alter most configuration settings. These powerful capabilities make accounts with administrative rights prime targets for attackers. In addition, many vulnerabilities affect only accounts with administrative rights. Therefore, employees who need administrative powers on a particular computer should be assigned two accounts: one with administrative rights and another that has only limited privileges. These employees should be trained to log in under their limited account to perform routine daily duties and to log in to their administrative account only when they need to perform some action, such as installing new software, that requires administrative rights. It is especially important that the employee use a limited regular user account when browsing the Web or reading e-mail. This way, if the user visits a compromised Web site or opens an infected e-mail, the attacker will acquire only limited rights on the machine. Although the attacker can use other tools to eventually obtain administrative rights on that machine, other security controls might detect and thwart such attempts to escalate privileges before they can be completed. Finally, it is important to change the default passwords on all administrative accounts that are created during initial installation of any software or hardware because those account names and their default passwords are publicly available on the Internet and thus provide attackers with an easy way to compromise a system.

3 SOFTWARE DESIGN As organizations have increased the effectiveness of their perimeter security controls, attackers have increasingly targeted vulnerabilities in application programs. Buffer overflows, SQL injection, and cross-site scripting are common examples of attacks against the software running on Web sites. These attacks all exploit poorly written software that does not thoroughly check user-supplied input prior to further processing. Consider the common task of soliciting user input such as name and address. Most programs set aside a fixed amount of memory, referred to as a buffer, to hold user input. However, if the program does not carefully check the size of data being input, an attacker may enter many times the amount of data that was anticipated and overflow the buffer. The excess data may be written to an area of memory normally used to store and execute commands. In such cases, an attacker may be able to take control of the machine by sending carefully crafted commands in the excess data. Similarly, SQL injection attacks occur whenever Web application software that interfaces with a database server does not filter user input, thereby permitting an attacker to embed SQL commands within a data entry request and have those commands executed on the database server. Cross-site scripting attacks occur when Web application software does not carefully filter user input before returning any of that data to the browser, in which case the victim's browser will execute any embedded malicious script.

The common theme in all of these attacks is the failure to "scrub" user input to remove potentially malicious code. Therefore, programmers must be trained to treat all input from external users as untrustworthy and to carefully check it before performing further actions. Poor programming techniques affect not only internally created code but also software purchased from third parties. Consequently, several sections of the COBIT framework are devoted to control objectives for application software. Section AI 2 specifies the need to carefully design security into all new applications. Section AI 7 stresses the importance of thoroughly testing new applications before deployment. Sections DS 1 and DS 2 enumerate specific control objectives that should be followed when contracting with vendors.

Detective Controls

As noted earlier, preventive controls are never 100% effective in blocking all attacks. Therefore, COBIT control objective DS 5.5 stresses that organizations also need to implement controls designed to detect intrusions in a timely manner. Detective controls enhance security by monitoring the effectiveness of preventive controls and detecting incidents in which preventive controls have been successfully circumvented. This section discusses the four types of detective controls listed in Table 2: log analysis, intrusion detection systems, managerial reports, and security testing.

Log Analysis

Most systems come with extensive capabilities for logging who accesses the system and what specific actions each user performed. These logs form an audit trail of system access. Like any other audit trail, logs are of value only if they are routinely examined. *Log analysis* is the process of examining logs to identify evidence of possible attacks.

It is especially important to analyze logs of failed attempts to log on to a system and failed attempts to obtain access to specific information resources. For example, Figure 6 presents a portion of security log from a computer running the Windows operating system that shows that a user named "rjones" unsuccessfully tried to log onto a computer named "payroll server." The goal of log analysis is to determine the reason for this failed log-on attempt. One possible explanation is that rjones is a legitimate user who forgot his or her password. Another possibility is that rjones is a legitimate user but is not authorized to access the payroll server. Yet another possibility is that this may represent an attempted attack by an external intruder.

It is also important to analyze changes to the logs themselves (i.e., "to audit the audit trail"). Logs records are routinely created whenever the appropriate event occurs. However, log records are not normally deleted or updated. Therefore, finding such changes to a log file indicate that the system has likely been compromised.

Logs need to be analyzed regularly to detect problems in a timely manner. This is not easy, because logs can quickly grow in size. Another problem is that many devices produce logs with proprietary formats, making it hard to correlate and summarize logs from different devices. Software tools such as log management systems and security information management systems attempt to address these issues by converting vendor-specific log formats into common representations and producing reports that correlate and summarize information from multiple sources. Nevertheless, log analysis ultimately requires human judgment to interpret the reports and identify situations that are not "normal".

FIGURE 6
Example of a System Log

Intrusion Detection Systems

Intrusion detection systems (IDSs) consist of a set of sensors and a central monitoring unit that create logs of network traffic that was permitted to pass the firewall and then analyze those logs for signs of attempted or successful intrusions. Like an IPS, an IDS functions by comparing observed traffic to a database of signatures of known attacks or to a model of "normal" traffic on a particular network. In addition, an IDS can be installed on a specific device to monitor unauthorized attempts to change that device's configuration. The main difference between an IDS and an IPS is that the former only produces a warning alert when it detects a suspicious pattern of network traffic, whereas the latter not only issues an alert but also automatically takes steps to stop a suspected attack.

Managerial Reports

COBIT sections ME 1 and ME 2 address the need for management to monitor and evaluate both system performance and controls. The COBIT framework provides management guidelines that identify critical success factors associated with each control objective and suggests key performance indicators that management can use to monitor and assess control effectiveness. For example, the COBIT management guidelines suggest that key performance indicators relevant to DS 5, information security, include such things as:

1. Number of incidents with business impact
2. Percentage of users who do not comply with password standards
3. Percentage of cryptographic keys compromised and revoked

Nevertheless, despite its importance, surveys indicate that many organizations fail to regularly monitor security. This is clearly an area where accountants can help by using the COBIT framework to design security effectiveness scorecards and encouraging management to regularly review such reports.

Security Testing

COBIT control objective DS 5.5 notes the need to periodically test the effectiveness of existing security procedures. We already discussed the use of vulnerability scanners to identify potential weaknesses in system configuration. Penetration testing provides a more rigorous way to test the effectiveness of an organization's information security. A **penetration test** is an *authorized* attempt by either an internal audit team or an external security consulting firm to break into the organization's information system. These teams try everything possible to compromise a company's system. Because there are numerous potential attack vectors, penetration tests almost always succeed. Thus, their value is not so much in demonstrating that a system *can* be broken into, but in identifying where additional protections are most needed to increase the time and effort required to compromise the system.

Corrective Controls

Detecting attempted and successful intrusions is not enough. Organizations also need procedures to undertake timely corrective actions. Many corrective controls, however, rely on human judgment. Consequently, their effectiveness depends to a great extent on proper planning and preparation. That is why COBIT control objective DS 5.6 prescribes the need to define and communicate characteristics of security incidents to facilitate their proper classification and treatment. In addition, COBIT sections DS 8 and DS 10 outline specific control objectives for effectively managing incidents and problems. This section discusses three particularly important corrective controls listed in Table 2: (1) establishment of a computer incident response team, (2) designation of a specific individual, typically referred to as the Chief Information Security Officer (CISO), with organization-wide responsibility for information security, and (3) an well-designed patch management system

Computer Incident Response Team

A key component to being able to respond to security incidents promptly and effectively is the establishment of a *computer incident response team (CIRT)* responsible for dealing with major incidents. The CIRT should include not only technical specialists but also senior operations management, because some potential responses to security incidents have significant economic consequences. For example, it may be necessary to temporarily shut down an e-commerce server. The decision to do so is too important to leave to the discretion of IT security staff; only operations management possesses the breadth of knowledge to properly evaluate the costs and benefits of such an action, and only it should have the authority to make that decision.

The CIRT should lead the organization's incident response process through the following four steps:

1. *Recognition* that a problem exists. Typically, this occurs when an IPS or IDS signals an alert or as a result of log analysis by a systems administrator.
2. *Containment* of the problem. Once an intrusion is detected, prompt action is needed to stop it and to contain the damage.
3. *Recovery.* Damage caused by the attack must be repaired. This may involve restoring data from backup and reinstalling corrupted programs. We will discuss backup and disaster recovery procedures in more detail in chapter entitled, "Information Systems Controls for Systems Reliability—Part 3: Processing Integrity and Availability."
4. *Follow-up.* Once recovery is in process, the CIRT should lead the analysis of how the incident occurred. Steps may need to be taken to modify existing security policy and procedures to minimize the likelihood of a similar incident occurring in the future. An important decision that needs to be made is whether to attempt to catch and punish the perpetrator. If the organization decides that it wants to prosecute the attacker(s), it needs to immediately involve forensic experts to ensure that all possible evidence is collected and maintained in a manner that makes it admissible for use in court.

Communication is vital throughout all four steps in the incident response process. Therefore, multiple methods of notifying members of the CIRT are necessary. For example, IPSs and IDSs might be configured to send e-mail alerts. However, if the system goes down or is compromised, the e-mail alerts may not work. Traditional telephones and cell phones provide good alternative channels for sending the initial alerts and subsequent communications.

It is also important to practice the incident response plan, including the alert process. It is much better to discover a gap in the plan during a practice run than when a real incident occurs. Regular practice helps identify the need for change in response to technological changes. For example, many organizations are switching from a traditional telephone system to one based on voice-over IP (VoIP). This can save considerable money, but it also means that if the computer network goes down, so, too, does the phone system. This side effect may not be noticed until the incident response plan is practiced.

Chief Information Security Officer (CISO)

COBIT control objective PO 4.8 specifies that responsibility for information security be assigned to someone at an appropriate senior level. One way to satisfy this objective is to create the position of chief information security officer (CISO), who should be independent of other information systems functions and should report to either the chief operating officer (COO) or the CEO. The CISO must understand the company's technology environment and work with the CIO to design, implement, and promote sound security policies and procedures. The CISO should also be an impartial assessor and evaluator of the IT environment. Accordingly, the CISO should have responsibility for ensuring that vulnerability and risk assessments are performed regularly and that security audits are carried out periodically. The CISO also needs to work closely with the person in charge of physical security, because unauthorized physical access can allow an intruder to bypass the most elaborate logical access controls. To facilitate integrating physical and information security, some organizations have created a new position, the chief security officer (CSO), who is in charge of both functions.

Patch Management

COBIT control objective DS 5.9 stresses the need to fix known vulnerabilities by installing the latest updates to both security programs (e.g., antivirus and firewall software) and to operating systems and other applications programs in order to protect the organization from viruses and other types of malware. This is important because the number of reported vulnerabilities rises each year. A primary cause of the rise in reported vulnerabilities is the ever-increasing size and complexity of software. Many widely used programs now contain millions of lines of code. This means that even if 99.99% of the code is "bug-free," there are still 100 possible vulnerabilities for each million lines of code. Hackers and security consulting firms constantly search for vulnerabilities in widely used software. Once a vulnerability has been identified, the next step is to explore and document how to take advantage of it to compromise a system. The set of instructions for taking advantage of a vulnerability is called an *exploit*. Although the creation of an exploit takes considerable skill, once an exploit is published on the Internet it can be easily used by anyone who runs that code.

The widespread availability of many exploits and their ease of use make it important for organizations to take steps to quickly correct known vulnerabilities in software they use. A *patch* is code released by software developers that fixes a particular vulnerability. *Patch management* is the process for regularly applying patches and updates to all software used by the organization. This is not as straightforward as it sounds. Patches represent modifications to already complex software. Consequently, patches sometimes create new problems because of unanticipated side effects. Therefore, organizations need to carefully test the effect of patches prior to deploying them; otherwise, they run the risk of crashing important applications. Further complicating matters is the fact that there are likely to be multiple patches released each year for each software program used by an organization. Thus, organizations may face the task of applying hundreds of patches to thousands of machines every year. This is one area where intrusion prevention systems (IPSs) hold great promise. If an IPS can be quickly updated with the information needed to respond to new vulnerabilities and block new exploits, the organization can use the IPS to buy the time needed to thoroughly test patches before applying them.

Security Implications of Virtualization and the Cloud

Recently, many organizations have embraced virtualization and cloud computing to enhance both efficiency and effectiveness. *Virtualization* takes advantage of the power and speed of modern computers to run multiple systems simultaneously on one physical computer. This cuts hardware costs, because fewer servers need to be purchased. Fewer machines mean lower maintenance costs. Data center costs also fall because less space needs to be rented, which also reduces utility costs.

Cloud computing takes advantage of the high bandwidth of the modern global telecommunication network to enable employees to use a browser to remotely access software (software as a service), data storage devices (storage as a service), hardware (infrastructure as a service), and entire application environments (platform as a service). The arrangement is referred to as a "private," "public," or "hybrid" cloud depending upon whether the remotely accessed resources are entirely owned by the organization, a third party, or a mix of the two, respectively. Cloud computing can potentially generate significant cost savings. For example, instead of purchasing, installing, and maintaining separate copies of software for each end user, an organization can purchase one copy, install it on a central server, and pay for the right of a specified number of employees to simultaneously use a browser to remotely access and use that software. Public clouds actually eliminate the need for making major capital investments in IT, with organizations purchasing (and expensing) their use of computing resources on a pay-for-use or subscription basis. In addition to reducing costs, the centralization of computing resources with cloud computing (whether public, private, or hybrid) makes it easier to change software and hardware, thereby improving flexibility.

Virtualization and cloud computing alter the risk of some information security threats. For example, unsupervised physical access in a virtualization environment exposes not just one device but the entire virtual network to the risk of theft or destruction and compromise. Similarly, compromising a cloud provider's system may provide unauthorized access to multiple systems. Moreover, in cloud computing authentication often relies solely on passwords. Thus, the only thing protecting one cloud customer's data from unauthorized access by another cloud customer is the strength of the passwords used to sign onto the system. Public clouds also raise concerns about the other aspects of systems reliability (confidentiality, privacy, processing integrity, and availability) because the organization is outsourcing control of its data and computing resources to a third party.

Although virtualization and cloud computing can increase the risk of some threats, they also offer the opportunity to significantly improve overall security. For example, implementing strong access controls in the cloud or over the server that hosts a virtual network provides good security over all the systems contained therein. The important point is that all of the controls discussed previously in this chapter remain relevant in the context of virtualization and cloud computing. Strong user access controls, ideally involving the use of multifactor authentication, and physical access controls are essential. Virtual firewalls, IPS, and IDS need to be deployed to isolate virtual machines and cloud customers from one another. The need for timely detection of problems continues to exist, as does the need for corrective controls such as patch management. Thus, virtualization and cloud computing can have either positive or negative effects on the overall level of information security, depending upon how well the organization or the cloud provider implements the various layers of preventive, detective, and corrective controls.

Summary and Case Conclusion

Jason Scott finished his review of the company's information systems security procedures and prepared an interim report for his supervisor. The report began by explaining that security was one of five principles of systems reliability. Because absolute security is not practical, the report noted that Northwest Industries' goal should be to adopt the time-based model of security and employ a combination of detective and corrective controls that would allow the company to detect and respond to attacks in less time than it would take an intruder to break through its preventive controls and successfully attack the system. In addition, the report pointed out the value of deploying redundant, overlapping controls to provide layers of defense-in-depth.

Jason's report then described and evaluated the various security procedures in place at Northwest Industries. Physical access to the company's office is limited to one main entrance, which is staffed at all times by a security guard. All visitors have to sign in at the security desk and are escorted at all times by an employee. Access to rooms with computing equipment requires insertion of an employee badge in a card reader plus entry of a PIN in a keypad lock on the door. Remote access controls include a main firewall that performs stateful packet filtering and additional internal firewalls that segregate different business functions from one another. The information security staff regularly scans all equipment for vulnerabilities and makes sure that every employee's workstation is running a current version of the company's A-V software as well as a firewall. To improve security awareness, all employees attend monthly hour-long workshops that cover a different current security issue each month. The company uses intrusion detection systems, and top management receives monthly reports on the effectiveness of system security. Corrective controls include a computer incident response team and quarterly practice of an incident response plan.

Jason's report concluded by emphasizing that information security is primarily a management issue, not an IT issue. Jason explained how management's attitude and philosophy about security are critical determinants of an organization's overall security. He noted that when top management considers information security to be an integral part of the organization's processes, similar to quality, security is more likely to be proactive and effective. In contrast, if top management considers information security to be primarily an issue of compliance with regulatory requirements, security is more likely to be reactive in nature and less effective.

Jason's supervisor was pleased with his interim report. She asked Jason to continue his review of the company's information systems by examining two of the other principles of systems reliability in the AICPA's Trust Services framework: confidentiality and privacy.

Key Terms

defense-in-depth	demilitarized zone (DMZ)	war dialing
time-based model of security	Transmission Control Protocol (TCP)	endpoints
social engineering	Internet Protocol (IP)	vulnerabilities
authentication	routers	vulnerability scanners
biometric identifier	access control list (ACL)	hardening
multifactor authentication	static packet filtering	log analysis
multimodal authentication	stateful packet filtering	intrusion detection system (IDS)
authorization	deep packet inspection	penetration test
access control matrix	intrusion prevention system (IPS)	computer incident response team (CIRT)
compatibility test	Remote Authentication Dial-In User Service (RADIUS)	exploit
border router		patch
firewall		patch management
		virtualization
		cloud computing

AIS IN ACTION

Chapter Quiz

1. Which of the following statements is true?
   a. The concept of defense-in-depth reflects the fact that security involves the use of a few sophisticated technical controls.
   b. Information security is necessary for protecting confidentiality, privacy, integrity of processing, and availability of information resources.

   c. The time-based model of security can be expressed in the following formula: $P < D + C$

   d. Information security is primarily an IT issue, not a managerial concern.

2. Which of the following is a preventive control?
   - a. training
   - b. log analysis
   - c. CIRT
   - d. virtualization

3. The control procedure designed to restrict what portions of an information system an employee can access and what actions he or she can perform is called _____.
   - a. authorization
   - b. authentication
   - c. intrusion prevention
   - d. intrusion detection

4. A weakness that an attacker can take advantage of to either disable or take control of a system is called a(n) _____.
   - a. exploit
   - b. patch
   - c. vulnerability
   - d. attack

5. Which of the following is a corrective control designed to fix vulnerabilities?
   - a. virtualization
   - b. patch management
   - c. penetration testing
   - d. authorization

6. Which of the following is a detective control?
   - a. hardening endpoints
   - b. physical access controls
   - c. penetration testing
   - d. patch management

7. A firewall that implements perimeter defense by examining only information in the packet header of a single IP packet in isolation is using a technique referred to as _____.
   - a. deep packet inspection
   - b. static packet filtering
   - c. stateful packet filtering
   - d. single packet inspection

8. Which of the following techniques is the most effective way to protect the perimeter?
   - a. deep packet inspection
   - b. static packet filtering
   - c. stateful packet filtering
   - d. All of the above are equally effective.

9. Which of the following combinations of credentials is an example of multifactor authentication?
   - a. voice recognition and a fingerprint reader
   - b. a PIN and an ATM card
   - c. a password and a user ID
   - d. all of the above

10. Modifying default configurations to turn off unnecessary programs and features to improve security is called _____.
    - a. user account management
    - b. defense-in-depth
    - c. vulnerability scanning
    - d. hardening

Discussion Questions

1. Explain why an organization would want to use all of the following information security controls: firewalls, intrusion prevention systems, intrusion detection systems, and a CIRT.

2. What are the advantages and disadvantages of having the person responsible for information security report directly to the chief information officer (CIO), who has overall responsibility for all aspects of the organization's information systems?

3. Reliability is often included in service level agreements (SLAs) when an organization is outsourcing. The toughest thing is to decide how much reliability is enough. Consider an application such as e-mail. If an organization outsources its e-mail to a cloud provider, what is the difference between 95%, 99%, 99.99%, and 99.9999% reliability?

4. What is the difference between authentication and authorization?

5. What are the limitations, if any, of relying on the results of penetration tests to assess the overall level of security?

6. Security awareness training is necessary to teach employees "safe computing" practices. The key to effectiveness, however, is that it changes employee behavior. How can organizations maximize the effectiveness of their security awareness training programs?

7. What is the relationship between COSO, COBIT, and the AICPA's Trust Services frameworks?

Problems

1. Match the following terms with their definitions:

Term	Definition
____ **1.** Vulnerability	a. Code that corrects a flaw in a program
____ **2.** Exploit	b. Verification of claimed identity
____ **3.** Authentication	c. The firewall technique that filters traffic by comparing the information in packet headers to a table of established connections
____ **4.** Authorization	d. A flaw or weakness in a program
____ **5.** Demilitarized zone (DMZ)	e. A test that determines the time it takes to compromise a system
____ **6.** Deep packet inspection	f. A subnetwork that is accessible from the Internet but separate from the organization's internal network
____ **7.** Router	g. The device that connects the organization to the Internet
____ **8.** Social engineering	h. The rules (protocol) that govern routing of packets across networks
____ **9.** Firewall	i. The rules (protocol) that govern the division of a large file into packets and subsequent reassembly of the file from those packets
____ **10.** Hardening	j. An attack that involves deception to obtain access
____ **11.** CIRT	k. A device that provides perimeter security by filtering packets
____ **12.** Patch	l. The set of employees assigned responsibility for resolving problems and incidents
____ **13.** Virtualization	m. Restricting the actions that a user is permitted to perform
____ **14.** Transmission Control Protocol (TCP)	n. Improving security by removal or disabling of unnecessary programs and features
____ **15.** Static packet filtering	o. A device that uses the Internet Protocol (IP) to send packets across networks
____ **16.** Border router	p. A detective control that identifies weaknesses in devices or software
____ **17.** Vulnerability scan	q. A firewall technique that filters traffic by examining the packet header of a single packet in isolation
____ **18.** Penetration test	r. The process of applying code supplied by a vendor to fix a problem in that vendor's software
____ **19.** Patch management	s. Software code that can be used to take advantage of a flaw and compromise a system

Term	Definition
_____ 20. Cloud computing	t. A firewall technique that filters traffic by examining not just packet header information but also the contents of a packet
	u. The process of running multiple machines on one physical server
	v. An arrangement whereby a user remotely accesses software, hardware, or other resources via a browser.

2. Install and run the latest version of the Microsoft Baseline Security Analyzer (MBSA) on your home computer or laptop. Write a report explaining the weaknesses identified by the tool and how to best correct them. Attach a copy of the MBSA output to your report.

3. The following table lists the actions that various employees are permitted to perform:

Employee	Permitted Actions
Able	Check customer account balances
	Check inventory availability
Baker	Change customer credit limits
Charley	Update inventory records for sales and purchases
Denise	Add new customers
	Delete customers whose accounts have been written off as uncollectible
	Add new inventory items
	Remove discontinued inventory items
Ellen	Review audit logs of employee actions

Complete the following access control matrix so that it enables each employee to perform those specific activities:

Employee	Customer Master file	Inventory Master File	Payroll Master File	System Log Files
Able				
Baker				
Charley				
Denise				
Ellen				

Use the following codes:

0 = No access

1 = Read-only access

2 = Read and modify records

3 = Read, modify, create, and delete records

4. Which preventive, detective, and/or corrective controls would best mitigate the following threats?
   a. An employee's laptop was stolen at the airport. The laptop contained personal information about the company's customers that could potentially be used to commit identity theft.
   b. A salesperson successfully logged into the payroll system by guessing the payroll supervisor's password.
   c. A criminal remotely accessed a sensitive database using the authentication credentials (user ID and strong password) of an IT manager. At the time the attack occurred, the IT manager was logged into the system at his workstation at company headquarters.
   d. An employee received an e-mail purporting to be from her boss informing her of an important new attendance policy. When she clicked on a link embedded in the e-mail to view the new policy, she infected her laptop with a keystroke logger.

257

e. A company's programming staff wrote custom code for the shopping cart feature on its Web site. The code contained a buffer overflow vulnerability that could be exploited when the customer typed in the ship-to address.

f. A company purchased the leading "off-the-shelf" e-commerce software for linking its electronic storefront to its inventory database. A customer discovered a way to directly access the back-end database by entering appropriate SQL code.

g. Attackers broke into the company's information system through a wireless access point located in one of its retail stores. The wireless access point had been purchased and installed by the store manager without informing central IT or security.

h. An employee picked up a USB drive in the parking lot and plugged it into his laptop to "see what was on it." As a result, a keystroke logger was installed on that laptop.

i. Once an attack on the company's Web site was discovered, it took more than 30 minutes to determine who to contact to initiate response actions.

j. To facilitate working from home, an employee installed a modem on his office workstation. An attacker successfully penetrated the company's system by dialing into that modem.

k. An attacker gained access to the company's internal network by installing a wireless access point in a wiring closet located next to the elevators on the fourth floor of a high-rise office building that the company shared with seven other companies.

5. What are the advantages and disadvantages of the three types of authentication credentials (something you know, something you have, and something you are)?

6. a. Apply the following data to evaluate the time-based model of security for the XYZ Company. Does the XYZ Company satisfy the requirements of the time-based model of security? Why?
   • Estimated time for attacker to successfully penetrate system = 25 minutes
   • Estimated time to detect an attack in progress and notify appropriate information security staff = 5 minutes (best case) to 10 minutes (worst case)
   • Estimated time to implement corrective actions = 6 minutes (best case) to 20 minutes (worst case)

   b. Which of the following security investments to you recommend? Why?
   1. Invest $50,000 to increase the estimated time to penetrate the system by 4 minutes
   2. Invest $50,000 to reduce the time to detect an attack to between 2 minutes (best case) and 6 minutes (worst case)
   3. Invest $50,000 to reduce the time required to implement corrective actions to between 4 minutes (best case) and 14 minutes (worst case)

7. Explain how the following items individually and collectively affect the overall level of security provided by using a password as an authentication credential.
   a. Length
   b. Complexity requirements (which types of characters are required to be used: numbers, alphabetic, case-sensitivity of alphabetic, special symbols such as $ or !)
   c. Maximum password age (how often password must be changed)
   d. Minimum password age (how long a password must be used before it can be changed)
   e. Maintenance of password history (how many prior passwords the system remembers to prevent reselection of the same password when the user is required to change passwords)
   f. account lockout threshold (how many failed log-in attempts are allowed before the account is locked)
   g. time frame during which account lockout threshold is applied (i.e., if lockout threshold is five failed log-in attempts, the time frame is the period during which those five failures must occur: within 15 minutes, 1 hour, 1 day, etc.).
   h. account lockout duration (how long the account remains locked after the user exceeds the maximum allowable number of failed log-in attempts)

8. The chapter briefly discussed the following three common attacks against applications:
   a. Buffer overflows
   b. SQL injection
   c. Cross-site scripting

Required

Research each of these three attacks, and write a report explaining in detail how each attack actually works and describing suggested controls for reducing the risks that these attacks will be successful.

9. Physical security is extremely important. Read the article "19 Ways to Build Physical Security into a Data Center," which appeared in the November 2005 issue of *CSO Magazine* (you can find the article at www.csoonline.com/read/110105/datacenter.html). Which methods would you expect almost any major corporation to use? Which might likely be justified only at a financial institution?

Case 1 Costs of Preventive Security

Firewalls are one of the most fundamental and important security tools. You are likely familiar with the software-based host firewall that you use on your laptop or desktop. Such firewalls should also be installed on every computer in an organization. However, organizations also need corporate-grade firewalls, which are usually, but not always, dedicated special-purpose hardware devices. Conduct some research to identify three different brands of such corporate-grade firewalls, and write a report that addresses the following points:

- Cost
- Technique (deep packet inspection, static packet filtering, or stateful packet filtering)
- Ease of configuration and use

Case 2 Developing an Information Security Checklist

Obtain a copy of COBIT (available at www.isaca.org), and read section DS 5. Design a checklist for assessing each of the 11 detailed information security control objectives. The checklist should contain questions to which a yes response represents a control strength, a no response represents a control weakness, plus a possible N/A response. Provide a brief reason for asking each question. Organize your checklist as follows:

Question	Yes	No	N/A	Reason for asking
1. Is there regular security awareness training?				Training is one of the most important preventive controls because many security incidents happen due to either human error or social engineering.

AIS IN ACTION SOLUTIONS

Quiz Key

1. Which of the following statements is true?
   a. The concept of defense-in-depth reflects the fact that security involves the use of a few sophisticated technical controls. (Incorrect. The concept of defense-in-depth is based on the idea that, given enough time and resources, any single control, no matter how sophisticated, can be overcome—therefore, the use of redundant, overlapping controls maximizes security.)

   ▶ b. Information security is necessary for protecting confidentiality, privacy, integrity of processing, and availability of information resources. (Correct. As Figure 2 shows, security is the foundation for achieving the other four components of system reliability.)

   c. The time-based model of security can be expressed in the following formula: $P < D + C$ (Incorrect. The formula is $P > D + C$.)

   d. Information security is primarily an IT issue, not a managerial concern. (Incorrect. Security is primarily a managerial issue because only management can choose the most appropriate risk response to protect the organization's information resources.)

2. Which of the following is a preventive control?

   ▶ a. training (Correct. Training is designed to prevent employees from falling victim to social engineering attacks and unsafe practices such as clicking on links embedded in e-mail from unknown sources.)

   b. log analysis (Incorrect. Log analysis involves examining a record of events to discover anomalies. Thus, it is a detective control.)

   c. CIRT (Incorrect. The purpose of a computer incident response team is to respond to and remediate problems and incidents. Thus, it is a corrective control.)

   d. virtualization (Incorrect. Virtualization involves using one physical computer to run multiple virtual machines. It is primarily a cost-control measure, not an information security control procedure.)

3. The control procedure designed to restrict what portions of an information system an employee can access and what actions he or she can perform is called _____.

   a. authentication (Incorrect. Authentication is the process of verifying a user's identity to decide whether or not to grant that person access.)

   ▶ b. authorization (Correct. Authorization is the process of controlling what actions—read, write, delete, etc.—a user is permitted to perform.)

   c. intrusion prevention (Incorrect. Intrusion prevention systems monitor patterns in network traffic to identify and stop attacks.)

   d. intrusion detection (Incorrect. Intrusion detection is a detective control that identifies when an attack has occurred.)

4. A weakness that an attacker can take advantage of to either disable or take control of a system is called a(n) _____.

   a. exploit (Incorrect. An exploit is the software code used to take advantage of a weakness.)

   b. patch (Incorrect. A patch is code designed to fix a weakness.)

   ▶ c. vulnerability (Correct. A vulnerability is any weakness that can be used to disable or take control of a system.)

   d. attack (Incorrect. An attack is the action taken against a system. To succeed, it exploits a vulnerability.)

5. Which of the following is a corrective control designed to fix vulnerabilities?

   a. virtualization (Incorrect. Virtualization involves using one physical computer to run multiple virtual machines. It is primarily a cost-control measure, not an information security control procedure.)

   ▶ b. patch management (Correct. Patch management involves replacing flawed code that represents a vulnerability with corrected code, called a patch.)

   c. penetration testing (Incorrect. Penetration testing is detective control.)

   d. authorization (Incorrect. Authorization is a preventive control used to restrict what users can do.)

6. Which of the following is a detective control?

   a. Endpoint hardening (Incorrect. Hardening is a preventive control that seeks to eliminate vulnerabilities by reconfiguring devices and software.)

   b. Physical access controls (Incorrect. Physical access controls are a preventive control designed to restrict access to a system.)

   ▶ c. Penetration testing (Correct. Penetration testing is a detective control designed to identify how long it takes to exploit a vulnerability.)

    d. Patch management (Incorrect. Patch management is a corrective control that fixes vulnerabilities.)

7. A firewall that implements perimeter defense by examining only information in the packet header of a single IP packet in isolation is using a technique referred to as _____.

    a. deep packet inspection (Incorrect. Deep packet inspection examines the contents of the data in the body of the IP packet, not just the information in the packet header.)

  ▶ **b.** static packet filtering (Correct. Static packet filtering examines the headers of individual IP packets.)

    c. stateful packet filtering (Incorrect. Stateful packet filtering examines not only the headers of individual IP packets but also a state table to determine whether incoming packets are part of an already established connection.)

    d. single packet inspection (Incorrect. There is no such thing.)

8. Which of the following techniques is the most effective way to protect the perimeter?

  ▶ **a.** deep packet inspection (Correct. Deep packet inspection examines the contents of the data in the body of the IP packet, not just the information in the packet header. This is the best way to catch malicious code.)

    b. static packet filtering (Incorrect. Static packet filtering examines the headers of individual IP packets. It can be fooled by attacks that pretend to be sending a response to earlier outbound messages.)

    c. stateful packet filtering (Incorrect. Stateful packet filtering maintains information about "state" or connections initiated by the organization, but it examines only the information in the packet header. Therefore, it cannot detect malware in the payload of a message.)

    d. All of the above are equally effective (Incorrect. Choices b and c are less effective than choice a.)

9. Which of the following combinations of credentials is an example of multifactor authentication?

    a. voice recognition and a fingerprint reader (Incorrect. This is a combination of two biometric credentials and is an example of multimodal authentication.)

  ▶ **b.** a PIN and an ATM card (Correct. The PIN is something a person knows, the ATM card is something the person has.)

    c. password and a user ID (Incorrect. These are both things a person knows and thus represent an example of multimodal authentication.)

    d. all of the above (Incorrect. Only choice b is correct.)

10. Modifying default configurations to turn off unnecessary programs and features to improve security is called _____.

    a. user account management (Incorrect. User account management is a preventive control that limits what a user can do.)

    b. defense-in-depth (Incorrect. Defense-in-depth is the general security principle of using multiple overlapping controls to protect a system.)

    c. vulnerability scanning (Incorrect. Vulnerability scanning is a detective control designed to identify weaknesses.)

  ▶ **d.** hardening (Correct. This is the definition of hardening.)

Chapter 9

Information Systems Controls for Systems Reliability—Part 2: Confidentiality and Privacy

From Chapter 9 of *Accounting Information Systems*, 12/e. Marshall B. Romney. Paul John Steinbart. Copyright © 2012 by Pearson Education. Published by Prentice Hall. All rights reserved.

Information Systems Controls for Systems Reliability—Part 2: Confidentiality and Privacy

Learning Objectives

After studying this chapter, you should be able to:

1. Identify and explain controls designed to protect the confidentiality of sensitive corporate information.

2. Identify and explain controls designed to protect the privacy of customers' personal information.

3. Explain how the two basic types of encryption systems work.

INTEGRATIVE CASE NORTHWEST INDUSTRIES

Jason Scott was preparing for his meeting with the company's chief information security officer (CISO). Although Jason was satisfied that Northwest Industries' computer security policies and procedures provided the company with adequate protection against intrusions, he was concerned about other aspects of systems reliability. In particular, he wanted to learn what Northwest Industries was doing to address the following issues:

1. Protecting the confidentiality of sensitive corporate information, such as marketing plans and trade secrets
2. Protecting the privacy of personal information collected from customers

Jason planned to use his interview with the CISO to obtain a general understanding of the company's information systems controls. He then planned to follow up by collecting evidence about the effectiveness of those controls.

Introduction

This chapter covers two important principles of reliable systems in the Trust Services Framework: preserving the confidentiality of an organization's intellectual property and protecting

264

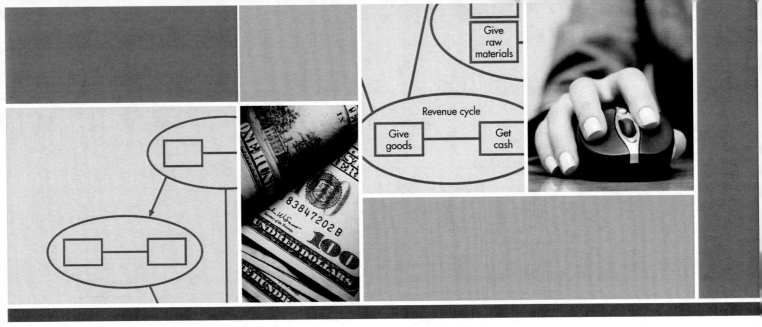

the privacy of personal information it collects from customers. We also discuss the topic of encryption in detail, because it is a critical tool to protecting both confidentiality and privacy.

Preserving Confidentiality

Organizations possess a myriad of sensitive information, including strategic plans, trade secrets, cost information, legal documents, and process improvements. This intellectual property often is crucial to the organization's long-run competitive advantage and success. Consequently, preserving the confidentiality of the organization's intellectual property, and similar information shared by its business partners, has long been recognized as a basic objective of information security. This section discusses the actions that must be taken to preserve confidentiality: (1) identification and classification of the information to be protected, (2) encryption of sensitive information, (3) controlling access to sensitive information, and (4) training.

Identification and Classification of Information to be Protected

The first step to protect the confidentiality of intellectual property and other sensitive business information is to identify where such information resides and who has access to it. This sounds easy, but undertaking a thorough inventory of every digital and paper store of information is both time-consuming and costly because it involves examining more than just the contents of the organization's financial systems. For example, manufacturing firms typically employ large-scale factory automation. Those systems contain instructions that may provide significant cost advantages or product quality enhancements over those of competitors and, therefore, must be protected from unauthorized disclosure or tampering.

After the information that needs to be protected has been identified, the next step, as discussed in the Control Objectives for Information and Related Technology (COBIT) control objective PO 2.3, is to classify the information in terms of its value to the organization. Information classification is not a task to be delegated solely to information systems professionals; to properly recognize the information's value, the process also needs input from senior management. Once the information has been classified, the appropriate set of controls can be deployed to protect it.

Protecting Confidentiality with Encryption

Encryption (to be discussed later in this chapter) is an extremely important and effective tool to protect confidentiality. It is the only way to protect information in transit over the Internet. It is also a necessary part of defense-in-depth to protect information stored on Web sites or in a public cloud. For example, many accounting firms have created secure portals that they use to share sensitive audit, tax, or consulting information with clients. The security of such portals, however, is limited by the strength of the authentication methods used to restrict access. In most cases, this involves only single factor authentication via a password. Encrypting the client's data that is stored on the portal provides an additional layer of protection in the event of unauthorized access to the portal. Similarly, encrypting information stored in a public cloud protects it from unauthorized access by employees of the cloud service provider or by anyone else who is using that same cloud.

Encryption, however, is not a panacea. Some sensitive information, particularly "know-how" such as process shortcuts, may not be stored digitally and, therefore, cannot be protected by being encrypted. In addition, encryption protects information only in specific situations. For example, full disk encryption protects the information stored on a laptop in the event that it is lost or stolen. The person who steals or finds such a laptop will not be able to read any of the encrypted information, *unless* he or she can log on as the legitimate owner. That is why strong authentication is also needed. In addition, the information on the laptop is decrypted whenever the owner has logged on, which means that anyone who can sit down at the keyboard can view the sensitive information. Therefore, physical access controls are also needed. Similarly, in enterprise systems, encrypting information while it is stored in the database protects it from being viewed by people who have access to the system but not to the database. However, the database has to decrypt the information in order to process it; therefore, anyone who can log on to the database can potentially see confidential information. That is why strong access controls are also needed. In summary, sensitive information is exposed in plain view whenever it is being processed by a program, displayed on a monitor, or included in printed reports. Consequently, protecting confidentiality requires application of the principle of defense-in-depth: supplementing encryption with access controls and training.

Controlling Access to Sensitive Information

The previous chapter discussed how organizations use authentication and authorization controls to restrict access to information systems that contain sensitive information. *Information rights management (IRM)* software provides an additional layer of protection to specific information resources, offering the capability not only to limit access to specific files or documents, but also to specify the actions (read, copy, print, download to USB devices, etc.) that individuals who are granted access to that resource can perform. Some IRM software even has the capability to limit those privileges to a specific period of time and to remotely erase protected files. Either the creator of the information or the person responsible for managing it must assign the access rights. To access an IRM-protected resource, a person must first authenticate to the IRM server, which then downloads code containing the access-limiting instructions to that person's computer.

CoBIT control objectives DS 12.2 and DS 12.3 address physical access controls, which are also important in preventing someone with unsupervised access from quickly downloading and copying gigabytes of confidential information onto a USB drive, an iPod, a cell phone, or other portable device. It is especially important to restrict access to rooms that contain printers, digital copiers, and fax machines because such devices typically possess large amounts of RAM, which may store any confidential information that was printed. Laptops and workstations should run password-protected screen savers automatically after a few minutes of inactivity, to prevent unauthorized viewing of sensitive information. Screen protection devices that limit the distance and angle from which information on a laptop or workstation monitor can be seen are also useful.

In addition, CoBIT control objective DS 11.4 addresses the importance of controlling the *disposal* of information resources. Printed reports and microfilm containing confidential information should be shredded before being thrown out. Special procedures are needed to destroy information stored on magnetic and optical media. Using built-in operating system commands to delete that information is insufficient, because many utility programs exist that can recover such deleted files. Frequently, people who have purchased used computers, cell phones, digital copy machines, and other devices discover information that the previous owner thought had been deleted. Proper disposal of computer media requires use of special software designed to "wipe" the media clean by repeatedly overwriting the disk or drive with random patterns of data. Probably the safest alternative is to physically destroy (e.g., by incineration) magnetic and optical media that have been used to store extremely sensitive data.

Today, organizations constantly exchange information with their business partners and customers. Therefore, protecting confidentiality also requires controls over outbound communications. One tool for accomplishing that is *data loss prevention (DLP)* software, which works like antivirus programs in reverse, blocking outgoing messages (whether e-mail, IM, or other means) that contain key words or phrases associated with the intellectual property or other sensitive data the organization wants to protect. DLP software is a preventive control. It can and should be supplemented by embedding code called a *digital watermark* in documents. The digital watermark is a detective control that enables an organization to identify confidential information that has been disclosed. When an organization discovers documents containing its digital watermark on the Internet, it has evidence that the preventive controls designed to protect its sensitive information have failed. It should then investigate how the compromise occurred and take appropriate corrective action.

Access controls designed to protect confidentiality must be continuously reviewed and modified to respond to new threats created by technological advances. For example, the incorporation of digital cameras in cell phones makes it possible for visitors to surreptitiously capture confidential information. Consequently, many organizations now prohibit visitors from using cell phones while touring manufacturing facilities or other areas likely to contain confidential information. Because camera phones are so easy to hide, most organizations also require that visitors always be escorted by employees to further reduce the risk that the visitors photograph sensitive information.

Telephone conversations are another area affected by advances in technology. In the past, wiretaps were the only serious threat to the confidentiality of telephone conversations, and the difficulty of setting them up meant that the risk of that threat was relatively low. The use of voice-over-the-Internet (VoIP), however, means that telephone conversations are now routed as packets over the Internet. This means that VoIP telephone conversations are as vulnerable to interception as any other information sent over the Internet. Therefore, VoIP conversations about sensitive topics should be encrypted.

Virtualization and cloud computing also affect the risk of unauthorized access to sensitive or confidential information. An important control in virtual environments, including internally managed "private" clouds, is to use virtual firewalls to restrict access between different virtual machines that coexist on the same physical server. In addition, virtual machines that store highly sensitive or confidential data should not be hosted on the same physical server with virtual machines that are accessible via the Internet because of the risk that a skilled attacker might be able to break out of the latter and compromise the former. With public clouds, the data is stored elsewhere, and access occurs over the Internet via browsers. Therefore, all communication between users and the cloud must be encrypted. Browser software, however, often contains numerous vulnerabilities. Consequently, highly sensitive and confidential data probably should not be stored in a public cloud because of lack of control over where that information is actually stored and because of the risk of unauthorized access by other cloud customers, who may include competitors, or even by employees of the cloud provider.

Training

Training is arguably the most important control for protecting confidentiality. Employees need to know what information they can share with outsiders and what information needs to be protected. They also need to be taught how to protect confidential data. For example, employees need to know how to use encryption software. They also need to learn to always log out of applications before leaving their laptop or workstation unattended, to prevent other employees from obtaining unauthorized access to that information. Employees also need to know how to code reports they create to reflect the importance of the information contained therein so that other employees will know how to handle those reports. They also need to be taught not to leave reports containing sensitive information in plain view on their desks when they leave.

Training is particularly important concerning the proper use of e-mail, instant messaging (chat), and blogs because it is impossible to control the subsequent distribution of information once it has been sent or posted through any of those methods. For example, it is important to teach employees not to routinely use the "reply all" option with e-mail because doing so may disclose sensitive information to people who should not see it. Employees also need to be taught how to participate in discussions at conferences or professional education courses so that they do not inadvertently disclose information that might compromise their employer's competitive advantage. Employees often do not realize the importance of information they possess, such as time-saving steps or undocumented features they have discovered when using a particular software program. Therefore, it is important for management to inform employees who will attend external training courses, trade shows, or conferences whether they can discuss such information or whether it should be protected because it provides the company a cost savings or quality improvement advantage over its competitors.

With proper training, employees can play an important role in protecting the confidentiality of an organization's information and enhance the effectiveness of related controls. For example, if employees understand their organization's data classification scheme, they may recognize situations in which sensitive information has not been properly protected and proactively take appropriate corrective actions. Training in how to protect the confidentiality of an organization's intellectual property can also enhance its efforts to protect the privacy of personal information it collects from its customers.

Privacy

The Trust Services framework privacy principle is closely related to the confidentiality principle, differing primarily in that it focuses on protecting personal information about customers rather than organizational data. Consequently, the controls that need to be implemented to protect privacy are the same ones used to protect confidentiality: identification of the information that needs to be protected, encryption, access controls, and training.

Privacy Controls

As is the case for confidential information, the first step to protect the privacy of personal information collected from customers is to identify what information is collected, where it is stored, and who has access to it. It is then important to implement controls to protect that information because incidents involving the unauthorized disclosure of customers' personal information, whether intentional or accidental, can be costly. For example, the Massachusetts Data Security Law (201 CMR 17.00) fines companies $5,000 per record for data breaches. Governments may also restrict the daily business operations of companies that suffer a breach. For example, after Citibank's online credit card application in Taiwan was hacked and personal customer data compromised in November 2003, the Taiwanese government imposed a one-month moratorium on issuing new credit cards and a three-month suspension of the online application, until Citibank's online security could be independently verified.

Encryption is a fundamental control for protecting the privacy of personal information that organizations collect from their customers. That information needs to be encrypted both while it is in transit over the Internet and while it is in storage (indeed, the Massachusetts law mandates encryption of personal information at all times, whether in transit or in storage). Encrypting customers' personal information not only protects it from unauthorized disclosure, but also can save organizations money. Many states have passed data breach notification laws that require organizations to notify customers after any event, such as the loss or theft of a laptop or portable media device, that may have resulted in the unauthorized disclosure of customer personal information. This can be expensive for businesses that have hundreds of thousands or millions of customers. The costly notification requirement is usually waived, however, if the lost or stolen customer information was encrypted.

However, customers' personal information is not encrypted during processing or when it is displayed either on a monitor or in a printed report. Consequently, as with confidentiality, protecting customers' privacy requires supplementing encryption with access controls and training. Strong authentication and authorization controls restrict who can access systems that contain customers' personal information and the actions the users can perform once they are granted access. It is especially important to prevent programmers from having access to personal information, such as credit card numbers, telephone numbers, and Social Security numbers. In developing new applications, programmers often have to use "realistic" data to test the new system. It is tempting, and easy, to provide them with a copy of the data in the organization's transaction processing system. Doing so, however, gives programmers access to customers' personal information. To protect privacy, organizations should run *data masking* programs that replace customers' personal information with fake values (e.g., replace a real Social Security number with a different set of numbers that have the same characteristics, such as 123-45-6789) before sending that data to the program development and testing system.

Organizations also need to train employees on how to manage and protect personal information collected from customers. This is especially important for medical and financial information. Obviously, intentional misuse of such information can have serious negative economic consequences, including significant declines in stock prices. Unintentional disclosure of such personal information can also create costly problems, however. For example, someone denied health or life insurance because of improper disclosure of personal information is likely to sue the organization that was supposed to restrict access to that data.

Privacy Concerns

Two major privacy-related concerns are spam and identity theft.

SPAM   *Spam* is unsolicited e-mail that contains either advertising or offensive content. Spam is a privacy-related issue because recipients are often targeted as a result of unauthorized access to e-mail address lists and databases containing personal information. The volume of spam is overwhelming many e-mail systems. Spam not only reduces the efficiency benefits of e-mail but also is a source of many viruses, worms, spyware programs, and other types of malware. To deal with this problem, the U.S. Congress passed the Controlling the Assault of Non-Solicited Pornography and Marketing (CAN-SPAM) Act in 2003. CAN-SPAM provides both criminal and civil penalties for violations of the law. CAN-SPAM applies to commercial e-mail, which is defined as any e-mail that has the primary purpose of advertising or promotion. This covers much of the legitimate e-mail that many organizations send to their customers, suppliers, and, in the case of nonprofit organizations, their donors. Thus, organizations need to be sure to follow CAN-SPAM's guidelines or risk sanctions. Key provisions include the following:

- The sender's identity must be clearly displayed in the header of the message.
- The subject field in the header must clearly identify the message as an advertisement or solicitation.
- The body of the message must provide recipients with a working link that can be used to opt out of future e-mail. After receiving an opt-out request, organizations have 10 days to implement steps to ensure they do not send any additional unsolicited e-mail to that address. This means that organizations need to assign someone responsibility for processing opt-out requests.
- The body of the message must include the sender's valid postal address. Although not required, best practice would be to also include full street address, telephone, and fax numbers.
- Organizations should not send commercial e-mail to randomly generated addresses, nor should they set up Web sites designed to "harvest" e-mail addresses of potential customers. Experts recommend that organizations redesign their own Web sites to include a visible means for visitors to opt in to receive e-mail, such as checking a box.

IDENTITY THEFT   Another privacy-related issue that is of growing concern is identity theft. *Identity theft* is the unauthorized use of someone's personal information for the perpetrator's benefit. Often, identity theft is a financial crime, in which the perpetrator obtains loans or opens new credit cards in the victim's name and sometimes loots the victim's bank accounts. However, a growing portion of identity theft cases involve fraudulently obtaining medical care and services. Medical identity theft can have life-threatening consequences because of errors it may create in the victim's medical records, such as changing information about drug allergies or prescriptions. It may even cause victims to lose their insurance coverage if the thief has used up their annual or lifetime cap for coverage of a specific illness.

Focus 1 discusses the steps that individuals should take to minimize the risk of identity theft. Organizations, however, also have a role to play in preventing identity theft. Customers entrust them with personal information. Organizations economically benefit from having access to that information. Therefore, organizations have an ethical and moral obligation to implement controls to protect the personal information that they collect from and about their customers.

FOCUS 1 — Protecting Yourself from Identity Theft

Victims of identity theft often spend much time and money to recover from it. Fortunately, there are a number of simple steps you can take to minimize your risk of becoming a victim of identity theft.

- Shred all documents that contain personal information, especially unsolicited credit card offers, before discarding them. Cross-cut shredders are much more effective than strip-cut shredders.
- Never send personal information (Social Security number, passport number, etc.) in unencrypted e-mail.
- Beware of e-mail, telephone, and print requests to "verify" personal information that the requesting party should already possess. For example, credit card companies will never need to ask you for the three- or four-digit security code on your card. Similarly, the IRS will never e-mail you asking to send personally identifying information in response to an audit.
- Do not carry your Social Security card with you. Be wary of requests to reveal the last four digits of your Social Security number. The first three and middle two digits are assigned based on the location and date you applied for a Social Security number and, therefore, can be discovered through research, but the last four digits are assigned randomly.

- Print only your initials and last name, rather than your full name, on checks. This prevents a thief from knowing how you sign your name.
- Limit the amount of other information (address and phone number) preprinted on checks, and consider totally eliminating such information.
- Do not place outgoing mail containing checks or personal information in your mailbox for pickup.
- Do not carry more than a few blank checks with you.
- Use special software to thoroughly clean any digital media prior to disposal, or physically destroy the media. It is especially important to thoroughly erase or destroy hard drives (for computers, printers, *and* copy machines) prior to donating or disposing of obsolete equipment because they likely contain information about online financial transactions.
- Monitor your credit reports regularly.
- File a police report as soon as you discover that your purse or wallet was lost or stolen.
- Make photocopies of driver's licenses, passports, and credit cards. Store this information, along with the telephone numbers of all your credit cards, in a safe location to facilitate notifying appropriate authorities in the case that those documents are lost or stolen.
- Immediately cancel any stolen or lost credit cards.

Privacy Regulations and Generally Accepted Privacy Principles

Concerns about spam, identity theft, and protecting individual privacy have resulted in numerous government regulations. In addition to state disclosure laws, a number of federal regulations, including the Health Insurance Portability and Accountability Act (HIPAA), the Health Information Technology for Economic and Clinical Health Act (HITECH), and the Financial Services Modernization Act (commonly referred to as the Gramm–Leach–Bliley Act, representing the names of its three Congressional sponsors), impose specific requirements on organizations to protect the privacy of their customers' personal information. Many other countries also have regulations concerning the use and protection of customers' personal information.

To help organizations cost-effectively comply with these myriad requirements, the American Institute of Certified Public Accountants (AICPA) and the Canadian Institute of Chartered Accountants (CICA) jointly developed a framework called *Generally Accepted Privacy Principles (GAPP)*. GAPP identifies and defines the following 10 internationally recognized best practices for protecting the privacy of customers' personal information:

1. *Management.* Organizations need to establish a set of procedures and policies for protecting the privacy of personal information they collect from customers, as well as information about their customers obtained from third parties such as credit bureaus. They should assign responsibility and accountability for implementing those policies and procedures to a specific person or group of employees.
2. *Notice.* An organization should provide notice about its privacy policies and practices at or before the time it collects personal information from customers, or as soon as practicable thereafter. The notice should clearly explain what information is being collected, the reasons for its collection, and how the information will be used.
3. *Choice and consent.* Organizations should explain the choices available to individuals and obtain their consent prior to the collection and use of their personal information. The

nature of the choices offered differs across countries. In the United States, the default policy is called opt-out, which allows organizations to collect personal information about customers unless the customer explicitly objects. In contrast, the default policy in Europe is opt-in, meaning that organizations cannot collect personally identifying information unless customers explicitly give them permission to do so. However, even in the United States, GAPP recommends that organizations follow the opt-in approach and obtain explicit positive consent prior to collecting and storing sensitive personal information, such as financial or health records, political opinions, religious beliefs, and prior criminal history.

4. *Collection.* An organization should collect only the information needed to fulfill the purposes stated in its privacy policies. One particular issue of concern is the use of cookies on Web sites. A *cookie* is a text file created by a Web site and stored on a visitor's hard disk. Cookies store information about what the user has done on the site. Most Web sites create multiple cookies per visit in order to make it easier for visitors to navigate to relevant portions of the Web site. It is important to note that cookies are text files, which means that they cannot "do" anything besides store information. They do, however, contain personal information that may increase the risk of identity theft and other privacy threats. Browsers can be configured to not accept cookies, and GAPP recommends that organizations employ procedures to accede to such requests and not surreptitiously use cookies.

5. *Use and retention.* Organizations should use customers' personal information only in the manner described in their stated privacy policies and retain that information only as long as it is needed to fulfill a legitimate business purpose. This means that organizations need to create retention policies and assign someone responsibility for ensuring compliance with those policies.

6. *Access.* An organization should provide individuals with the ability to access, review, correct, and delete the personal information stored about them.

7. *Disclosure to third parties.* Organizations should disclose their customers' personal information to third parties only in the situations and manners described in the organization's privacy policies and only to third parties who provide the same level of privacy protection as does the organization which initially collected the information. This principle has implications for using cloud computing, because storing customers' personal information in the cloud may make it accessible to the cloud provider's employees; hence such information should be encrypted at all times.

8. *Security.* An organization must take reasonable steps to protect its customers' personal information from loss or unauthorized disclosure. Indeed, it is not possible to protect privacy without adequate information security. Therefore, organizations must use the various preventive, detective, and corrective controls discussed in the previous chapter to restrict access to their customers' personal information. However, achieving an acceptable level of information security is not sufficient to protect privacy. It is also necessary to train employees to avoid practices that can result in the unintentional or inadvertent breach of privacy. One sometimes overlooked issue concerns the disposal of computer equipment. It is important to follow the suggestions presented in the section on protecting confidentiality for properly erasing all information stored on computer media. Perhaps one of the most famous incidents of failing to properly erase information on a hard drive involved the disposal of an obsolete personal computer by a British bank. It was sold at an auction; the buyer found that it contained personal information about the financial affairs of Paul McCartney. E-mail presents a second threat vector to consider. For example, in 2002 drug manufacturer Eli Lilly sent an e-mail about its antidepressant drug Prozac to 669 patients. However, because it used the cc: function to send the message to all patients, the e-mails revealed the identities of other patients. A third often overlooked area concerns the release of electronic documents. Just as special procedures are used to black out (redact) personal information on paper documents, organizations should train employees to use procedures to remove such information on electronic documents in a manner that prevents the recipient of the document from recovering the redacted information.

9. *Quality.* Organizations should maintain the integrity of their customers' personal information and employ procedures to ensure that it is reasonably accurate. Providing customers with a way to review the personal information stored by the organization (GAPP principle 6) can be a cost-effective way to achieve this objective.

10. *Monitoring and enforcement.* An organization should assign one or more employees to be responsible for ensuring compliance with its stated privacy policies. Organizations must also periodically verify that their employees are complying with stated privacy policies. In addition, organizations should establish procedures for responding to customer complaints, including the use of a third-party dispute resolution process.

In summary, GAPP shows that protecting the privacy of customers' personal information requires first implementing a combination of policies, procedures, and technology, then training everyone in the organization to act in accordance with those plans, and subsequently monitoring compliance. Only senior management possesses the authority and the resources to accomplish this, which reinforces the fact that all aspects of systems reliability are, at bottom, a managerial issue and not just an IT issue. Because accountants and auditors serve as trusted advisors to senior management, they too need to be knowledgeable about these issues.

Encryption

Encryption is a preventive control that can be used to protect both confidentiality and privacy. Encryption protects data that is being sent over the Internet and it provides one last barrier that must be overcome by an intruder who has obtained unauthorized access to stored information. As we will see later, encryption also strengthens authentication procedures and plays an essential role in ensuring and verifying the validity of e-business transactions. Therefore, it is important for accountants, auditors, and systems professionals to understand encryption.

As shown in Figure 1, *encryption* is the process of transforming normal content, called **plaintext,** into unreadable gibberish, called **ciphertext. Decryption** reverses this process,

FIGURE 1

Steps in the Encryption and Decryption Process

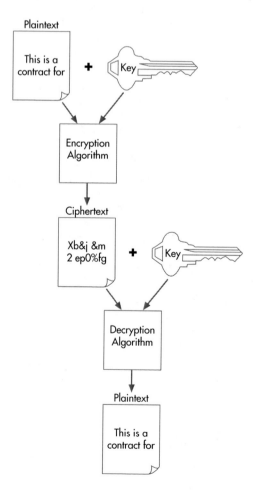

transforming ciphertext back into plaintext. Both encryption and decryption involve use of a key and an algorithm. Computers represent both plaintext and ciphertext as a series of binary digits (0s and 1s). The key is also a string of binary digits of a fixed length; for example, a 128-bit key consists of a string of 128 0s and 1s. The algorithm is a formula for combining the key and the text. Most documents are longer than the key, so the encryption process begins by dividing the plaintext into blocks, each block being of equal length to the key. Then the algorithm is applied to the key and the block of plaintext. For example, if a 128-bit key is being used, the computer first divides the document or file into 128-bit-long blocks and then combines each block with the key in the manner specified by the algorithm (for example, by adding them). The result is a ciphertext version of the document or file, equal in size to the original. To reproduce the original document, the computer first divides the ciphertext into 128-bit blocks and then applies the decryption key to each block.

Factors that Influence Encryption Strength

Three important factors determine the strength of any encryption system: (1) key length, (2) encryption algorithm, and (3) policies for managing the cryptographic keys.

KEY LENGTH   Longer keys provide stronger encryption by reducing the number of repeating blocks in the ciphertext. This makes it harder to spot patterns in the ciphertext that reflect patterns in the original plaintext. For example, a 24-bit key encrypts plaintext in blocks of 24 bits. In English, each letter is represented by 8 bits. Thus, a 24-bit key encrypts English plaintext in chunks of three letters. This makes it easy to use information about relative word frequencies, such as the fact that *the* is one of the most common three-letter words in English, to "guess" that the most commonly recurring pattern of 24 bits in the ciphertext probably represents the English word *the* and proceed to "break" the encryption. That's why most encryption keys are at least 256 bits long (corresponding to 42 English letters), and are often 1024 bits or longer.

ENCRYPTION ALGORITHM   The nature of the algorithm used to combine the key and the plaintext is important. A strong algorithm is difficult, if not impossible, to break by using brute-force guessing techniques. Secrecy is not necessary for strength. Indeed, the procedures used by the most accepted and widely used encryption algorithms are publicly available. Their strength is due not to the secrecy of their procedures, but to the fact that they have been rigorously tested and demonstrated to resist brute-force guessing attacks. Therefore, organizations should not attempt to create their own "secret" encryption algorithm, but instead should purchase products that use widely accepted standard algorithms whose strength has been proven.

POLICIES FOR MANAGING CRYPTOGRAPHIC KEYS   COBIT control objective DS 5.8 stresses the importance of sound practices for managing cryptographic keys. Indeed, this is often the most vulnerable aspect of encryption systems. No matter how long the keys are, or how strong an encryption algorithm is, if the keys have been compromised, the encryption can be easily broken. Therefore, cryptographic keys must be stored securely and protected with strong access controls. Best practices include not storing cryptographic keys in a browser or any other file that other users of that system can readily access and using a strong (and long) passphrase to protect the keys.

Organizations must also have a way to decrypt the data in the event that the employee who encrypted it is no longer present. One way to do this is to use encryption software that creates a built-in master key that can be used to decrypt anything encrypted by that software. An alternative is a process called *key escrow,* which involves making copies of all encryption keys used by employees and storing those copies securely. Organizations also need sound policies and procedures for issuing and revoking keys. Keys should be issued only to employees who handle sensitive data and, therefore, need the ability to encrypt it. It is also important to promptly revoke (cancel) keys when an employee leaves or when there is reason to believe the key has been compromised and to notify everyone who has relied upon those keys that they are no longer valid.

Types of Encryption Systems

There are two basic types of encryption systems. *Symmetric encryption systems* use the same key both to encrypt and to decrypt. DES and AES are examples of symmetric encryption systems. *Asymmetric encryption systems* use two keys. One key, called the *public key,* is widely distributed and available to everyone; the other, called the *private key,* is kept secret and known only to the owner of that pair of keys. Either the public or private key can be used to encrypt, but only the other key can decrypt the ciphertext. RSA and PGP are examples of asymmetric encryption systems.

Symmetric encryption is much faster than asymmetric encryption, but it has two major problems. First, both parties (sender and receiver) need to know the shared secret key. This means that the two parties need to have some method for securely exchanging the key that will be used to both encrypt and decrypt. E-mail is not a solution, because anyone who can intercept the e-mail would know the secret key. Thus, some other method of exchanging keys is needed. Although this could be done by telephone, postal mail, or private delivery services, such techniques quickly become cost-prohibitive, particularly for global communications. The second problem is that a separate secret key needs to be created for use by each party with whom the use of encryption is desired. For example, if company A wants to encrypt information it shares with companies B and C, but prevent B and C from having access to the other's information, it needs to create two encryption keys, one for use with company B and the other for use with company C. Otherwise, if Company A shared only one common secret key with both B and C, either company could decrypt any information to which it obtained access, even if intended for the other company. Thus, secure management of keys quickly becomes more complex as the number of participants in a symmetric encryption system increases.

Asymmetric encryption systems solve these problems. It does not matter who knows the public key, because any text encrypted with it can be decrypted only by using the corresponding private key. Therefore, the public key can be distributed by e-mail or even be posted on a Web site so that anyone who wants to can send encrypted information to the owner of that public key. Also, any number of parties can use the same public key to send encrypted messages because only the owner of the corresponding private key can decrypt the messages. In addition, information can be encrypted with the private key and then decrypted with the corresponding public key. Since only one party possesses the private key, asymmetric encryption systems make it possible to prove who created a document, thereby providing a means for creating legally binding electronic agreements.

The main drawback to asymmetric encryption systems is speed. Asymmetric encryption is much (thousands of times) slower than symmetric encryption, making it impractical for use to exchange large amounts of data over the Internet. Consequently, e-business uses both types of encryption systems. Symmetric encryption is used to encode most of the data being exchanged, and asymmetric encryption is used to safely send the symmetric key to the recipient for use in decrypting the ciphertext. In addition, as will be discussed later, asymmetric encryption is also used in combination with a process called hashing to create digital signatures.

Hashing

Hashing is a process that takes plaintext of any length and transforms it into a short code called a *hash*. For example, the SHA-256 algorithm creates a 256-bit hash, regardless of the size of the original plaintext. As Table 1 shows, hashing differs from encryption in two important aspects. First, encryption always produces ciphertext similar in length to the original plaintext, but hashing always produces a hash that is of a fixed short length, regardless of the length of the original

TABLE 1 Comparison of Hashing and Encryption

Hashing	Encryption
1. One-way function (cannot reverse, or "unhash").	1. Reversible (can decrypt back to plaintext).
2. Any size input yields same fixed-size output. For example, SHA-256 hashing algorithm produces a 256-bit hash for each of the following: + a one-sentence document + a one-page document + a ten-page document	2. Output size approximately the same as input size. For example: + a one-sentence document becomes a one-sentence encrypted document + a one-page document becomes a one-page encrypted document + a ten-page document becomes a ten-page encrypted document

plaintext. The second difference is that encryption is reversible, but hashing is not. Given the decryption key and the algorithm, ciphertext can be decrypted back into the original plaintext. In contrast, it is not possible to transform a hash back into the original plaintext, because hashing throws away information. For example, using SHA-256 to hash a 10,000-character document produces a string of 256 bits. There is no way to recover the 79,744 bits that were discarded and convert the short 256-bit hash back into the original document.

Hashing algorithms have another interesting property: They use every bit in the original plaintext to calculate the hash value. Therefore, changing any character in the document being hashed, such as replacing a 1 with a 7, adding or removing a single space, or even switching from upper- to lowercase produces a different hash value. This property of hashing algorithms provides a means to verify that the contents of a message have not been altered.

Digital Signatures

An important issue for business transactions has always been **nonrepudiation,** or how to create legally binding agreements that cannot be unilaterally repudiated by either party. Traditionally, this has been accomplished by signing contracts and other documents and then making photocopies so that each party can retain an identical copy. Today, however, many business transactions occur digitally using the Internet. How can businesses obtain the same level of assurance about the enforceability of a digital transaction that a signed original or photocopy provides for a paper-based transaction? The answer is to use both hashing and asymmetric encryption to create a digital signature.

As Figure 2 shows, a *digital signature* is a hash of a document (or file) that is encrypted using the document creator's private key. Digital signatures provide proof about two important issues: (1) that a copy of a document or file has not been altered, and (2) who created the original version of a digital document or file. Thus, digital signatures provide assurance that someone cannot enter into a digital transaction and then subsequently deny they had done so and refuse to fulfill their side of the contract.

How do digital signatures provide this assurance? First, remember that an important property of a hash is that it reflects every bit in a document. Therefore, if two hashes are identical, it means that two documents or files are identical. Consequently, just as a photocopy can be compared to an original to verify that it has not been altered, comparing a hash of a document on one computer to a hash of a document on another computer provides a way to determine whether two documents are identical. Second, remember that in asymmetric encryption systems, something encrypted with a private key can only be decrypted with the corresponding public key. Therefore, if something can be decrypted with an entity's public key, it must have been encrypted with the corresponding private key, which proves that it had to have been encrypted by the owner of that pair of public and private keys.

Let us now see how both of these facts work together to provide nonrepudiation. For example, a supplier receives a purchase order along with a digital signature of that purchase order from a customer. The supplier can hash its copy of the purchase order using the same hashing algorithm that the customer used to create its digital signature. The supplier can then use the customer's public key to decrypt the digital signature, thereby producing a hash of some document that must have existed in the customer's information system. If the hash resulting from decrypting the customer's digital signature matches the hash of the purchase order in the supplier's possession, it proves that (1) the supplier's copy of the purchase order is an exact copy of a purchase order that exists on some other system (otherwise, the two hashes would not match) and (2) that

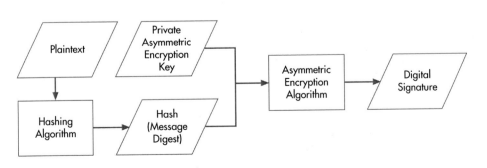

FIGURE 2

Creating a Digital Signature

the purchase order must have existed on the *customer's* information system (otherwise, decrypting the digital signature with the customer's public key would not have produced the hash).

One question still remains, however. Successfully using a public key to decrypt a document or file proves that it was created by the party possessing the corresponding private key. But how can the recipient be sure of the other party's identity? Returning to our prior example, how can a supplier know that the public key purportedly belonging to a customer really belongs to a legitimate customer and not to a criminal who created that pair of public and private keys? For that matter, how does the supplier obtain the customer's public key? The answers to these questions involve the use of digital certificates and a public key infrastructure.

Digital Certificates and Public Key Infrastructure

A *digital certificate* is an electronic document that contains an entity's public key and certifies the identity of the owner of that particular public key. Thus, digital certificates function like the digital equivalent of a driver's license or passport. Just as passports and drivers licenses are issued by a trusted independent party (the government) and employ mechanisms such as holograms and watermarks to prove that they are genuine, digital certificates are issued by an organization called a *certificate authority* and contain the certificate authority's digital signature to prove that they are genuine. Digital certificates intended for e-business use are typically issued by commercial certificate authorities, such as Thawte and VeriSign. These certificate authorities charge a fee to issue a pair of public and private keys and collect evidence to verify the claimed identity of the person or organization purchasing those keys and the corresponding digital certificate.

This system for issuing pairs of public and private keys and corresponding digital certificates is called a *public key infrastructure (PKI)*. The entire PKI system hinges on trusting the certificate authorities that issue the keys and certificates. The AICPA's Trust Services framework contains a list of criteria that can be used to evaluate the overall reliability of a particular certificate authority. One important factor concerns the procedures the certificate authority uses to verify the identity of an applicant for a digital certificate. Several classes of digital certificates exist. The cheapest, and least trustworthy, may involve nothing more than verifying the applicant's e-mail address. The most expensive certificates may require verification of the applicant's identity through use of credit reports and tax returns. Digital certificates are valid for only a specified period of time. Thus, a second important criterion for assessing the reliability of a certificate authority is the procedures it uses to update certificates and revoke expired digital certificates.

Digital certificates provide a mechanism for securely obtaining and verifying the validity of another party's public key. Organizations can store their digital certificates on their Web sites. Browsers are designed to automatically obtain a copy of a Web site's digital certificate to acquire the site's public key. (You can manually examine the contents of a Web site's digital certificate by double-clicking on the lock icon that appears in your browser window when you visit a Web site). Browsers also are designed to automatically check the validity of a Web site's digital certificate. Recall that a digital certificate is signed by the issuing certificate authority. All browsers come preloaded with the public keys of widely recognized certificate authorities. (In Internet Explorer, you can view the list of certificate authorities trusted by your browser by opening your browser, selecting Internet Options on the Tools menu, then moving to the Content tab and then clicking the Publishers button). The browser uses that key to decrypt the certificate authority's digital signature, which yields a hash of the digital certificate. The browser then creates its own hash of the digital certificate; if the two hashes match, the certificate is valid.

Illustrative Example: The Role of Encryption and Hashing in E-Business

To illustrate how hashing, symmetric encryption, and asymmetric encryption techniques are all used together in an e-business transaction, Figure 3 uses the example of Northwest Industries submitting a competitive bid to provide services to a local government agency. The example assumes that both Northwest Industries and the government agency have previously acquired digital certificates from a mutually trusted certificate authority.

Step 1. A Northwest Industries employee connects to the government agency's Web site and clicks on the button for submitting bids on open contracts. *The browser moves to a secure Web page displaying the familiar lock icon. The browser software on the*

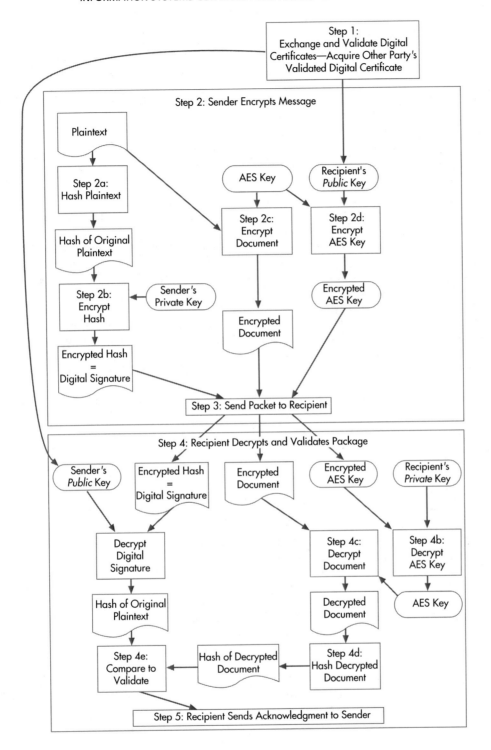

FIGURE 3

Using Encryption and Hashing for E-Business

employee's computer obtains the Web site's digital certificate, verifies its validity, and opens it to get the agency's public key. The government Web site software follows similar steps to acquire Northwest Industries' public key.

Step 2. The employee clicks a button to attach and submit the company's bid. *Behind the scenes, the encryption software performs the following actions:*

  a. Uses a hashing algorithm, such as SHA-256, to create a hash of the bid.

  b. Encrypts the hash using Northwest Industries' private key. This creates a digital signature for the bid.

277

     c. Encrypts the bid using the AES symmetric key algorithm. This protects the confidentiality of the bid, because only someone who knows the AES key can decrypt it.

     d. Uses the government agency's public key to encrypt the AES key used in step 2c. This ensures that only the intended recipient (the government agency) will be able to decrypt the AES key needed to decrypt the bid.

Step 3. The encrypted bid (created in step 2c), the AES key needed to decrypt that bid (created in step 2d), and Northwest Industries' digital signature (created in step 2b) are all sent over the Internet to the government agency.

Step 4. The government agency's computer receives the package of information and performs the following steps:

     a. Uses Northwest Industries' public key, obtained in step 1, to decrypt the digital signature created in step 2b. This yields the hash of the original bid that was created by the sender.

     b. Uses its private key to decrypt the AES key sent by Northwest Industries in step 2d.

     c. Uses the AES key from step 4b to decrypt the encrypted bid produced in step 2c. This produces a plaintext version of Northwest Industries' bid.

     d. Uses the same hashing algorithm used by Northwest Industries in step 2a to hash the plaintext copy of the bid created in step 4c.

     e. Compares the hash created in step 4d to that produced by step 4a. If the two match, the government agency knows that (1) the copy of the bid it recreated in step 4c was created by Northwest Industries, and (2) the bid has not been altered or garbled during transmission.

Step 5. The agency sends Northwest Industries an acknowledgement that its bid has been received.

Virtual Private Networks (VPNs)

To protect confidentiality and privacy, information must be encrypted not only within a system, but also when it is in transit over the Internet. As Figure 4 shows, encrypting information while it traverses the Internet creates a *virtual private network (VPN)*, so named because it provides the functionality of a privately owned secure network without the associated costs of leased telephone lines, satellites, and other communication equipment. Using VPN software to encrypt information while it is in transit over the Internet in effect creates private communication channels, often referred to as *tunnels*, which arc accessible only to those parties possessing the appropriate encryption and decryption keys. VPNs also include controls to authenticate the parties exchanging information and to create an audit trail of the exchange. Thus, VPNs satisfy COBIT control objective DS 5.11, which identifies the need to ensure that sensitive information is exchanged securely and in a manner that can provide proof of its authenticity.

Organizations typically use two types of VPNs. One type uses SSL and browser software to give employees remote access to the corporate network when traveling or working at home. The other type of VPN uses IPSec, a version of the IP protocol that incorporates encryption, to securely connect two offices. Both types of VPNs provide a secure means of exchanging sensitive information over the Internet but create problems for other components of information security. For example, firewalls function by inspecting the contents of packets. Firewalls, however, cannot examine packets that are encrypted. There are three

FIGURE 4
Virtual Private Networks (VPNs)

VPN = Encrypted Tunnel

INTERNET

commonly used approaches to dealing with this problem. One is to configure the firewall to send encrypted packets to a computer in the DMZ that decrypts them; that computer then sends the decrypted packets back through the firewall for filtering before being allowed into the internal network. Although this approach allows the firewall to screen all incoming packets, it means that sensitive information is unencrypted both in the DMZ and within the internal network. A second approach is to configure the main firewall to allow encrypted packets to enter the internal network and decrypt them only at their final destination. Although this approach protects the confidentiality of sensitive information until it reaches the appropriate destination, it creates potential holes in access controls because not all incoming packets are filtered by the firewall. The third approach is to have the firewall also function as the VPN termination point, decrypting all incoming traffic and then inspecting the content. This approach is costly, creates a single point of failure (if the firewall goes down, so too does the VPN), and means that sensitive information is not encrypted while traveling on the internal corporate network. Thus, organizations must choose which systems reliability objective is more important: confidentiality (privacy) or security. Unfortunately, this type of dilemma is not limited to firewalls; antivirus programs, intrusion prevention systems, and intrusion detection systems also have difficulty in dealing with encrypted packets. This necessity of making trade-offs among different components of systems reliability is another reason that information security and controls is a managerial concern, and not just an IT issue.

Summary and Case Conclusion

Jason Scott reviewed what he had learned about Northwest Industries' information systems controls to protect confidentiality and privacy. Confidential information about business plans and personal information collected from customers was encrypted both in storage and whenever it was transmitted over the Internet. Employee laptops were configured with VPN software so that they could securely access the company's information systems when they worked at home or while traveling on business. Northwest Industries employed a key escrow system to manage the encryption keys; Jason had tested and verified that it worked as planned. The CISO had used GAPP to develop procedures to protect personal information collected from customers. Jason verified that employees received detailed training on how to handle such information when initially hired and attended mandatory "refresher" courses every six months. Multifactor authentication was used to control access to the company's databases. Jason also verified that Northwest Industries digitally signed transactions with its business partners and required customers to digitally sign all orders that exceeded $10,000.

Based on his report, Jason's supervisor and the CIO were satisfied with Northwest Industries' measures to protect confidentiality and privacy. They asked Jason next to examine the controls in place to achieve the remaining two principles of systems reliability in the AICPA's Trust Services framework: processing integrity and availability.

Key Terms

information rights management (IRM)	plaintext	hashing
data loss prevention (DLP)	ciphertext	hash
digital watermark	decryption	nonrepudiation
data masking	key escrow	digital signature
spam	symmetric encryption systems	digital certificate
identity theft	asymmetric encryption systems	certificate authority
cookie	public key	public key infrastructure (PKI)
encryption	private key	virtual private network (VPN)

AIS IN ACTION

Chapter Quiz

1. Which of the following statements is true?
   a. Encryption is sufficient to protect confidentiality and privacy.
   b. Cookies are text files that only store information. They cannot perform any actions.
   c. The controls for protecting confidentiality are not effective for protecting privacy.
   d. All of the above are true.

2. A digital signature is _____.
   a. created by hashing a document and then encrypting the hash with the signer's private key
   b. created by hashing a document and then encrypting the hash with the signer's public key
   c. created by hashing a document and then encrypting the hash with the signer's symmetric key
   d. none of the above

3. Able wants to send a file to Baker over the Internet and protect the file so that only Baker can read it and can verify that it came from Able. What should Able do?
   a. Encrypt the file using Able's public key, and then encrypt it again using Baker's private key.
   b. Encrypt the file using Able's private key, and then encrypt it again using Baker's private key.
   c. Encrypt the file using Able's public key, and then encrypt it again using Baker's public key.
   d. Encrypt the file using Able's private key, and then encrypt it again using Baker's public key.

4. Which of the following statements is true?
   a. Encryption and hashing are both reversible (can be decoded).
   b. Encryption is reversible, but hashing is not.
   c. Hashing is reversible, but encryption is not.
   d. Neither hashing nor encryption is reversible.

5. Confidentiality focuses on protecting _____.
   a. personal information collected from customers
   b. a company's annual report stored on its Web site
   c. merger and acquisition plans
   d. all of the above

6. Which of the following statements about obtaining consent to collect and use a customer's personal information is true?
   a. The default policy in Europe is opt-out, but in the United States the default is opt-in.
   b. The default policy in Europe is opt-in, but in the United States the default is opt-out.
   c. The default policy in both Europe and the United States is opt-in.
   d. The default policy in both Europe and the United States is opt-out.

7. One of the ten Generally Accepted Privacy Principles concerns security. According to GAPP, what is the nature of the relationship between security and privacy?
   a. Privacy is a necessary, but not sufficient, precondition to effective security.
   b. Privacy is both necessary and sufficient to effective security.
   c. Security is a necessary, but not sufficient, precondition to protect privacy.
   d. Security is both necessary and sufficient to protect privacy.

8. Which of the following statements is true?
   a. Symmetric encryption is faster than asymmetric encryption and can be used to provide nonrepudiation of contracts.
   b. Symmetric encryption is faster than asymmetric encryption but cannot be used to provide nonrepudiation of contracts.

    c. Asymmetric encryption is faster than symmetric encryption and can be used to provide nonrepudiation of contracts.

    d. Asymmetric encryption is faster than symmetric encryption but cannot be used to provide nonrepudiation of contracts.

9. Which of the following statements is true?
    a. VPNs protect the confidentiality of information while it is in transit over the Internet.
    b. Encryption limits firewalls' ability to filter traffic.
    c. A digital certificate contains that entity's public key.
    d. All of the above are true.

10. Which of the following can organizations use to protect the privacy of a customer's personal information when giving programmers a realistic data set with which to test a new application?
    a. digital signature
    b. digital watermark
    c. data loss prevention
    d. data masking

Discussion Questions

1. From the viewpoint of the customer, what are the advantages and disadvantages to the opt-in versus the opt-out approaches to collecting personal information? From the viewpoint of the organization desiring to collect such information?

2. What risks, if any, does offshore outsourcing of various information systems functions pose to satisfying the principles of confidentiality and privacy?

3. Should organizations permit personal use of e-mail systems by employees during working hours?

4. What privacy concerns might arise from the use of biometric authentication techniques? What about the embedding of radio frequency identification (RFID) tags in products such as clothing? What other technologies might create privacy concerns?

5. What do you think an organization's duty or responsibility to protect the privacy of its customers' personal information should be? Why?

6. Assume you have interviewed for a job online and now receive an offer of employment. The job requires you to move across the country. The company sends you a digital signature along with the contract. How does this provide you with enough assurance to trust the offer so that you are willing to make the move?

Problems

1. Match the terms with their definitions:

____	1. Virtual private network (VPN)	a. A hash encrypted with the creator's private key
____	2. Data loss prevention (DLP)	b. A company that issues pairs of public and private keys and verifies the identity of the owner of those keys
____	3. Digital signature	c. A secret mark used to identify proprietary information
____	4. Digital certificate	d. An encrypted tunnel used to transmit information securely across the Internet
____	5. Data masking	e. Replacing real data with fake data
____	6. Symmetric encryption	f. Unauthorized use of facts about another person to commit fraud or other crimes

____ 7. Spam	g.	The process of turning ciphertext into plaintext
____ 8. Plaintext	h.	Unwanted e-mail
____ 9. Hashing	i.	A document or file that can be read by anyone who accesses it
____ 10. Ciphertext	j.	Used to store an entity's public key, often found on Web sites
____ 11. Information rights management	k.	A procedure to filter outgoing traffic to prevent confidential information from leaving
____ 12. Certificate authority	l.	A process that transforms a document or file into a fixed-length string of data
____ 13. Nonrepudiation	m.	A document or file that must be decrypted to be read
____ 14. Digital watermark	n.	A copy of an encryption key stored securely to enable decryption if the original encryption key becomes unavailable
____ 15. Asymmetric encryption	o.	An encryption process that uses a pair of matched keys, one public and the other private; either key can encrypt something, but only the other key in that pair can decrypt
____ 16. Key escrow	p.	An encryption process that uses the same key to both encrypt and decrypt
	q.	The inability to unilaterally deny having created a document or file or having agreed to perform a transaction
	r.	Software that limits what actions (read, copy, print, etc.) that users granted access to a file or document can perform.

2. Cost-effective controls to provide confidentiality require valuing the information that is to be protected. This involves classifying information into discrete categories. Propose a minimal classification scheme that could be used by any business, and provide examples of the type of information that would fall into each of those categories.

3. Download a hash calculator from the course web site that can create hashes for both files and text input. Use it to create SHA-256 (or any other hash algorithm your instructor assigns) hashes for the following:
   a. A document that contains this text: "Congratulations! You earned an A+"
   b. A document that contains this text: "Congratulations! You earned an A−"
   c. A document that contains this text: "Congratulations! You earned an a−"
   d. A document that contains this text: "Congratulations! You earned an A+" (this message contains two spaces between the exclamation point and the capital letter Y).
   e. Make a copy of the document used in step a, and calculate its hash value.
   f. Hash any multiple-page text file on your computer.

4. Accountants often need to print financial statements with the words "CONFIDENTIAL" or "DRAFT" appearing in light type in the background.
   a. Create a watermark with the word "CONFIDENTIAL" in a Word document. Print out a document that displays that watermark.
   b. Create the same watermark in Excel, and print out a spreadsheet page that displays that watermark.
   c. Can you make your watermark "invisible" so that it can be used to detect whether a document containing sensitive information has been copied to an unauthorized location? How? How could you use that "invisible" watermark to detect violation of copying policy?

5. Create a spreadsheet to compare current monthly mortgage payments versus the new monthly payments if the loan were refinanced, as shown:

Refinancing Calculator

Instructions: Only enter data into borderless cells; DO NOT enter data into cells with borders
Current loan amount   500000
Current term (years)   30

Current interest rate	5%
Current monthly payment	$2,684.11
New Loan amount	400000
New Loan term (years)	25
New interest rate	4.50%
New monthly payment	$2,223.33

Required

a. Restrict access to the spreadsheet by encrypting it.
b. Further protect the spreadsheet by limiting users to the ability to select and enter data only in the six cells without borders.

Hint: The article "Keeping Secrets: How to Protect Your Computer from Snoops and Spies," by Theo Callahan in the July 2007 issue of the *Journal of Accountancy* explains how to do this using Excel 2003. Review the article, and then use Excel's built-in help function to learn how to do this with later versions of Excel.

6. Research the information rights management software that may be available for your computer. What are its capabilities for limiting access rights? Write a report of your findings.

   Optional: If you can download and install IRM software from Microsoft, use it to prevent anyone from being able to copy or print your report.

7. The principle of confidentiality focuses on protecting an organization's intellectual property. The flip side of the issue is ensuring that employees respect the intellectual property of other organizations. Research the topic of software piracy and write a report that explains the following:
   a. What software piracy is
   b. How organizations attempt to prevent their employees from engaging in software piracy
   c. How software piracy violations are discovered
   d. The consequences to both individual employees and to organizations who commit software piracy

8. Practice encryption.

   Required

   a. Use your computer operating system's built-in encryption capability to encrypt a file. Create another user account on your computer, and log in as that user. Which of the following actions can you perform?

      1. Open the file
      2. Copy the file to a USB drive
      3. Move the file to a USB drive
      4. Rename the file
      5. Delete the file

   b. TruCrypt is one of several free software programs that can be used to encrypt files stored on a USB drive. Download and install a copy of TruCrypt (or another program recommended by your professor) from the course web site. Use it to encrypt some files on a USB drive. Compare its functionality to that of the built-in encryption functionality provided by your computer's operating system.

9. Research the problem of identity theft and write a report that explains the following:
   a. Whether the problem of identity theft is increasing or decreasing
   b. What kind of identity theft protection services or insurance products are available. Compare and contrast at least two products

10. Certificate authorities are an important part of a public key infrastructure (PKI). Research at least two certificate authorities, and write a report that explains the different types of digital certificates that they offer.

11. Obtain a copy of COBIT (available at www.isaca.org), and read the control objectives that relate to encryption (DS5.8 and DS5.11). What are the essential control procedures that organizations should implement when using encryption?

Case 1 Protecting Privacy of Tax Returns

The department of taxation in your state is developing a new computer system for processing individual and corporate income-tax returns. The new system features direct data input and inquiry capabilities. Taxpayers are identified by Social Security number (for individuals) and federal tax identification number (for corporations). The new system should be fully implemented in time for the next tax season.

The new system will serve three primary purposes:

1. Tax return data will automatically input into the system either directly (if the taxpayer files electronically) or by a clerk at central headquarters scanning a paper return received in the mail.
2. The returns will be processed using the main computer facilities at central headquarters. Processing will include four steps:
   a. Verifying mathematical accuracy
   b. Auditing the reasonableness of deductions, tax due, and so on, through the use of edit routines, which also include a comparison of current and prior years' data
   c. Identifying returns that should be considered for audit by department revenue agents
   d. Issuing refund checks to taxpayers

3. Inquiry services. A taxpayer will be allowed to determine the status of his or her return or get information from the last three years' returns by calling or visiting one of the department's regional offices or by accessing the department's Web site and entering his or her Social Security number.

The state commissioner of taxation and the state attorney general are concerned about protecting the privacy of personal information submitted by taxpayers. They want to have potential problems identified *before* the system is fully developed and implemented so that the proper controls can be incorporated into the new system.

Required

Describe the potential privacy problems that could arise in each of the following three areas of processing, and recommend the corrective action(s) to solve each problem identified:

   a. Data input
   b. Processing of returns
   c. Data inquiry

(CMA examination, adapted)

Case 2 Generally Accepted Privacy Principles

Obtain the practitioner's version of Generally Accepted Privacy Principles from the AICPA's Web site (www.aicpa.org). Use it to answer the following questions:

1. What is the difference between confidentiality and privacy?
2. How many categories of personal information exist? Why?
3. In terms of the principle of choice and consent, what does GAPP recommend concerning opt-in versus opt-out?
4. Can organizations outsource their responsibility for privacy?
5. What does principle 1 state concerning top management's and the board of directors' responsibility for privacy?
6. What does principle 1 state concerning the use of customers' personal information when organizations test new applications?
7. Obtain a copy of your university's privacy policy statement. Does it satisfy GAPP criterion 2.2.3? Why?

8. What does GAPP principle 3 say about the use of cookies?
9. What are some examples of practices that violate management criterion 4.2.2?
10. What does management criterion 5.2.2 state concerning retention of customers' personal information? How can organizations satisfy this criterion?
11. What does management criterion 5.2.3 state concerning the disposal of personal information? How can organizations satisfy this criterion?
12. What does management criterion 6.2.2 state concerning access? What controls should organizations use to achieve this objective?
13. According to GAPP principle 7, what should organizations do if they wish to share personal information they collect with a third party?
14. What does GAPP principle 8 state concerning the use of encryption?
15. What is the relationship between GAPP principles 9 and 10?

AIS IN ACTION SOLUTIONS

Quiz Key

1. Which of the following statements is true?
   a. Encryption is sufficient to protect confidentiality and privacy. (Incorrect. Encryption is not sufficient, because sensitive information cannot be encrypted at all times—it must be decrypted during processing, when displayed on a monitor, or included in a printed report.)
   ▶ b. Cookies are text files that only store information. They cannot perform any actions. (Correct. Cookies are text files, not executable programs. They can, however, store sensitive information, so they should be protected.)
   c. The controls for protecting confidentiality are not effective for protecting privacy. (Incorrect. The same set of controls—encryption, access controls, and training—can be used to protect both confidentiality and privacy.)
   d. All of the above are true. (Incorrect. Statements a and c are false.)

2. A digital signature is _____.
   ▶ a. created by hashing a document and then encrypting the hash with the signer's private key (Correct. Creating a hash provides a way to verify the integrity of a document, and encrypting it with the signer's private key provides a way to prove that the sender created the document.)
   b. created by hashing a document and then encrypting the hash with the signer's public key (Incorrect. Anyone could encrypt something with the signer's public key. Therefore, this process cannot be used to prove who created a document.)
   c. created by hashing a document and then encrypting the hash with the signer's symmetric key (Incorrect. A symmetric key is possessed by more than one party, so encrypting something with it does not provide a means to prove who created a document).
   d. none of the above (Incorrect. Only choices b and c are incorrect; choice a is correct.)

3. Able wants to send a file to Baker over the Internet and protect the file so that only Baker can read it and can verify that it came from Able. What should Able do?
   a. Encrypt the file using Able's public key, and then encrypt it again using Baker's private key. (Incorrect. Able does not know Baker's private key.)
   b. Encrypt the file using Able's private key, and then encrypt it again using Baker's private key. (Incorrect. Able does not know Baker's private key.)
   c. Encrypt the file using Able's public key, and then encrypt it again using Baker's public key. (Incorrect. Baker does not know Able's private key and therefore cannot decrypt the file encrypted with Able's public key.)
   ▶ d. Encrypt the file using Able's private key, and then encrypt it again using Baker's public key. (Correct. Encrypting it with Baker's public key means that only Baker can decrypt it. Then, Baker can use Able's public key to decrypt the file—if the result is understandable, it had to have been created by Able and encrypted with Able's private key.)

4. Which of the following statements is true?
   a. Encryption and hashing are both reversible (can be decoded). (Incorrect. Hashing is irreversible.)
   ▶ b. Encryption is reversible, but hashing is not. (Correct. Encryption can be reversed to decrypt the ciphertext, but hashing cannot be reversed.)
   c. Hashing is reversible, but encryption is not. (Incorrect. Hashing is irreversible, but encryption is reversible.)
   d. Neither hashing nor encryption is reversible. (Incorrect. Encryption is reversible, a process called decryption.)

5. Confidentiality focuses on protecting _____.
   a. personal information collected from customers (Incorrect. Protecting customers' personal information relates to the principle of privacy.)

    b. a company's annual report stored on its Web site (Incorrect. A company's annual report is meant to be available to the public.)

▶ **c.** merger and acquisition plans (Correct. Merger and acquisition plans are sensitive information that should not be made public until the deal is consummated.)

    d. all of the above (Incorrect. Statements a and b are false.)

6. Which of the following statements about obtaining consent to collect and use a customer's personal information is true?

    a. The default policy in Europe is opt-out, but in the United States the default is opt-in. (Incorrect. The default policy in Europe is opt-in, and in the United States it is opt-out.)

▶ **b.** The default policy in Europe is opt-in, but in the United States the default is opt-out. (Correct.)

    c. The default policy in both Europe and the United States is opt-in. (Incorrect. The default policy in Europe is opt-in, and in the United States it is opt-out.)

    d. The default policy in both Europe and the United States is opt-out. (Incorrect. The default policy in Europe is opt-in and in the U.S. it is opt-out.)

7. One of the ten Generally Accepted Privacy Principles concerns security. According to GAPP, what is the nature of the relationship between security and privacy?

    a. Privacy is a necessary, but not sufficient, precondition to effective security. (Incorrect. Security is one of the ten criteria in GAPP because you need security in order to have privacy. Security alone, however, is not enough—that is why there are nine other criteria in GAPP.)

    b. Privacy is both necessary and sufficient to effective security. (Incorrect. Security is one of the ten criteria in GAPP because you need security in order to have privacy. Security alone, however, is not enough—that is why there are nine other criteria in GAPP.)

▶ **c.** Security is a necessary, but not sufficient, precondition to protect privacy. (Correct.)

    d. Security is both necessary and sufficient to protect privacy. (Incorrect. Security is one of the ten criteria in GAPP because you need security in order to have privacy. Security alone, however, is not enough—that is why there are nine other criteria in GAPP.)

8. Which of the following statements is true?

    a. Symmetric encryption is faster than asymmetric encryption and can be used to provide nonrepudiation of contracts. (Incorrect. Symmetric encryption cannot be used for nonrepudiation because both parties share the key, so there is no way to prove who created and encrypted a document.)

▶ **b.** Symmetric encryption is faster than asymmetric encryption but cannot be used to provide nonrepudiation of contracts. (Correct. Symmetric encryption is faster than asymmetric encryption, but it cannot be used for nonrepudiation; the key is shared by both parties, so there is no way to prove who created and encrypted a document.)

    c. Asymmetric encryption is faster than symmetric encryption and can be used to provide nonrepudiation of contracts. (Incorrect. Symmetric encryption is faster than asymmetric encryption.)

    d. Asymmetric encryption is faster than symmetric encryption but cannot be used to provide nonrepudiation of contracts. (Incorrect. Symmetric encryption is faster than asymmetric encryption. Also, asymmetric encryption can be used to provide nonrepudiation, because encrypting a contract with the creator's private key proves that the encrypter did indeed create the contract.)

9. Which of the following statements is true?

    a. VPNs protect the confidentiality of information while it is in transit over the Internet. (Incorrect. This statement is true, but so are the others.)

    b. Encryption limits firewalls' ability to filter traffic. (Incorrect. This statement is true—firewalls cannot apply their rules to encrypted packets—but so are the others.)

    c. A digital certificate contains that entity's public key. (Incorrect. This statement is true, but so are the others.)

▶ **d.** All of the above are true. (Correct. All three statements are true.)

10. Which of the following can organizations use to protect the privacy of a customer's personal information when giving programmers a realistic data set with which to test a new application?

   a. digital signature (Incorrect. A digital signature is used for nonrepudiation. However, because it is an encrypted hash, it cannot be used to test programming logic.)

   b. digital watermark (Incorrect. A digital watermark is used to identify proprietary data, but it does not protect privacy.)

   c. data loss prevention (Incorrect. Data loss prevention is designed to protect confidentiality by filtering outgoing messages to prevent sensitive data from leaving the company.)

   ▶ d. data masking (Correct. Masking replaces actual values with fake ones, but the result is still the same type of data, which can then be used to test program logic.)

Chapter 10

Information Systems Controls for Systems Reliability—Part 3: Processing Integrity and Availability

Information Systems Controls for Systems Reliability—Part 3: Processing Integrity and Availability

Learning Objectives

After studying this chapter, you should be able to:

1. Identify and explain controls designed to ensure processing integrity.
2. Identify and explain controls designed to ensure systems availability.

INTEGRATIVE CASE NORTHWEST INDUSTRIES

Jason Scott began his review of Northwest Industries' processing integrity and availability controls by meeting with the CFO and the CIO. The CFO mentioned that she had just read an article about how spreadsheet errors had caused several companies to make poor decisions that cost them millions of dollars. She wanted to be sure that such problems did not happen to Northwest Industries. She also stressed the need to continue to improve the monthly closing process so that management would have more timely information. The CIO expressed concern about the company's lack of planning for how to continue business operations in the event of a major natural disaster such as the recent floods in the Midwest, which had forced several small businesses to close. Jason thanked them for their input and set about collecting evidence about the effectiveness of Northwest Industries' procedures for ensuring processing integrity and availability.

Introduction

This chapter addresses two principles of reliable systems: processing integrity and availability. We conclude with a discussion of the importance of controlling changes to systems to ensure that the

- Authorized ID numbers (such as employee numbers) can contain a *check digit* that is computed from the other digits. For example, the system could assign each new employee a nine-digit number, then calculate a tenth digit from the original nine and append that calculated number to the original nine to form a ten-digit ID number. Data entry devices can then be programmed to perform *check digit verification* by using the first nine digits to calculate the tenth digit each time an ID number is entered. If an error is made in entering any of the ten digits, the calculation made on the first nine digits will not match the tenth, or check digit.

The preceding data entry tests are used for both batch processing and online real-time processing. Additional data input controls differ for the two processing methods.

ADDITIONAL BATCH PROCESSING DATA ENTRY CONTROLS

- Batch processing works more efficiently if the transactions are sorted so that the accounts affected are in the same sequence as records in the master file. For example, accurate batch processing of sales transactions to update customer account balances requires that the transactions first be sorted by customer account number. A *sequence check* tests whether a batch of input data is in the proper numerical or alphabetical sequence.
- An error log that identifies data input errors (date, cause, problem) facilitates timely review and resubmission of transactions that cannot be processed.
- *Batch totals* summarize important values for a batch of input records. The following are three commonly used batch totals:
    1. A *financial total* sums a field that contains monetary values, such as the total dollar amount of all sales for a batch of sales transactions.
    2. A *hash total* sums a nonfinancial numeric field, such as the total of the quantity ordered field in a batch of sales transactions.
    3. A *record count* is the number of records in a batch.

These batch totals are calculated and stored by the system when data is initially entered. They will be recalculated later to verify that all input was processed correctly.

ADDITIONAL ONLINE DATA ENTRY CONTROLS

- *Prompting*, in which the system requests each input data item and waits for an acceptable response, ensures that all necessary data are entered (i.e., prompting is an online completeness check).
- *Closed-loop verification* checks the accuracy of input data by using it to retrieve and display other related information. For example, if a clerk enters an account number, the system could retrieve and display the account name so that the user could verify that the correct account number had been entered.
- A transaction log includes a detailed record of all transactions, including a unique transaction identifier, the date and time of entry, and who entered the transaction. If an online file is damaged, the transaction log can be used to reconstruct the file. If a malfunction temporarily shuts down the system, the transaction log can be used to ensure that transactions are not lost or entered twice.

Processing Controls

Controls are also needed to ensure that data is processed correctly. Important processing controls include the following:

- *Data matching.* In certain cases, two or more items of data must be matched before an action can take place. For example, before paying a vendor, the system should verify that information on the vendor invoice matches information on both the purchase order and the receiving report.
- *File labels.* File labels need to be checked to ensure that the correct and most current files are being updated. Both external labels that are readable by humans and internal labels that are written in machine-readable form on the data recording media should be used. Two important types of internal labels are header and trailer records. The *header record* is located at the beginning of each file and contains the file name, expiration date, and other

identification data. The *trailer record* is located at the end of the file and contains the batch totals calculated during input. Programs should be designed to read the header record *prior* to processing, to ensure that the correct file is being updated. Programs should also be designed to read the information in the trailer record *after* processing, to verify that all input records have been correctly processed.

- *Recalculation of batch totals.* Batch totals should be recomputed as each transaction record is processed, and the total for the batch should then be compared to the values in the trailer record. Any discrepancies indicate a processing error. Often, the nature of the discrepancy provides a clue about the type of error that occurred. For example, if the recomputed record count is smaller than the original, one or more transaction records were not processed. Conversely, if the recomputed record count is larger than the original, either additional unauthorized transactions were processed, or some transaction records were processed twice. If a financial or hash total discrepancy is evenly divisible by 9, the likely cause is a *transposition error*, in which two adjacent digits were inadvertently reversed (e.g., 46 instead of 64). Transposition errors may appear to be trivial but can have enormous financial consequences. For example, consider the effect of misrecording the interest rate on a loan as 6.4% instead of 4.6%.

- *Cross-footing and zero-balance tests.* Often totals can be calculated in multiple ways. For example, in spreadsheets a grand total can be computed either by summing a column of row totals or by summing a row of column totals. These two methods should produce the same result. A *cross-footing balance test* compares the results produced by each method to verify accuracy. A *zero-balance test* applies this same logic to control accounts. For example, the payroll clearing account is debited for the total gross pay of all employees in a particular time period. It is then credited for the amount of all labor costs allocated to various expense categories. The payroll clearing account should have a zero balance after both sets of entries have been made; a nonzero balance indicates a processing error.

- *Write-protection mechanisms.* These protect against overwriting or erasing of data files stored on magnetic media. Write-protection mechanisms have long been used to protect master files from accidentally being damaged. Technological innovations also necessitate the use of write-protection mechanisms to protect the integrity of transaction data. For example, radio frequency identification (RFID) tags used to track inventory need to be write-protected so that unscrupulous customers cannot change the price of merchandise.

- *Concurrent update controls.* Errors can occur when two or more users attempt to update the same record simultaneously. *Concurrent update controls* prevent such errors by locking out one user until the system has finished processing the transaction entered by the other.

Output Controls

Careful checking of system output provides additional control over processing integrity. Important output controls include the following:

- *User review of output.* Users should carefully examine system output to verify that it is reasonable, that it is complete, and that they are the intended recipients.
- *Reconciliation procedures.* Periodically, all transactions and other system updates should be reconciled to control reports, file status/update reports, or other control mechanisms. In addition, general ledger accounts should be reconciled to subsidiary account totals on a regular basis. For example, the balance of the inventory control account in the general ledger should equal the sum of the item balances in the inventory database. The same is true for the accounts receivable, capital assets, and accounts payable control accounts.
- *External data reconciliation.* Database totals should periodically be reconciled with data maintained outside the system. For example, the number of employee records in the payroll file can be compared with the total number of employees in the human resources database to detect attempts to add fictitious employees to the payroll database. Similarly, inventory on hand should be physically counted and compared to the quantity on hand recorded in the database.

- *Data transmission controls.* Organizations also need to implement controls designed to minimize the risk of data transmission errors. Whenever the receiving device detects a data transmission error, it requests the sending device to retransmit that data. Generally, this happens automatically, and the user is unaware that it has occurred. For example, the Transmission Control Protocol (TCP) assigns a sequence number to each packet and uses that information to verify that all packets have been received and to reassemble them in the correct order. Two other common data transmission controls are checksums and parity bits.
  1. *Checksums.* When data are transmitted, the sending device can calculate a hash of the file, called a *checksum*. The receiving device performs the same calculation and sends the result to the sending device. If the two hashes agree, the transmission is presumed to be accurate. Otherwise, the file is resent.
  2. *Parity bits.* Computers represent characters as a set of binary digits called bits. Each bit has two possible values: 0 or 1. Many computers use a seven-bit coding scheme, which is more than enough to represent the 26 letters in the English alphabet (both upper- and lowercase), the numbers 0 through 9, and a variety of special symbols ($, %, &, etc.). A **parity bit** is an extra digit added to the beginning of every character that can be used to check transmission accuracy. Two basic schemes are referred to as *even parity* and *odd parity*. In even parity, the parity bit is set so that each character has an even number of bits with the value 1; in odd parity, the parity bit is set so that an odd number of bits in the character have the value 1. For example, the digits 5 and 7 can be represented by the seven-bit patterns 0000101 and 0000111, respectively. An even parity system would set the parity bit for 5 to 0, so that it would be transmitted as 00000101 (because the binary code for 5 already has two bits with the value 1). The parity bit for 7 would be set to 1 so that it would be transmitted as 10000111 (because the binary code for 7 has 3 bits with the value 1). The receiving device performs **parity checking**, which entails verifying that the proper number of bits are set to the value 1 in each character received.

Illustrative Example: Credit Sales Processing

We now use a credit sale to illustrate how many of the application controls that have been discussed actually function. The following transaction data are used: sales order number, customer account number, inventory item number, quantity sold, sale price, and delivery date. If the customer purchases more than one product, there will be multiple inventory item numbers, quantities sold, and prices associated with each sales transaction. Processing these transactions includes the following steps: (1) entering and editing the transaction data; (2) updating the customer and inventory records (the amount of the credit purchase is added to the customer's balance; for each inventory item, the quantity sold is subtracted from the quantity on hand); and (3) preparing and distributing shipping and/or billing documents. Examples for both batch and online processing are presented.

BATCH PROCESSING INTEGRITY CONTROLS   Figure 1 shows the application controls that should be applied at each step of processing a batch of credit sales transactions:

1. *Prepare batch totals.* The sum of all sales amounts is calculated as a financial total and recorded on batch control forms that accompany each group of sales documents.
2. *Deliver the transactions to the computer operations department for processing.* Each batch is checked for proper authorization and recorded in a control log.
3. *Enter the transaction data into the system.* As data are entered, the system performs several preliminary validation tests. Check digit verification identifies transactions with invalid account numbers or invalid inventory item numbers. Field checks verify that the quantity ordered and price fields contain only numbers and that the date field follows the correct MM/DD/YYYY format. A sequence check on sales order numbers and reconciliation of the batch totals calculated in step 1 verifies that no transactions are missing.

   A control report lists all data entry errors. Data entry errors that occurred because an operator read a source document incorrectly or accidentally struck the wrong key can usually be corrected immediately after being detected. Incorrect source data, such as an

FIGURE 1

Application Controls in Batch Processing of Credit Sales

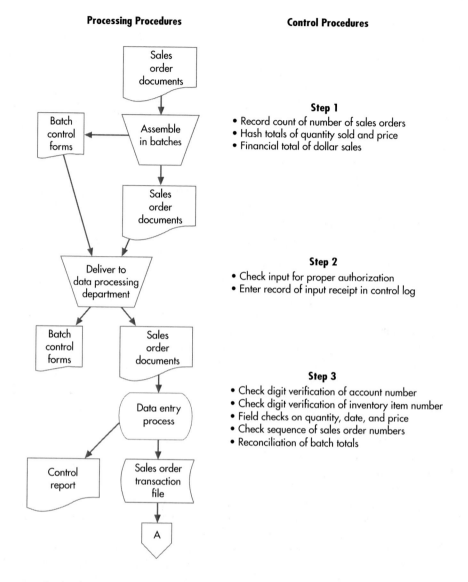

Processing Procedures

Control Procedures

Step 1
- Record count of number of sales orders
- Hash totals of quantity sold and price
- Financial total of dollar sales

Step 2
- Check input for proper authorization
- Enter record of input receipt in control log

Step 3
- Check digit verification of account number
- Check digit verification of inventory item number
- Field checks on quantity, date, and price
- Check sequence of sales order numbers
- Reconciliation of batch totals

unauthorized sales transaction or an invalid account number, are more problematic and should be returned to the sales department for correction.

4. *Sort and edit the transaction file.* The transaction file is now sorted by customer account number. Additional validation checks are performed, including sign checks that both the quantity ordered and price fields contain positive numbers, and a range check on promised delivery dates to verify that it is not earlier than the date of the order nor later than the company's advertised policies. Rejected transactions are listed on a control report along with the computed batch totals. Data control reconciles the batch totals, investigates and corrects any errors, and submits the corrected transactions for processing.

5. *Update the master files.* The sales transaction file is processed against customer (accounts receivable) and inventory databases or master files. The operator reads the external label, and the program reads the internal header record to ensure that the correct master file is being updated. Sales transactions with customer numbers or item numbers that do not exist in the corresponding master file are not processed; instead, they are entered on an error report. After a sales transaction is processed, a sign check is performed to ensure that the quantity-on-hand field in the inventory master record is not negative. Tests are also performed to ensure that sales prices fall within normal ranges, that the order does not exceed the customer's credit limit, and that the quantity ordered is reasonable given the nature of the item and the customer's order history. Redundant data checks—for example, comparing inventory item number and description—are used to ensure that the correct master file

Processing Procedures　　　　**Control Procedures**　　　　**FIGURE 1** Continued

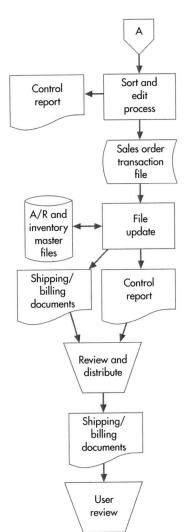

Step 4
- Sequence check on account number
- Limit checks on quantity and price
- Range check on delivery date
- Completeness test on entire record
- Reconciliation of batch totals
- Review errors identified by edit checks
- Investigation and correction of erroneous input

Step 5
- Security of master files in file library
- Protection of master files with file labels
- Maintenance of backup copies of master files
- Validity check of customer account number
- Validity check of inventory item number
- Sign check of inventory quantity on hand
- Limit check of sale amount versus credit limit
- Range check on sale price
- Reasonableness test of quantity ordered
- Redundant data check on customer data
- Redundant data check on inventory data

Step 6
- Reconciliation of batch totals
- Review of errors identified by edit checks
- Investigation and correction of erroneous input
- Distribution of billing and shipping documents
- Recording of output distribution in control log
- Return of master files to file library

Step 7
- Visual inspection of output
- Reconciliation of batch totals

record is updated. The total change in customer balances is computed; this financial total is compared to the total sales amount of all transactions that were processed.

6. *Prepare and distribute output.* Outputs include billing and/or shipping documents and a control report. The control report contains batch totals accumulated during the file update run and a list of transactions rejected by the update program.

7. *User review.* Users in the shipping and billing departments perform a limited review of the documents for incomplete data or other obvious deficiencies. They also compare the system-generated batch totals to those calculated in step 1 to verify that all transactions were processed.

ONLINE PROCESSING INTEGRITY CONTROLS Online real-time processing records each credit sales transaction individually as it occurs (Figure 2). This enables more timely detection and correction of errors. The various application controls discussed in this chapter are applied at each stage (input, processing, output) of online transaction processing, as follows.

Online Data Entry Controls

- When an employee accesses the online system, logical access controls confirm the identity of the data entry device (personal computer, terminal) and the validity of the employee's user ID number and password.

FIGURE 2

Application Controls in Online Processing of Credit Sales

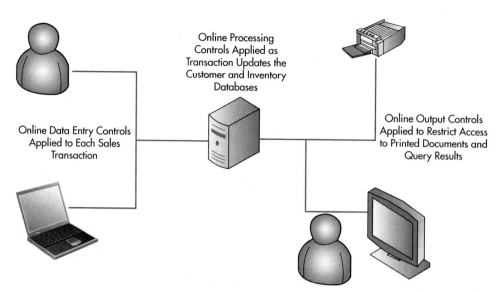

Online Processing Controls Applied as Transaction Updates the Customer and Inventory Databases

Online Data Entry Controls Applied to Each Sales Transaction

Online Output Controls Applied to Restrict Access to Printed Documents and Query Results

- A compatibility test ensures that the employee is authorized to perform that task.
- The system automatically assigns the transaction the next sequential sales order number and the current date as the date of the invoice.
- The system prompts for all required input (completeness test). After each prompt, the system waits for a response.
- Each response is tested using one or more of the following controls: validity checks (valid customer and inventory numbers), field and sign checks (only positive, numeric characters in the quantity, date, and price fields), and limit or range checks (delivery date versus current date).
- When the customer number is entered, the system retrieves the corresponding customer name from the database and displays it on the screen (closed-loop verification). The operator visually examines the customer name. If it matches the name on the sales order document, the operator signals the system to proceed with the transaction. If not, the operator rechecks the customer number and enters the correct value.
- When the inventory item number is entered, the system and the operator go through the same procedures as they do with the customer number.

Online Processing Controls. Because the file update program accesses the customer and inventory database records, it performs additional input validation tests by comparing data in each transaction record with data in the corresponding database record. These tests often include the following:

- Validity checks on the customer and inventory item numbers
- Sign checks on inventory-on-hand balances (after subtracting quantities sold)
- Limit checks that compare each customer's total amount due with the credit limit
- Range checks on the sale price of each item sold relative to the permissible range of prices for that item
- Reasonableness tests on the quantity sold of each item relative to normal sales quantities for that customer and that item

Online Output Controls. Outputs of this process include billing and/or shipping documents and a control report. The following output controls are used:

- Billing and shipping documents are forwarded electronically only to preauthorized users.
- Users in the shipping and billing departments perform a limited review of the documents by visually inspecting them for incomplete data or other obvious errors.
- The control report is sent automatically to its intended recipients, or the recipients can query the system for the report. If they query the system, logical access controls confirm the identity of the device making the query and the validity of the user's ID number and password.

298

FOCUS 1 — Ensuring the Processing Integrity of Electronic Voting

Electronic voting may eliminate some of the types of problems that occur with manual or mechanical voting. For example, electronic voting software could use limit checks to prevent voters from attempting to select more candidates than permitted in a particular race. A completeness check would identify a voter's failure to make a choice in every race, and closed-loop verification could then be used to verify whether that was intentional. (This would eliminate the "hanging chad" problem created when voters fail to punch out the hole completely on a paper ballot.)

Nevertheless, there are concerns about electronic voting, particularly its audit trail capabilities. At issue is the ability to verify that only properly registered voters did indeed vote and that they voted only once. Although no one disagrees with the need for such authentication, there is debate over whether electronic voting machines can create adequate audit trails without risking the loss of voters' anonymity.

There is also debate about the overall security and reliability of electronic voting. Some security experts suggest that election officials should adopt the methods used by the state of Nevada to ensure that electronic gambling machines operate honestly and accurately, which include the following:

- **Access to the source code.** The Nevada Gaming Control Board keeps copies of all software. It is illegal for casinos to use any unregistered software. Similarly, security experts recommend that the government should keep copies of the source code of electronic voting software.
- **Hardware checks.** Frequent on-site spot checks of the computer chips in gambling machines are made to verify compliance with the Nevada Gaming Control Board's records. Similar tests should be done to voting machines.
- **Tests of physical security.** The Nevada Gaming Control Board extensively tests how machines react to stun guns and large electric shocks. Voting machines should be similarly tested.
- **Background checks.** All gambling machine manufacturers are carefully scrutinized and registered. Similar checks should be performed on voting machine manufacturers, as well as election software developers.

The preceding example illustrated the use of application controls to ensure the integrity of processing business transactions. Focus 1 explains the importance of processing integrity controls in nonbusiness settings, too.

Processing Integrity Controls in Spreadsheets

Most organizations have thousands of spreadsheets that are used to support decision making. The importance of spreadsheets to financial reporting is reflected in the fact that the ISACA document *IT Control Objectives for Sarbanes-Oxley* contains a separate appendix that specifically addresses processing integrity controls that should be used in spreadsheets. Yet, because spreadsheets are almost always developed by end users, they seldom contain adequate application controls. Therefore, it is not surprising that many organizations have experienced serious problems caused by spreadsheet errors. For example, an August 17, 2007, article in *CIO Magazine*[1] describes how spreadsheet errors caused companies to lose money, issue erroneous dividend payout announcements, and misreport financial results.

These kinds of costly mistakes could have been prevented by careful testing of spreadsheets before use. Although most spreadsheet software contains built-in "audit" features that can easily detect common errors, spreadsheets intended to support important decisions need more thorough testing to detect subtle errors. Nevertheless, a survey of finance professionals[2] indicates that only 2% of firms use multiple people to examine every spreadsheet cell, which is the only reliable way to effectively detect spreadsheet errors. It is especially important to check for *hardwiring*, where formulas contain specific numeric values (e.g., sales tax = 8.5% × A33), instead of referencing a cell that contains the current value for that variable (e.g., sales tax = A8 × A33). The problem with hardwiring is that the spreadsheet initially produces correct answers, but when the hardwired variable (e.g., the sales tax rate in the preceding example) changes, the formula may not be corrected.

---

[1] Thomas Wailgum, "Eight of the Worst Spreadsheet Blunders," *CIO Magazine* (August 2007), available at www.cio.com/article/131500/Eight_of_the_Worst_Spreadsheet_Errors
[2] Raymond R. Panko, "Controlling Spreadsheets," *Information Systems Control Journal-Online* (2007): Volume 1. Accessible at www.isaca.org/publications

Availability

Interruptions to business processes due to the unavailability of systems or information can cause significant financial losses. Consequently, COBIT section DS 4 addresses the importance of ensuring that systems and information are available for use whenever needed. The primary objective is to minimize the risk of system downtime. It is impossible, however, to completely eliminate the risk of downtime. Therefore, organizations also need controls designed to enable quick resumption of normal operations after an event disrupts system availability. Table 2 summarizes the key controls related to these two objectives.

Minimizing Risk of System Downtime

Organizations can undertake a variety of actions to minimize the risk of system downtime. COBIT control objective DS 13.5 identifies the need for preventive maintenance, such as cleaning disk drives and properly storing magnetic and optical media, to reduce the risk of hardware and software failure. The use of redundant components provides *fault tolerance*, which is the ability of a system to continue functioning in the event that a particular component fails. For example, many organizations use *redundant arrays of independent drives (RAID)* instead of just one disk drive. With RAID, data is written to multiple disk drives simultaneously. Thus, if one disk drive fails, the data can be readily accessed from another.

COBIT section DS 12 addresses the importance of locating and designing the data centers housing mission-critical servers and databases so as to minimize the risks associated with natural and human-caused disasters. Common design features include the following:

- Raised floors provide protection from damage caused by flooding.
- Fire detection and suppression devices reduce the likelihood of fire damage.
- Adequate air-conditioning systems reduce the likelihood of damage to computer equipment due to overheating or humidity.
- Cables with special plugs that cannot be easily removed reduce the risk of system damage due to accidental unplugging of the device.
- Surge-protection devices provide protection against temporary power fluctuations that might otherwise cause computers and other network equipment to crash.
- An *uninterruptible power supply (UPS)* system provides protection in the event of a prolonged power outage, using battery power to enable the system to operate long enough to back up critical data and safely shut down. (However, it is important to regularly inspect and test the batteries in a UPS to ensure that it will function when needed.)
- Physical access controls reduce the risk of theft or damage.

Training can also reduce the risk of system downtime. Well-trained operators are less likely to make mistakes and will know how to recover, with minimal damage, from errors they do commit. That is why COBIT control objective DS 13.1 stresses the importance of defining and documenting operational procedures and ensuring that IT staff understand their responsibilities.

System downtime can also occur because of computer malware (viruses and worms). Therefore, it is important to install, run, and keep current antivirus and anti-spyware programs. These programs should be automatically invoked not only to scan e-mail, but also any removable

TABLE 2 Availability: Objectives and Key Controls

Objective	Key Controls
1. To minimize risk of system downtime	• Preventive maintenance • Fault tolerance • Data center location and design • Training • Patch management and antivirus software
2. Quick and complete recovery and resumption of normal operations	• Backup procedures • Disaster recovery plan (DRP) • Business continuity plan (BCP)

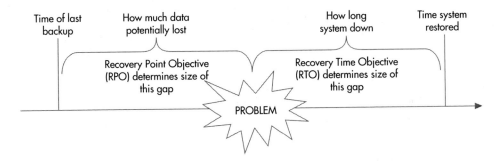

FIGURE 3

Relationship of Recovery Point Objective and Recovery Time Objective

computer media (CDs, DVDs, USB drives, etc.) that are brought into the organization. A patch management system provides additional protection by ensuring that vulnerabilities that can be exploited by malware are fixed in a timely manner.

Recovery and Resumption of Normal Operations

The preventive controls discussed in the preceding section can minimize, but not entirely eliminate, the risk of system downtime. Hardware malfunctions, software problems, or human error can cause data to become inaccessible. That's why backup procedures are necessary. A *backup* is an exact copy of the most current version of a database, file, or software program that can be used in the event that the original is no longer available. Natural disasters or terrorist acts can destroy not only data but also the entire information system. That's why organizations also need disaster recovery and business continuity plans.

An organization's backup procedures and disaster recovery and business continuity plans reflect management's answers to two fundamental questions:

1. How much data are we willing to recreate from source documents (if they exist) or potentially lose (if no source documents exist)?
2. How long can the organization function without its information system?

Figure 3 shows the relationship between these two questions. When a problem occurs, data about everything that has happened since the last backup is lost unless it can be reentered into the system. Thus, management's answer to the first question determines the organization's *recovery point objective (RPO)*, which represents the maximum amount of data that the organization is willing to potentially lose. The answer to the second question determines the organization's *recovery time objective (RTO)*, which represents the length of time that the organization is willing to attempt to function without its information system.

For some organizations, the answer to both questions is close to zero. Airlines and financial institutions, for example, cannot operate without their information systems, nor can they afford to lose information about transactions. For such organizations, the goal is not quick recovery from problems, but resiliency. The solution is to employ real-time mirroring. *Real-time mirroring* involves maintaining two copies of the database at two separate data centers at all times and updating both copies in real-time as each transaction occurs. In the event that something happens to one data center, the organization can immediately switch all daily activities to the other.

For other organizations, however, acceptable RPO and RTO may be measured in hours or even days. Achieving those goals requires data backup procedures plus disaster recovery and business continuity plans.

DATA BACKUP PROCEDURES   Data backup procedures are designed to deal with situations where information is not accessible because the relevant files or databases have become corrupted as a result of hardware failure, software problems, or human error, but the information system itself is still functioning. Several different backup procedures exist. A *full backup* is an exact copy of the entire database. Full backups are time-consuming, so most organizations only do full backups weekly and supplement them with daily partial backups. Figure 4 compares the two types of daily partial backups:

1. An *incremental backup* involves copying only the data items that have changed since the last partial backup. This produces a set of incremental backup files, each containing the

FIGURE 4

Comparison of Incremental and Differential Daily Backups

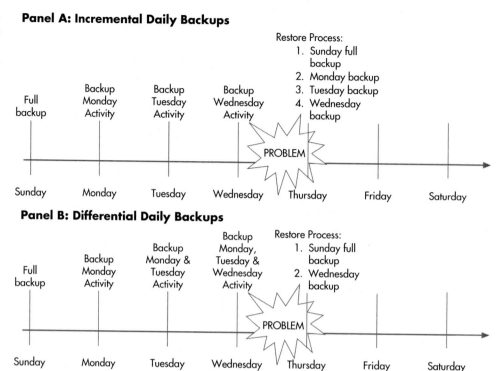

results of one day's transactions. Restoration involves first loading the last full backup and then installing each subsequent incremental backup in the proper sequence.

2. A *differential backup* copies all changes made since the last full backup. Thus, each new differential backup file contains the cumulative effects of all activity since the last full backup. Consequently, except for the first day following a full backup, daily differential backups take longer than incremental backups. Restoration is simpler, however, because the last full backup needs to be supplemented with only the most recent differential backup, instead of a set of daily incremental backup files.

No matter which backup procedure is used, multiple backup copies should be created. One copy can be stored on-site, for use in the event of relatively minor problems, such as failure of a hard drive. In the event of a more serious problem, such as a fire or flood, any backup copies stored on-site will likely be destroyed or inaccessible. Therefore, a second backup copy needs to be stored off-site. These backup files can be transported to the remote storage site either physically (e.g., by courier) or electronically. In either case, the same security controls need to be applied to backup files as are used to protect the original copy of the information. This means that backup copies of sensitive data should be encrypted both in storage and during electronic transmission. Access to backup files also needs to be carefully controlled and monitored.

It is also important to periodically practice restoring a system from its backups. This verifies that the backup procedure is working correctly and that the backup media (tape or disk) can be successfully read by the hardware in use.

Backups are retained for only a relatively short period of time. For example, many organizations maintain only several months of backups. Some information, however, must be stored much longer. An *archive* is a copy of a database, master file, or software that is retained indefinitely as an historical record, usually to satisfy legal and regulatory requirements. As with backups, multiple copies of archives should be made and stored in different locations. Unlike backups, archives are seldom encrypted because their long retention times increase the risk of losing the decryption key. Consequently, physical and logical access controls are the primary means of protecting archive files.

What media should be used for backups and archives, tape or disk? Disk backup is faster, and disks are less easily lost. Tape, however, is cheaper, easier to transport, and more durable. Consequently, many organizations use both media. Data are first backed up to disk, for speed, and then transferred to tape.

Special attention needs to be paid to backing up and archiving e-mail, because it has become an important repository of organizational behavior and information. Indeed, e-mail often contains solutions to specific problems. E-mail also frequently contains information relevant to lawsuits. It may be tempting for an organization to consider a policy of periodically deleting all e-mail, to prevent a plaintiff's attorney from finding a "smoking gun" and to avoid the costs of finding the e-mail requested by the other party. Most experts, however, advise against such policies, because there are likely to be copies of the e-mail stored in archives outside the organization. Therefore, a policy of regularly deleting all e-mail means that the organization will not be able to tell its side of the story; instead, the court (and jury) will only read the e-mail created by the other party to the dispute. There have also been cases where the courts have fined organizations millions of dollars for failing to produce requested e-mail. Therefore, organizations need to back up and archive important e-mail while also periodically purging the large volume of routine, trivial e-mail.

DISASTER RECOVERY AND BUSINESS CONTINUITY PLANNING   Backups are designed to mitigate problems when one or more files or databases become corrupted because of hardware, software, or human error. Disaster recovery and business continuity plans are designed to mitigate more serious problems.

A *disaster recovery plan (DRP)* outlines the procedures to restore an organization's IT function in the event that its data center is destroyed by a natural disaster or act of terrorism. Organizations have three basic options for replacing their IT infrastructure, which includes not just computers, but also network components such as routers and switches, software, data, Internet access, printers, and supplies. The first option is to contract for use of a *cold site*, which is an empty building that is prewired for necessary telephone and Internet access, plus a contract with one or more vendors to provide all necessary equipment within a specified period of time. A cold site still leaves the organization without the use of its information system for a period of time, so it is appropriate only when the organization's RTO is one day or more. A second option is to contract for use of a *hot site*, which is a facility that is not only prewired for telephone and Internet access but also contains all the computing and office equipment the organization needs to perform its essential business activities. A hot site typically results in an RTO of hours.

A problem with both cold and hot sites is that the site provider typically oversells its capacity, under the assumption that at any one time only a few clients will need to use the facility. That assumption is usually warranted. In the event of a major disaster, such as Hurricane Katrina, that affects all organizations in a geographic area, however, some organizations may find that they cannot obtain access to their cold or hot site. Consequently, a third infrastructure replacement option for organizations with a very short RTO is to establish a second data center as a backup and use it to implement real-time mirroring.

A *business continuity plan (BCP)* specifies how to resume not only IT operations, but all business processes, including relocating to new offices and hiring temporary replacements, in the event that a major calamity destroys not only an organization's data center but also its main headquarters. Such planning is important, because more than half of the organizations without a DRP and a BCP never reopen after being forced to close down for more than a few days because of a disaster. Thus, having both a DRP and a BCP can mean the difference between surviving a major catastrophe such as Hurricane Katrina or 9/11 and going out of business. Focus 2 describes how planning helped NASDAQ survive the complete destruction of its offices in the World Trade Center on September 11, 2001.

Simply having a DRP and a BCP, however, is not enough. Both plans must be well documented. The documentation should include not only instructions for notifying appropriate staff and the steps to take to resume operations, but also vendor documentation of all hardware and software. It is especially important to document the numerous modifications made to default configurations, so that the replacement system has the same functionality as the original. Failure to do so can create substantial costs and delays in implementing the recovery process. Detailed operating instructions are also needed, especially if temporary replacements have to be hired. Finally, copies of all documentation need to be stored both on-site and off-site so that it is available when needed.

Periodic testing and revision are probably the most important components of effective disaster recovery and business continuity plans. Most plans fail their initial test because it is impossible

How NASDAQ Recovered from September 11

Thanks to its effective disaster recovery and business continuity plans, NASDAQ was up and running six days after the September 11, 2001, terrorist attack that destroyed the twin towers of the World Trade Center. NASDAQ'S headquarters were located on the 49th and 50th floors of One Liberty Plaza, just across the street from the World Trade Center. When the first plane hit, NASDAQ'S security guards immediately evacuated personnel from the building. Most of the employees were out of the building by the time the second plane crashed into the other tower. Although employees were evacuated from the headquarters and the office in Times Square had temporarily lost telephone service, NASDAQ was able to relocate to a backup center at the nearby Marriott Marquis hotel. Once there, NASDAQ executives went through their list of priorities: first, their employees; next, the physical damage; and last, the trading industry situation.

Effective communication became essential in determining the condition of these priorities. NASDAQ attributes much of its success in communicating and coordinating with the rest of the industry to its dress rehearsals for Y2K. While preparing for the changeover, NASDAQ had regular nationwide teleconferences with all the exchanges. This helped it organize similar conferences after the 9/11 attack. NASDAQ had

already planned for one potential crisis, and this proved helpful in recovering from a different, unexpected, crisis. By prioritizing and teleconferencing, the company was able to quickly identify problems and the traders who would need extra help before NASDAQ could open the market again.

NASDAQ'S extremely redundant and dispersed systems also helped it quickly reopen the market. Executives carried more than one mobile phone so that they could continue to communicate in the event one carrier lost service. Every trader was linked to two of NASDAQ's 20 connection centers located throughout the United States. The centers are connected to each other using two separate paths and sometimes two distinct vendors. Servers are kept in different buildings and have two network topologies. In addition to Manhattan and Times Square, NASDAQ had offices in Maryland and Connecticut. This decentralization allowed it to monitor the regulatory processes throughout the days following the attack. It also lessened the risk of losing all NASDAQ'S senior management.

NASDAQ also invested in interruption insurance to help defer the costs of closing the market. All of this planning and foresight saved NASDAQ from losing what could have been tens of millions of dollars.

to fully anticipate everything that could go wrong. The time to discover such problems is not during an actual emergency, but rather in a setting in which weaknesses can be carefully and thoroughly analyzed and appropriate changes in procedures made. Therefore, disaster recovery and business continuity plans need to be tested on at least an annual basis to ensure that they accurately reflect recent changes in equipment and procedures. It is especially important to test the procedures involved in the transfer of actual operations to cold or hot sites. Finally, DRP and BCP documentation needs to be updated to reflect any changes in procedures made in response to problems identified during tests of those plans.

EFFECTS OF VIRTUALIZATION AND CLOUD COMPUTING   A virtual machine is just a collection of software files. Therefore, if the physical server hosting that machine fails, the files can be installed on another host machine within minutes. Thus, virtualization significantly reduces the time needed to recover (RTO) from hardware problems. Note that virtualization does not eliminate the need for backups; organizations still need to create periodic "snapshots" of desktop and server virtual machines and then store those snapshots on a network drive so that the machines can be recreated. Virtualization can also be used to support real-time mirroring in which two copies of each virtual machine are run in tandem on two separate physical hosts. Every transaction is processed on both virtual machines. If one fails, the other picks up without any break in service.

Cloud computing has both positive and negative effects on availability. Cloud computing typically utilizes banks of redundant servers in multiple locations, thereby reducing the risk that a single catastrophe could result in system downtime and the loss of all data. However, if a public cloud provider goes out of business, it may be difficult, if not impossible, to retrieve any data stored in the cloud. Therefore, a policy of making regular backups and storing those backups somewhere other than with the cloud provider is critical. In addition, accountants need to assess the long-run financial viability of a cloud provider before their organization commits to outsource any of its data or applications to a public cloud.

Change Control

COBIT sections AI 6, AI 7, and DS 9 address different aspects of the critically important topic of change control. Organizations constantly modify their information systems to reflect new business practices and to take advantage of advances in information technology. *Change control* is the formal process used to ensure that modifications to hardware, software, or processes do not reduce systems reliability. In fact, good change control often results in overall *better* operating performance: careful testing prior to implementation reduces the likelihood of making changes that cause system downtime, and thorough documentation facilitates quicker "trouble-shooting" and resolution of any problems that do occur. Companies with a good change control process are also less likely to suffer financial or reputational harm from security incidents.

Effective change control procedures require regularly monitoring for unauthorized changes and sanctioning anyone who intentionally introduces such changes. Other principles of a well-designed change control process include the following:

- All change requests should be documented and follow a standardized format that clearly identifies the nature of the change, the reason for the request, the date of the request, and the outcome of the request.
- All changes should be approved by appropriate levels of management. Approvals should be clearly documented to provide an audit trail. Managers should consult with the CISO or other IT managers about the effects of the proposed changes on systems reliability.
- To assess the impact of the proposed change on all five principles of systems reliability, changes should be thoroughly tested prior to implementation in a separate, nonproduction environment, not the system actually used for daily business processes. (Virtualization technology can be used to reduce the costs of creating a separate testing and development system). As data from old files and databases are entered into new data structures, conversion controls are needed to ensure that the new data storage media are free of errors. The old and new systems should be run in parallel at least once and the results compared to identify discrepancies. Internal auditors should review data conversion processes for accuracy.
- All documentation (program instructions, systems descriptions, backup and disaster recovery plans, etc.) should be updated to reflect authorized changes to the system.
- "Emergency" changes or deviations from standard operating policies must be documented and subjected to a formal review and approval process as soon after implementation as practicable. All emergency changes need to be logged to provide an audit trail.
- "Backout" plans need to be developed for reverting to previous configurations in case approved changes need to be interrupted or abandoned.
- User rights and privileges must be carefully monitored *during* the change process to ensure that proper segregation of duties is maintained.

Probably the most important change control is adequate monitoring and review by top management to ensure that proposed and implemented changes are consistent with the organization's multiyear strategic plan. The objective of this oversight is to make certain that the organization's information system continues to effectively support its strategy. Many organizations create IT steering committees to perform this important monitoring function.

Summary and Case Conclusion

Jason's report assessed the effectiveness of Northwest Industries' controls designed to ensure processing integrity. To minimize data entry, and the opportunity for mistakes, Northwest Industries mailed turnaround documents to customers, which were returned with their payments. All data entry was done online, with extensive use of input validation routines to ensure the accuracy of the information entering the system. Managers reviewed output for reasonableness, and the accuracy of key components of financial reports was regularly cross-validated with independent sources. For example, inventory was counted quarterly, and the results of the physical counts were reconciled to the quantities stored in the system.

Jason was concerned about the effectiveness of controls designed to ensure systems availability, however. He noted that although Northwest Industries had developed a disaster recovery and business continuity plan, those plans had not been reviewed or updated for three years. Of even greater concern was the fact that many portions of the plan, including arrangements for a cold site located in California, had never been tested. Jason's biggest concern, however, related to backup procedures. All files were backed up weekly, on Saturdays, onto DVDs, and incremental backups were made each night, but no one had ever practiced restoring the data. In addition, the backups were not encrypted, and one copy was stored on-site in the main server room on a shelf by the door.

Jason also documented evidence of weaknesses related to change control. One point of concern was the finding that "emergency" changes made during the past year were not documented. Another was the fact that in order to save money, Northwest Industries gave programmers access to its transaction processing system to make changes, rather than using a separate testing and development system.

Jason concluded his report with specific recommendations to address the weaknesses he had found. He recommended that Northwest Industries immediately test its backup restoration procedures and encrypt its backup files. Jason also recommended testing the DRP and BCP plans. Another recommendation was to purchase a server that would use virtualization software to create a testing and development system and restrict programmers' access to only that virtual system. Finally, he suggested the CIO should assign someone to update the documentation to record the effects of "emergency changes" made during the past year and implement procedures to ensure that all future changes be documented. Jason felt confident that once those recommendations were implemented, management could be reasonably assured that Northwest Industries' information systems had satisfied the AICPA's Trust Services framework criteria and principles for systems reliability.

Key Terms

turnaround document	header record	recovery point objective
field check	trailer record	(RPO)
sign check	transposition error	recovery time objective
limit check	cross-footing balance	(RTO)
range check	test	real-time mirroring
size check	zero-balance test	incremental backup
completeness check	concurrent update	differential backup
validity check	controls	archive
reasonableness test	checksum	disaster recovery plan
check digit	parity bit	(DRP)
check digit verification	parity checking	cold site
sequence check	fault tolerance	hot site
batch totals	redundant arrays of	business continuity plan
financial total	independent drives	(BCP)
hash total	(RAID)	change control
record count	uninterruptible power supply	
prompting	(UPS)	
closed-loop verification	backup	

AIS IN ACTION

Chapter Quiz

1. Which of the following measures the amount of data that might be potentially lost as a result of a system failure?
   a. recovery time objective (RTO)
   b. recovery point objective (RPO)
   c. disaster recovery plan (DRP)
   d. business continuity plan (BCP)

2. Which data entry application control would detect and prevent entry of alphabetic characters as the price of an inventory item?
   a. field check
   b. limit check
   c. reasonableness check
   d. sign check

3. Which of the following controls would prevent entry of a nonexistent customer number in a sales transaction?
   a. field check
   b. completeness check
   c. validity check
   d. batch total

4. Which disaster recovery strategy involves contracting for use of a physical site to which all necessary computing equipment will be delivered within 24 to 36 hours?
   a. virtualization
   b. cold site
   c. hot site
   d. data mirroring

5. Which of the following statements is true?
   a. Incremental daily backups are faster to perform than differential daily backups, but restoration is slower and more complex.
   b. Incremental daily backups are faster to perform than differential daily backups, and restoration is faster and simpler.
   c. Differential daily backups are faster to perform than incremental daily backups, but restoration is slower and more complex.
   d. Differential daily backups are faster to perform than incremental daily backups, and restoration is faster and simpler.

6. Information that needs to be stored securely for 10 years or more would most likely be stored in which type of file?
   a. backup
   b. archive
   c. encrypted
   d. log

7. Which of the following is an example of the kind of batch total called a hash total?
   a. the sum of the purchase amount field in a set of purchase orders
   b. the sum of the purchase order number field in a set of purchase orders
   c. the number of completed documents in a set of purchase orders
   d. all of the above

8. Which of the following statements is true?
   a. "Emergency" changes need to be documented once the problem is resolved.
   b. Changes should be tested in a system separate from the one used to process transactions.
   c. Change controls are necessary to maintain adequate segregation of duties.
   d. All of the above are true.

9. Which of the following provides detailed procedures to resolve the problems resulting from a flash flood that completely destroys a company's data center?
   a. backup plan
   b. disaster recovery plan (DRP)
   c. business continuity plan (BCP)
   d. archive plan

10. Which of the following is a control that can be used to verify the accuracy of information transmitted over a network?
    a. completeness check
    b. check digit
    c. parity bit
    d. size check

Discussion Questions

1. Two ways to create processing integrity controls in Excel spreadsheets are to use the built-in Data Validation tool or to write custom code with IF statements. What are the relative advantages and disadvantages of these two approaches?

2. What is the difference between using check digit verification and using a validity check to test the accuracy of an account number entered on a transaction record?

3. For each of the three basic options for replacing IT infrastructure (cold sites, hot sites, and real-time mirroring), give an example of an organization that could use that approach as part of its DRP. Be prepared to defend your answer.

4. Use the numbers 10–19 to show why transposition errors are always divisible by 9.

5. What are some business processes for which an organization might use batch processing?

6. Why do you think that surveys continue to find that a sizable percentage of organizations either do not have formal disaster recovery and business continuity plans or have not tested and revised those plans for more than a year?

Problems

1. Match the following terms with the appropriate definition or example:

____	**1.** Business continuity plan (BCP)	a. A file used to store information for long periods of time
____	**2.** Completeness check	b. A plan that describes how to resume IT functionality after a disaster
____	**3.** Hash total	c. An application control that verifies that the quantity ordered is greater than 0
____	**4.** Incremental daily backup	d. A control that counts the number of odd or even bits in order to verify that all data were transmitted correctly
____	**5.** Archive	e. An application control that tests whether a customer is 18 or older
____	**6.** Field check	f. A daily backup plan that copies all changes since the last full backup
____	**7.** Sign check	g. A disaster recovery plan that contracts for use of an alternate site that has all necessary computing and network equipment, plus Internet connectivity
____	**8.** Change control	h. A disaster recovery plan that contracts for use of another company's information system
____	**9.** Cold site	i. A disaster recovery plan that contracts for use of an alternate site that is prewired for Internet connectivity but has no computing or network equipment
____	**10.** Limit check	j. An application control that ensures that a customer's ship-to address is entered in a sales order
____	**11.** Zero-balance test	k. An application control that involves use of an account that should not have a balance after processing
____	**12.** Recovery point objective (RPO)	l. An application control that involves comparing the sum of a set of columns to the sum of a set of rows
____	**13.** Recovery time objective (RTO)	m. A measure of the length of time that an organization is willing to function without its information system
____	**14.** Record count	n. A measure of the amount of data that an organization is willing to reenter or possibly lose in the event of a disaster
____	**15.** Validity check	o. A batch total that does not have any intrinsic meaning
____	**16.** Check digit verification	p. A batch total that represents the number of transactions processed

____ 17. Closed-loop
verification

q. An application control that validates the correctness of one data item in a transaction record by comparing it to the value of another data item in that transaction record

____ 18. Parity checking

r. An application control that verifies that an account number entered in a transaction record matches an account number in the related master file

____ 19. Reasonableness test

s. A plan that describes how to resume business operations after a major calamity, such as Hurricane Katrina, that destroys not only an organization's data center but also its headquarters

____ 20. Financial total

t. A data entry application control that verifies the accuracy of an account number by recalculating the last number as a function of the preceding numbers

____ 21. Turnaround
document

u. A daily backup procedure that copies only the activity that occurred on that particular day

v. A data entry application control that could be used to verify that only numeric data are entered into a field

w. A plan to ensure that modifications to an information system do not reduce its security

x. A data entry application control in which the system displays the value of a data item and asks the user to verify that the system has accessed the correct record

y. A batch total that represents the total dollar value of a set of transactions

z. A document sent to an external party and subsequently returned so that preprinted data can be scanned rather than manually reentered.

2. Excel Problem
Enter the following data into a spreadsheet, and then perform the following tasks:

Employee Number	Pay Rate	Hours Worked	Gross Pay	Deductions	Net Pay
12355	10.55	38	400.90	125.00	275.90
2178g	11.00	40	440.00	395.00	45.00
24456	95.00	90	8550.00	145.00	8405.00
34567	10.00	40	400.00	105.00	505.00

a. Calculate examples of these batch totals:
   • A hash total
   • A financial total
   • A record count
b. Assume the following rules govern normal data:
   • Employee numbers are five digits in length and range from 10000 through 99999.
   • Maximum pay rate is $25, and minimum is $9.
   • Hours worked should never exceed 40.
   • Deductions should never exceed 40% of gross pay.
Give a specific example of an error or probable error in the data set that each of the following controls would detect:
   • Field check
   • Limit check
   • Reasonableness test
   • Cross-footing balance test
c. Create a control procedure that would prevent, or at least detect, each of the errors in the data set.

3. Excel Problem

The Moose Wings Cooperative Flight Club owns a number of airplanes and gliders. It serves fewer than 2,000 members, who are numbered sequentially from the founder, Tom Eagle (0001), to the newest member, Jacques Noveau (1368). Members rent the flying machines by the hour, and all must be returned on the same day. The following six records were among those entered for the flights taken on September 1, 2010:

Member #	Flight Date MM/DD/YY	Plane Used*	Takeoff Time	Landing Time
1234	09/10/10	G	6:25	8:46
4111	09/01/10	C	8:49	10:23
1210	09/01/10	P	3:42	5:42
0023	09/01/10	X	1:59	12:43
012A	09/01/10	P	12:29	15:32
0999	09/01/10	L	15:31	13:45

*C = Cessna, G = Glider, L = Lear Jet, P = Piper Cub

Required

a. Identify and describe any errors in the data.
b. For each of the five data fields, suggest one or more input edit controls that could be used to detect input errors.
c. Enter the data in a spreadsheet, and create appropriate controls to prevent or at least detect the input errors.
d. Suggest other controls to minimize the risk of input errors.

(SMAC adapted)

4. The first column in Table 3 lists transaction amounts that have been summed to obtain a batch total. Assume that all data in the first column are correct. Cases A through D each contain an input error in one record, along with a batch total computed from that set of records.

Required

For each case (a through d), compute the difference between the correct and erroneous batch totals, and explain how this difference could help identify the cause of the error.

TABLE 3 Data for Problem 4

	Correct Transactions	Case A	Case B	Case C	Case D
	$3,630.62	$3,630.62	$3,630.62	$3,630.62	$3,630.62
	1,484.86	1,484.86	1,484.86	1,484.86	1,484.86
	1,723.46	1,723.46	1,723.46	1,723.46	1,723.46
	9,233.25	9,233.25	9,233.25	9,233.25	9,233.25
	123.45	123.45	123.45	123.45	123.45
	7,832.44	7,832.44	1,832.44	7,832.44	7,832.44
	2,398.33	2,398.33	2,398.33	2,398.33	2,398.33
	3,766.24	3,766.24	3,766.24	3,766.24	3,766.24
	4,400.00	4,400.00	4,400.00	−4,400.00	4,400.00
	2,833.00	2,833.00	2,833.00	2,833.00	2,833.00
	1,978.95	1,987.95	1,978.95	1,978.95	1,978.95
	654.32	654.32	654.32	654.32	9,876.23
	9,876.23	9,876.23	9,876.23	9,876.23	2,138.10
	2,138.10	2,138.10	2,138.10	2,138.10	5,533.99
	5,533.99	5,533.99	5,533.99	5,533.99	
Batch total	$57,607.24	$57,616.24	$51,607.24	$48,807.24	$56,952.92

5. Excel Problem

    Create a spreadsheet with the following columns:

    - Plaintext character
    - ASCII code (seven bits, binary number)
    - First bit
    - Second bit
    - Third bit
    - Fourth bit
    - Fifth bit
    - Sixth bit
    - Seventh bit
    - Number of bits with value = 1
    - Parity bit for odd parity coding
    - Parity bit for even parity coding

    Required

    a. Enter a-e, A-E, 0-9, ?, !,%, &, and ; in the plaintext column.

    b. The ASCII column should convert the plaintext character to the binary code used by your computer.

    c. The next seven columns should each display one bit of the ASCII code, beginning with the leftmost digit. (*Hint:* Excel provides text functions that can select individual characters from a string.)

    d. The tenth column should sum the number of bits that have the value 1. (*Hint:* The text functions used to populate columns 3–9 return a text string that you will need to convert to a numeric value.)

    e. Column 11 should have a 1 if the number in column 10 is odd, and 0 if the number in column 10 is even.

    f. Column 12 should have a 1 if the number in column 10 is even, and a 0 if the number in column 10 is odd.

6. The ABC Company is considering the following options for its backup plan:

    1. Daily full backups:
       - Time to perform backup = 60 minutes
       - Size of backup = 50 GB
       - Time to restore from backup = 30 minutes
    2. Weekly full backups plus daily incremental backup:
       - Same requirements as option 1 to do a full backup on Friday, plus
       - Time to perform daily backup = 10 minutes
       - Size of daily backup = 10 GB
       - Time to restore each daily backup file = 5 minutes
    3. Weekly full backups plus daily differential backup:
       - Same requirements as option 1 to do a full backup on Friday, plus
       - Time to perform daily backup = 10 minutes first day, growing by 5 minutes each day thereafter
       - Size of daily backup = 10 GB first day, growing by 10 GB each day
       - Time to restore differential backup file = 5 minutes first day, increasing by 2 minutes each subsequent day

       Which approach would you recommend? Why?

7. Which control(s) would best mitigate the following threats?

    a. The hours-worked field in a payroll transaction record contained the value 400 instead of 40. As a result, the employee received a paycheck for $6,257.24 instead of $654.32.

    b. The accounts receivable file was destroyed because it was accidentally used to update accounts payable.

    c. During processing of customer payments, the digit 0 in a payment of $204 was mistakenly typed as the letter "O." As a result, the transaction was not processed correctly, and the customer erroneously received a letter that the account was delinquent.

d. A salesperson mistakenly entered an online order for 50 laser printers instead of 50 laser printer toner cartridges.

e. A 20-minute power brownout caused a mission-critical database server to crash, shutting down operations temporarily.

f. A fire destroyed the data center, including all backup copies of the accounts receivable files.

g. After processing sales transactions, the inventory report showed a negative quantity on hand for several items.

h. A customer order for an important part did not include the customer's address. Consequently, the order was not shipped on time, and the customer called to complain.

i. When entering a large credit sale, the clerk typed in the customer's account number as 45982 instead of 45892. That account number did not exist. The mistake was not caught until later in the week, when the weekly billing process was run. Consequently, the customer was not billed for another week, delaying receipt of payment.

j. A visitor to the company's Web site entered 400 characters into the five-digit Zip code field, causing the server to crash.

k. Two traveling sales representatives accessed the parts database at the same time. Salesperson A noted that there were still 55 units of part 723 available and entered an order for 45 of them. While salesperson A was keying in the order, salesperson B, in another state, also noted the availability of 55 units for part 723 and entered an order for 33 of them. Both sales reps promised their customer next-day delivery. Salesperson A's customer, however, learned the next day that the part would have to be back-ordered. The customer canceled the sale and vowed to never again do business with the company.

l. The warranty department manager was upset because special discount coupons were mailed to every customer who had purchased the product within the past three years, instead of to only those customers who had purchased the product within the past three months.

m. The clerk entering details about a large credit sale mistakenly typed in a nonexistent account number. Consequently, the company never received payment for the items.

n. A customer filled in the wrong account number on the portion of the invoice being returned with payment. Consequently, the payment was credited to another customer's account.

o. A batch of 73 time sheets was sent to the payroll department for weekly processing. Somehow, one of the time sheets did not get processed. The mistake was not caught until payday, when one employee complained about not receiving a paycheck.

p. Sunspot activity resulted in the loss of some data being sent to the regional office. The problem was not discovered until several days later, when managers attempted to query the database for that information.

8. MonsterMed Inc. (MMI) is an online pharmaceutical firm. MMI has a small systems staff that designs and writes MMI's customized software. The data center is installed in the basement of its two-story headquarters building. The data center is equipped with halon-gas fire suppression equipment and an uninterruptible power supply system.

   The computer operations staff works a two-shift schedule, five days per week. MMI's programming staff, located in the same building, has access to the data center and can test new programs and program changes when the operations staff is not available. Programmers make changes in response to oral requests by employees using the system. Because the programming staff is small and the work demands have increased, systems and programming documentation is developed only when time is available. Backups are made whenever time permits. The backup files are stored in a locked cabinet in the data center. Unfortunately, due to several days of heavy rains, MMI's building recently experienced serious flooding that destroyed not only the computer hardware but also all the data and program files that were on-site.

Required

a. Identify at least five weaknesses in MonsterMed Inc.'s backup and DRP procedures.

b. Evaluate change controls at MonsterMed Inc.

(CMA exam, adapted)

9. Excel Problem

Create data validation rules in a spreadsheet to perform each of the following controls:

a. Limit check—that values in the cell are < 70

b. Range check—that values in the cell are between 15 and 65

c. Sign check—that values in the cell are positive

d. Field check—that values in a cell are only numeric

e. Size check—that the cell accepts no more than 40 characters of text

f. Reasonableness check—that the cell's value is less than 75% of the cell to its left

g. Validity check—that a value exists in a list of allowable values

10. Excel Problem

Creating and testing check digits.

Required

a. Create a spreadsheet that will take as input a five-digit account number, and calculate a check digit using this formula: (5 × left-most digit + 4 × next digit + 3 × third digit + 2 × fourth digit + fifth digit) modulus division by 7. (Modulus division returns the remainder—for example: 11 modulus division by 3 = 2). The check digit then becomes the sixth (right-most) digit in the account number. Your spreadsheet should look like this:

Check digits—creation and use

a. Creating check digits Formula = (5x left-most digit + 4x next digit + 3x third digit + 2x fourth digit + fifth digit) mod 7

Raw account#	First digit	Second digit	Third digit	Fourth digit	Fifth digit	Check digit calculation	Actual account #
12345	1	2	3	4	5	0	123450
12346	1	2	3	4	6	1	123461
12347	1	2	3	4	7	2	123472
12348	1	2	3	4	8	3	123483
12349	1	2	3	4	9	4	123494
12350	1	2	3	5	0	4	123504
12351	1	2	3	5	1	5	123515
12352	1	2	3	5	2	6	123526
12353	1	2	3	5	3	0	123530

b. Add another panel to the spreadsheet that takes as input a six-digit account number and uses the check digit formula in part a to test whether or not the account number is valid. Your solution should look like this:

b. Testing check digits

Account number	First digit	Second digit	Third digit	Fourth digit	Fifth digit	Check digit	Valid? (Y/N)
123530	1	2	3	5	3	0	Y
123534	1	2	3	5	3	4	N

11. For each of the following scenarios, determine whether the company's current backup procedures enable it to meet its recovery objectives, and explain why:

a. Scenario 1:

   • Recovery point objective = 24 hours

   • Daily backups at 3:00 A.M., process takes 2 hours

   • Copy of backup tapes picked up daily at 8:00 A.M. for storage off-site

b. Scenario 2: Company makes daily incremental backups Monday through Saturday at 7:00 P.M. each night. Company makes full backup weekly, on Sunday at 1:00 P.M.
   - Recovery time objective = 2 hours
   - Time to do full backup = 3 hours
   - Time to restore from full backup = 1 hour
   - Time to make incremental daily backup = 1 hour
   - Time to restore each incremental daily backup = 30 minutes
c. Scenario 3: Company makes daily differential backups Monday through Friday at 8:00 P.M. each night. Company makes full backup weekly, on Saturdays, at 8:00 A.M.
   - Recovery time objective = 6 hours
   - Time to do full backup = 4 hours
   - Time to restore from full backup = 3 hours
   - Time to do differential daily backups = 1 hour on Monday, increasing by 30 minutes each successive day
   - Time to restore differential daily backup = 30 minutes for Monday, increasing by 15 minutes each successive day

Case 1 Ensuring Systems Availability

The *Journal of Accountancy* (available at www.aicpa.org) has published a series of articles that address different aspects of disaster recovery and business continuity planning:

1. J. A. Gerber and E. R. Feldman, "Is Your Business Prepared for the Worst?" *Journal of Accountancy* (April 2002): 61–64.
2. E. McCarthy, "The Best-Laid Plans," *Journal of Accountancy* (May 2004): 46–54.
3. R. Myers, "Katrina's Harsh Lessons," *Journal of Accountancy* (June 2006): 54–63.
4. S. Phelan and M. Hayes, "Before the Deluge—and After," *Journal of Accountancy* (April 2003): 57–66.

Required

Read one or more of these articles that your professor assigns, plus section DS 4 of COBIT version 4.1 (available at www.isaca.org), to answer the following questions:

1. What does COBIT suggest as possible metrics for evaluating how well an organization is achieving the objective of DS 4? Why do you think that metric is useful?

2. For each article assigned by your professor, complete the following table, summarizing what each article said about a specific COBIT control objective (an article may not address all 10 control objectives in DS 4):

COBIT Control Objective	Points Discussed in Article
DS 4.1	
DS 4.2	
DS 4.3	
DS 4.4	
DS 4.5	
DS 4.6	
DS 4.7	
DS 4.8	
DS 4.9	
DS 4.10	

Case 2 Change Controls

Read section AI 6 in version 4.1 of COBIT (available at www. isaca.org), and answer the following questions:

1. What is the purpose of each detailed control objective—why is it important?
2. How is each of the suggested metrics useful?

AIS IN ACTION SOLUTIONS

Quiz Key

1. Which of the following measures the amount of data that might be potentially lost as a result of a system failure?
   a. recovery time objective (RTO) (Incorrect. The RTO measures the time that an organization may have to function without its information system.)
   ▶ b. recovery point objective (RPO) (Correct. The RPO measures the time between the last data backup and the occurrence of a problem.)
   c. disaster recovery plan (DRP) (Incorrect. A DRP specifies the procedures to restore IT operations.)
   d. business continuity plan (BCP) (Incorrect. A BCP specifies the procedures to resume business processes.)

2. Which data entry application control would detect and prevent entry of alphabetic characters as the price of an inventory item?
   ▶ a. field check (Correct. Field checks test whether data are numeric or alphabetic.)
   b. limit check (Incorrect. A limit check compares an input value against a fixed number.)
   c. reasonableness check (Incorrect. A reasonableness check compares two data items to determine whether the values of both are reasonable.)
   d. sign check (Incorrect. A sign check determines whether a numeric field is positive or negative.)

3. Which of the following controls would prevent entry of a nonexistent customer number in a sales transaction?
   a. field check (Incorrect. A field check tests only whether data are numeric or alphabetic.)
   b. completeness check (Incorrect. A completeness check would ensure that a customer number was entered, but it does not test whether the customer number exists.)
   ▶ c. validity check (Correct. A validity check compares a customer number entered into a transaction record against the customer numbers that exist in the master file or database.)
   d. batch total (Incorrect. A batch total is used to verify completeness of data entry.)

4. Which disaster recovery strategy involves contracting for use of a physical site to which all necessary computing equipment will be delivered within 24 to 36 hours?
   a. virtualization (Incorrect. Virtualization is a strategy to make better use of resources by running multiple virtual machines on one physical host. It is not a disaster recovery strategy.)
   ▶ b. cold site (Correct.)
   c. hot site (Incorrect. A hot site is an infrastructure replacement strategy which contracts for use of a physical site that contains all necessary computer and network equipment.)

    d. data mirroring (Incorrect. Data mirroring is a fault-tolerant backup strategy in which the organization maintains a second data center and all transactions are processed on both systems as they occur.)

5. Which of the following statements is true?
  ▶ a. Incremental daily backups are faster to perform than differential daily backups, but restoration is slower and more complex. (Correct.)
    b. Incremental daily backups are faster to perform than differential daily backups, and restoration is faster and simpler. (Incorrect. Incremental daily backups produce separate backup files for each day since the last full backup, making restoration more complex.)
    c. Differential daily backups are faster to perform than incremental daily backups, but restoration is slower and more complex. (Incorrect. Differential daily backups are slower than incremental daily backups, but restoration is faster and simpler because only the most recent differential daily backup and the last full backup files are required.)
    d. Differential daily backups are faster to perform than incremental daily backups, and restoration is faster and simpler. (Incorrect. Differential daily backups are slower to perform than incremental daily backups.)

6. Information that needs to be stored securely for 10 years or more would most likely be stored in which type of file?
    a. backup (Incorrect. Backups are for short-term storage; archives are for long-term storage.)
  ▶ b. archive (Correct.)
    c. encrypted (Incorrect. Long-term retention uses archives, which are usually not encrypted.)
    d. log (Incorrect. A log is part of an audit trail.)

7. Which of the following is an example of the kind of batch total called a hash total?
    a. the sum of the purchase amount field in a set of purchase orders (Incorrect. This is an example of a financial total.)
  ▶ b. the sum of the purchase order number field in a set of purchase orders (Correct. The sum of purchase order numbers has no intrinsic meaning.)
    c. the number of completed documents in a set of purchase orders (Incorrect. This is an example of a record count.)
    d. all of the above (Incorrect. Choices a and c are incorrect.)

8. Which of the following statements is true?
    a. "Emergency" changes need to be documented once the problem is resolved. (Incorrect. This statement is true, but so are b and c.)
    b. Changes should be tested in a system separate from the one used to process transactions. (Incorrect. This statement is true, but so are a and c.)
    c. Change controls are necessary to maintain adequate segregation of duties. (Incorrect. This statement is true, but so are a and b.)
  ▶ d. All of the above are true. (Correct.)

9. Which of the following provides detailed procedures to resolve the problems resulting from a flash flood that completely destroys a company's data center?
    a. backup plan (Incorrect. Backup plans focus solely on making a duplicate copy of files in the event that the original becomes corrupted because of hardware malfunctions, software problems, or human error.)
  ▶ b. disaster recovery plan (DRP) (Correct. A DRP focuses on restoring an organization's IT functionality.)
    c. business continuity plan (BCP) (Incorrect. A BCP focuses on restoring not only IT, but all aspects business processes.)
    d. archive plan (Incorrect. An archive plan deals with long-term retention of data.)

10. Which of the following is a control that can be used to verify the accuracy of information transmitted over a network?
    a. completeness check (Incorrect. A completeness check is a data input control to ensure that all necessary data are entered.)
    b. check digit (Incorrect. A check digit is a data input control designed to detect miskeying of account numbers.)
    ▶ c. parity bit (Correct. A parity bit is a communications control that counts the number of bits in order to verify the integrity of data sent and received.)
    d. size check (Incorrect. A size check is a data input control to ensure that the amount of data entered does not exceed the space set aside for it. Size checks are especially important for programs that accept input from users, because they can prevent buffer overflow attacks.)

Chapter 11

Auditing Computer-Based Information Systems

Auditing Computer-Based Information Systems

Learning Objectives

After studying this chapter, you should be able to:

1. Describe the scope and objectives of audit work, and identify the major steps in the audit process.

2. Identify the objectives of an information system audit, and describe the four-step approach necessary for meeting these objectives.

3. Design a plan for the study and evaluation of internal control in an AIS.

4. Describe computer audit software, and explain how it is used in the audit of an AIS.

5. Describe the nature and scope of an operational audit.

INTEGRATIVE CASE SEATTLE PAPER PRODUCTS

Seattle Paper Products (SPP) is modifying its sales department payroll system to change the way it calculates sales commissions. Under the old system, commissions were a fixed percentage of dollar sales. The new system is considerably more complex, with commission rates varying according to the product sold and the total dollar volume of sales.

Jason Scott was assigned to use audit software to write a parallel simulation test program to calculate sales commissions and compare them with those generated by the new system. Jason obtained the necessary payroll system documentation and the details on the new sales commission policy and prepared his program.

Jason used the sales transaction data from the last payroll period to run his program. To his surprise, his calculations were $5,000 less than those produced by SPP's new program. Individual differences existed for about half of the company's salespeople. Jason double-checked his program code but could not locate any errors. He

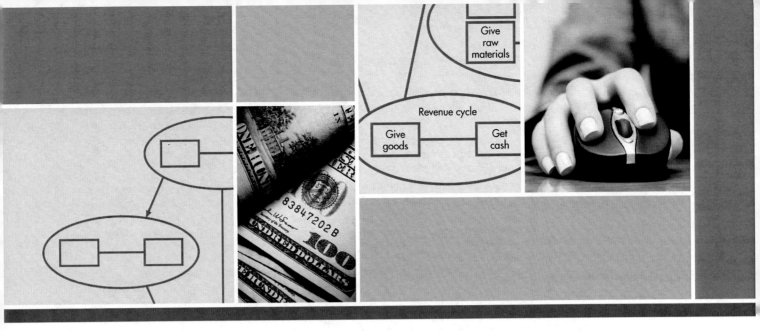

selected a salesperson with a discrepancy and calculated the commission by hand. The result agreed with his program. He reviewed the new commission policy with the sales manager, line by line, and concluded that he understood the new policy completely. Jason is now convinced that his program is correct and that the error lies with SPP's new program. He is now asking himself the following questions:

1. How could a programming error of this significance be overlooked by experienced programmers who thoroughly reviewed and tested the new system?
2. Is this an inadvertent error, or could it be a fraud?
3. What can be done to find the error in the program?

Introduction

This chapter focuses on auditing an accounting information system (AIS). *Auditing* is the systematic process of obtaining and evaluating evidence regarding assertions about economic actions and events in order to determine how well they correspond with established criteria. The results of the audit are then communicated to interested users. Auditing requires careful planning and the collection, review, and documentation of audit evidence. In developing recommendations, the auditor uses established criteria, such as the principles of control described in previous chapters, as a basis for evaluation.

Many organizations in the United States employ internal auditors to evaluate company operations. Governments employ auditors to evaluate management performance and compliance with legislative intent. The Department of Defense employs auditors to review the financial records of companies with defense contracts. Publicly held companies hire external auditors to provide an independent review of their financial statements.

This chapter is written from the perspective of an internal auditor. *Internal auditing* is an independent, objective assurance and consulting activity designed to add value and improve organizational effectiveness and efficiency, including assisting in the design and implementation of an AIS. Internal auditing helps an organization accomplish its objectives by bringing a systematic, disciplined approach to evaluate and improve the effectiveness of risk management, control, and governance processes.

There are several different types of internal audits:

1. A *financial audit* examines the reliability and integrity of financial transactions, accounting records, and financial statements.

2. An *information systems*, or *internal control*, **audit** reviews the controls of an AIS to assess its compliance with internal control policies and procedures and its effectiveness in safeguarding assets. The audits usually evaluate system input and output; processing controls; backup and recovery plans; system security; and computer facilities.
3. An *operational* **audit** is concerned with the economical and efficient use of resources and the accomplishment of established goals and objectives.
4. A *compliance audit* determines whether entities are complying with applicable laws, regulations, policies, and procedures. These audits often result in recommendations to improve processes and controls used to ensure compliance with regulations.
5. An *investigative audit* examines incidents of possible fraud, misappropriation of assets, waste and abuse, or improper governmental activities.

In contrast, external auditors are responsible to corporate shareholders and are mostly concerned with gathering the evidence needed to express an opinion on the financial statements. They are only indirectly concerned with the effectiveness of a corporate AIS. However, external auditors are required to evaluate how audit strategy is affected by an organization's use of information technology (IT). External auditors may need specialized skills to (1) determine how the audit will be affected by IT, (2) assess and evaluate IT controls, and (3) design and perform both tests of IT controls and substantive tests.

Despite the distinction between internal and external auditing, many of the internal audit concepts and techniques discussed in this chapter also apply to external audits.

The first section of this chapter provides an overview of auditing and the steps in the auditing process. The second section describes a methodology and set of techniques for evaluating internal controls in an AIS and conducting an information system audit. The third section discusses the computer software and other techniques for evaluating the reliability and integrity of information in an AIS. Finally, operational audits of an AIS are reviewed.

The Nature of Auditing

Overview of the Audit Process

All audits follow a similar sequence of activities. Audits may be divided into four stages: planning, collecting evidence, evaluating evidence, and communicating audit results. Figure 1 is an overview of the auditing process and lists many of the procedures performed within each of these stages.

AUDIT PLANNING   Audit planning determines why, how, when, and by whom the audit will be performed. The first step is to establish the audit's scope and objectives. For example, an audit of a publicly held corporation determines whether its financial statements are presented fairly. In contrast, an internal audit may examine a specific department or a computer application. It may focus on internal controls, financial information, operating performance, or some combination of the three.

An audit team with the necessary experience and expertise is formed. They become familiar with the auditee by conferring with supervisory and operating personnel, reviewing system documentation, and reviewing prior audit findings.

An audit is planned so the greatest amount of audit work focuses on the areas with the highest risk factors. There are three types of audit risk:

1. *Inherent risk* is the susceptibility to material risk in the absence of controls. For example, a system that employs online processing, networks, databases, telecommunications, and other forms of advanced technology has more inherent risk than a batch processing system.
2. *Control risk* is the risk that a material misstatement will get through the internal control structure and into the financial statements. A company with weak internal controls has a higher control risk than one with strong controls. Control risk can be determined by reviewing the control environment, testing internal controls, and considering control weaknesses identified in prior audits and evaluating how they have been rectified.

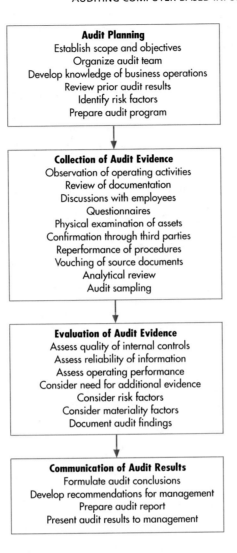

FIGURE 1

Overview of the
Auditing Process

3. *Detection risk* is the risk that auditors and their audit procedures will fail to detect a material error or misstatement.

To conclude the planning stage, an audit program is prepared to show the nature, extent, and timing of the procedures needed to achieve audit objectives and minimize audit risks. A time budget is prepared, and staff members are assigned to perform specific audit steps.

COLLECTION OF AUDIT EVIDENCE Most audit effort is spent collecting evidence. Because many audit tests cannot be performed on all items under review, they are often performed on a sample basis. The following are the most common ways to collect audit evidence:

- *Observation* of the activities being audited (e.g., watching how data control personnel handle data processing work as it is received)
- *Review of documentation* to understand how a particular process or internal control system is supposed to function
- *Discussions* with employees about their jobs and about how they carry out certain procedures
- *Questionnaires* that gather data
- *Physical examination* of the quantity and/or condition of tangible assets, such as equipment and inventory
- *Confirmation* of the accuracy of information, such as customer account balances, through communication with independent third parties
- *Reperformance* of calculations to verify quantitative information (e.g., recalculating the annual depreciation expense)

- *Vouching* for the validity of a transaction by examining supporting documents, such as the purchase order, receiving report, and vendor invoice supporting an accounts payable transaction
- *Analytical review* of relationships and trends among information to detect items that should be further investigated. For example, an auditor for a chain store discovered that one store's ratio of accounts receivable to sales was too high. An investigation revealed that the manager was diverting collected funds to her personal use.

A typical audit has a mix of audit procedures. For example, an internal control audit makes greater use of observation, documentation review, employee interviews, and reperformance of control procedures. A financial audit focuses on physical examination, confirmation, vouching, analytical review, and reperformance of account balance calculations.

EVALUATION OF AUDIT EVIDENCE   The auditor evaluates the evidence gathered and decides whether it supports a favorable or unfavorable conclusion. If inconclusive, the auditor performs sufficient additional procedures to reach a definitive conclusion.

Because errors exist in most systems, auditors focus on detecting and reporting those that significantly impact management's interpretation of the audit findings. Determining **materiality**, what is and is not important in an audit, is a matter of professional judgment. Materiality is more important to external audits, where the emphasis is fairness of financial statement, than to internal audits, where the focus is on adherence to management policies.

The auditor seeks **reasonable assurance** that no material error exists in the information or process audited. Because it is prohibitively expensive to seek complete assurance, the auditor has some risk that the audit conclusion is incorrect. When inherent or control risk is high, the auditor must obtain greater assurance to offset the greater uncertainty and risks.

In all audit stages, findings and conclusions are documented in audit working papers. Documentation is especially important at the evaluation stage, when conclusions must be reached and supported.

COMMUNICATION OF AUDIT RESULTS   The auditor submits a written report summarizing audit findings and recommendations to management, the audit committee, the board of directors, and other appropriate parties. Afterwards, auditors often do a follow-up study to ascertain whether recommendations were implemented.

The Risk-Based Audit Approach

The following internal control evaluation approach, called the risk-based audit approach, provides a framework for conducting information system audits:

1. *Determine the threats (fraud and errors) facing the company.*   This is a list of the accidental or intentional abuse and damage to which the system is exposed.
2. *Identify the control procedures that prevent, detect, or correct the threats.*   These are all the controls that management has put into place and that auditors should review and test, to minimize the threats.
3. *Evaluate control procedures.*   Controls are evaluated two ways:
   a. A *systems review* determines whether control procedures are actually in place.
   b. *Tests of controls* are conducted to determine whether existing controls work as intended.
4. *Evaluate control weaknesses to determine their effect on the nature, timing, or extent of auditing procedures.*   If the auditor determines that control risk is too high because the control system is inadequate, the auditor may have to gather more evidence, better evidence, or more timely evidence. Control weaknesses in one area may be acceptable if there are *compensating controls* in other areas.

The risk-based approach provides auditors with a clearer understanding of the fraud and errors that can occur and the related risks and exposures. It also helps them plan how to test and evaluate internal controls, as well as how to plan subsequent audit procedures. The result is a sound basis for developing recommendations to management on how the AIS control system should be improved.

Information Systems Audits

The purpose of an information systems audit is to review and evaluate the internal controls that protect the system. When performing an information systems audit, auditors should ascertain that the following six objectives are met:

1. Security provisions protect computer equipment, programs, communications, and data from unauthorized access, modification, or destruction.
2. Program development and acquisition are performed in accordance with management's general and specific authorization.
3. Program modifications have management's authorization and approval.
4. Processing of transactions, files, reports, and other computer records is accurate and complete.
5. Source data that are inaccurate or improperly authorized are identified and handled according to prescribed managerial policies.
6. Computer data files are accurate, complete, and confidential.

Figure 2 depicts the relationship among these six objectives and information systems components. Each of these objectives is discussed in detail in the following sections. Each description includes an audit plan to accomplish each objective, as well as the techniques and procedures to carry out the plan.

Objective 1: Overall Security

Table 1 uses the risk-based approach to present a framework for auditing overall computer security. It shows that overall system security threats include accidental or intentional damage to system assets; unauthorized access, disclosure, or modification of data and programs; theft; and interruption of crucial business activities.

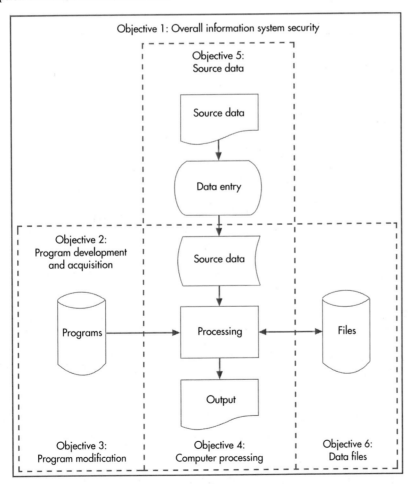

FIGURE 2

Information Systems Components and Related Audit Objectives

TABLE 1 Framework for Audit of Overall Computer Security

Types of Errors and Fraud
- Theft of or accidental or intentional damage to hardware
- Loss, theft, or unauthorized access to programs, data, and other system resources
- Loss, theft, or unauthorized disclosure of confidential data
- Unauthorized modification or use of programs and data files
- Interruption of crucial business activities

Control Procedures
- Information security/protection plan
- Limiting of physical access to computer equipment
- Limiting of logical access to system using authentication and authorization controls
- Data storage and transmission controls
- Virus protection procedures
- File backup and recovery procedures
- Fault-tolerant systems design
- Disaster recovery plan
- Preventive maintenance
- Firewalls
- Casualty and business interruption insurance

Audit Procedures: System Review
- Inspect computer sites
- Review the information security/protection and disaster recovery plans
- Interview information system personnel about security procedures
- Review physical and logical access policies and procedures
- Review file backup and recovery policies and procedures
- Review data storage and transmission policies and procedures
- Review procedures employed to minimize system downtime
- Review vendor maintenance contracts
- Examine system access logs
- Examine casualty and business interruption insurance policies

Audit Procedures: Tests of Controls
- Observe and test computer-site access procedures
- Observe the preparation of and off-site storage of backup files
- Test assignment and modification procedures for user IDs and passwords
- Investigate how unauthorized access attempts are dealt with
- Verify the extent and effectiveness of data encryption
- Verify the effective use of data transmission controls
- Verify the effective use of firewalls and virus protection procedures
- Verify the use of preventive maintenance and an uninterruptible power supply
- Verify amounts and limitations on insurance coverage
- Examine the results of disaster recovery plan test simulations

Compensating Controls
- Sound personnel policies, including segregation of incompatible duties
- Effective user controls

Control procedures to minimize these threats include developing an information security/protection plan, restricting physical and logical access, encrypting data, protecting against viruses, implementing firewalls, instituting data transmission controls, and preventing and recovering from system failures or disasters.

Systems review procedures include inspecting computer sites; interviewing personnel; reviewing policies and procedures; and examining access logs, insurance policies, and the disaster recovery plan.

Auditors test security controls by observing procedures, verifying that controls are in place and work as intended, investigating errors or problems to ensure they were handled correctly, and examining any tests previously performed. For example, one way to test logical access controls is to try to break into a system. During a U.S. government security audit, auditors used agency terminals to gain unauthorized access to its computer system, disable its security-checking procedures, and control the system from the terminal. The security breakdown was possible because of poor administrative controls and inadequate security software.

Sound personnel policies and effective segregation of incompatible duties can partially compensate for poor computer security. Good user controls will also help, provided that user personnel can recognize unusual system output. Because it is unlikely these controls can compensate indefinitely for poor computer security, auditors should strongly recommend that security weaknesses be corrected.

Objective 2: Program Development and Acquisition

The auditor's role in systems development should be limited to an independent review of systems development activities. To maintain objectivity, auditors should not help develop the system.

Two things can go wrong in program development: (1) inadvertent programming errors due to misunderstanding system specifications or careless programming and (2) unauthorized instructions deliberately inserted into the programs.

These problems can be controlled by requiring management and user authorization and approval, thorough testing, and proper documentation.

During systems review, auditors should discuss development procedures with management, system users, and information system personnel. They should also review the policies, procedures, standards, and documentation listed in Table 2.

TABLE 2 Framework for Audit of Program Development

Types of Errors and Fraud
- Inadvertent programming errors or unauthorized program code

Control Procedures
- Review of software license agreements
- Management authorization for program development and software acquisition
- Management and user approval of programming specifications
- Thorough testing of new programs, including user acceptance tests
- Complete systems documentation, including approvals

Audit Procedures: System Review
- Independent review of the systems development process
- Review of systems development/acquisition policies and procedures
- Review of systems authorization and approval policies and procedures
- Review of programming evaluation standards
- Review of program and system documentation standards
- Review of test specifications, test data, and test results
- Review of test approval policies and procedures
- Review of acquisition of copyright license agreement policies and procedures
- Discussions with management, users, and information system personnel regarding development procedures

Audit Procedures: Tests of Controls
- Interview users about their systems acquisition/development and implementation involvement
- Review minutes of development team meetings for evidence of involvement
- Verify management and user sign-off approvals at development milestone points
- Review test specifications, test data, and systems test results
- Review software license agreements

Compensating Controls
- Strong processing controls
- Independent processing of test data by auditor

To test systems development controls, auditors should interview managers and system users, examine development approvals, and review development team meeting minutes. The auditor should review all documentation relating to the testing process to make sure all program changes were tested. The auditor should examine the test specifications and the test data and evaluate the test results. Auditors should ascertain how unexpected test result problems were resolved.

Strong processing controls may compensate for inadequate development controls if auditors obtain persuasive evidence of compliance with processing controls, using techniques such as independent test data processing. If this evidence is not obtained, auditors may have to conclude that a material internal control weakness exists and that the risk of significant threats in application programs is unacceptably high.

Objective 3: Program Modification

Table 3 presents a framework for auditing changes to application programs and system software. The same threats that occur during program development occur during program modification. For example, a programmer assigned to modify his company's payroll system inserted a command to erase all company files if he was terminated. When he was fired, the system crashed and erased key files.

TABLE 3 Framework for Audit of Program Modifications

Types of Errors and Fraud
- Inadvertent programming errors or unauthorized program code

Control Procedures
- List program components to be modified
- Management authorization and approval of program modifications
- User approval of program change specifications
- Thorough test of program changes, including user acceptance tests
- Complete program change documentation, including approvals
- Separate development, test, and production versions of programs
- Changes implemented by personnel independent of users and programmers
- Logical access controls

Audit Procedures: System Review
- Review program modification policies, standards, and procedures
- Review documentation standards for program modification
- Review final documentation of program modifications
- Review program modification testing and test approval procedures
- Review test specifications, test data, and test results
- Review test approval policies and procedures
- Review programming evaluation standards
- Discuss modification policies and procedures with management, users, and systems personnel
- Review logical access control policies and procedures

Audit Procedures: Tests of Controls
- Verify user and management signoff approval for program changes
- Verify that program components to be modified are identified and listed
- Verify that program change test procedures and documentation comply with standards
- Verify that logical access controls are in effect for program changes
- Observe program change implementation
- Verify that separate development, test, and production versions are maintained
- Verify that changes are not implemented by user or programming personnel
- Test for unauthorized or erroneous program changes using a source code comparison program, reprocessing, and parallel simulation

Compensating Controls
- Independent audit tests for unauthorized or erroneous program changes
- Strong processing controls

When a program change is submitted for approval, a list of all required updates should be compiled and approved by management and program users. All program changes should be tested and documented. During the change process, the developmental program must be kept separate from the production version. After the modified program is approved, the production version replaces the developmental version.

During systems review, auditors should discuss the change process with management and user personnel. The policies, procedures, and standards for approving, modifying, testing, and documenting the changes should be examined. All final documentation materials for program changes, including test procedures and results, should be reviewed. The procedures used to restrict logical access to the developmental program should be reviewed.

An important part of tests of controls is to verify that program changes were identified, listed, approved, tested, and documented. The auditor should verify that separate development and production programs are maintained and that changes are implemented by someone independent of the user and programming functions. The development program's access control table is reviewed to verify that only authorized users had access to the system.

Auditors should test programs on a surprise basis to guard against an employee inserting unauthorized program changes after the audit is completed and removing them prior to the next audit. There are three ways auditors test for unauthorized program changes:

1. After testing a new program, auditors keep a copy of its source code. Auditors use a *source code comparison program* to compare the current version of the program with the source code. If no changes were authorized, the two versions should be identical; any differences should be investigated. If the difference is an authorized change, auditors examine program change specifications to ensure that the changes were authorized and correctly incorporated.
2. In the *reprocessing* technique, auditors reprocess data using the source code and compare the output with the company's output. Discrepancies in the output are investigated.
3. In *parallel simulation*, the auditor writes a program instead of using the source code, compares the outputs, and investigates any differences. Parallel simulation can be used to test a program during the implementation process. For example, Jason used this technique to test a portion of SPP's new sales department payroll system.

For each major program change, auditors observe testing and implementation, review authorizations and documents, and perform independent tests. If this step is skipped and program change controls subsequently prove to be inadequate, it may not be possible to rely on program outputs.

If program change controls are deficient, a compensating control is source code comparison, reprocessing, or parallel simulation performed by the auditor. Sound processing controls, independently tested by the auditor, can partially compensate for such deficiencies. However, if the deficiencies are caused by inadequate restrictions on program file access, the auditor should strongly recommend actions to strengthen the organization's logical access controls.

Objective 4: Computer Processing

Table 4 provides a framework for auditing the processing of transactions, files, and related computer records to update files and databases and to generate reports.

During computer processing, the system may fail to detect erroneous input, improperly correct input errors, process erroneous input, or improperly distribute or disclose output. Table 4 shows the control procedures to detect and prevent these threats and the systems review and tests of controls used to understand the controls, evaluate their adequacy, and test whether they function properly.

Auditors periodically reevaluate processing controls to ensure their continued reliability. If they are unsatisfactory, user and source data controls may be strong enough to compensate. If not, a material weakness exists, and steps should be taken to eliminate the control deficiencies.

Several specialized techniques are used to test processing controls, each of which has its own advantages and disadvantages. No technique is effective for all circumstances; all are more appropriate in some situations and less so in others. Auditors should not disclose which technique they use, because doing so may lessen their effectiveness. Each of these procedures is now explained.

TABLE 4 Framework for Audit of Computer Processing Controls

Types of Errors and Fraud
- Failure to detect incorrect, incomplete, or unauthorized input data
- Failure to properly correct errors flagged by data editing procedures
- Introduction of errors into files or databases during updating
- Improper distribution or disclosure of computer output
- Intentional or unintentional inaccuracies in reporting

Control Procedures
- Data editing routines
- Proper use of internal and external file labels
- Reconciliation of batch totals
- Effective error correction procedures
- Understandable operating documentation and run manuals
- Competent supervision of computer operations
- Effective handling of data input and output by data control personnel
- Preparation of file change listings and summaries for user department review
- Maintenance of proper environmental conditions in computer facility

Audit Procedures: System Review
- Review administrative documentation for processing control standards
- Review systems documentation for data editing and other processing controls
- Review operating documentation for completeness and clarity
- Review copies of error listings, batch total reports, and file change lists
- Observe computer operations and data control functions
- Discuss processing and output controls with operators and information system supervisors

Audit Procedures: Tests of Controls
- Evaluate adequacy of processing control standards and procedures
- Evaluate adequacy and completeness of data editing controls
- Verify adherence to processing control procedures by observing computer and data control operations
- Verify that application system output is properly distributed
- Reconcile a sample of batch totals; follow up on discrepancies
- Trace a sample of data edit routines errors to ensure proper handling
- Verify processing accuracy of sensitive transactions
- Verify processing accuracy of computer-generated transactions
- Search for erroneous or unauthorized code via analysis of program logic
- Check accuracy and completeness of processing controls using test data
- Monitor online processing systems using concurrent audit techniques
- Recreate selected reports to test for accuracy and completeness

Compensating Controls
- Strong user controls and effective controls of source data

PROCESSING TEST DATA   One way to test a program is to process a hypothetical set of valid and invalid transactions. The program should process all valid transactions correctly and reject all invalid ones. All logic paths should be checked by one or more test transactions. Invalid data include records with missing data, fields containing unreasonably large amounts, invalid account numbers or processing codes, nonnumeric data in numeric fields, and records out of sequence.

The following resources are helpful when preparing test data:

- A list of actual transactions
- The test transactions the company used to test the program
- A *test data generator*, which prepares test data based on program specifications

In a batch processing system, the company's program and a copy of relevant files are used to process the test data. Results are compared with the predetermined correct output; discrepancies indicate processing errors or control deficiencies to be investigated.

In an online system, auditors enter test data and then observe and log the system's response. If the system accepts erroneous test transactions, the auditor reverses the effects of the transactions, investigates the problem, and recommends that the deficiency be corrected.

Processing test transactions has two disadvantages. First, the auditor must spend considerable time understanding the system and preparing the test transactions. Second, the auditor must ensure that test data do not affect company files and databases. The auditor can reverse the effects of the test transactions or process the transactions in a separate run using a copy of the file or database. However, a separate run removes some of the authenticity obtained from processing test data with regular transactions. Because the reversal procedures may reveal the existence and nature of the auditor's test to key personnel, it can be less effective than a concealed test.

CONCURRENT AUDIT TECHNIQUES   Because transactions can be processed in an online system without leaving an audit trail, evidence gathered after data is processed is insufficient for audit purposes. In addition, because many online systems process transactions continuously, it is difficult to stop the system to perform audit tests. Thus, auditors use *concurrent audit techniques* to continually monitor the system and collect audit evidence while live data are processed during regular operating hours. Concurrent audit techniques use *embedded audit modules*, which are program code segments that perform audit functions, report test results, and store the evidence collected for auditor review. Concurrent audit techniques are time-consuming and difficult to use but are less so if incorporated when programs are developed.

Auditors commonly use five concurrent audit techniques.

1. An *integrated test facility (ITF)* inserts fictitious records that represent a fictitious division, department, customer, or supplier in company master files. Processing test transactions to update them will not affect actual records. Because fictitious and actual records are processed together, company employees are unaware of the testing. The system distinguishes ITF records from actual records, collects information on the test transactions, and reports the results. The auditor compares processed data with expected results to verify that the system and its controls operate correctly. In a batch processing system, the ITF eliminates the need to reverse test transactions. ITF effectively tests online processing systems, because test transactions can be submitted frequently, processed with actual transactions, and traced through every processing stage without disrupting regular processing operations. The auditor must take care not to combine dummy and actual records during the reporting process.

2. In the *snapshot technique*, selected transactions are marked with a special code. Audit modules record these transactions and their master file records before and after processing and store the data in a special file. The auditor reviews the data to verify that all processing steps were properly executed.

3. *System control audit review file (SCARF)* uses embedded audit modules to continuously monitor transaction activity, collect data on transactions with special audit significance, and store it in a SCARF file or *audit log*. Transactions recorded include those exceeding a specified dollar limit, involving inactive accounts, deviating from company policy, or containing write-downs of asset values. Periodically, the auditor examines the audit log to identify and investigate questionable transactions.

4. *Audit hooks* are audit routines that notify auditors of questionable transactions, often as they occur. State Farm's use of audit hooks, including how the company detected a major fraud, is explained in Focus 1.

5. *Continuous and intermittent simulation (CIS)* embeds an audit module in a database management system (DBMS) that examines all transactions that update the database using criteria similar to those of SCARF. If a transaction has special audit significance, the CIS module independently processes the data (in a manner similar to parallel simulation), records the results, and compares them with those obtained by the DBMS. When discrepancies exist, they are stored in an audit log for subsequent investigation. If the discrepancies are serious, the CIS may prevent the DBMS from executing the update.

ANALYSIS OF PROGRAM LOGIC   If auditors suspect that a program contains unauthorized code or serious errors, a detailed analysis of program logic may be necessary. This is time-consuming and requires proficiency in the appropriate programming language, so it should be used as a last

FOCUS 1   Using Audit Hooks at State Farm Life Insurance Company

The State Farm Life Insurance Company computer system has a host computer in Bloomington, Illinois, and smaller computers in regional offices. The system processes more than 30 million transactions per year for over 4 million individual policies worth more than $7 billion.

This online, real-time system updates files and databases as transactions occur. Paper audit trails have virtually vanished, and documents supporting changes to policyholder records have been eliminated or are held only a short time before disposition.

Because anyone with access and a working knowledge of the system could commit fraud, the internal audit staff was asked to identify all the ways fraud was possible. They brainstormed ways to defraud the system and interviewed system users, who provided extremely valuable insights.

Auditors implemented 33 embedded audit hooks to monitor 42 different types of transactions. One audit hook monitors unusual transactions in transfer accounts, which are clearing accounts for temporarily holding funds that are to be credited to multiple accounts.

The audit hooks have been very successful. One employee fraudulently processed a loan on her brother's life insurance policy, forged her brother's signature, and cashed the check. To conceal the fraud, she had to repay the loan before the annual status report was sent to her brother. She used a series of fictitious transactions involving a transfer account. The fraud was uncovered almost immediately when the transfer account audit hook recognized the first of these fictitious transactions and notified the auditor. Within a month of the notification, the case had been investigated and the employee terminated.

Source: Linda Marie Leinicke, W. Max Rexroad, and John D. Ward, "Computer Fraud Auditing: It Works," *Internal Auditor* (August 1990).

---

resort. Auditors analyze development, operating, and program documentation as well as a printout of the source code. They also use the following software packages:

- *Automated flowcharting programs* interpret source code and generate a program flowchart.
- *Automated decision table programs* interpret source code and generate a decision table.
- *Scanning routines* search a program for all occurrences of specified items.
- *Mapping programs* identify unexecuted program code. This software could have uncovered the program code that an unscrupulous programmer inserted to erase all computer files when he was terminated.
- *Program tracing* sequentially prints all program steps executed when a program runs, intermingled with regular output so the sequence of program execution events can be observed. Program tracing helps detect unauthorized program instructions, incorrect logic paths, and unexecuted program code.

Objective 5: Source Data

An **input controls matrix** is used to document the review of source data controls. The matrix in Figure 3 shows the control procedures applied to each input record field.

The data control function should be independent of other functions, maintain a data control log, handle errors, and ensure the overall efficiency of operations. It is usually not economically feasible for small businesses to have an independent data control function. To compensate, user department controls must be stronger with respect to data preparation, batch control totals, edit programs, restrictions on physical and logical access, and error-handling procedures. These procedures should be the focus of the auditor's systems review and tests of controls when there is no independent data control function.

Although source data controls may not change often, how strictly they are applied may change, and auditors should regularly test them. The auditor tests the system by evaluating source data samples for proper authorization, reconciling batch controls, and evaluating whether data edit errors were resolved and resubmitted for processing.

If source data controls are inadequate, user department and data processing controls may compensate. If not, auditors should recommend that source data control deficiencies be corrected.

Table 5 shows the internal controls that prevent, detect, and correct inaccurate or unauthorized source data. It also shows the system review and tests of control procedures auditors use. In an online system, the source data entry and processing functions are one operation. Therefore, source data controls are integrated with processing controls in Table 4.

FIGURE 3

Input Controls Matrix

Record Name: Employee Weekly Time Report — Input Controls	Employee number	Last name	Department number	Transaction code	Week ending (date)	Regular hours	Overtime hours		Comments
Financial totals									
Hash totals	✓				✓	✓			
Record counts									Yes
Cross-footing balance									No
Visual inspection									All fields
Check digit verification	✓								
Prenumbered forms									No
Turnaround document									No
Edit program									Yes
Sequence check	✓								
Field check	✓	✓			✓	✓			
Sign check									
Validity check	✓	✓	✓	✓					
Limit check						✓	✓		
Reasonableness test						✓	✓		
Completeness check				✓	✓	✓	✓		
Overflow procedure									
Other:									

Objective 6: Data Files

The sixth objective concerns the accuracy, integrity, and security of data stored on machine-readable files. Table 6 summarizes the errors, controls, and audit procedures for this objective. If file controls are seriously deficient, especially with respect to physical or logical access or to backup and recovery procedures, the auditor should recommend they be rectified.

TABLE 5 Framework for Audit of Source Data Controls

Types of Errors and Fraud

- Inaccurate or unauthorized source data

Control Procedures

- Effective handling of source data input by data control personnel
- User authorization of source data input
- Preparation and reconciliation of batch control totals
- Logging the receipt, movement, and disposition of source data input
- Check digit verification
- Key verification
- Use of turnaround documents
- Data editing routines
- User department review of file change listings and summaries
- Effective procedures for correcting and resubmitting erroneous data

Audit Procedures: System Review

- Review documentation about data control function responsibilities
- Review administrative documentation for source data control standards
- Review authorization methods and examine authorization signatures
- Review documentation to identify processing steps and source data content and controls
- Document source data controls using an input control matrix
- Discuss source data controls with data control personnel, system users, and managers

(Continued)

TABLE 5 Continued

Audit Procedures: Tests of Controls

- Observe and evaluate data control department operations and control procedures
- Verify proper maintenance and use of data control log
- Evaluate how error log items are dealt with
- Examine source data for proper authorization
- Reconcile batch totals and follow up on discrepancies
- Trace disposition of errors flagged by data edit routines

Compensating Controls

- Strong user and data processing controls

TABLE 6 Framework for Audit of Data File Controls

Types of Errors and Fraud

- Destruction of stored data due to errors, hardware or software malfunctions, and intentional acts of sabotage or vandalism
- Unauthorized modification or disclosure of stored data

Control Procedures

- Storage of data in a secure file library and restriction of physical access to data files
- Logical access controls and an access control matrix
- Proper use of file labels and write-protection mechanisms
- Concurrent update controls
- Data encryption for confidential data
- Virus protection software
- Off-site backup of all data files
- Checkpoint and rollback procedures to facilitate system recovery

Audit Procedures: System Review

- Review documentation for file library operation
- Review logical access policies and procedures
- Review standards for virus protection, off-site data storage, and system recovery procedures
- Review controls for concurrent updates, data encryption, file conversion, and reconciliation of master file totals with independent control totals
- Examine disaster recovery plan
- Discuss file control procedures with managers and operators

Audit Procedures: Tests of Controls

- Observe and evaluate file library operations
- Review records of password assignment and modification
- Observe and evaluate file-handling procedures by operations personnel
- Observe the preparation and off-site storage of backup files
- Verify the effective use of virus protection procedures
- Verify the use of concurrent update controls and data encryption
- Verify completeness, currency, and testing of disaster recovery plans
- Reconcile master file totals with separately maintained control totals
- Observe the procedures used to control file conversion

Compensating Controls

- Strong user and data processing controls
- Effective computer security controls

The auditing-by-objectives approach is a comprehensive, systematic, and effective means of evaluating internal controls. It can be implemented using an audit procedures checklist for each objective. The checklist helps auditors reach a separate conclusion for each objective and suggests compensating controls as appropriate. Each of the six checklists should be completed for each significant application.

Audit Software

Computer-assisted audit techniques (CAATS) refer to audit software, often called *generalized audit software (GAS)*, that uses auditor-supplied specifications to generate a program that performs audit functions, thereby automating or simplifying the audit process. Two of the most popular software packages are Audit Control Language (ACL) and Interactive Data Extraction and Analysis (IDEA). CAATS is ideally suited for examining large data files to identify records needing further audit scrutiny.

The U.S. government discovered that computer-assisted audit techniques are a valuable tool in reducing massive federal budget deficits. The software is used to identify fraudulent Medicare claims and pinpoint excessive charges by defense contractors. The General Accounting Office (GAO) cross-checked figures with the IRS and discovered that thousands of veterans lied about their income to qualify for pension benefits. Some 116,000 veterans who received pensions based on need did not disclose $338 million in income from savings, dividends, or rents. More than 13,600 underreported income; one did not report income of over $300,000. When the Veterans Administration (VA) notified beneficiaries that their income would be verified with the IRS and the Social Security Administration, pension rolls dropped by more than 13,000, at a savings of $9 million a month. The VA plans to use the same system for checking income levels of those applying for medical care. If their income is found to be above a certain level, patients will be required to make copayments.

In another example, a new tax collector in a small New England town requested a tax audit. Using CAATS, the auditor accessed tax collection records for the previous four years, sorted them by date, summed collections by month, and created a report of monthly tax collections. The analysis revealed that collections during January and July, the two busiest months, had declined by 58% and 72%, respectively. Auditors then used CAATS to compare each tax collection record with property records. They identified several discrepancies, including one committed by the former tax collector, who used another taxpayer's payment to cover her own delinquent tax bills. The former tax collector was arrested for embezzlement.

To use CAATS, auditors decide on audit objectives, learn about the files and databases to be audited, design the audit reports, and determine how to produce them. This information is recorded on specification sheets and entered into the system. The CAATS program uses the specifications to produce an auditing program. The program uses a copy of the company's live data (to avoid introducing any errors) to perform the auditing procedures and produce the specified audit reports. CAATS cannot replace the auditor's judgment or free the auditor from other phases of the audit. For example, the auditor must still investigate items on exception reports, verify file totals against other sources of information, and examine and evaluate audit samples.

CAATS are especially valuable for companies with complex processes, distributed operations, high transaction volumes, or a wide variety of applications and systems.

The following are some of the more important uses of CAATS:

- Querying data files to retrieve records meeting specified criteria
- Creating, updating, comparing, downloading, and merging files
- Summarizing, sorting, and filtering data
- Accessing data in different formats and converting the data into a common format
- Examining records for quality, completeness, consistency, and correctness
- Stratifying records, selecting and analyzing statistical samples
- Testing for specific risks and identifying how to control for that risk
- Performing calculations, statistical analyses, and other mathematical operations
- Performing analytical tests, such as ratio and trend analysis, looking for unexpected or unexplained data patterns that may indicate fraud

- Identifying financial leakage, policy noncompliance, and data processing errors
- Reconciling physical counts to computed amounts, testing clerical accuracy of extensions and balances, testing for duplicate items
- Formatting and printing reports and documents
- Creating electronic work papers

Operational Audits of an AIS

The techniques and procedures used in operational audits are similar to audits of information systems and financial statements. The basic difference is audit scope. An information systems audit is confined to internal controls and a financial audit to systems output, whereas an operational audit encompasses all aspects of systems management. In addition, objectives of an operational audit include evaluating effectiveness, efficiency, and goal achievement.

The first step in an operational audit is audit planning, during which the scope and objectives of the audit are established, a preliminary system review is performed, and a tentative audit program is prepared. The next step, evidence collection, includes the following activities:

- Reviewing operating policies and documentation
- Confirming procedures with management and operating personnel
- Observing operating functions and activities
- Examining financial and operating plans and reports
- Testing the accuracy of operating information
- Testing controls

At the evidence evaluation stage, the auditor measures the system against one that follows the best systems management principles. One important consideration is that the results of management policies and practices are more significant than the policies and practices themselves. That is, if good results are achieved through policies and practices that are theoretically deficient, then the auditor must carefully consider whether recommended improvements would substantially improve results. Auditors document their findings and conclusions and communicate them to management.

The ideal operational auditor has audit training and experience as well as a few years' experience in a managerial position. Auditors with strong auditing backgrounds but weak management experience often lack the perspective necessary to understand the management process.

Summary and Case Conclusion

Jason is trying to determine how his parallel simulation program generated sales commission figures that were higher than those generated by SPP's program. Believing that this discrepancy meant there was a systematic error, he asked to review a copy of SPP's program.

The program was lengthy, so Jason used a scanning routine to search the code for occurrences of "40000," because that was the point at which the commission rate changes, according to the new policy. He discovered a commission rate of 0.085 for sales in excess of $40,000, whereas the policy called for only 0.075. Some quick calculations confirmed that this error caused the differences between the two programs.

Jason's audit manager met with the embarrassed development team, who acknowledged and corrected the coding error.

The audit manager called Jason to congratulate him. He informed Jason that the undetected programming error would have cost over $100,000 per year in excess sales commissions. Jason was grateful for the manager's praise and took the opportunity to point out deficiencies in the development team's programming practices. First, the commission rate table was embedded in the program code; good programming practice requires that it be stored in a separate table to be used by the program when needed. Second, the incident called into question the quality of SPP's program development and testing practices. Jason asked whether a more extensive operational audit of those practices was appropriate. The audit manager agreed it was worth examining and promised to raise the issue at his next meeting with Northwest's director of internal auditing.

Key Terms

auditing
internal auditing
financial audit
information systems audit
internal control audit
operational audit
compliance audit
investigative audit
inherent risk
control risk
detection risk
materiality
reasonable assurance
systems review
tests of control

compensating controls
source code comparison
   program
reprocessing
parallel simulation
test data generator
concurrent audit techniques
embedded audit modules
integrated test facility (ITF)
   snapshot technique
system control audit review
   file (SCARF)
audit log

audit hooks
continuous and intermittent
   simulation (CIS)
automated flowcharting
   programs
automated decision table
   programs
scanning routines
mapping programs
program tracing
input controls matrix
computer-assisted audit
   techniques (CAATS)
generalized audit software
   (GAS)

AIS IN ACTION

Chapter Quiz

1. Which of the following is a characteristic of auditing?
   a. Auditing is a systematic, step-by-step process.
   b. Auditing involves the collection and review of evidence.
   c. Auditing involves the use of established criteria to evaluate evidence.
   d. All of the above are characteristics of auditing.

2. Which of the following is NOT a reason an internal auditor should participate in internal control reviews during the design of new systems?
   a. It is more economical to design controls during the design stage than to do so later.
   b. It eliminates the need for testing controls during regular audits.
   c. It minimizes the need for expensive modifications after the system is implemented.
   d. It permits the design of audit trails while they are economical.

3. Which type of audit involves a review of general and application controls, with a focus on determining whether there is compliance with policies and adequate safeguarding of assets?
   a. information systems audit
   b. financial audit
   c. operational audit
   d. compliance audit

4. At what step in the audit process do the concepts of reasonable assurance and materiality enter into the auditor's decision process?
   a. planning
   b. evidence collection
   c. evidence evaluation
   d. they are important in all three steps.

5. What is the four-step approach to internal control evaluation that provides a logical framework for carrying out an audit?
   a. inherent risk analysis
   b. systems review
   c. tests of controls
   d. risk-based approach to auditing

6. Which of the following procedures is NOT used to detect unauthorized program changes?
   a. source code comparison
   b. parallel simulation
   c. reprocessing
   d. reprogramming code

7. Which of the following is a concurrent audit technique that monitors all transactions and collects data on those that meet certain characteristics specified by the auditor?
   a. integrated test facility
   b. snapshot techniques
   c. SCARF
   d. audit hooks

8. Which of the following is a computer technique that assists an auditor in understanding program logic by identifying all occurrences of specific variables?
   a. mapping program
   b. program tracing
   c. automated flowcharting
   d. scanning routine

9. Which of the following is a computer program written especially for audit use?
   a. GAS
   b. CATAS
   c. ITF
   d. CIS

10. The focus of an operational audit is on which of the following?
    a. reliability and integrity of financial information
    b. all aspects of information systems management
    c. internal controls
    d. safeguarding assets

Discussion Questions

1. Auditing an AIS effectively requires that an auditor have some knowledge of computers and their accounting applications. However, it may not be feasible for every auditor to be a computer expert. Discuss the extent to which auditors should possess computer expertise in order to be effective auditors.

2. Should internal auditors be members of systems development teams that design and implement an AIS? Why or why not?

3. Berwick Industries is a fast-growing corporation that manufactures industrial containers. The company has a sophisticated AIS that uses advanced technology. Berwick's executives have decided to pursue listing the company's securities on a national stock exchange, but they have been advised that their listing application would be stronger if they were to create an internal audit department.

   At present, no Berwick employees have auditing experience. To staff its new internal audit function, Berwick could (a) train some of its computer specialists in auditing, (b) hire experienced auditors and train them to understand Berwick's information system, (c) use a combination of the first two approaches, or (d) try a different approach. Which approach would you support, and why?

4. The assistant finance director for the city of Tustin, California, was fired after city officials discovered that she had used her access to city computers to cancel her daughter's $300 water bill. An investigation revealed that she had embezzled a large sum of money from Tustin over a long period. She was able to conceal the embezzlement for so long because the amount embezzled always fell within a 2% error factor used by the city's internal auditors. What weaknesses existed in the audit approach? How could the audit plan be improved? What internal control weaknesses were present in the system? Should Tustin's internal auditors have discovered this fraud earlier?

5. Lou Goble, an internal auditor for a large manufacturing enterprise, received an anonymous note from an assembly-line operator who has worked at the company's West Coast factory for the past 15 years. The note indicated that there are some fictitious employees on the payroll as well as some employees who have left the company. He offers no proof or names. What computer-assisted audit technique could Lou use to substantiate or refute the employee's claims? *(CIA Examination, adapted)*

6. Explain the four steps of the risk-based audit approach, and discuss how they apply to the overall security of a company.

7. Compare and contrast the frameworks for auditing program development/acquisition and for auditing program modification.

Problems

1. You are the director of internal auditing at a university. Recently, you met with Issa Arnita, the manager of administrative data processing, and expressed the desire to establish a more effective interface between the two departments. Issa wants your help with a new computerized accounts payable system currently in development. He recommends that your department assume line responsibility for auditing suppliers' invoices prior to payment. He also wants internal auditing to make suggestions during system development, assist in its installation, and approve the completed system after making a final review.

   Required

   Would you accept or reject each of the following? Why?
   a. The recommendation that your department be responsible for the preaudit of suppliers' invoices
   b. The request that you make suggestions during system development
   c. The request that you assist in the installation of the system and approve the system after making a final review
   (CIA Examination, adapted)

2. As an internal auditor for the Quick Manufacturing Company, you are participating in the audit of the company's AIS. You have been reviewing the internal controls of the computer system that processes most of its accounting applications. You have studied the company's extensive systems documentation. You have interviewed the information system manager, operations supervisor, and other employees to complete your standardized computer internal control questionnaire. You report to your supervisor that the company has designed a successful set of comprehensive internal controls into its computer systems. He thanks you for your efforts and asks for a summary report of your findings for inclusion in a final overall report on accounting internal controls.

   Required

   Have you forgotten an important audit step? Explain. List five examples of specific audit procedures that you might recommend before reaching a conclusion.

3. As an internal auditor, you have been assigned to evaluate the controls and operation of a computer payroll system. To test the computer systems and programs, you submit independently created test transactions with regular data in a normal production run.

   Required

   List four advantages and two disadvantages of this technique.
   (CIA Examination, adapted)

4. You are involved in the audit of accounts receivable, which represent a significant portion of the assets of a large retail corporation. Your audit plan requires the use of the computer, but you encounter the following reactions:
   a. The computer operations manager says the company's computer is running at full capacity for the foreseeable future and that the auditor will not be able to use the system for audit tests.
   b. The scheduling manager suggests that your computer program be stored in the computer program library so that it can be run when computer time becomes available.
   c. You are refused admission to the computer room.

d. The systems manager tells you that it will take too much time to adapt the auditor's computer audit program to the computer's operating system and that company programmers will write the programs needed for the audit.

Required

For each situation, state how the auditor should proceed with the accounts receivable audit. *(CIA Examination, adapted)*

5. You are a manager for the CPA firm of Dewey, Cheatem, and Howe (DC&H). While reviewing your staff's audit work papers for the state welfare agency, you find that the test data approach was used to test the agency's accounting software. A duplicate program copy, the welfare accounting data file obtained from the computer operations manager, and the test transaction data file that the welfare agency's programmers used when the program was written were processed on DC&H's home office computer. The edit summary report listing no errors was included in the working papers, with a notation by the senior auditor that the test indicates good application controls. You note that the quality of the audit conclusions obtained from this test is flawed in several respects, and you decide to ask your subordinates to repeat the test.

Required

Identify three existing or potential problems with the way this test was performed. For each problem, suggest one or more procedures that might be performed during the revised test to avoid flaws in the audit conclusions.

6. You are performing an information system audit to evaluate internal controls in Aardvark Wholesalers' (AW) computer system. From an AW manual, you have obtained the following job descriptions for key personnel:

Director of information systems: Responsible for defining the mission of the information systems division and for planning, staffing, and managing the IS department.

Manager of systems development and programming: Reports to director of information systems. Responsible for managing the systems analysts and programmers who design, program, test, implement, and maintain the data processing systems. Also responsible for establishing and monitoring documentation standards.

Manager of operations: Reports to director of information systems. Responsible for management of computer center operations, enforcement of processing standards, and systems programming, including implementation of operating system upgrades.

Data entry supervisor: Reports to manager of operations. Responsible for supervision of data entry operations and monitoring data preparation standards.

Operations supervisor: Reports to manager of operations. Responsible for supervision of computer operations staff and monitoring processing standards.

Data control clerk: Reports to manager of operations. Responsible for logging and distributing computer input and output, monitoring source data control procedures, and custody of programs and data files.

Required

a. Prepare an organizational chart for AW's information systems division.
b. Name two positive and two negative aspects (from an internal control standpoint) of this organizational structure.
c. What additional information would you require before making a final judgment on the adequacy of AW's separation of functions in the information systems division?

7. Robinson's Plastic Pipe Corporation uses a data processing system for inventory. The input to this system is shown in Table 7. You are using an input controls matrix to help audit the source data controls.

TABLE 7 Parts Inventory Transaction File

Field Name	Field Type
Item number	Numeric
Description	Alphanumeric
Transaction date	Date
Transaction type	Alphanumeric
Document number	Alphanumeric
Quantity	Numeric
Unit cost	Monetary

Required

Prepare an input controls matrix using the format and input controls shown in Figure 3; however, replace the field names shown in Figure 3 with those shown in Table 7. Place checks in the matrix cells that represent input controls you might expect to find for each field.

8. As an internal auditor for the state auditor's office, you are assigned to review the implementation of a new computer system in the state welfare agency. The agency is installing an online computer system to maintain the state's database of welfare recipients. Under the old system, applicants for welfare assistance completed a form giving their name, address, and other personal data, plus details about their income, assets, dependents, and other data needed to establish eligibility. The data are checked by welfare examiners to verify their authenticity, certify the applicant's eligibility for assistance, and determine the form and amount of aid.

Under the new system, welfare applicants enter data on the agency's Web site or give their data to clerks, who enter it using online terminals. Each applicant record has a "pending" status until a welfare examiner can verify the authenticity of the data used to determine eligibility. When the verification is completed, the examiner changes the status code to "approved," and the system calculates the aid amount.

Periodically, recipient circumstances (income, assets, dependents, etc.) change, and the database is updated. Examiners enter these changes as soon as their accuracy is verified, and the system recalculates the recipient's new welfare benefit. At the end of each month, payments are electronically deposited in the recipient's bank accounts.

Welfare assistance amounts to several hundred million dollars annually. You are concerned about the possibilities of fraud and abuse.

Required

a. Describe how to employ concurrent audit techniques to reduce the risks of fraud and abuse.
b. Describe how to use computer audit software to review the work welfare examiners do to verify applicant eligibility data. Assume that the state auditor's office has access to other state and local government agency databases.

9. Melinda Robinson, the director of internal auditing at Sachem Manufacturing Company, believes the company should purchase software to assist in the financial and procedural audits her department conducts. Robinson is considering the following software packages:

- A generalized audit software package to assist in basic audit work, such as the retrieval of live data from large computer files. The department would review this information using conventional audit investigation techniques. The department could perform criteria selection, sampling, basic computations for quantitative analysis, record handling, graphical analysis, and print output (i.e., confirmations).
- An ITF package that uses, monitors, and controls dummy test data processed by existing programs. It also checks the existence and adequacy of data entry and processing controls.
- A flowcharting package that graphically presents the flow of information through a system and pinpoints control strengths and weaknesses.

- A parallel simulation and modeling package that uses actual data to conduct the same tests using a logic program developed by the auditor. The package can also be used to seek answers to difficult audit problems (involving many comparisons) within statistically acceptable confidence limits.

Required

a. Without regard to any specific computer audit software, identify the general advantages of using computer audit software.

b. Describe the audit purpose facilitated and the procedural steps followed when using the following:

- Generalized audit software
- Integrated test facility
- Flowcharting
- Parallel simulation and modeling

(CMA Examination, adapted)

10. The fixed-asset master file at Thermo-Bond includes the following data items:

Asset number	Date of retirement (99/99/2099 for assets still in service)
Description	Depreciation method code
Type code	Depreciation rate
Location code	Useful life (years)
Date of acquisition	Accumulated depreciation at beginning of year
Original cost	Year-to-date depreciation

Required

Explain how generalized audit software can be used in a financial audit of Thermo-Bond's fixed assets.

11. You are auditing the financial statements of a cosmetics distributor that sells thousands of individual items. The distributor keeps its inventory in its distribution center and in two public warehouses. At the end of each business day, it updates its inventory file, whose records contain the following data:

Item number	Cost per item
Item description	Date of last purchase
Quantity-on-hand	Date of last sale
Item location	Quantity sold during year

You will use audit software to examine inventory data as of the date of the distributor's physical inventory count. You will perform the following audit procedures:

1. Observe the distributor's physical inventory count at year-end and test a sample for accuracy.
2. Compare the auditor's test counts with the inventory records.
3. Compare the company's physical count data with the inventory records.
4. Test the mathematical accuracy of the distributor's final inventory valuation.
5. Test inventory pricing by obtaining item costs from buyers, vendors, or other sources.
6. Examine inventory purchase and sale transactions on or near the year-end date to verify that all transactions were recorded in the proper accounting period.
7. Ascertain the propriety of inventory items located in public warehouses.
8. Analyze inventory for evidence of possible obsolescence.
9. Analyze inventory for evidence of possible overstocking or slow-moving items.
10. Test the accuracy of individual data items listed in the distributor's inventory master file.

Required

Describe how an audit software package and a copy of the inventory file can help you perform each auditing procedure.

(AICPA Examination, adapted)

12. Which of the following should have the primary responsibility to detect and correct data processing errors? Explain why that function should have primary responsibility and why the others should not.
    a. The data processing manager
    b. The computer operator
    c. The corporate controller
    d. The independent auditor

    (CPA Examination, adapted)

Case 1 Preston Manufacturing

You are performing a financial audit of the general ledger accounts of Preston Manufacturing. As transactions are processed, summary journal entries are added to the general ledger file at the end of the day. At the end of each day, the general journal file is processed against the general ledger control file to compute a new current balance for each account and to print a trial balance.

The following resources are available as you complete the audit:

- Your firm's generalized computer audit software
- A copy of the general journal file for the entire year
- A copy of the general ledger file as of fiscal year-end (current balance = year-end balance)
- A printout of Preston's year-end trial balance listing the account number, account name, and balance of each account on the general ledger control file

Create an audit program for Preston Manufacturing. For each audit step, list the audit objectives and the procedures you would use to accomplish the audit program step.

General Journal

Field Name	Field Type
Account number	Numeric
Amount	Monetary
Debit/credit code	Alphanumeric
Date (MM/DD/YY)	Date
Reference document type	Alphanumeric
Reference document number	Numeric

General Ledger Control

Field Name	Field Type
Account number	Numeric
Account name	Alphanumeric
Beginning balance/year	Monetary
Beg-bal-debit/credit code	Alphanumeric
Current balance	Monetary
Cur-bal-debit/credit code	Alphanumeric

AIS IN ACTION SOLUTIONS

Quiz Key

1. Which of the following is a characteristic of auditing?
   a. Auditing is a systematic, step-by-step process. (Incorrect. While this is true, it is not the only correct answer.)
   b. Auditing involves the collection and review of evidence. (Incorrect. While this is true, it is not the only correct answer.)
   c. Auditing involves the use of established criteria to evaluate evidence. (Incorrect. While this is true, it is not the only correct answer.)

▶ **d.** All of the above are characteristics of auditing. (Correct. Auditing is a systematic, step-by-step process that involves the collection and review of evidence and uses established criteria to evaluate evidence.)

2. Which of the following is NOT a reason an internal auditor should participate in internal control reviews during the design of new systems?
    a. It is more economical to design controls during the design stage than to do so later. (Incorrect. Internal audit should participate in internal control reviews because it is far less expensive to design controls during systems design than to try and implement controls after the system has been designed.)
    ▶ **b.** It eliminates the need for testing controls during regular audits. (Correct. Even if the auditor participates in internal control reviews, the auditor will still have to test controls to determine whether they are in place and working as intended.)
    c. It minimizes the need for expensive modifications after the system is implemented. (Incorrect. Internal auditors should participate in internal control reviews because it reduces the likelihood of post-system-implementation modifications.)
    d. It permits the design of audit trails while they are economical. (Incorrect. Internal auditors should participate in internal control reviews because their participation in systems design does facilitate the design of effective audit trails.)

3. Which type of audit involves a review of general and application controls, with a focus on determining if there is compliance with policies and adequate safeguarding of assets?
    ▶ **a.** information systems audit (Correct. An information systems audit reviews general and application controls, with a focus on determining whether there is compliance with policies and adequate safeguarding of assets.)
    b. financial audit (Incorrect. A financial audit examines the reliability of accounting records.)
    c. operational audit (Incorrect. An operational audit is concerned with the efficient use of resources and the accomplishment of entity objectives.)
    d. compliance audit (Incorrect. A compliance audit is concerned with reviewing whether an entity is meeting prescribed policies, rules, and laws.)

4. At what step in the audit process do the concepts of reasonable assurance and materiality enter into the auditor's decision process?
    a. planning (Incorrect. Although materiality and reasonable assurance enter into the auditor's decision process during planning, they are also important in other steps in the audit process.)
    b. evidence collection (Incorrect. Although materiality and reasonable assurance enter into the auditor's decision process during evidence collection, they are also important in other steps in the audit process.)
    c. evidence evaluation (Incorrect. Although materiality and reasonable assurance enter into the auditor's decision process during evidence evaluation, they are also important in other steps in the audit process.)
    ▶ **d.** They are important in all three steps. (Correct. Materiality and reasonable assurance are important when the auditor plans an audit and when the auditor collects and evaluates evidence.)

5. What is the four-step approach to internal control evaluation that provides a logical framework for carrying out an audit?
    a. inherent risk analysis (Incorrect. Inherent risk is the susceptibility to material risk in the absence of controls.)
    b. systems review (Incorrect. Systems review involves reviewing system documentation and interviewing appropriate personnel to determine whether the necessary procedures are in place.)
    c. tests of controls (Incorrect. Tests of controls are conducted to determine whether control policies and procedures are satisfactorily followed.)

▶ **d.** risk-based approach to auditing (Correct. The risk-based audit approach is a four-step approach to carrying out an audit. The four steps are determining threats, identifying control procedures, evaluating control procedures, and evaluating weaknesses.)

6. Which of the following procedures is NOT used to detect unauthorized program changes?
   a. source code comparison (Incorrect. Source code comparison is used to detect unauthorized program changes by thoroughly testing a newly developed program and keeping a copy of its source code.)
   b. parallel simulation (Incorrect. To use parallel simulation to detect unauthorized program changes, an auditor writes a version of the program, reprocesses the company's data, compares the results to the company's results, and investigates any differences.)
   c. reprocessing (Incorrect. To use reprocessing to detect unauthorized program changes, the auditor verifies the integrity of an application program, saves it, and on a surprise basis uses the program to reprocess data and compare that output with the company's output.)
   ▶ **d.** reprogramming code (Correct. Reprogramming code is not used to test for unauthorized program changes.)

7. Which of the following is a concurrent audit technique that monitors all transactions and collects data on those that meet certain characteristics specified by the auditor?
   a. integrated test facility (Incorrect. An integrated test facility inserts a dummy company or division into a computer system to test transaction data without affecting real data.)
   b. snapshot techniques (Incorrect. The snapshot technique records the content of both a transaction record and a related master file record before each processing step.)
   ▶ **c.** SCARF (Correct. System control audit review file is a concurrent audit technique that embeds audit modules into application software to monitor continuously all transaction activity.)
   d. audit hooks (Incorrect. An audit hook is a concurrent audit technique that embeds audit routines into application software to flag certain kinds of transactions that might be indicative of fraud.)

8. Which of the following is a computer technique that assists an auditor in understanding program logic by identifying all occurrences of specific variables?
   a. mapping program (Incorrect. Mapping programs are activated during regular processing and provide information about portions of the application program that were not executed.)
   b. program tracing (Incorrect. Program tracing is a technique used to determine application program logic in order to test program controls.)
   c. automated flowcharting (Incorrect. Automated flowcharting interprets source code and generates a flowchart of that program.)
   ▶ **d.** scanning routine (Correct. Scanning routine software programs search for particular variable names or specific characters.)

9. Which of the following is a computer program written especially for audit use?
   ▶ **a.** GAS (Correct. Generalized audit software is a software program written especially for audit uses, such as testing data files. Examples are ACL and IDEA.)
   b. CATAS (Incorrect. CATAS has no meaning in information systems auditing. Computer-assisted audit techniques (CAATS) is the name given to all computer-assisted techniques used to audit computers.)
   c. ITF (Incorrect. An integrated test facility places a small set of fictitious records in master files. Transactions are processed for these records, and the actual and expected results are compared.)
   d. CIS (Incorrect. Continuous and intermittent simulation embeds an audit module in a DBMS that examines all transactions that update the database.)

10. The focus of an operational audit is on which of the following?
    a. reliability and integrity of financial information (Incorrect. A financial audit examines the reliability and integrity of financial information.)
    ▶ b. all aspects of information systems management (Correct. An operational audit is concerned with all aspects of information systems management.)
    c. internal controls (Incorrect. The focus of an operational audit is much broader than just internal controls.)
    d. safeguarding assets (Incorrect. The focus of an operational audit is much broader than just the safeguarding of assets.)

Index